The New Sabin

To

Fermín Peraza Sarausa

1907-1969

The New Sabin;

Books Described by Joseph Sabin and His

Successors, Now Described Again on the

Basis of Examination of Originals,

and Fully Indexed by Title, Subject,

Joint Authors, and Institutions and Agencies

by

Lawrence S. Thompson

Entries 17946—21752

Volume VIII

The Whitston Publishing Company
Troy, New York

PREFACE

This is the first of a series of volumes of *The New Sabin* covering Latin American and Caribbean publications which Sabin would have included if the original set were current today. They have been selected mainly from the "Recent Books" section of the *Revista Interamericana de Bibliografía* and they represent a sound collection of the best Latin American and Caribbean books from the last quarter of a century. All are available on 35 mm microfilm or microfiche from the General Microfilm Company of Watertown, Massachusetts, also in eye-legible copy.

There are likely to be five or six more volumes to record existing material in the collection, but they will not be consecutive. Volume IX will contain material from the original Sabin, now available from the Lost Cause Press of Louisville. However, we will have cumulative indexes after each five volumes. The cumulative index after Volume XV should contain a guide to the most important Latin American and Caribbean publications of the previous three decades. Over the years there will be additional volumes of Latin American and Caribbean material.

Lawrence S. Thompson
Lexington, Kentucky
October 1981

A

17946   Abad, José Ramón.
        Puerto Rico en la Feria-exposición de Ponce en 1882.
        Memoria redactada de orden de la Junta directiva de la
        misma, por Don José Ramón Abad. Ponce, Establecimiento
        tipográfica El Comercio, 1885.
        351 p.   24 cm.

17947   Aballi, Angel Arturo.
        Dr. Joaquín L. Dueñas y Pinto. La Habana, Ministerio
        de Salud Pública, 1967.
        110 p.   front. (port.)   23 cm.   (Cuadernos de
        Historia de la Salud Pública, 36)

17948   Abalos, Jorge W
        ¿Qué sabe usted de víboras? [Por] J. W. Abalos.
        [Buenos Aires] E[ditorial] U[niversitaria] de B[uenos]
        A[ires, 1964]
        93 p.   illus.   16 cm.   (Libros del Caminante, 1)

17949   Abbot, Gordham Dummer.
        Mexico and the United States; their mutual relations
        and common interests. By Gordham D. Abbot...
        New York, G. P. Putnam & son, 1869.
        xvi, 391 p.   front., port., map.   23½ cm.

17950   Aben Athar, J   1914-
        Curso de previdência social; programa da Cátedra de
        Direito do Trabalho da Universidade do Brasil.
        Prefácio do Professor Javert de Souza Lima. [Rio de
        Janeiro] Distribuidora Record Editôra, 1961.
        177 p.   21 cm.

17951   Aboal Amaro, José Alberto.
        Amerigho Vespucci; ensayo de bibliografía crítica.
        Madrid, Librería para Bibliófilos, 1962.
        149 p.   facsims.   25 cm.   (Publicaciones de
        la Biblioteca Colombina, no. 3)

17952   Abouhamad H   , Jeannette.
        Apuntes de introducción a la sociología: Max Weber,
        Talcott Parsons [por] Jeannette Abouhamad H.
        Caracas, Instituto de Investigaciones, Facultad de
        Economía, Universidad Central de Venezuela, 1966.
        55 p.   24 cm.   (Colección "Esquemas")
        Includes bibliographies.

17953   Abouhamad H   , Jeannette.
        Apuntes de métodos de investigación de ciencias
        sociales. Caracas, Instituto de Investigaciones,
        Facultad de Economía, Universidad Central de Venezuela,
        1965.
        112 p.   24 cm.   (Colección "Esquemas")
        Includes bibliographical references.

17954   Abrahams, Roger D
        Charles Walters -- West Indian Autolycus [by] Roger
        D. Abrahams. Austin, Institute of Latin American
        Studies, University of Texas [1968]
        77-95 p.   23 cm.   (Offprint series, 75)
        "Reprinted from Western Folklore, XXVII, 77-95."

17955   Abrahams, Roger D
        Public drama and common values in two Caribbean
        islands [by] Roger D. Abrahams. [Austin, Institute
        of Latin American Studies, University of Texas, 1968]
        [62-71] p.   illus., map.   28 cm.   (Offprint
        series, 82)

17956   Abrahams, Roger D
        Speech mas' [masquerade] on Tobago [by] Roger D.
        Abrahams. Austin, Institute of Latin American
        Studies, University of Texas, 1968.
        125-144 p.   23 cm.   (Offprint series, 77)
        "Reprinted from Tire Shrinker to Dragster. Public-
        ations of the Texas Folklore Society, XXXIV (Austin,
        1968)"

17957   Abrego, Leopoldo.
        Plagas y enfermedades del cafeto en El Salvador.
        Santa Tecia, 1960.
        48 p.

17958   Abreu, Adilson Avansi.
        As funções urbanas da zona do mercado central de
        São Paulo. São Paulo, 1966.
        17 p.   illus., maps. 32 cm.   (Geografia
        econômica, 2)

At head of title: Instituto de Geografia,
Universidade de São Paulo.
On cover: Setor de pesquisas.

17959 Abreu, Casimiro de Abreu, 1837-1860.
Camões e o Jáo, cena dramática. Rio de Janeiro,
Serviço Nacional de Teatro, 1972.
vi, 18 p. 21 cm.

17960 Abreu, Cid T
Poemas I. [Belo Horizonte, Difusão Pan-Americana
do Livro, 1962]
[37] p. 21 cm.

17961 Abreu, Florencio de.
Ensaios e estudos historicos. Rio de Janeiro,
Irmãos Pongetti, 1964.
270 p. plate. 22 cm.
Contents. - A constituinte e o projecto de Consti-
tuição da Republica Rio-Grandense. - Recursos finan-
ceiros da Republica do Piratini. - O gado bovino e
sua influência na antropogeografia do R. G. do Sul. -
Govêrno de José Marcelino de Figueiredo, fundador de
Porto Alegre, no continente de S. Pedro, 1760 a 1780. -
Silveira Martins, o tribuno. - Octavio Augusto de
Faria Corrêa (estatistica, geografia & literatura) -
O movimento positivista no Rio Grande do Sul. -
Importancia da colonização açoriana no Rio Grande do
Sul. - Aureliano Pinto e a poesia gauchesca.

17962 Abreu, Jayme.
Educação, sociedade e desenvolvimento. Rio de
Janeiro, Centro Brasileiro de Pesquisas Educacionais,
1968.
237 p. 21 cm. (Publicações do Centro Brasileiro
de Pesquisas Educacionais. Série 6: Sociedade e
educação, v. 8)

17963 Abreu, Modesto de.
Correção de textos para exames e concursos. Rio
de Janeiro e São Paulo, Livraria Freitas Bastos S.A.
[n.d.]
236 p. 18 cm.

17964 Abreu, Nelson de.
O processo civil no tribunal de justiça de Santa
Catarina; jurisprudência civil. Florianópolis,
Imprensa Universitária, 1967.
503 p. 21 cm.

17965   Abreu, Oldemar Cardim.
Pesquisas relativas à incubação artificial e natural
dos ovos do Bombyx mori L [por] Oldemar Cardim Abreu
e Nivaldo Alves Bonilha. Campinas, Serviço de Sericicultura, 1968.
69 p.   illus., fold. tables.   23 cm.   (Boletim
técnico de sericicultura no. 31)
Summary in English.
Bibliography: p. 69.

17966   Abreu Gómez, Ermilo, 1894-
Diálogo del buen decir; y otros ensayos. [1. ed.]
San Salvador, Editorial Universitaria [1961]
203 p.   19 cm.
Contents. - Diálogo del buen decir. - Diálogo de
Don Quijote. - Evolución de la prosa castellana. -
Sor Juana: unas obras completas y una vida incompleta. -
Justo Sierra. - Martín Luis Guzmán.

17967   Abreu Gómez, Ermilo, 1894-
Discurso del estilo. Mexico, Dirección General de
Publicaciones, 1963.
57 p.   18 cm.
"Francisco Monterde: Contestación al discurso de
recepción de Ermilo Abreu Gómez...": p. 39-57.

17968   Abusada-Salah, Roberto.
Industrialization policies in Peru, 1970-1976 by
Roberto Abusada-Salah. [Austin] Office for Public
Sector Studies, Institute of Latin American Studies,
University of Texas at Austin, 1978.
15 p.   tables.   28 cm.

17969   Academia Campinense de Letras.
Antologia; obra comemorativa do décimo aniversário
da Academia Campinense de Letras. Campinas, 1966.
375 p.   23 cm.   (Publicação, no. 16)
Includes bio-bibliographical sketches of the authors.

17970   Academia Colombiana de Historia.
Segundo centenario del nacimiento de Don Antonio
Nariño, 1765-1965. Bogotá, Kelly [1965]
213 p.   illus., ports.   25 cm.   (Biblioteca
de historia nacional, 106)

17971   Academia Costarricense de la Historia.
IV [Cuarto] centenario de la entrada de Cavallón
a Costa Rica, 1561-1861. San José, Imprenta Nacional,
1961.

140 p.   illus., maps.   26 cm.
Cover-title: Cavallón en Costa Rica.

17972 Academia de Ciencias de Cuba. Instituto de Geología.
Actas. Resúmenes del Tercer Consejo Científico.
La Habana, 1972.
2 v.   maps (1 fold.), diagrs.   28½ cm.

17973 Academia de Ciencias de Cuba. Instituto de Geología.
Conmemoración del V aniversario de la fundación del
Instituto de Geología de la Academia de Ciencias de
Cuba. La Habana, 1973.
23 p.   28½ cm.   (Serie actividades, no. 25)

17974 Academia de Ciencias de Cuba. Instituto de Geología.
Geología de los minerales útiles de Cuba. La Habana,
1974.
161 p.   illus., fold. map, fold. table.   27 cm.
(Publicación especial, no. 3)
Abstracts in English.

17975 Academia de Ciencias de Cuba. Instituto de Suelos.
Aplicación de la fotografía aerea en el reconocimiento y en la cartografía de los suelos. Grupo
asesor chino del Instituto de Suelos de la Academia
de Ciencias de Cuba. La Habana, 1970.
26 p.   illus., diags.   28½ cm.   (Serie suelos,
no. 11)

17976 Academia Española, Madrid.
Ortografía. Edición que incorpora al texto tradicional las nuevas normas declaradas de ampliación
preceptiva desde el 1º. enero de 1969. [Bogotá,
1977]
40 p.   23 cm.
"Separata. Revista de las Fuerzas Armadas, no. 85,
v. XXIX."

17977 Academia Nacional de la Historia, Buenos Aires.
Periódicos de la época de la Revolución de Mayo.
Reproducción facsimilar publicada con el auspicio y
fondos de la Comisión Nacional Ejecutiva del 150.
Aniversario de la Revolución de Mayo. Introducción
por Guillermo Fúrlong y Enrique de Gandía [Buenos
Aires, 19]
v.   facsims.   24 cm.
Contents. - 2. El Grito del sud (1812) - 4. El
Independiente (1815-1816) - 5. Los Amigos de la patria
y de la juventud, 1815-1816.

5

17978 Academia Nacional de la Historia, Caracas.
        Biblioteca de la Academia Nacional de la Historia.
        Caracas.
        v.   23 cm.
        Library has v. 23 (1960) - 91, 94, 104-105 (1971)

17979 Academia Nacional de la Historia, Caracas.
        Biblioteca de la Academia Nacional de la Historia.
        Catálogo. Caracas, 1968.
        31 p.   13½ cm.

17980 Academia Nacional de la Historia, Caracas.
        Descubrimiento y conquista de Venezuela (textos
        históricos contemporáneos y documentos fundamentales)
        Caracas, 1962.
        2 v.   23 cm.   (Biblioteca de la Academia
        Nacional de la Historia, 54-55)
        "Estudio preliminar por Joaquín Gabaldón Márquez":
        vol. 1, p. xix-xxxv; vol. 2, p. xi-xviii.
        Contents. - v. 1. Cristóbal Colón. Américo Vespucio.
        Fray Bartolomé de las Casas. Martín Fernández de
        Navarrete. Diversos apéndices documentales. -
        v. 2. Capítulos de Jerónimo Benzoni relativos a la
        isla de Cubaqua, Cumaná y los Belzares. Cédulas
        selectas y ordenanzas referentes a la isla de Cubaqua.
        "Historia indiana" o primer viaje de Nicolas Fenerman.
        Relaciones diversas relativas a la expedición de
        Alfinger. "Diario" y cartas de Felipe de Hutten.
        Carta de un joven alemán: Titus Neukomm.

17981 Academia Nacional de la Historia, Caracas.
        Discursos de incorporación. Caracas, 1966.
        4 v.   col. map.   22 cm.

17982 Academia Nacional de la Historia, Caracas.
        Documentos de cancillerias europeas sobre
        independencia venezolana. Estudio preliminar por
        Caracciolo Parra-Pérez. Caracas, 1962.
        2 v.   23 cm.   (Biblioteca de la Academia
        Nacional de la Historia, 45-46)
        "Fuentes utilizadas": v. 1, p. [67]-68.

17983 Academia Nacional de la Historia, Caracas.
        Epistolario de la Primera Républica. Estudio
        preliminar por la Fundación John Boulton. Caracas,
        1960.
        2 v.   23 cm.   (Biblioteca de la Academia
        Nacional de la Historia, 35-36)
        Bibliographical footnotes.

17984   Academia Nacional de la Historia, Caracas.
        El pensamiento constitucional de Latinoamérica,
        1810-1830. Caracas, 1962.
        5 v.   fold. facsims.   23 cm.   (Biblioteca de
        la Academia Nacional de la Historia, 47-51)
        "Se recogen en cinco volumenes las actas, documentos
        y ponencias relativas al Congreso de Academias e
        Institutos Históricos, sobre 'El Pensamiento Constitu-
        cional de Latinoamérica (1810-1830)', organizado por
        la Academia Nacional de la Historia en Caracas...
        durante los dias del veintiseis de junio al cuatro
        de julio de 1961."

17985   Academia Nacional de la Historia, Caracas.
        El pensamiento constitucional hispanoamericano
        hasta 1830; compilación de constituciones sancionadas
        y proyectos constitucionales. Caracas, 1961.
        5 v.   22 cm.   (Biblioteca de la Academia
        Nacional de la Historia, 40-44)
        Spanish, Portuguese or French.
        Includes bibliographies.
        Contents. - v. 1. Argentina, Bolivia, Brasil, Centro
        America, Colombia. - v. 2. Colombia (continuación)
        Costa Rica, Cuba, Chile. - v. 3. Ecuador, Guatemala,
        Haiti, Honduras, Nicaragua, Mexico, Nueva Granada. -
        v. 4. Nueva Granada (continuación) Paraguay, Perú,
        Santo Domingo, Uruguay. - v. 5. Venezuela. Consti-
        tución de Cádiz, 1812.

17986   Academia Nacional de la Historia, Caracas.
        Proceso político [de Francisco Isnardy. Estudio
        preliminar por Joaquín Gabaldón Márquez] Caracas,
        1959.
        382 p.   23 cm.   (Biblioteca de la Academia
        Nacional de la Historia, 24)

17987   Academia Nacional de la Historia, Caracas.
        Testimonios de la época emancipadora. Estudio
        preliminar por Arturo Uslar Pietri. Caracas, 1961.
        xxxvii, 529 p.   facsims.   22 cm.   (Biblioteca
        de la Academia Nacional de la Historia, 37)
        Contents. - Testimonios de próceres. - Documentos
        y correspondencia de Juntas Provinciales. - Periódicos
        de la Primera República. - Impresos de la época.

17988   Academia Nacional de la Historia, Caracas.
        Venezuela en los cronistas generales de Indias.
        [Estudio preliminar por Carlos Felice Cardot]
        Caracas, 1962.

7

2 v.   23 cm.   (Biblioteca de la Academia
Nacional de la Historia, 58-59)
Contents. - v. 1. Décadas del Nuevo Mundo, por
P. Mártir de Anglería. Historia general y natural
de las Indias, islas y Tierra-Firme del Mar Océano,
por G. Fernández de Oviedo y Valdés. Historia
general de las Indias, por F. López de Gómara. -
v. 2. Historia general de los hechos de los castellanos
en las islas y Tierra Firme, por A. de Herrera.
Historia general de las conquistas del Nuevo Reino
de Granada, por L. Fernández de Piedrahita. Historia
de la Provincia de San Antonio del Nuevo Reino de
Granada, por A. de Zamora. Cualidades y riquezas
del Nuevo Reino de Granada, por B. V. de Oviedo.

17989   Academia Nacional de San Carlos, México.
Catálogos de las exposiciones de la antigua Academia
de San Carlos de México; 1850-1898. México, 1963.
690 p.   illus.   24 cm.   (Instituto de Investigaciones Estéticas. Universidad Nacional Autónoma
de México. Estudios y fuentes del arte en México, 14)

17990   Acasuso, Rubén.
Achtung. ¡Peligro!   Montevideo, Ediciones Estrella,
1961.
38 p.   20 cm.

17991   Accioli, Roberto.
Non rex sed Caesar.   Sintese da vida e da obra
de Caio Julio César.   [Rio de Janeiro] Edições o
Cruzeiro [1968]
156 p.   19½ cm.

17992   Accioly, Marcus.
Cancioneiro.   Recife, Universidade Federal de
Pernambuco, 1968.
44 p.   22 cm.

17993   Acción para el Desarrollo.
Lineamientos básicos para una política económica
peruana: 5 conferencias de Emilio Castañón [y otros]
Lima, Biblioteca de Acción para el Desarrollo [1965]
135 p.   21 cm.

17994   Acción Popular (Peru) Secretaría Nacional de
Propaganda.
El hombre de la bandera: Fernando Belaúnde Terry
[por el Departamento de Publicaciones de la Secretaría
Nacional de Propaganda. 1. ed.] Lima, Ediciones

Tawantinsuyu, 1962.
136 p.   illus., ports.   17 cm.

17995   Acedo, Pedro Perdomo, 1897-
Pedro Perdomo Acedo, par René L.-F. Durand. Dakar,
Centre de Hautes Études Afro-Ibéro-Américaines,
Faculté des Lettres et Sciences Humaines, Université
de Dakar, 1973.
80 p.   22½ cm.   (Cahiers de poésie des Îles
Canaries, IV)

17996   Acevedo, Edberto Oscar.
Informe sobre la documentación histórica relativo
a Cuyo existente en el Archivo (y Biblioteca) Nacional
de Santiago de Chile. Mendoza, Argentina, Universidad
Nacional de Cuyo, 1963.
232 p.   fold. maps.   20 cm.   (Serie I [Fuentes
documentales] no. 1)

17997   Acevedo, Edberto Oscar.
La rebelión de 1767 en el Tucumán. Mendoza,
Argentina, Instituto de Historia, Facultad de Filosofía
y Letras, Universidad Nacional de Cuyo, 1969.
232 p.   19½ cm.   (Serie II, Monografías, 2)
Bibliography: p. [227]

17998   Achury Valenzuela, Darío.
Palabras con azar: glosas. Bogotá, Instituto
Caro y Cuervo, 1975.
185 p.   21½ cm.   (La Granada entreabierta, 8)

17999   Acioli, J   L
The $K+\mu 3$ and $K+\epsilon 3$ decay through a current of
definite isotopic rank, by J. L. Acioli and S. W.
MacDowell. Rio de Janeiro, Centro Brasileiro de
Pesquisas Físicas, 1961.
163-175 p.   diagrs.   28 cm.   (Notas de física,
v. 8, no. 9)

18000   Ackermann, Fritz.
A obra poética de Antônio Gonçalves Dias. Tradução
de Egon Schaden. São Paulo, Comissão de Literatura,
Conselho Estadual de Cultura, 1964.
176 p.   22 cm.   (Coleção Ensaio, 32)
Translation of Die Versdichtung des Brasiliers
Antônio Gonçalves Dias.
Issued also as thesis, Hamburg, 1937.

18001 Acosta, Cecilio, 1818-1881.
Cecilio Acosta: estudio preliminar de Oscar
Sambrano Urdaneta. [Caracas] Academia Venezolana de
la Lengua, 1963.
211 p. illus. 23 cm. (Colección clásicos
venezolanos de la Academia Venezolana de la Lengua, 3)
Includes bibliography.

18002 Acosta, Ricardo.
Teatro. El asfalto de los infiernos. El baile de
los cautivos. Agonía y muerte del Caravaggio. La
vida es sueño (versión moderna) Caracas, Dirección
de Cultura, Universidad Central de Venezuela, 1969.
211 p. 21 cm. (Letras de Venezuela, 19)

18003 Acosta Hermoso, Eduardo.
Análisis histórico de la O.P.E.P. Mérida, Venezuela,
Universidad de los Andes, Facultad de Economía, 1969.
129 p. tables (part fold.) 24 cm.

18004 Acosta Hoyos, Luis Eduardo, ed.
Un temperamento: Edmundo Medina Madroñero.
Compilado por Luis Eduardo Acosta Hoyos. Pasto,
Editorial Sur Colombiana, 1965.
184 p. port. 23 cm.
At head of title: Universidad de Narino. Biblioteca
General.
Contents. - Introducción. - Datos biográficos y
curriculum vitae. - El medio ambiente, por I.
Rodríguez Guerrero. - La batalla, por G. A. Jurado. -
La conquista, por A. Quijano Guerrero. - Proposi-
ciones, acuerdos y decretos expedidos con motivo de
su deceso. - Discursos pronunciados ante los despojos
mortales del escritor. - La prensa escrita de la
ciudad y del país hace eco al dolor producido por
la muerte del escritor nariñense, en la siguiente
forma. - Carta a "Marcucho Landi," por K. A. Melo. -
Entrega de su colección particular a la Biblioteca
General por voluntad del escritor. - Antología y
reseña bibliografía de su obra.

18005 Acosta Hoyos, Luis Eduardo.
Manual para auxiliares de biblioteca. Edición
preliminar. Medellín, Colombia, Departamento de
Bibliotecas, Universidad de Antioquia, 1969.
v, 45 ℓ. 24 cm.

18006 Acosta Saignes, Miguel.
Breve historia del Instituto de Antropología e

Historia [por] Miguel Acosta Saignes [y] Edgard
Rodríguez Leal. [Caracas, Imprenta Universitaria,
1962?]
    15, 59 p.   23 cm.
"Separata de Archivos venezolanos de folklore,
años X y XI, no. 7, 1961-1962)"

18007 Acosta Saignes, Miguel.
    Cerámica de la luna en los Andes venezolanos.
Mérida [1957]
    23 p.   illus.   24 cm.   (Publicaciones de la
Dirección de Cultura de la Universidad de Los Andes,
no. 59)

18008 Acosta Saignes, Miguel.
    Estudios de folklore venezolano. Caracas, Instituto
de Antropología e Historia, Facultad de Humanidades y
Educación, Universidad Central de Venezuela, 1962.
    289 p.   illus.   24 cm.   (Serie de folklore)

18009 Acosta Saignes, Miguel.
    La vivienda rural en Paraguaná y en Margarita.
Caracas, Instituto de Antropología e Historia, Facultad
de Humanidades y Educación, Universidad Central de
Venezuela, 1961.
    18 p.   illus.   24 cm.
"Separata del no. 6 de 'Archivos venezolanos de
folklore.'"

18010 Acosta y Lara, Eduardo F
    La guerra de los Charrúas en la Banda Oriental
(periodo hispánico)   Montevideo, Impresores F.
Monteverde, 1961.
    251 p.   illus.   25 cm.
    Includes bibliography.

18011 Acqua, Amadeo dell', ed.
    La caricatura política argentina; antología.
[Selección y presentación de Amadeo dell' Acqua.
Buenos Aires] Editorial Universitaria de Buenos Aires
[1960]
    149 p.   illus.   19 cm.   (Serie del siglo y
medio, 19)

18012 Acquaviva, Edelmira Duarte de.
    Adolescencia e identidad. [Maracaibo] Facultad de
Humanidades e Educación, Universidad del Zulia [1968]
    26 p.   21 cm.
    Bibliography: p. 25-26.

18013   Acquaviva, Edelmira Duarte de.
         Orientación y educación. Maracaibo, Facultad de
         Humanidades y Educación, Universidad del Zulia, 1972.
         237 p.   29 cm.

18014   Acquaviva, Edelmira Duarte de.
         Situación del profesor guía en el nivel de educación
         media en Venezuela. Trabajo presentado por la Lic.
         Edelmira Duarte de Acquaviva, para su ascenso en la
         categoría de profesor agregado en el escalafón del
         personal docente de la Universidad del Zulia.
         [Maracaibo] Facultad de Humanidades y Educación,
         Universidad del Zulia [1968]
            [90] p.   graphs.   22 cm.
         Bibliography: p. 87.

18015   Acta amazonica. ano 1-   abril 1971-
         [Manaus, Instituto Nacional de Pesquisas da Amazônia]
            v.   illus.   29 cm.   3 no. a year.
         English or Portuguese with summary in the other
         language.
         Library has v. 1, 2.

18016   Acuña B   , Olda María.
         La familia en Costa Rica [por] Olda M. Acuña B. [y]
         Carlos F. Denton L. [San José, Costa Rica] Ministerio
         de Cultura, Juventud y Deportes e Instituto de Estudios
         Sociales en Población (IDESPO) 1979.
            101 p.   19½ cm.
         Ports. on back cover.
         Bibliography: p. 94-98.

18017   Acuña de Figueroa, Francisco Esteban.
         Antología. Prólogo de Armando D. Pirotto. Monte-
         video [Ministerio de Instrucción Pública y Previsión
         Social] 1965.
            lxxxviii, 182 p.   19 cm.   (Biblioteca Artigas.
         Colección de clásicos uruguayos, 82)

18018   Acuña Galé, Julián.
         Flora de las ciénagas de Cuba. La Habana,
         Academia de Ciencias de Cuba, Instituto de Biología,
         1964.
            10 p.   24 cm.   (Poeyana, serie A, no. 3)
         Caption title.
         Summary in English.

18019   Adam, Félix, 1925-
         La educación de adultos y los planes de desarrollo

12

económico y social en Venezuela [por Félix Adam y
Pedro Tomás Vásquez] Caracas [Ministerio de Educación,
Oficina de Educación de Adultos, 1965]
71 p.   illus.   24 cm.   (Ediciones ODEA)

18020   Adami, João Spadari, 1897-
História de Caxias do Sul. Primeiro tomo.   Caxias
do Sul, Brazil, Editora São Miguel [1962?]
414 p.   illus.   24 cm.

18021   Adams, Richard Newbold, 1924-
La brecha tecnológica.   Algunas de sus conse-
cuencias en el desarrollo de América Latina [por]
Richard N. Adams.   [Austin, Institute of Latin
American Studies, University of Texas, 1969]
28-40 p.   22 cm.   (Offprint series, 96)
"Sobretiro de Foro Internacional, vol. X, no. 1,
El Colegio de México, 1969."

18022   Adams, Richard Newbold, 1924-
The development of the Guatemalan military [by]
Richard N. Adams.   [Austin, Institute of Latin
American Studies, University of Texas, 1969]
91-110 p.   tables.   28½ cm.   (Offprint series,
90)
Reprinted from Studies in Comparative international
development, vol. IV, no. 5, 1968-1969.

18023   Adams, Richard Newbold, 1924-
Introducción a la antropología aplicada; libro de
texto y manual para trabajadores de bienestar social
en América Latina.   Versión castellana y prólogo de
Jorge Skinner Klée.   Guatemala, Centro Editorial
"José de Pineda Ibarra," Ministerio de Educación
Pública, 1964.
382 p.   20 cm.   (Seminario de Integración
Social Guatemalteca.   Publicación, no. 13)

18024   Adams, Richard Newbold, 1924-
Nationalization [by] Richard N. Adams.   Austin,
Institute of Latin American Studies, University of
Texas [196-]
468-489 p.   table.   27 cm.   (Offprint
series, 60)
"Reprinted from Social anthropology, ed. Manning
Nash, vol. VI of Handbook of Middle American Indians,
gen. ed. Robert Wauchope."

13

18025   Adato Green, Victoria.
        Reflexiones sobre la reforma penal mexicana;
        parte general. México, 1963.
        125 p.   map.   24 cm.
        Bibliography: p. 123-124.

18026   Adem, J
        La Isla Socorro, archipiélago de las Revillagigedo.
        México, Instituto de Geofísica, Universidad Nacional,
        1960.
        234 p.   illus., plates, maps, diagrs.   24 cm.
        (Monografías, 2)

18027   Adet, Walter.
        En el sendero gris, sonetos. Salta [República
        Argentina] Ediciones Cepa [1962]
        1 v. (unpaged)   22 cm.

18028   Adler, John Hans, 1913-
        Recursos financieros y reales para el desarrollo.
        México, 1961.
        148 p.   fold. charts.   21 cm.   (Centro de
        Estudios Monetarios Latinoamericanos. Conferencias)

18029   Adonias, Isa.
        A cartografía da região amazônica; catálogo
        descritivo: 1500-1961 [por] Isa Adonias [com a cola-
        boração da Sra. Maria de Lourdes Jovita] Rio de
        Janeiro, Conselho Nacional de Pesquisas, Instituto
        Nacional de Pesquisas da Amazônia, 1963.
        2 v.   fold. maps (part. col.) plates.   27 cm.

18030   Adorno Benitez, Felix.
        Relato de episodios de la guerra del Paraguay
        con Bolivia, 1932-1935. Asunción, Paraguay, El Arte,
        1963.
        171 p.   illus., maps, ports.   23 cm.

18031   Agency for International Development. Regional
        Technical Aids Center.
        ... 1969-1970 Spanish-language film catalog.
        Catálogo de películas en español, 1969-1970.
        México/Buenos Aires, Centro Regional de Ayuda Técnica,
        Agencia para el Desarrollo Internacional (A.I.D.)
        [n.d.]
        212 p.   23 cm.
        Parallel English and Spanish text.

18032 Agor, Weston H   1939-
       The decisional role of the Senate in the Chilean
       political system, by Weston H. Agor. Madison, Land
       Tenure Center, University of Wisconsin, 1969.
       44 ℓ.   28 cm.   (University of Wisconsin. Land
       Tenure Center. LTC no. 66)
       Includes bibliographical references.

18033 Agostini, Victor.
       Dos viajes. La Habana, Ediciones Revolución, 1965.
       291 p.   21½ cm.

18034 Agraz García de Alba, Gabriel.
       Datos biográficos del presbítero, profesor y escritor
       Higinio Vázquez Santa Ana. México, 1963.
       53 p.   illus., ports.   20 cm.
       Bibliography: p. 49.

18035 A Agricultura subdesenvolvida [por] Caio Prado Jr.
       [et al] Petrópolis, Editôra Vozes [1969]
       275 p.   illus.   19 cm.   (Coleção Caminhos
       brasileiros, 2)
       Bibliographical footnotes.
       Contents. - Contribuição para a análise da questão
       agrária no Brasil, por C. Prado Jr. - A situação rural
       na América Latina, por J. Medina Echevarria. - As
       formas sociais da utilização da terra e os setores
       agrícolas predominantes, por M. Paixão. - Estrutura
       interna do latifúndio, pelo Comité Interamericano de
       Desenvolvimento Agrário (CIDA) da OEA. - Reflexões
       sôbre as tendências da produção, da produtividade,
       e dos preços do setor agrícola do Brasil, por R.
       Miller Paiva. - Bases de uma política para a melhoria
       técnica da agricultura brasileira, por R. Miller Paiva. -
       Reflexão da estrutura agrícola, por M. Averbug.

18036 Aguado, Pedro de, 16th cent.
       Recopilación historial de Venezuela. Estudio
       preliminar de Guillermo Morón. Caracas, Academia
       Nacional de la Historia, 1963.
       2 v.   23 cm.   (Biblioteca de la Academia Nacional
       de la Historia, 62-63)
       Bibliography: v. 1, p. [lxxvii]-lxxx.

18037 Aguado-Andreut, Salvador.
       Por el mundo poético de Rubén Darío. Guatemala,
       Editorial Universitaria, 1966.
       307 p.   18 cm.   (Publicación 54)

15

18038   Aguayo, Carlos Guillermo.
        Una lista de los moluscos terrestres y fluviales de
        Puerto Rico. Rio Piedras, Puerto Rico, Museum of
        Biology, University of Puerto Rico, 1966.
        16 p.   25½ cm.   (Stahlia 5)

18039   Agudo Freites, Raúl.
        Pío Tamayo y la vanguardia. Caracas, Ediciones de
        la Biblioteca, Universidad Central de Venezuela,
        1969.
        207 p.   22 cm.   (Colección temas)

18040   Aguiar, Luis Cristóvão Dias de, 1940-
        Mãos vazias; poemas [por] Cristóvão Aguiar.   Coimbra,
        Livraria Almedina, 1965.
        61 p.   21 cm.

18041   Aguilar, Antonio.
        Del yo al mí. [San Juan, Argentina] Editorial
        Sanjuanina, 1966.
        149 p.   22 cm.   (Editorial Sanjuanina.
        [Publicaciones] 15)
        Bibliography: p. 149.

18042   Aguilar, Carlos H
        Religión y magia entre los indios de Costa Rica de
        origen sureño.   Ciudad Universitaria Rodrigo Facio,
        Universidad de Costa Rica, 1965.
        83 p.   20 cm.   (Serie Historia y geografía, 6)

18043   Aguilar, Esperanza.
        Eliot el hombre, no el viejo gato. [Santiago de
        Chile, Editorial Universitaria, 1962]
        103 p.   port.   19 cm.   (El Espejo de papel)
        Bibliography: p. 103.

18044   Aguilar, Luis A
        Algunas anotaciones sobre el programa de subsidios
        conservacionistas que actualmente se desarrollan en
        los estados Táchira y Mérida.   Caracas, Taller
        Gráfica M.A.C., 1962.
        25 p.   illus.   32 cm.   (Publicaciones del
        Ministerio de Agricultura y Cría)
        At head of title: Dirección de Recursos Naturales
        Renovables.   División de Protección y Parques Nacionales
        Sección de Conservación de Suelos y Aguas.

18045   Aguilar, Santiago.
        Tinieblas elegidas.   Trujillo [Perú] Ediciones

"Grupo Trilce" [1964]
56 p.   17 cm.
Poems.

18046   Aguilar Arroyo, Mario Roberto.
La función notarial en nuestro medio. Guatemala,
1965.
33 p.   23 cm.
Tesis (licenciatura en ciencias jurídicas y sociales) -
Universidad de San Carlos de Guatemala.
Bibliography: p. 33.

18047   Aguilar Barroso, Francisco.
Violación de correspondencia; estudio dogmático.
México, Universidad Nacional Autónoma de México,
Seminario de Derecho Penal, Facultad de Derecho, 1964.
120 p.   24 cm.
Bibliography: p. 119-120.

18048   Aguilar Bulgarelli, Oscar, ed.
El desarrollo nacional en 150 años de vida independiente. Ciudad Universitaria "Rodrigo Facio,"
Universidad de Costa Rica, 1971.
401 p.   26 cm.   (Publicaciones de la Universidad
de Costa Rica. Serie historia y geografía, 12)

18049   Aguilar Chávez, M
Puros cuentos. San Salvador, Departamento Editorial,
Ministerio de Cultura, 1959.
145 p.   18 cm.   (Contemporáneos, 13)

18050   Aguilar Gorrondona, José Luis.
Derecho civil. Caracas, 1963-
v.   23 cm.   (Universidad Católica Andrés
Bello. Manuales de derecho)
Contents. - v. 1. Personas.

18051   Aguilar Gorrondona, José Luis.
Necesidad, apertura y constitución de la tutela
ordinaria de menores en el derecho venezolano.
Caracas, 1962.
334 p.   24 cm.   (Universidad Central. Publicaciones de la Facultad de Derecho, v. 26)
Continuation of Teoría general de la tutela de
menores en el derecho venezolano.
Bibliographical footnotes.

18052   Aguilar Merlo, Carlos de, 1930-
Un alcalde bajo los álamos; comedia dramática en

17

cuatro cuadros. Panamá, Ediciones del Departamento
de Bellas Artes, 1964.
88 p.   23 cm.
With, as issued (inverted) Martínez, José de Jesús.
Aurora y el mestizo. Panamá, 1964.

18053 Aguilar Villa, Mario Alberto.
Contrato individual de trabajo. Bogotá, Editorial
Kelly, 1963.
111 p.   24 cm.
Tesis - Pontificia Universidad Javeriana, Bogotá.
Bibliography: p. 107-108.

18054 Aguilera, Francisco, comp.
The archive of Hispanic literature on tape: a
descriptive guide. Compiled by Francisco Aguilera.
Edited by Georgette Magassy Dorn... Washington,
Library of Congress, 1974.
xii, 516 p.   24 cm.

18055 Aguilera, Julio Fausto.
10 [i.e. Diez] poemas fieles. Guatemala, 1964.
30 p.   23 cm.

18056 Aguilera Ripoll, Ana Margarita.
El cancionero infantil de Hispanoamericanos. La
Habana, Biblioteca Nacional José Marti, 1960.
92 p.   22 cm.
Includes melodies with words.
Bibliography: p. 91-92.

18057 Aguinsky de Iribarne, Esther.
Justicia y derecho. Montevideo, Facultad de
Derecho y Ciencias Sociales de la Universidad de la
República, 1965.
162 p.   22 cm.   (Publicaciones, Sección III,
XXX)

18058 Aguirre, Angel M
Viaje de J. R. Jiménez a la Argentina [por] Angel
M. Aguirre. [Austin, Institute of Latin American
Studies, University of Texas, 1969]
19 p.   24 cm.   (Offprint series, 92)
"Trabajo publicado en la revista 'Cuadernos Hispano-
americanos' Marzo 1969, no. 231, Madrid."

18059 Aguirre, J   M
Calisto y Melibea, amantes cortesanos, por J. M.
Aguirre. Zaragoza, 1962.

94 p.   18 cm.   (Colección de ensayos Almenara, 1)
Bibliographical references included in "Notas":
p. 85-94.

18060   Aguirre, J   M
José de Valdivielso y la poesía religiosa tradicional
[por] J. M. Aguirre. Toledo, Diputación Provincial,
1965.
222 p.   21 cm.   (Publicaciones del Instituto
Provincial de Investigaciones y Estudios Toledanos.
Sección primera: Monografías, v. 2)
At head of title: Patronato "José María Quadrado"
del Consejo Superior de Investigaciones Científicas.
Bibliography: p. [181]-214.

18061   Aguirre, Manuel J
La intervención francesa y el imperio en México.
Guadalajara, México, Gobierno del Estado de Jalisco,
1969.
349 p.   20½ cm.

18062   Aguirre, Nataniel, 1843-1888.
Juan de la Rosa; memorias del último soldado de la
independencia. [5. ed. Buenos Aires] Editorial
Universitaria de Buenos Aires [1964]
270 p.   18 cm.   (Serie del Nuevo Mundo)

18063   Aguirre Beltrán, Gonzalo.
The Indian economic service development of Guatemala
[by Gonzalo Aguirre Beltrán and Emil J. Sady. New
York, United Nations] 1960.
46 p.   22 cm.

18064   Aguirre Beltrán, Gonzalo.
La universidad latinoamericana, y otros ensayos.
[1. ed.] Xalapa, México, Universidad Veracruzana,
1961.
203 p.   23 cm.   (Biblioteca de la Facultad de
Filosofía y Letras, 10)

18065   Aguirre Gamio, Hernando.
Liquidación histórica del Apra y del colonialismo
neoliberal. Lima, 1962.
239 p.   17 cm.

18066   Aguirre Godoy, Mario.
La declaración unilateral de voluntad como fuente
de obligaciones. Guatemala, Editorial Universitaria,
1960.

233 p. 24 cm. (Universidad de San Carlos de
Guatemala. Editorial Universitaria. [Publicaciones]
v. 36)

18067 Aguirre Godoy, Mario.
La prueba en el proceso civil guatemalteco.
Guatemala, Universidad de San Carlos de Guatemala,
Facultad de Ciencias Jurídicas y Sociales, Profesorado
de Medio Tiempo, 1965.
171 p. 22 cm.
Bibliographical footnotes.

18068 Aguirre Prieto, Javier.
Los puertos libres mexicanos. México, 1963.
104 p. 23 cm.
Tesis (licenciatura en derecho) - Universidad
Nacional Autónoma de México.
Bibliography: p. 99-101.

18069 Agulla, Juan Carlos.
La educación y las ciencias en la sociedad de
masas. Córdoba, Argentina, Dirección General de
Publicidad, Universidad Nacional, 1961.
144 p. 20 cm. (Grandes problemas contemporáneos)

18070 Agustini, Delmira, 1886-1914.
Antología. Selección y prólogo de Esther de
Cáceres. Montevideo [Ministerio de Instrucción Pública
y Previsión Social] 1965.
xiv, 65 p. 20 cm. (Biblioteca Artigas.
Colección de clásicos uruguayos, v. 69)
"La mayor parte de los poemas... fueron cotejados
con los que figuran en Los cálices vacíos, Montevideo,
O. M. Bertani, 1913... conservándose en ellos fiel-
mente la puntuación y el empleo de los signos
admirativos e interrogativos."

18071 Agustini, Delmira, 1886-1914.
Correspondencia íntima. Estudio, ordenación y
prólogo de Arturo Sergio Visca. Montevideo, Departamento de Investigaciones, Biblioteca Nacional, 1969.
53 p. illus. 25 cm.

18072 Ahumada, Juan Antonio.
Estados para un alba en sí. Córdoba, Distribuye
Assandri, 1969.
93 p. 22 cm.
Poems.

20

18073   Ahumada B   , J
        Estudio radiométrico ambiental de la sabana de
        Bogotá; preliminar, por J. Ahumada B. Bogotá,
        Instituto de Asuntos Nucleares, División de Radiofísica
        Sanitaria, 1965.
        55 ℓ.   illus., maps.   27 cm.   (IAN-RS-ERA-1)
        Bibliography: leaf 54.

18074   Aires de Menezes, Durval, 1922-
        Barra da solidão; novela-reportagem [por] Durval
        Aires. Fortaleza, Imp. Universitária, 1968.
        93 p.   20 cm.

18075   Ajofrín, Francisco de, 18th cent.
        ... Diario del viaje que hicimos a México fray
        Francisco de Ajofrín y fray Fermín de Olite, capuchinos;
        con una introducción por Genero Estrada. México,
        Antiqua librería Robredo de J. Porrúa e hijos, 1936.
        32 p., 1 ℓ.   illus.   23½ cm.   (Biblioteca
        histórica mexicana de obras inéditas, 1)

18076   Akademiīa nauk SSSR.   Institut Latinskoĭ Ameriki.
        Освободительное движение в Латинской Америке. ¡От-
        ветственный редактор С. С. Михайлов₎ Москва, Наука, 1964.
        426 p.   21 cm.
        Bibliographical footnotes.

18077   Akademiīa nauk SSSR.   Institut mirovoĭ ėkonomiki i
        mezhdunarodnykh otnosheniĭ.
        Аграрно-крестьянский вопрос на современном этапе
        национально-освободительного движения в странах Азии,
        Африки и Латинской Америки. ¡Ответственный редактор
        В. А. Мартынов₎ Москва, Наука: Глав. ред. восточной
        лит-ры, 1965.
        214 p.   20 cm.
        Bibliographical footnotes.

18078   Alabama.   Agricultural Experiment Station.   International
        Center for Aquaculture.
        Annual report. Auburn, Ala., 1974-
        v.   illus., tables.   28 cm.
        Library has 1973, 1974, 1975, 1976.

18079   Alamán, Lucas, 1792-1853.
        Disertaciones sobre la historia de la República
        Megicana, desde la época de la conquista que los
        Españoles hicieron, a fines del siglo XV y principios
        del XVI, de las islas y continente americano, hasta
        la independencia. Por D. Lucas Alamán... Mégico,
        Impr. de J. M. Lara, 1844-49.

21

3 v.   plates (1 col.)   ports., double map,
plans, fold. facsims.   23½ cm.
Vols. 1-2 have each an appendix of "Documentos
raros ó ineditos relativos a la historia de Megico."

18080   Alarco, Luis Felipe.
Guía didáctica.   [1. ed.   Lima] Universidad Nacional
Mayor de San Marcos [1960]
180 p.   music.   17 cm.   (Biblioteca de
cultura general.   Serie Educación, 6)

18081   Alarcón, José C
Compendio de historia del departamento del Magdalena
de 1525 hasta 1895.   [Bogotá, Editorial El Voto
Nacional, 1963]
455 p.   illus.   21 cm.

18082   Alarcón de Folgar, Romelia.
Poemas de la vida simple.   Guatemala, Centro
Editorial "José de Pineda Ibarra," Ministerio de
Educación Pública, 1963.
174 p.   20 cm.   (Colección Contemporáneos, 73)

18083   Alario di Filippo, Mario, 1920-
Lexicón de colombianismos [por] M. Alario di
Filippo.   Cartagena, Colombia, Impreso en la Editora
Bolívar, 1964.
viii, 391 p.   24 cm.
Bibliography: p. [387]-391.

18084   Alayo Delmau, Pastor.
Estudios sobre los himenópteros de Cuba.   La
Habana, Academia de Ciencias de Cuba, Instituto de
Biología, 1968.
4 v.   illus.   25 cm.   (Poeyana, serie A,
54, 58, 59, 61)

18085   Alayo Delmau, Pastor.
Estudios sobre los himenópteros de Cuba.   VII.
Dos nuevas especies para la fauna mirmecológica
cubana [por] Pastor Alayo D. y Lorenzo Zayas Montero.
La Habana, Academia de Ciencias de Cuba, Instituto
de Zoología, 1977.
5 p.   illus.   23 cm.   (Poeyana, 174)

18086   Alayo Delmau, Pastor.
Los neurópteros de Cuba.   La Habana, Academia
de Ciencias de Cuba, 1968.
127 p.   illus. (part col.)   28 cm.   (Poeyana,

serie B, 2)
Summary in English.
Bibliography: p. 79-80.

18087   Alayo Soto, Rafael.
Introducción al estudio de los coccoideos de Cuba
[por] Rafael Alayo Soto. La Habana, Academia de
Ciencias de Cuba, Instituto de Zoología, 1976.
19 p., 6 pl.   26½ cm.   (Serie biológica, 61)

18088   Alayón García, Giraldo.
Descripción del macho de Nops ludovicorum y redes-
cripción de la hembra de Nops guanabacoae (Arachnida:
Araneae, Caponiidae) [por] Giraldo Alayón García.
La Habana, Academia de Ciencias de Cuba, Instituto de
Zoología, 1977.
8 p.   illus., tables.   23 cm.   (Poeyana, 169)
Abstract in English: p. 1.

18089   Alayón García, Giraldo.
Nueva especie de Nops Mac Leay, 1839 (Araneae:
Caponiidae) de Isla de Pinos, Cuba. La Habana,
Instituto de Zoología, Academia de Ciencias de Cuba,
1976.
6 p.   illus.   23 cm.   (Poeyana, 148)
Abstract in English.

18090   Alayón García, Giraldo.
Nuevas especies de Scytodes Latreille, 1804
(Araneae: Scytodidae) de Cuba [por] Giraldo Alayón
García. La Habana, Instituto de Zoología, Academia
de Ciencias de Cuba, 1977.
20 p.   illus., tables.   23 cm.   (Poeyana, 177)
"Literatura citada": p. 20.
Abstract in English: p. 1.

18091   Alazragui Alonso, Jaime A
La industria azucarera Argentina; la industria de
la caña de azúcar. [Buenos Aires?] 1960.
2 v.   illus., maps.   22 cm.
At head of title: Banco Industrial de la República
Argentina. Dirección de Promoción y Desarrollo
Industrial. Gerencia de Investigaciones Técnicas.
Includes bibliographies.

18092   Alba, Victor.
Populism and national awareness in Latin America.
Lawrence, Center of Latin American Studies, University

of Kansas, 1966.
24 p.   24 cm.   (Occasional publications, 6)

18093   Albano, José.
Rimas. Fortaleza, Imprensa Universitária do Ceará, 1966.
240 p.   ports.   18 cm.

18094   Albear, Jesús Francisco de.
Las formaciones geológicas y su importancia en la solución de algunos problemas geológicos, por Jesús Francisco de Albear, Irina V. Jvorova, Elena A. Sokolova, Amelia Brito y Pablo Donis Coutin. La Habana, 1968.
16 p.   28 cm.   (Academia de Ciencias de Cuba. Instituto de Geología. Serie geológica, no. 2)
Résumés in English and French.

18095   Alberdi, Juan Bautista, 1810-1884.
Bases y puntos de partida para la organización política de la República Argentina. [Buenos Aires] Editorial Universitaria de Buenos Aires [1966]
237 p.   18 cm.   (Serie del siglo y medio, 115)

18096   Alberini, Coriolano.
Escritos de ética. Mendoza, Instituto de Filosofía, Facultad de Filosofía y Letras, Universidad Nacional de Cuyo, 1973.
227 p.   illus.   23 cm.

18097   Alberini, Coriolano.
Problemas de la historia de las ideas filosóficas en la Argentina. La Plata, Instituto de Estudios Sociales y del Pensamiento Argentino, Universidad Nacional de La Plata, 1966.
140 p.   23 cm.   (Col. Pensamiento argentino)

18098   Alberione, Santiago.
Elementos de sociología cristiana. [Florida, Argentina, 1963]
216 p.   20 cm.

18099   Albertazzi Avendaño, José, 1892-
Canto a la amada viva y muerta; [poemas. San José, Costa Rica, A. Lehmann, Librería e Imprenta, 1962]
59 p.   20 cm.

18100   Alberti, Giorgio.
The breakdown of provincial urban power structure

24

and the rise of peasant movements. Madison, Land
Tenure Center, University of Wisconsin, 1973.
315-333 p.   23 cm.   (LTC reprint no. 103)
Reprinted from Sociología ruralis, v. 12, no. 3/4,
1972.

18101 Alberti, Rafael, 1902-
Los viejos olivos. [Poemas] Homenaje de la revista
nacional de cultura. [Caracas] Ministerio de Educación,
Dirección de Cultura y Bellas Artes, Departamento de
Publicaciones [1960]
unpaged.   illus.   31 cm.

18102 Albiol Estapé, Enrique.
Una madre caminó de los altares; la sierva de Dios
Práxedes Fernández. 2. ed., completamente revisada,
por Enrique Fernández. [Bogotá] Ediciones Paulinas
[1962]
248 p.   illus., ports.   17 cm.

18103 Albornoz, Orlando, 1932-
¿Qué es la sociología? y otros ensayos. Caracas,
Universidad Central de Venezuela, Organización de
Bienestar Estudiantil, 1964.
171 p.   25 cm.

18104 Albornoz, Orlando, 1932-
La sociología en Venezuela. Caracas, Universidad
Central de Venezuela, Facultad de Economía, Escuela
de Sociología y Antropología [1962]
240 p.   20 cm.   (Colección Estudios sociales,
v. 1)
Bibliography: p. 239-240.

18105 Albornoz, Victor Manuel.
Alberto Muñoz Vernaza. Cuenca, Núcleo del Azuay,
Casa de la Cultura Ecuatoriana, 1969.
216 p.   ports.   23 cm.

18106 Albornoz de la Escosura, Alvaro de.
Trayectoria y ritmo del crédito agrícola en México
[por] Alvaro de Albornoz. [1. ed.] México,
Instituto Mexicano de Investigaciones Económicas,
1966.
497 p.   24 cm.
Bibliography: p. [489]-493.

18107 Albuquerque, Byron Wilson Pereira de.
Contribuição ao conhecimento das Aspidosperma da

25

Amazônia Brasileira (Apocynaceae) [Belém] 1971.
9-20 p. illus., table. 29½ cm.
Reprinted from Acta Amazônica, v. 1, no. 2.
"Bibliografia citada": p. 16-17.
Summary in English: p. 16.

18108 Albuquerque, Byron Wilson Pereira de.
Contribuição ao conhecimento de Aspidosperma album
(Vahl) R. Ben. e Aspidosperma obscurinervium Azamcuja,
da Amazônia-apocynaceae. Manaus, Brazil, Instituto
Nacional de Pesquisas da Amazônia, 1968.
16 p., 30 pl. fold. pl. 24 cm. (Instituto
Nacional de Pesquisas da Amazônia. Publicação.
Botânica, no. 26)

18109 Albuquerque, Byron Wilson Pereira de.
Contribuição ao conhecimento de Couma macrocarpa
Barb. Rodr. e C. utilis (Mart.) M. Arg. (Apocynaceae)
da Amazônia. [Belém] 1973.
7-15 p. illus. 29½ cm.
Reprinted from Acta Amazônica, v. 3, no. 2.
"Bibliografia citada": p. 14-15.
Summary in English: p. 14.

18110 Albuquerque, Byron Wilson Pereira de.
Contribuição ao estudo da nervação de plantas da
flora amazônica. II. Fagara Prancei Alubq. (Rutaceae)
[Belém] 1971.
11-13 p. illus. 29½ cm.
Reprinted from Acta Amazônica, v. 1, no. 1.
"Bibliografia citada": p. 12.
Summary in English: p. 12.

18111 Albuquerque, Byron Wilson Pereira de.
Contribuição ao estudo da nervação foliar de
plantas da flora amazônica, I -- gênero Fagara
(Rutaceae) Manaus, Instituto Nacional de Pesquisas
da Amazônia, 1969.
18 p., 18 unnumb. ℓ. illus. 23 cm. (Boletim
do INPA, Botânica, no. 33)
Summary in English: p. 13.
"Literatura citada": p. 13-14.

18112 Albuquerque, Byron Wilson Pereira de.
Contribuição ao estudo da nervação foliar de
plantas da flora amazônica. [Belém] 1972.
21-22 p. illus. 29½ cm.
Reprinted from Acta Amazônica, v. 2, no. 1.

"Bibliografía citada": p. 22.
"Summary in English": p. 22.

18113 Albuquerque, Byron Wilson Pereira de.
Revisão taxonômica das Rutaceae do estado do
Amazônas [por] Byron W. P. de Albuquerque. Manaus,
Instituto Nacional de Pesquisas da Amazônia, 1978.
67 p. illus., maps. 29 cm. (Acta amazônica,
v. 6, no. 3: Suplemento)

18114 Albuquerque, Francisco Uchoa de.
Noções de filosofia, para o vestibular. Fortaleza,
Ceará, Imprensa Universitária do Ceará, 1966.
215 p. 24 cm.
"Segunda edição."

18115 Albuquerque, Isolda Rocha e Silva.
Check-list dos Blattaria brasileiros. Manaus,
Brazil, 1964.
37 p. 24 cm. (Boletim do Museu Paraense
Emílio Goeldi, Nova série, Zoologia, no. 41)

18116 Albuquerque, Isolda Rocha e Silva.
... Sôbre quatro espécies novas de baratas da
Amazônia (dictioptera blattaria). Belém, Pará,
Conselho Nacional de Pesquisas, Instituto Nacional
de Pesquisas da Amazônia, Museu Paraense Emílio
Goeldi, 1967.
11 p. illus. 23 cm. (Boletim do Museu
Paraense Emílio Goeldi, Nova série, Zoologia,
no. 65, Agôsto 16, 1967)

18117 Albuquerque, Olavo A   L   Pires e.
Fresadoras, por Olavo A. L. Pires e Albuquerque.
Belo Horizonte, 1952.
30, [1] p. illus. 22 cm. (Instituto de
Tecnologia Industrial do Estado de Minas Gerais.
Boletim, no. 13)
Bibliography: p. [31]

18118 Albuquerque, Sérgio Moacir de.
Murais da morte. Apresentação de Renato Carneiro
Campos. Il de Vicente Monteiro. Recife, Universidade
Federal de Pernambuco, 1968.
69 p. 22 cm.
Poems.

18119 Albuquerque, Tereza Tenório de.
Parábola (poesía) Recife, Edição da revista

27

Estudos universitários, Universidade Federal de
Pernambuco, 1970.
38 p.   24 cm.

18120   Alcalá González, María Guadalupe.
La expropiación por causa de utilidad pública, en
las ejecutorias de la H. Suprema Corte de Justicia
de la Nación. México, 1961.
147 p.   23 cm.
Tesis (licenciatura en derecho) - Universidad
Nacional Autónoma de México.
Bibliography: p. 147.

18121   Alcántara, José Salvador.
Clavo en la voz. Presentación postuma. Monterrey,
Mexico, Ediciones Sierra Madre [1960]
47 p.   26 cm.   (Poesía en el mundo, 4)

18122   Alcaraz Gomes, Flávio.
A rebelião dos jovens. Pôrto Alegre, Editôra
Globo [1968]
142 p.   illus.   21 cm.

18123   Alcaraz Vieco, Hernan.
Normas para evaluación de las poblaciones
insectiles y control de las plagas del algodonero y
cultivos de rotación. Bogotá, 1968.
ii, 30 ℓ.   28 cm.
At head of title: Federación Nacional de Algodoneros. División Asistencia Técnica.

18124   Alcedo, Antonio de, 1736-1812.
Bibliotheca americana; catálogo de los autores que
han escrito de la América en diferentes idiomas y
noticia de su vida y patria, años en que vivieron,
y obras que escribieron. Introducción de Jorge A.
Garcés G. [Quito, 1964-   ]
v.   27 cm.   (Publicaciones del Museo
Municipal de Arte e Historia, v. 32)

18125   Alcira Altavista, Ana.
El teatro y su ámbito cultural; desde Grecia hasta
el siglo XX. Chascomús [Argentina] Municipalidad
de Chascomús, Dirección de Cultura, Centro de
Publicaciones Municipales, 1968.
43 p.   23 cm.

18126   Alckmin, José Geraldo Rodrigues de.
Problemas atuais do inquilinato; palestras proferidas

pelos conferencistas José Geraldo Rodrigues de
Alckmin, Luiz Antônio de Andrade [e] José Frederico
Marques. Acompanhadas da coletânea da legislação
vigente sôbre inquilinato. [São Paulo, 1966]
55, lxi ℓ.   21 cm.
At head of title: Associação dos Advogados de
São Paulo. Departamento de Cultura.

18127   Alcorta, Jorge Alberto.
La tarea de hemeroteca; selección, adquisición,
accesión y tratamiento técnico de publicaciones
periódicas. Santa Fé, Argentina, Departamento de
Pedagogía Universitaria, Universidad Nacional del
Litoral, 1961.
77 p.   19 cm.   (Extensión cultural, 3)

18128   Aldarondo Galván, Etiony.
Programas para el desarrollo profesional del
maestro en la Universidad de Puerto Rico. San Juan,
1963.
8 ℓ.   27 cm.

18129   Alday, Francisco.
De la poesía mexicana contemporánea. Monterrey,
México, Ediciones Sierra Madre, 1960.
622-636 p.   25½ cm.   (Poesía en el mundo, 27)

18130   Aldrey, Fausto Teodoro de, 1825-1886.
Rasgos biográficos para la historia de la vida
pública del general Guzmán Blanco. Artículos editoriales de "La Opinión nacionale," diario de Caracas,
publicados desde el 2 de agosto de 1872 hasta el 18
de febrero de 1873, cuyos redactores eran Fausto
Teodoro de Aldrey y Rafael Hernández Gutiérrez.
Caracas, Impr. de "La Opinión nacional" por F. T.
de Aldrey, 1876.
644 p.   port.   27½ cm.

18131   Alegre, Rodolfo.
Surcos y chimeneas; crónicas políticas y descriptivas.
Buenos Aires, 1963.
156 p.   20 cm.

18132   Alegría, Alfredo.
Velas contra el viento; [poemas] Managua,
Nicaragua, 1963.
82 p.   22 cm.

18133   Alegría, Ciro, 1909-
        Novelas completas. Prólogo de Arturo del Hoyo.
        [Madrid] Aguilar [1963]
        xl, 966 p.   illus.   19 cm.

18134   Alegria, Paula.
        La educación en México antes y después de la
        conquista. [Mexico, Instituto Federal de Capacitación,
        del Magisterio, Secretaría de Educación Pública] 1963.
        175 p.   20 cm.   (Biblioteca pedagógica de
        perfeccionamiento profesional, 13)
        "Bibliografía":   p. 173-175.

18135   Aleixo, Pedro.
        Imunidades parlamentares. [Belo Horizonte]
        Revista brasileira de estudos politicos, 1961.
        180 p.   24 cm.   (Estudos sociais e politicos, 18)

18136   Alemán Alemán, Eloisa.
        Investigación socioeconómica directa de los ejidos
        de San Luis Potosí. México, Instituto Mexicano de
        Investigaciones Económicas, 1966.
        191 p.   19 cm.

18137   Alemann, Juan Ernesto.
        La inversión bursátil. Buenos Aires, Selección
        Constable [1962]
        188 p.   illus.   24 cm.

18138   Alencar, Hunald de.
        "Uma vez, em Olduvai..." (antropoema) Aracaju,
        Brazil, 1973.
        29 p.   illus.   25 cm.
        "Visalização de Nicholas Almeida."
        Poems.

18139   Alencar, Joaquim Eduardo de.
        Calazar canino; contribuição para o estudo da
        epidemiologia do calazar no Brazil. Ceará, Imprensa
        Oficial, 1959.
        342 p.   illus.
        Running title: Leishmaniose canino.
        "Autores citados ou consultados." - p. 277-342.

18140   Alencar, José Martiniano de, 1829-1877.
        Cartas e documentos de José de Alencar, no
        centenario do romance Iracema. [Ed. by] Raimundo
        de Menezes. São Paulo, Conselho Estadual de Cultura,

1967.
    154 p.   19½ cm.   (Colección Correspondência, 2)

18141 Alencar, José Martiniano de, 1829-1877.
    O Rio de Janeiro verso e reverso, comédia em 2 atos.
    Rio de Janeiro, Serviço Nacional de Teatro, 1972.
    vi, 42 p.   21 cm.

18142 Ales, Manuel.
    ... Remembranzas quilmeñas... [Quilmes, 1970]
    140 p.   plans in pocket at end.   20 cm.
    (Serie Archivos y fuentes de información, dirigida
    por Carlos G. Maier, 4)
    At head of title: Municipalidad de Quilmes,
    Secretaría de Gobierno y Cultura, Dirección de Cultura.

18143 Alfaro, Gustavo A
    La estructura de la novela picaresca. Bogotá,
    Instituto Caro y Cuervo, 1977.
    145 p.   20 cm.   (La Granada entreabierta, 16)

18144 Alfaro González, Anastasio, 1865-1951.
    El delfin de Corubibi; visión de Nicoya antes de
    la conquista española. [Novela. San José] Editorial
    Costa Rica, 1962.
    134 p.   illus., port., map.   18 cm.   (Colección
    popular, no. 1)
    Bibliography: p. [132]-134.

18145 Alfaro Monroy, Graciela.
    El régimen y personalidad de la sociedad conyugal.
    México, 1964.
    91, [7] ℓ.   24 cm.
    Tesis (licenciatura en derecho) - Universidad
    Nacional Autónoma de México.
    Bibliography: leaf [95]

18146 Alfaro R   , José F
    El suelo, el agua y el algodón. Bogotá, Instituto
    de Fomento Algodonero, 1963.
    23 p.   20 cm.   (Bogotá. Instituto de Fomento
    Algodonero. Boletín de divulgación)

18147 Alguiar Derpich, Juan, 1921-
    Guyana - another way to socialism. [Georgetown,
    Ministry of Information, Culture and Youth, n.d.]
    [7] p.   front. (port.)   25 cm.
    "A review of a penetrating new book by South American
    author, Juan Derpich."

18148 Aliança Renovadora Nacional. Comissão Coordenadora
de Éstudos do Nordeste.
Medidas e propostas para o desenvolvimento do
nordeste e sua integração à economia nacional.
Brasília, 1971.
333 p.   tables.   23 cm.   (Estudo no. 1)

18149 Alisky, Marvin.
Government of the Mexican state of Nuevo León...
Tempe, Arizona, Center for Latin American Studies,
Arizona State University, 1971.
60 p.   map.   24 cm.

18150 Alisky, Marvin.
Mexico's federal betterment boards: financial
mainstays of border municipalities. Tempe, Arizona,
Institute of Public Administration, Arizona State
University, 1970.
6 p.   tables.   29½ cm.   (Public affairs
bulletin, vol. 9, no. 4)

18151 Alisky, Marvin.
Peru's SINAMOS, governmental agency for coordinating
reforms. Tempe, Institute of Public Administration,
Arizona State University, 1972.
4 p.   29½ cm.   (Public affairs bulletin,
vol. 11, no. 1)

18152 Alisky, Marvin.
Peruvian political perspective. Tempe, Center
for Latin American Studies, Arizona State University,
1972.
33 p.   24 cm.

18153 Allende Arrau, Jorge de.
Puertos e caletas de Chile, 1622-1644. [Santiago
de Chile, 1973]
57-63 p.   24½ cm.
Reprinted from Revista chilena de historia y geografía
no. 141, 1973.

18154 Allende-Lezama, Luciano Pedro, 1887-
Hombre, mundo, transcendencia. [1. ed.] Buenos Aires
[1964]
399 p.   illus.   27 cm.
"Edición auspiciada por la Asociación Argentina de
Epistemología."

18155 Allevi, Aquiles, 1895-
La conducción estatal argentina; observaciones de
un hombre de empresa. Santa Fe, Librería Colmegna

Editorial [1968]
197 p.   20 cm.

18156   Alliance for Progress weekly newsletter. Washington,
        Organization of American States, 1963-1974.
        12 v.   30 cm.
        Library has v. 6, no. 52 (index); v. 7, nos. 1-20,
        22-43, 45-52; v. 8, nos. 1-3, 4-52; v. 9-12, no. 25.
        V. 12, no. 25, last issued.
        Partially superseded by IDB News of Inter-American
        Development Bank.
        Index is last number of each volume.

18157   Alliende, Felipe.
        Estudios de lengua y literatura como humanidades;
        homenaje a Juan Uribe Echevarría. Santiago, Chile,
        Seminario de Humanidades, 1960.
        131 p.   22 cm.

18158   Allison, Esther Margarita, 1922-
            Florerías (1964)   Monterrey, Mexico, Ediciones
        Sierra Madre, 1968.
        40 p.   22 cm.   (Poesía en el mundo, 59)

18159   Almanach royal d'Haiti... Présenté au roi par Buon.
        Sans-Souci, Imprimerie royale.
            v.   18½ cm.
        Library has 1818 and 1820.

18160   Almanaque brasileiro Garnier. Anno 1-11; 1903-14.
        [Rio de Janeiro, Garnier, 1902?-13?]
            11 v.   illus. (incl. ports.)   maps.   22½ cm.
        None issued for 1913.
        Editors: 1903-06, B. F. Ramiz Galvão. 1907-14,
        João Ribeiro.
        No more published?

18161   Almeida, Abílio Pereira de.
            "Santa Marta Fabril Sociedade Anônima;" comédia
        em 3 atos. Rio de Janeiro, Serviço Nacional de
        Teatro, 1973.
            vii, 63 p.   21 cm.   (Coleção Dramaturgia
        brasileira)

18162   Almeida, Aluisio de.
            Campina do Monte Alegre, romance. Petrópolis,
        Editora Vozes, 1964.
            112 p.   19 cm.

33

18163 Almeida, Antonio da Rocha, 1902-
Efemérides dos principais fatos relacionados com
a Campanha. Organizadas pelo professor Dr. Antônio
da Rocha Almeida. [Pôrto Alegre, Pontifícia Universidade Católica do Rio Grande do Sul] 1965.
124 p.   23 cm.

18164 Almeida, Dayl de.
Em defesa da Bacia do Paraíba. Brasília, Câmara
dos Deputados, 1967.
9 p.   23 cm.
"Discurso proferido na Sessão de 17 de março de
1967."

18165 Almeida, Elpidio de.
História de Campina Grande. Campina Grande,
Livraria Pedrosa [1962?]
424 p.   illus., ports.   23 cm.

18166 Almeida, Fernando Flavio Marques de.
Fundamentos geológicos do relévo paulista. São
Paulo, Instituto de Geografia, Universidade de São
Paulo, 1974.
110 p.   illus., map, diagr.   26 cm.   (Série
teses e monografias, no. 14)
"Transcrito de 'Geologia do Estado de São Paulo',
boletim no. 41 (1964) Instituto Geográfico e
Geológico (SP)"
"Obras citadas": p. 93-99.

18167 Almeida, Fernando Mendes de.
Mário de Andrade. São Paulo, Comissão de Literatura,
Conselho Estadual de Cultura, 1962.
105 p.   20 cm.   (Coleção Ensaio, 21)

18168 Almeida, Haroldo Ubirajara de.
A profundamento dos sulcos rasos. Belém,
Superintêndencia do Desenvolvimento da Amazônia,
Divisão de Documentação, 1974.
29 p.   illus., tables, diagrs.   28 cm.

18169 Almeida, Mauro Lauria de, 1928-
Filosofia dos pára-choques. Recife, Instituto
Joaquim Nabuco de Pesquisas Sociais, 1963.
126 p.   illus.   24 cm.

18170 Almeida, Nelly Alves de.
Análise literária de Homens de palha. [Goiânia]
Oriente, 1973.

310 p.   21 cm.
Bibliography: p. 307-310.

18171   Almeida, Paulo Mendes de.
De Anita ao Museu.   São Paulo, Conselho Estadual
Cultura, Comissão de Literatura [1961]
74 p.   22 cm.   (Coleção Ensaio, 13)
"Artigos publicados na imprensa local."

18172   Almeida, Pires de.
A escola byroniana no Brasil.   São Paulo, Conselho
Estadual de Cultura, Comissão de Literatura [1962]
224 p.   24 cm.   (Coleção Textos e documentos, 5)
Articles published in the Jornal do comercio,
July 2, 1903-Nov. 20, 1905.

18173   Almeida, Renato.
Danses africaines en Amérique Latine.   Rio de
Janeiro, Campanha de Defesa do Folclore Brasileiro,
Ministério da Educação e Cultura, 1969.
35 p.   24½ cm.

18174   Almeida, Renato.
Folclore.   [Rio de Janeiro, Ministerio da Educação
e Cultura, Campanha de Defesa do Folclore Brasileiro,
1976]
21 p.   23 cm.   (Cadernos de folclore.   Nova
série.   3)

18175   Almeida, Renato.
Música e dança folclóricas.   Rio de Janeiro,
Campanha de Defesa do Folclore Brasileiro, 1968.
8 p.   23 cm.   (Cadernos de folclore, 4)

18176   Almeida, Theodoro Figueira de, 1886-
Brasília, a cidade histórica da America.   Rio de
Janeiro, Departamento de Impr. Nacional, 1960.
72 p.   illus.   28 cm.
"Texto completo da monografia que ocupo cinco
páginas inteiras da edição de 30 de maio de 1930
do jornal a Ordem."

18177   Almeida Portugal, Luis de, 5° Conde de Avintes,
2° Marquês do Lavradio.
Cartas da Bahia 1768-1769.   [Rio de Janeiro?]
Ministerio da Justiça, Arquivo Nacional, 1972.
294 p.   23 cm.   (Brazil.   Arquivo Nacional.
Série de Publicações, no. 68)
Edited by Raul Lima.

35

18178 Almenar de Ochoa, Elena.
Funcionamiento del Registro Civil en Venezuela.
Caracas, 1964.
xi, 14 p.   29 cm.   (Venezuela. División de
Estadística Vital. Informe especial, no. 3)
At head of title: Ministerio de Sanidad y Asistencia
Social. Dirección de Salud Pública. Departamento
de Demografía y Epidemiología. División de Estadística
Vital.
Bibliography: p. xi.

18179 Alonso, Isidoro.
La Iglesia en América Latina; estructuras eclesiás-
ticas. Friburgo, Suiza, Oficina Internacional de
Investigaciones Sociales de FERES, 1964.
223 p.   illus., maps.   22 cm.   (Estudios
socio-religiosos latino-americanos, 21)
Bibliography: p. 223.

18180 Alonso, Isidoro.
La Iglesia en Perú y Bolivia; estructuras eclesiás-
ticas, por Isidora Alonso [et al.] Friburgo, Suiza,
Oficina Internacional de Investigaciones Sociales
de FERES [1962]
271 p.   illus., maps.   21 cm.   (Estudios
socio-religiosos latino-americanos, 3, t. 2)

18181 Alonso, María Rosa.
Apuntes de ortografía, con explicaciones de
léxico; para uso de principiantes. Mérida, Venezuela,
Universidad de los Andes, 1965.
53 p.   24 cm.   (Publicaciones de la Biblioteca
Central "Tulio Febres Cordero", no. 1)

18182 Alonso, María Rosa.
Apuntes sobre la conjugación española. Mérida,
Venezuela, Escuela de Letras, Facultad de Humanidades
y Educación, Universidad de los Andes, 1966.
18 p.   18 cm.

18183 Alonso, Rodolfo.
Hablar claro; [poemas] Buenos Aires, Editorial
Sudamericana [1964]
159 p.   illus.   21 cm.

18184 Alonso Avila, Antonio.
Violación de los derechos humanos por la legislación comunista de Castro. [Miami, Fla., La Voz

36

de Cuba, 1962]
vii, 72 p.   21 cm.

18185   Alonso de San Juan.
Viajes de fray Alonso Ponce al occidente de México.
Guadalajara, Corresponsalia del Seminario de Cultura
Mexicana [1968]
xv, 155 p.   24 cm.
Selections from Relacion breve y verdadera de
algunas cosas de las muchas que sucedieron al padre
fray Alonso Ponce en las provincias de la Nueva
España, published in Madrid in 1873, and attributed
to Alonso de San Juan and Antonio de Ciudad Real.

18186   Alonso Novo, Manuel.
... Análisis de los cromosomos de algunos cultivos
de importancia económica en Cuba. La Habana,
Academia de Ciencias de Cuba, Instituto de Biología,
1970.
11 p.   illus.   23½ cm.   (Poeyana, ser. A,
no. 70)

18187   Alor Leal, Ángel Luis.
El volcán Jorullo: tectonismo, vulcanismo,
morfología [por] Ángel Luis Alor Leal. México,
Colegio de Geografía, Facultad de Filosofía y Letras,
Universidad Nacional Autónoma de México, 1977.
95 p.   illus., fold. maps.   24 cm.

18188   Al'perovich, Moiseĭ Samoĭlovich.
Война за независимость Мексики, 1810–1824. Москва,
Наука, 1964.
476 p.   2 fold. maps.   21 cm.
At head of title: Академия наук СССР. Институт истории.
М. С. Альперович.
Table of contents also in Spanish; summary in
Spanish.
Bibliography: p. 434-[458]

18189   Altamirano, Carlos Luis.
Enlace de gritos. [1. ed.] San José, Costa Rica
[1962]
62 p.   21 cm.

18190   Altezor, Carlos.
Historia urbanística y edilicia de la ciudad de
Montevideo [por] Carlos Altezor [y] Hugo Baracchini.
Montevideo, Biblioteca "José Artigas," Junta Departa-

mental de Montevideo, 1971.
318 p.   illus., maps.   25 cm.

18191   Alvar, Elena.
Thesavrvs. Boletín del Instituto Caro y Cuervo.
Indices de los tomos I-XXV, 1945-1970. Bogotá, 1974.
518 p.   26 cm.

18192   Alvar López, Manuel.
Juan de Castellanos; tradición española y realidad
americana. Bogotá, Instituto Caro y Cuervo, 1972.
xxxi, 411 p.   illus.   23 cm.   (Publicaciones
del Instituto Caro y Cuervo, 30)
Includes bibliographical references.

18193   Alvar López, Manuel.
Leticia; estudios lingüísticos sobre la Amazonia
colombiana, con una monografía etnográfica de Elena
Alvar. Bogotá, Instituto Caro y Cuervo, 1977.
558 p.   illus., maps, diagrs.   24 cm.
(Publicaciones del Instituto Caro y Cuervo, XLIII)

18194   Alvar López, Manuel.
Unidad y evolución en la lírica de Unamuno [por]
Manuel Alvar. Ceuta, Instituto Nacional de Enseñanza
Media, 1960.
59 p.   15 cm.   (Colección Aula magna, 1)

18195   Alvarado, Arcilio.
Words expressed by the speaker of the House of
Representatives, Honorable Arcilio Alvarado; and by
the vice-speaker of the House of Representatives,
Honorable Aguedo Mojica, in sitting of Friday,
April 5, 1968, on the occasion of the death of
Doctor Martin Luther King. San Juan, Puerto Rico,
Commonwealth of Puerto Rico, House of Representatives
[1968]
3, 1-4, 4a, 5-11 p.   28 cm.

18196   Alvarado, Rafael.
El protócolo de Rio de Janeiro; lo que garan-
tizaron las potencias garantes. Quito, Editorial
Casa de la Cultura Ecuatoriana, 1961.
82 p.   illus.   20 cm.

18197   Alvarado Arellano, Carlos Raúl.
Los derechos humanos en el derecho constitucional
guatemalteco. Guatemala, 1962.
208 p.   23 cm.

38

Tesis (licenciatura en ciencias jurídicas y sociales) - Universidad de San Carlos de Guatemala. Bibliography: p. 207-208.

18198 Alvarado de Ricord, Elsie.
Escritores panameños contemporáneos; notas críticas y bio-bibliográficas. [Panamá, 1962]
35 p.   22 cm.

18199 Alvarado Garaicoa, Teodoro.
Derecho bolivariano. [Guayaquil] Universidad de Guayaquil, Departamento de Publicaciones, 1964.
51 p.   23 cm.

18200 Alvaraco Garaicoa, Teodoro.
Derecho internacional marítimo. Guayaquil, Ecuador, Academia de Guerra Naval, 1970.
232 p.   23 cm.

18201 Alvarado Garaicoa, Teodoro.
El dominio del mar. [Guayaquil] Departamento de Publicaciones de la Universidad de Guayaquil, 1968.
200 p.   23 cm.
Bibliographical footnotes.

18202 Alvarado Tezozomoc, Hernando, fl. 1598.
Crónica mexicana [por] Hernando Alvarado Tezozomoc. Prólogo y selección de Mario Mariscal. México, Ediciones de la Universidad Nacional Autónoma, 1943.
xlv, [1], 206, [1] p., 2 ℓ.   19½ cm.   (Biblioteca del estudiante universitario, 41)
"Notas": p. 185-[203]

18203 Alvarenga, Delamar.
Ah, vous dirai-je, maman. São Paulo, Universidade de São Paulo, Escola de Comunicações e Artes, 1972.
[7] ℓ.   32 cm.   (Série música, N4)
Chance composition; directions for possible realizations, in Portuguese, on 2d ℓ.

18204 Alvarenga, Luis de Melo.
Igrejas de São João del Rei, Minas Gerais. [Ilustrações do J. Fortuna] Petrópolis, Editôra Vozes, 1963.
62 p.   illus.   23 cm.

18205 Álvares, Walter T
Direito da energia. Volume I. Belo Horizonte,

39

Instituto de Direito da Eletricidade, 1974.
332 p.   23 cm.

18206   Alvares, Walter T
        Introdução aos direitos tecnológicos. Belo
        Horizonte, Instituto de Direito da Eletricidade,
        1972.
        124 p.   23½ cm.   (Cadernos jurídicos da
        eletricidade, 12)

18207   Álvares de Azevedo, Manoel Antonio, 1831-1852.
        Macário. Rio de Janeiro, Serviço Nacional de
        Teatro, 1972.
        vi, 46 p.   21 cm.

18208   Alvarez, Ignacio.
        Estudios sobre la historia general de México.
        Por el Licenciado Ignacio Alvarez... Zacatecas,
        Impr. económica de M. Ruíz de Esparza, 1870-77.
        6 v.   18 cm.
        "Suplemento al tomo I" (8 p.) has special t.-p.
        Tomo 4 has imprint: "Zacatecas, Tip. de Néstor
        de la Riva"; tomo 5-6: Zacatecas, Impr. económica de
        T. Macia a cargo de N. Raigosa.
        Tomo 5 includes: "Advertencia para la segunda
        edición".
        Contents: t. 1. Historia antigua. - t. 2. Historia
        de la conquista. - t. 3. Gobierno vireinal. - t. 4.
        Guerra de independencia. - t. 5. Gobiernos mexicanos
        después de la independencia. - t. 6. Revolución de
        la reforma.
        Errors in pagination.

18209   Alvarez, J
        Contribución al conocimiento de los bagres fósiles
        de Chapala, Zacoalco, Jalisco, México. México,
        Departamento de Prehistoria, Instituto Nacional de
        Antropología e Historia, 1966.
        24 p.   illus.   23 cm.   (Paleoecología, 1)
        Bibliography: p. [26]

18210   Alvarez, José Rogelio.
        Vidrio soplado, Guadalajara. [Guadalajara, México,
        Planeación y Promoción, 1960]
        51 p., 17 ℓ.   illus.   17 cm.   (Jalisco en
        el arte)
        Spanish and English.

18211   Alvarez, Martins d', 1904-
        Ritmos e legendas. [Fortaleza, 1963]
        193 p.   20 cm.

18212   Alvarez, Ticul.
        The recent mammals of Tamaulipas, Mexico.
        Lawrence, University of Kansas, 1963.
        365-473 p.   illus.   23 cm.   (University of
        Kansas publications. Museum of Natural History
        [publications] v. 14, no. 15)

18213   Alvarez Cáceres, Carlos.
        Las empresas semifiscales, con un estudio particular
        de la Compañía de Acero del Pacífico. Santiago,
        Editorial Universitaria, 1962.
        81 p.   22 cm.
        Tesis (licenciatura en ciencias jurídicas y
        sociales) - Universidad de Chile.
        Bibliography: p. 79-80.

18214   Alvarez Conde, José.
        Historia de la geografía de Cuba. Prólogo por
        Salvador Massip y Valdés. La Habana, 1961.
        xvi, 574 p.   illus., ports., maps (part fold.)
        facsims.   24 cm.   (Historia de las ciencias
        naturales de Cuba, v. 5)
        Publicaciones de la Junta Nacional de Arqueología
        y Etnología.
        "Datos biográficos de los principales investigadores
        y educadores que han realizado estudios geográficos
        en Cuba": p. [421]-574.

18215   Alvarez de Cienfuegos y Campos, José Alberto.
        Aspectos sociales de la imposición. [Texto de la
        lección inaugural del curso 1961-1962 de la Escuela
        Social de Granada, 6 de octubre de 1961. Granada]
        Escuela Social de Granada, 1961.
        25, [3] p.   25 cm.   (Publicaciones de la
        Escuela Social de Granada, 40)
        Bibliography: p. [26]

18216   Alvarez del Castillo, Miguel.
        El vuelo de las horas y Homenaje a la Francia
        Combatiente. Hommage à la France combattante.
        Estampas de Rafael Freyre. [1. ed.] México,
        1963.
        157 p.   illus., port.   24 cm.
        Verse and prose.

41

18217 Alvarez Diaz, José R
        Cuba; geopolítica y pensamiento económico de
        J. Alvarez Diaz [et al.] Miami, 1964.
        576 p.   21 cm.
        Bibliographical footnotes.

18218 Alvarez Nazario, Manuel.
        El elemento aforonegroide en el español de Puerto
        Rico; contribución al estudio del negro en América.
        San Juan, P. R., Instituto de Cultura Puertorriqueña,
        1961.
        453 p.   maps (1 col.)   23 cm.
        Errata slip inserted.
        Bibliography: p. [399]-431.

18219 Alvarez O   , Federico.
        Labor periodística de don Andrés Bello [por]
        Federico Alvarez O. Caracas, 1962.
        202 p.   24 cm.   (Universidad Central de
        Venezuela. Facultad de Humanidades y Educación.
        Escuela de Periodismo. Cuaderno 16)
        Tesis (periodista) - Universidad de Chile.
        Bibliography: p. 201-202.

18220 Alvarez Sosa, Arturo.
        Los frutos del tiempo. [Tucumán, Consejo Provincial
        de Difusión Cultural, 1960]
        [38] p.   illus.   22 cm.   (Cuadernos del
        tiempo y su canto)
        Colección El arco.
        Poems.

18221 Alvarez Tabío, Fernando, 1907-
        El recurso de inconstitucionalidad. La Habana,
        Editorial Librería Martí, 1960.
        xvii, 209 p.   24 cm.

18222 Alvarez Vásquez, Mario.
        Ema, Milo y yo. Libro primero de lectura.
        Tercera edición. Guatemala, Centro Editorial José
        de Pineda Ibarra, Ministerio de Educación Pública,
        1968.
        125 p.   illus.   22 cm.   (Colección libro
        didáctico de Guatemala)

18223 Alvear Acevedo, Carlos.
        La educación y la ley; la legislación en materia
        educativa. México, 1963.
        331 p.   20 cm.

18224 Alvear Acevedo, Carlos.
Síntesis de historia mexicana. [1. ed.] México,
Editorial Jus, 1962.
96 p. illus. 24 cm. (Figuras y episodios
de la historia de México, no. 112)

18225 Alves, Albérico Barroso, 1931-
Agente de ligação; romance. Rio de Janeiro,
O Cruzeiro [1967]
207 p. 21 cm. (Guerra, aventuras & espionagem)
Série O Agente da U. N. C. L. E.

18226 Alves, Gorgônio Barbosa.
Cenas dos envangelhos. Rio de Janeiro, Casa Publ.
Batista, 1967.
231 p. 18 cm.

18227 Alves, José Brito.
O mercado aberto no Brasil [por] J. Brito Alves.
[Rio de Janeiro, Sindicato dos Bancos do Estado da
Guanabara, 1973 or 4]
149 p. forms. 23 cm.
"Tese apresentada à VII Reunião do Conselho de
Governadores da Federação Latino Americana de Bancos
(FELABAN) - Bariloche, setembro-1973."
"Sindicato dos Bancos do Estado da Guanabara,
ano I - número 1."
"O mercado aberto: legislação": p. [93]-149.

18228 Alves, Maria Helena X
Manual da merendeira [por M. Helena X. Alves]
Rio de Janeiro, Ministério da Educação e Cultura,
Departamento Nacional de Educação, Campanha Nacional
de Alimentação Escolar, 1967.
75 p. illus. 22 cm.

18229 Alves, Marieta.
Mestres ourives de ouro e prata da Bahia.
Salvador, Brasil, Imprensa Oficial da Bahia, 1962.
83 p. illus. 24 cm. (Museu do Estado da
Bahia. Publicação no. 16) "Artigos... publicados
no Jornal a tarde."

18230 Alves, Rodrigues.
A ecologia do grupo afro-brasileiro. [Rio de
Janeiro] Ministério da Educação e Cultura, Serviço
de Documentação [1966]
106 p. 22 cm. (Coleção Aspectos [66])
Bibliography: p. 105-106.

18231 Alvim, Decio Ferraz, 1897-
Sociologia. Petrópolis, 1963.
217 p.   20 cm.

18232 Alzamora Valdez, Mario.
La educación peruana: crisis y perspectiva;
errores de una política educativa. Lima, Editorial
Universitaria, 1960.
53, lxxiv p.   22 cm.   (Perfil del Perú;
problemas básicos del pais. Cuadernos de divulgación,
1)
"Anexos: Proyectos de ley presentados por el autor
en la Cámara de Diputados hasta 1960": p. i-lxxiv.

18233 Amado, Jorge, 1912-
A morte e a morte de Quincas Berro Dágua. Ilus.
de Di Cavalcanti. [Rio de Janeiro] Sociedade dos
Cem Bibliófilos do Brasil, 1962 [i.e. 1963]
59 p.   6 col. plates.   46 cm.
In portfolio.
"Tiragem única de 120 exemplares em papel vélin
d'Arches... Exemplar letra K impresso para a
The Library of Congress of Washington."

18234 Aman-Jean, François.
O guarda dos passaros. 1 ato. Tradução de
Virginia Valli. Rio de Janeiro, Serviço Nacional
de Teatro, 1975.
24-32 p.   21 x 33 cm.
Reprinted from Cadernos de teatro, no. 64,
Jan.-Mar. 1975.

18235 Amaral, A
Estudio comparativo de la holocelulosa del bagazo
en diferentes variedades de caña. La Habana,
Instituto Cubano de Investigaciones Tecnológicas,
1959.
71 p.   25 cm.   (Serie de Estudios sobre
trabajos de investigación, no. 81)

18236 Amaral, Antônio Barreto do.
Prudente de Moraes, uma vida marcada. São Paulo,
Instituto Histórico e Geográfico de São Paulo, 1971.
400 p.   illus., facsims., ports.   24 cm.

18237 Amaral, Rubens do.
Lezes do planalto. São Paulo, Conselho Estadual
de Cultura, Comissão de Literatura [1962]
94 p.   22 cm.   (Coleção Ensaio, 20)

44

18238   Ambriano, John.
        Geology of Baja California. A bibliography of the
        holdings in Malcolm A. Love Library, California
        State University, San Diego. Compiled by John
        Ambriano, Sciences and Engineering Library. Revised
        edition. San Diego, 1972.
        3 p.l., 105 p.   21½ cm.

18239   América Latina: ensayos de interpretación económica
        [por] Andrés Bianchi [et al. Santiago de Chile]
        Editorial Universitaria [1969]
            277 p.   22 cm.   (Colección Tiempo latino-
        americano)
            Contents. - Advertencia, por A. B. - Introducción:
        notas sobre la teoría del desarrollo económico latino-
        americano, por A. Bianchi. - Problemas teóricos y
        prácticos del crecimiento económico, por R. Prebisch. -
        Una tentativa de interpretación del modelo histórico
        latinoamericano, por A. B. de Castro. - Desarrollo
        y estancamiento en América Latina, por C. Furtado. -
        El proceso de sustitución de importaciones como modelo
        de desarrollo reciente en América Latina, por M. da
        C. Tavares. - Concentración del progreso técnico y
        de sus frutos en el desarrollo latinoamericano, por
        A. Pinto Santa Cruz. - Política nacional de desarrollo
        y dependencia externa, por C. Sunkel.

18240   American International Association. Programa Inter-
        americano de Información Popular.
            Estudio de la prensa del interior de la República
        Argentina. Buenos Aires, Instituto Nacional de
        Tecnología Agropecuaria, 1966.
            201 p.   illus.   28½ cm.

18241   Ames, Glenn C   W
            Small farmer association and development program:
        case of the Dominican Republic [by] Glenn C. W.
        Ames. [Madison, Wis., 1976]
            14-21 p.   28 cm.
            Reprinted from Land Tenure Center Newsletter,
        no. 52, April-June 1976.

18242   Ames González, Edmundo.
            Hacia el estado de derecho auténtico, por la
        educación democrática integral; un planteamiento
        actual para la transformación profunda de la realidad
        cultural peruana. Lima, 1961.
            206 p.   18 cm.

18243   Amezquita de Almeida, Josefina.
        Regimen legal de baldíos en Colombia [por]
        Josefina Amezquita de Almeida [y] Wenceslao Tavar
        Mozo. Bogotá, Editorial Temis, 1961.
        xii, 293 p.   20 cm.

18244   Los amigos de la patria y de la juventud, 1815-1816.
        Reproducción facsimilar publicada con el auspicio
        de la Comisión Nacional Ejecutiva del 150°. aniver-
        sario de la Revolución de Mayo. Buenos Aires,
        Academia Nacional de la Historia, 1961.
        135 p.   facsims.   24 cm.   (Periódicos de la
        época de la Revolución de Mayo, V)
        "Introducción" by Guillermo Fúrlong and Enrique
        de Gandía: p. 9-23.

18245   Amis y Amiles; cantar de gesta francés del siglo XIII.
        Traducción, introducción y notas de Carlos Alvar.
        Bogotá, Instituto Caro y Cuervo, 1978.
        139 p.   (La Granada entreabierta, 20)

18246   Amora, Antonio Soares.
        História de literatura brasileira, séculos XVI-XX.
        Lisbon, Atica [1961]
        243 p.   19 cm.
        Includes bibliography.

18247   Amorim, Alaide Sardá de, 1909-
        Turismo a dois. Florianópolis [Imprensa Oficial
        do Estado] 1968.
        105 p.   illus., port.   22 cm.

18248   Amorim, Eduardo Guedes de, 1891-
        Aruanã. Goiânia, Departamento Estadual de Cultura,
        Editôra Oriente, 1973.
        288 p.   23 cm.

18249   Amorim, Enrique.
        Temas de amor. Buenos Aires, Instituto Amigos
        del Libro Argentino [1960]
        93 p.   19 cm.   (Colección Cuadernos del
        Instituto, IV)

18250   Amster, Mauricio.
        Técnica gráfica; evolución, procedimientos y
        aplicaciones. [5. ed. aumentada. Santiago de Chile]
        Editorial Universitaria [1966]
        218 p.   illus.   23 cm.
        Third ed. published in 1960 under title: Técnica
        gráfica del periodismo.

18251   Amunátegui, Miguel Luis, 1828-1888, ed.
        ... El diario de la Covadonga. Santiago, G. E.
        Miranda, 1902.
        52 p.   19½ cm.   (Biblioteca de autores chilenos.
        Vol. XI)
        A diary of the operations of the Spanish schooner
        Covadonga off the coast of South America, 1862-1865,
        extracted from the journal of an officer, Félix
        Gurrea; edited, with connective narrative, by M. L.
        Amunátegui.

18252   Amunátegui, Miguel Luis, 1828-1888.
        Vida de Don Andrés Bello, por Miguel Luis Amuná-
        tegui. Santiago de Chile, Impreso por P. G. Ramírez,
        1882.
        vi, 672 p.   25 cm.

18253   Ana, Marcos, pseud.
        Poemas desde la cárcel. 2. ed. ampliada. [Monte-
        video, Corporación Gráfica, 1963]
        30 p.   20 cm.
        Contents. - Autobiografía. - Prisión central. -
        Para las llaves aún falta. - Romance. - ¡Amnistía! -
        Pequeña carta al mundo. - A los católicos. - Mi
        corazón es patio. - Te llamo desde un muro. - El
        mensaje. - ¿La vida...? - La casa y el corazón. -
        Romance para las doce menos cuarto.

18254   Anabalón Ramírez, Carlos.
        Los testigos de oídas. Santiago, Editorial
        Universitaria, 1962.
        90 p.   22 cm.
        Tesis (licenciatura en ciencias jurídicas y
        sociales) - Universidad de Chile.
        Bibliography: p. 88-89.

18255   Anastasi, Atilio.
        Actualización del léxico español. Mendoza,
        Argentina, Instituto de Lengua Española, Facultad
        de Filosofía y Letras, Universidad Nacional de Cuyo,
        1967.
        92 p.   20 cm.

18256   Anaya Espinasse, José María.
        Archivos, historia e información. [Luján]
        Universidad Nacional de Luján, 1974.
        6 unnumb. l.   37 cm.

18257   Anaya Espinasse, José María.
        Hacia una tipología documental argentina. Buenos
        Aires, Subsecretaría de Coordinación Universitaria,
        Ministerio de Cultura y Educación, 1972.
        11 p.   22 cm.   (Serie "Temas archivísticos," 4)

18258   Anaya Espinasse, José María.
        Notas elementales para un relevamiento estadístico
        de los archivos argentinos. Buenos Aires, Sub-
        secretaría de Coordinación Universitaria, Ministerio
        de Cultura y Educación, 1972.
        18 p.   22 cm.   (Serie "Temas archivísticos," 3)

18259   Anaya Espinasse, José María.
        Noticia sinóptica sobre documentación en el archivo
        del Museo Colonial e Histórico "Enrique Udaondo"
        (Luján, Provincia de Buenos Aires) Buenos Aires,
        Subsecretaría de Coordinación Universitaria,
        Ministerio de Cultura y Educación, 1973.
        116 p.   22 cm.   (Serie "Temas archivísticos," 5)

18260   Anaya Espinasse, José María.
        Que es la archivística? Buenos Aires,
        Subsecretaría de Coordinación Universitaria,
        Ministerio de la Cultura y Educación, 1972.
        31 p.   22 cm.   (Serie "Temas archivísticos," 1)

18261   Anaya Monroy, Fernando.
        La toponimia indígena en la historia y la cultura
        de Tlaxcala. México, Universidad Nacional Autónoma
        de México, Instituto de Investigaciones Históricas,
        1965.
        187 p.   illus., maps (part fold.)   24 cm.
        (Universidad Nacional Autónoma de México. Instituto
        de Investigaciones Históricas. Serie de cultura
        náhuatl. Monografías, 4)
        Issued also as thesis (maestro en historia de
        México), Universidad Nacional Autónoma de México.
        Bibliography: p. [113]-118.

18262   Anchieta, José de, 1534-1597.
        Auto representado na festa de São Lourenço.
        (Livre adaptação de Walmir Ayala) Rio de Janeiro,
        Serviço Nacional de Teatro, 1973.
        vii, 44 p.   21 cm.

18263   Anderson, A   W
        La industria de carne en Colombia. Por A. W.
        Anderson, con asistencia de Julio Bejarano. Bogotá,

48

Ferrocarriles Nacionales de Colombia, 1961.
56 p.   20 cm.

18264   Anderson, Charles W
        Factores políticos en el desarrollo económico de
        América Latina. Madison, Land Tenure Center,
        University of Wisconsin, 1966.
        21 p.   28 cm.   (Land Tenure Center, University
        of Wisconsin. LTC reprint no. 26-S)
        Reprinted from Journal of International Affairs,
        vol. 20, no. 2, 1966.

18265   Anderson, Teresa J
        Chile's agricultural economy - a bibliography.
        A bibliography of materials dealing with Chile in the
        Land Tenure Center Library, University of Wisconson.
        Madison, 1970-1971.
        65, 21 p.   29 cm.   (Training and methods series,
        12)

18266   Anderson, Teresa J
        Land tenure and agrarian reform in Mexico - a
        bibliography. A bibliography of materials dealing
        with Mexico in the Land Tenure Center Library,
        University of Wisconsin. Madison, 1970-1971.
        51, 18 p.   29 cm.   (Training and methods series,
        10)

18267   Anderson, Teresa J
        Sources for legal and social science research on
        Latin America: land tenure and agrarian reform.
        Madison, Land Tenure Center Library, University of
        Wisconsin, 1970.
        34 p.   29 cm.   (Training and methods series, 11)

18268   Andersson, Theodore.
        Bilingual schooling: oasis or mirage? [By]
        Theodore Andersson. [Austin, Institute of Latin
        American Studies, University of Texas, 196-?]
        69-74 p.   25 cm.   (Offprint series, 88)
        Reprinted from Hispania.

18269   Andery, Paulo Abib.
        Concentração de apatita do carbonatito de Jacupi-
        ranga, Estado de São Paulo. São Paulo, Escola
        Politécnica, 1967.
        73 p.   illus., plates, tables.   31 cm.
        "Tese para concurso à cátedra no. 33 - 'Lavra de

minas e tratamento de minerais.'"
Bibliography: p. [71]-73.

18270 Andrada, Auro Moura.
Falando ao presidente eleito. Alocução proferida
na sessão conjunta do Congresso nacional, a 3 de
outubro de 1966, após proclamar eleito o presidente
da república para o período de 1967 a 1971. Brasília,
1967.
13 p.   21 cm.

18271 Andrada e Silva, José Bonifácio de, 1763-1838.
Obra política de José Bonifácio, comemorativa do
sesquicentenario da Independência. Introdução
historica de José Antônio Soares de Souza. Direção
do deputado José Bonifácio Lafayette de Andrade.
Organização de Octaciano Nogueira. Brasília, Centro
Gráfico do Senado Federal, 1973.
2 v.   port.   24½ cm.

18272 Andrada e Silva, José Bonifácio de, 1763-1838.
Poesias. Texto organizado e apresentado por
Alfredo Bosi e Nilo Scalzo. São Paulo, Comissão
de Literatura, Conselho Estadual de Cultura, 1962.
317 p.   20 cm.   (Colección Poesía, 5)

18273 Andrade, Antônio Ferreira de.
Educação: solução ou desatino, por Antônio
Ferreira de Andrade. Belo Horizonte, Serviço
Nacional de Aprendizagem Industrial, Departamento
Regional de Minas Gerais, 1976.
88 p.   illus.   23 cm.   (Assessoria de Plane-
jamento, 2)

18274 Andrade, Carlos Américo Morato de.
Métodos experimentais usados na determinação do
comportamento de diodos de túnel, função da tempe-
ratura e da frequência. São Paulo, Escola Politécnica,
1967.
126 p.   illus. (part fold.)   23 cm.
"Tese apresentada ao concurso para provimento do
cargo de professor, catedrático da Cadeira de Ele-
trônica Fundamental da Escola Politécnica da Universidade de São Paulo... 1967."
Bibliography: p. 123-126.

18275 Andrade, Frederico Alberto de.
Conjuntura da castanha do Pará; relatório preliminar.
Belém, Superintendência do Desenvolvimento da Amazônia,

1968.

23 ℓ.   tables.   27 cm.   (Brazil. Superin-
tendência do Desenvolvimento da Amazônia. Doc[umento]
GASPLAM, 68/10)
On cover: Castanha do Pará; relatório e estudo.

18276   Andrade, Gilberto Osório de Oliveira.
Montebelo, os males e os mascates; contribução para
a história de Pernambuco na segunda metade do século
XVII. Recife, Universidade Federal de Pernambuco,
1969.
181 p.   port.   21 cm.
Bibliography: p. [173]-181.

18277   Andrade, Gilberto Osório de Oliveira.
Panorama dos recursos naturais do Nordeste [por]
Gilberto Osório de Andrade. Recife, Universidade
Federal de Pernambuco, 1968.
61 p.   22 cm.

18278   Andrade, Jaime.
Arte popular del Ecuador [por] Jaime Andrade
[et al.] 26 dibujos seleccionados, 184 temas,
53 subgéneros, 29 áreas visitadas, 9 géneros.
Prólogos: Galo H. Montaño. Orientación, siste-
matización e introducción: Paulo de Carvalho-Neto.
Selección: Angel de Chavarri. Patrocinio:
C.E.N.D.E.S., O.C.E.P.A. [Quito] Alianza para el
Progreso [1965]
cccxiii p.   illus.   27 cm.

18279   Andrade, Jorge, 1922-
... A moratória. 2.a edição. Capa de Milton
Ribeiro. Rio de Janeiro, Livraria AGIR editôra,
1965.
188 p.   20½ cm.
At head of title: Teatro moderno, 8.

18280   Andrade, Jorge, 1922-
O telescópio. Peça em 1 ato. Rio de Janeiro,
Serviço Nacional de Teatro, 1973.
viii, 51 p.   21 cm.

18281   Andrade, Manuel Correia de.
Movimentos nativistas em Pernambuco: Septembrizada
e Novembrada. Recife, Universidade Federal de
Pernambuco, 1971.
135 p.   23 cm.

51

18282 Andrade, Manuel Correia de.
... Nordeste, espaço e tempo. Petrópolis, R. J.,
Editôra Vozes Limitada [n.d.]
182 p.   19½ cm.   (Coleção Caminhos brasileiros,
5)

18283 Andrade, Oswald de, 1890-1945.
A morta. Peça em 1 ato. Rio de Janeiro, Serviço
Nacional de Teatro, 1973.
viii, 31 p.   21 cm.

18284 Andrade Barrientos, Néstor.
Hacia el desarrollo económico de Chiloé. Santiago,
Editorial Universitaria, 1962.
242 p.   tables.   22 cm.
Tesis (licenciatura en ciencias jurídicas y sociales)
Universidad de Chile.

18285 Andrade-Lima, Dardano de.
Um pouco de ecologia para o Nordeste; parte geral.
Recife, Centro de Encino de Ciências do Nordeste,
Universidade Federal de Pernambuco, 1972.
76 p.   illus.   24 cm.

18286 Andrade Moscoso, Carlos.
Los inolvidables, por Carlos Andrade-Kanela.
5 crónicas ajenas, 45 crónicas del autor, 8 dibujos
del autor, 2 protestas. Quito, 1964.
339 p.   illus., ports.   22 cm.

18287 Andrade y Cordero, César.
Poesías. Cuenca [Núcleo del Azuay de la Casa de
la Cultura Ecuatoriana] 1977.
201 p.   20 cm.

18288 Andreazza, Mário David.
Programas especiais na área do Ministério dos
Transportes (objetivos e execução) [Rio de Janeiro]
1972.
47 p.   maps.   21½ cm.

18289 Andreazza, Mário David.
Os transportes no Brasil. Planejamento e execução.
Conferencia pronunciada pelo Ministro dos Transportes
Mário David Andreazza, em 26 de junho de 1972, na
Escola Superior de Guerra. [Rio de Janeiro] 1972.
63 p.   maps, tables.   21½ cm.

18290 Andreoli, Arturo.
       Panorama da energía elétrica no Brasil e no
       Paraná. Curitiba, Brasil, Companhia Paranaense
       da Energia Elétrica, 1972.
       various pagings.   illus.   28 cm.

18291 Andreoni, João Antonio, 1650-1716.
       Cultura e opulencia do Brasil por suas drogas e
       minas, com varias noticias curiosas do modo de fazer
       o assucar; plantar e beneficiar o tabaco; tirar ouro
       das minas, e descubrir as da prata; e dos grandes
       emolumentos que esta conquista da America Meridional
       dá ao Reyno de Portugal, com estes e outros generos,
       e contratos reaes: Obra de Andre João Antonil.
       Lisboa, Officina Real Deslandesiana, 1711.
       205 p.   illus.   20 cm.
       Filmed backwards in General Microfilm collection.

18292 Andreozzi, María Rosa.
       Curso audiovisual de bibliotecología. La experiencia
       de Tucumán. Tucumán, Universidad Nacional de Tucumán,
       Biblioteca Central, 1971.
       21 p.   24 cm.   (Ciencia de la documentación.
       Serie II: La biblioteca, no. 8)

18293 Andrés, Alfredo.
       Balada del saxofonista que perdió el tren de la
       frontera, 1960/62. [Buenos Aires, Bordas Montanari,
       Impresores, 1963]
       [11] p.   17 cm.   (Entregas del fantasma flaco)

18294 Andrés Octavio, José.
       Los elementos fundamentales del impuesto sobre la
       renta en la ley del 16 de diciembre de 1966. Caracas,
       Facultad de Derecho, Universidad Central de
       Venezuela, 1971.
       113 p.   24 cm.   (Colección Trabajos de ascenso,
       1)

18295 Andrews, David H   , comp.
       Latin America; a bibliography of paperback books.
       Edited by T. J. Hillmon. Washington, Hispanic
       Foundation, Library of Congress, 1964.
       v, 38 p.   27 cm.   (Hispanic Foundation biblio-
       graphical series, 9)

18296 Angarita Arvelo, Rafael.
       Tres tiempos de poesía en Venezuela, historia por

53

representación.   Caracas, "Adán Gráfica," 1962.
103 p.   21 cm.

18297   Angeles Caballero, César Augusto.
César Vallejo, su obra [por] César A. Angeles
Caballero.   [1. ed.]   Lima, 1964.
248, [4] p.   illus., map, port.   20 cm.
Bibliography: p. 241-[250]

18298   Angelescu, Victor.
... Alimentación de la merluza en la región del
Talud continental argentino, época invernal (merlu-
ciidae, merluccius merluccius hubbsi) por Victor
Angelescu y María B. Cousseau.   Mar del Plata,
Universidades nacionales, 1969.
87 p., 6 pl.   illus.   25½ cm.   (Universidades
nacionales de Buenos Aires, La Plata y del Sur.
Instituto de biología marina, Boletín, 19)
Résumés in German and English.

18299   Anghiera, Pietro Martire d', 1455-1526.
Décadas del Nuevo Mundo, vertidas del latín a la
lengua castellana por el Dr. D. Joaquín Torres
Asensio...   Buenos Aires, Editorial Bajel, 1944.
lii, 675 p.   24 cm.   (Colección de fuentes
para la historia de América)
"Bibliografía de Pedro Mártir":   p. xxiii-lii.

18300   Angulo V   , Jorge.
Un tlamanalli encontrado en Tlatelolco.   México,
Instituto Nacional de Antropología e Historia, 1966.
47 p.   illus.   18 cm.   (Departamento de Pre-
historia.   Publicaciones, 18)
Bibliography: p. 47.

18301   Anjos, Nelson da Franca Ribeiro dos.
Estudo das possibilidades hidrogeológicas de
Feira de Santana, Bahia.   Por Nelson da Franca
Ribeiro dos Anjos, Carlos Alberto de Miranda
Bastos.   Recife, Superintendência do Desenvolvimento
do Nordeste, 1968.
216 p.   tables (part fold.), maps (part fold.)
30 cm.   (Série: Brasil. SUDENE. Hidrogeologia,
20)

18302   Un Anónimo poema gauchesco de 1825 sobre la guerra
de la Independencia.   Bahía Blanca, Universidad
Nacional del Sur, Extensión Cultural [1968]
101 p.   facsims.   21 cm.   (Serie: El Viento)

Includes facsimile of original t. p.: Graciosa
y divertida conversación que tuvo Chano con señor
Ramón Contreras... Buenos Aires, En la Imprenta del
Estado, 1825.
Edited by Félix Weinberg.

18303 Antinucci, Alfonso Eduardo.
Mashíaj; [novela] Buenos Aires, Ediciones Siglo
Veinte [1969]
138 p. 21 cm.

18304 Antioquia (State) Departamento Administrativo de
Planeación Departamental.
Anuario estadístico de Antioquia, 1972. Medellín,
1974.
546 p. 28 cm.

18305 Antioquia (State) Departamento Administrativo de
Planeación Departamental.
... Organización del gobierno de Antioquia.
Medellín, Editado por el Departamento Administrativo
de Planeación Departamental, 1969.
230 p. tables, maps. 25 cm.
At head of title: República de Colombia.
Gobernación de Antioquia.

18306 Antioquia, tierra de trabajo y progreso. [Medellín]
1961.
221 p. 20 cm.

18307 Antología de costumbristas venezolanos del siglo XIX.
Caracas, Ediciones del Ministerio de Educación,
Dirección de Cultura y Bellas Artes, Departamento
de Publicaciones, 1964.
401 p. 18 cm. (Biblioteca popular venezolana,
95)
Includes biographical sketches of authors.

18308 Antología de poetas cearenses contemporâneos.
Fortaleza, Imprensa Universitaria do Ceará, 1965.
123 p. 20 cm.

18309 Uma antología do conto cearense. Com um estudo de
Braga Montenegro. Fortaleza, Imprensa Universitaria
do Ceará, 1965.
220 p. illus. 24 cm.
Bibliography: p. 45.
Contents. - Evolução e natureza do conto cearense,
por Braga Montenegró. - Ed. Isizaro, por A. E.

55

Benevides. - Os demonios, por Braga Montenegro. -
Joaninha De-Torto, por E. Campos. - Ventania, por
F. Martins. - A fuga, por J. C. Bezerra. - O estranho,
por J. Mala. - Retrato, por L. Fernandes Martins. -
Amanha, as cinco horas, por M. Sabola de Carvalho. -
Aquela que eu perdi, por M. Dias. - O banho, por
Moreira Campos. - Fim da pena, por S. Sa.

18310 Antologia poética do movimento antroponáutica.
Chagas Val, Luis Augusto Cassas, Valdelino Cécio,
Raimundo Fontenele, Viriato Gaspar. [São Luís?
Secretaria de Educação e Cultura, Departamento de
Cultura do Marãnhao, n.d.]
115 p.   18 cm.

18311 Anton, George F   1892-   ed.
Since the beginning of time; the history of the
College of Agriculture and Mechanic Arts, beginning
with the originators of the idea and up to 1962,
compiled by George F. Anton. [Mayaguez, Puerto Rico]
Office of Information, College of Agriculture and
Mechanic Arts, University of Puerto Rico [1963]
343 p.   illus., ports.   22 cm.
English or Spanish.
"Appeared serially in the Revista colegial."

18312 Antonioletti, Rodrigo.
El Baker: un enfoque sobre problemas de geografía
administrativa. [Santiago de Chile, 1969]
41-59 p.   maps.   24½ cm.
Reprinted from Revista chilena de historia y
geografía, no. 137, 1969.

18313 Antunes, Clóvis.
Wakona-Kariri-Xukuru. Aspectos sócio-antropológicos
dos romanescentes indígenas de Alagoas. [Maceió]
Universidade Federal de Alagoas, Imprensa Universitária, 1973.
159 p.   illus., music.   23 cm.

18314 Anuario bibliográfico colombiano "Rubén Pérez Ortiz".
Compilado por Francisco José Romero Rojas. Bogotá,
Instituto Caro y Cuervo, Departamento de Bibliografía.
v.   26 cm.
Library has 1967, 1969, 1971-1974.

18315 Anuario bibliográfico puertorriqueño; índice alfabético
de libros, folletos, revistas y periódicos publicados
en Puerto Rico, 1948-   Rio Piedras, Biblioteca
de la Universidad.

v.   28 cm.
Compiler: 1948-   G. Velázquez.
Library has 1959.

18316   Anuario de estudios centroamericanos. San José,
Costa Rica, Universidad de Costa Rica, 1974-
v.   24 cm.
Library has no. 1 (1974), no. 3 (1977) and no. 4
(1979)

18317   Anuário geográfico do Estado do Rio de Janeiro,
no. 12, 1959. Rio de Janeiro, Serviço Gráfico do
Instituto Brasileiro de Geografia e Estatística,
1960.
280 p.   illus.   25 cm.

18318   Anzalaz, Fermín Alfredo, ed.
Folklore de los valles calchaquíes. Estudio
preliminar, selección, notas y glosario de Fermín
Alfredo Anzalaz. Santa Fé [República Argentina]
Ediciones Colmegna [1961]
82 p.   19 cm.

18319   Anzola Gómez, Gabriel.
Como llegar hasta los campesinos por medio de la
educación; resultados de una experiencia en el CREFAL.
[Bogotá, Ministerio de Educación Nacional, 1962]
308 p.   illus.   20 cm.   (Biblioteca de
autores contemporáneos, 4)

18320   Aparicio, Luis.
Planeamiento integral de la educación; síntesis de
su doctrina. San Salvador, Dirección General de
Publicaciones, Ministerio de Educación, 1967.
213 p.   21 cm.   (Biblioteca del maestro, 1)
Bibliography: p. 211-213.

18321   Aparicio Laurencio, Angel.
Donde está el cadáver se reúnen los buitres;
crónicas de la persecución religiosa en Cuba.
Santiago de Chile, 1963,
206 p.   19 cm.
Bibliography: p. 195-206.

18322   Apgaua, Paulo.
Análise sistematica das normas gerais de direito
financeiro na legislação brasileira [por] Paulo
Apgaua, Manoel Duarte Ferreira Porto Sobrinho,
Mayesse Mahmud Ganem. Belo Horizonte, Assembléia

Legislativa do Estado de Minas Gerais, 1969.
73 p.   tables (part fold.)   24 cm.

18323   Apollinaire, Guillaume, 1880-1918.
De la poesía francesa contempóranea. Monterrey,
México, Ediciones Sierra Madre, 1962.
25 p.   25½ cm.   (Poesía en el mundo, 38)
Parallel French and Spanish texts.
Translation by Georges Londeix.

18324   Appelbaum, Richard P
San Ildefonso Ixtabuacán, Guatemala; un estudio
sobre la migración temporal, sus causas y conse-
cuencias. Versión española de Fernando Cruz Sandoval.
Guatemala, Departamento Editorial José de Pineda
Ibarra, Ministerio de Educación, 1967.
82 p.   20½ cm.   (Seminario de Integración
Social Guatemalteca. Cuadernos, 17)
Bibliography: pp. 81-82.

18325   Appun, Karl Ferdinand, 1820-1872.
En los trópicos [traducción del alemán: Federica
de Ritter] Caracas, Universidad Central de Venezuela,
Ediciones de la Biblioteca, 1961.
519 p.   illus., fold. map.   23 cm.
(Ediciones de la Biblioteca, 2. Colección Ciencias
sociales, 1)
Translation of v. 1, entitled Venezuela, and
other selections from v. 2, entitled British Guyana,
of the author's Unter den Tropen.
"Traducción publicada por primera vez en los
Anales de la Universidad Central de Venezuela,
números xxxii-xxxix, enero 1953 - abril-diciembre
1954."

18326   Ara, Guillermo.
Fray Mocho; estudio y antología. [Buenos Aires]
Ediciones Culturales Argentinas, Dirección General
de Cultura, Ministerio de Educación y Justicia,
Dirección General de Cultura [1963]
149 p.   20 cm.   (Biblioteca del sesqui-
centenario. Colección Antologías)
Bibliography: p. 149.

18327   Ara, Guillermo.
Literatura nacional y libertad expresiva. Bahía
Blanca [Argentina, Instituto de Humanidades,
Universidad Nacional del Sur] 1960.
19 p.   24 cm.   (Cuadernos del Sur)

18328   Arai, Alberto T
        La arquitectura de Bonampak; ensayo de inter-
        pretación del arte maya. Viaje a las ruinas de
        Bonampak. [l. ed. Mexico] I[nstituto] N[acional de]
        B[ellas] A[rtes, 1960]
        196 p.   illus.   23 cm.

18329   Aramayo Alzérreca, Oscar, 1915-
        Régimen legal del comercio exterior chileno [por]
        Oscar Aramayo. 2. ed. actualizada. [Santiago de
        Chile] Editorial Jurídica de Chile, 1968.
        139 p.   27 cm.
        Bibliographical footnotes.

18330   Arámburu de la Cuesta, Juan B
        Medidas administrativas de protección a la industria
        mexicana [por] Juan B. Arámbaru de la Cuesta.
        México, 1961.
        105 p.   23 cm.
        Tesis (licenciatura en derecho) - Universidad
        Nacional Autónoma de México.
        Bibliography: p. 105.

18331   Arana, V   M
        Ni invasión ni golpe itrabajar! Exposición cívica
        [por] V. M. Arana. [Lima, 1964?]
        142, iii p.   21 cm.

18332   Arana Sánchez, Jorge.
        Márgenes de comercialización y algunos aspectos
        del mercadeo de arroz, maiz, frijol, trigo, papa.
        [Bogotá?] 1961.
        102 ℓ.   28 cm.

18333   Aranda Alvarez, Guillermo.
        Ensayo sobre el seguro social campesino en Bolivia.
        [La Paz, 1964]
        159 p.   21 cm.

18334   Aranda Sánchez, Francisco.
        La organización de los tribunales y la implantación
        de la carrera judicial en México. Mexico, 1964.
        125 p.   24 cm.
        Tesis (licenciatura en derecho) - Universidad
        Nacional Autónoma de México.
        Bibliography: p. 115.

18335   Araneda Bravo, Fidel, 1906-
        La iglesia catedral de Santiago. [Santiago de Chile,

1973]
159-203 p. 24½ cm.
Reprinted from Revista chilena de historia y
geografía, no. 141, 1973.

18336 Araneda Bravo, Fidel, 1906-
El obispo José Hipólito Salas. Santiago [de Chile,
Editorial U.C.] 1963.
128 p. 19 cm.
Bibliography: p. 125-126.

18337 Araneda Dörr, Hugo.
La administración financiera del Estado. [Santiago
de Chile] Editorial Jurídica de Chile, 1966.
217 p. 23 cm. (Colección de estudios jurídicos
y sociales, v. 53)

18338 Arango Cano, Jesús.
Capitalismo, comunismo y libertad. Bogotá, Editorial
Kelly, 1962.
311 p. 17 cm.

18339 Arango Cano, Jesús.
Geografía física y económica del Quindo. Primera
edición. [Quindio? Publicaciones Cultural] 1966.
[136] p. illus., maps. 23 cm.

18340 Arango R   , Mariano.
La estructura económica del Departamento de Antioquia. [Por] Mariano Arango R., Francisco Gómez P.
[y] Rocío Herrera C. Medellín, Colombia, Centro de
Investigaciones Económicas, Universidad de Antioquia,
1973.
xii, 345 p. tables, diagrs. 25 cm. (Serie
DPP-07-03-73)

18341 Aránguiz Donoso, Horacio.
... Bibliografía histórica (1959-1967) Santiago
de Chile, 1970.
86 p. 27½ cm.
At head of title: Universidad Católica de Chile.
Instituto de Historia. Horacio Aránguiz Donoso.
Carmen Gloria Duhart. Mariana Aylwin. Leonor Silva.
Carlos Bascuñán.

18342 Aránguiz Lezaeta, Eliana.
El delito de rapto. Santiago de Chile [Editorial
Universitaria] 1966.
54 p. 21 cm.

Memoria de prueba (licenciatura en ciencias jurídicas
y sociales) - Universidad de Chile, Santiago.
Bibliography: p. 51-52.

18343   Aranha, Graça.
Páginas seletas.   Edição comemorativa do centenário
do nascimento de Graça Aranha 21-6-1868 - 21-6-1968.
Maranhão, S.E.N.E.C., Departamento de Cultura do Estado,
1968.
78 p.   front.   (port.)   19 cm.

18344   Araquistain, Luis, 1886-1959.
El pensamiento español contemporáneo;   prólogo de
Luis Jiménez de Asúa.   Buenos Aires, Editorial Losada
[1962]
192 p.   21 cm.   (Cristal del tiempo)
Bibliographical footnotes.

18345   Araújo, Acrísio Tôrres.
Geografia de Sergipe.   Aracaju, Livraria Regina,
1969.
135 p.   illus., maps.   19 cm.
Includes bibliographical references.

18346   Araújo, Aloyr Queiroz de.
Técnicas audiovisuais nas escolas de educação física.
Rio de Janeiro, Ministério da Educação e Cultura,
Divisão de Educação Física, 1968.
27 p.   illus., plates.   22 cm.
Bibliography: p. [27]

18347   Araújo, Delio Moreira de.
A bitola métrica no sistema ferroviário brasileiro;
tentativa de caracterização econômico-qualitativa.
Tese de doutoramento, maio de 1970.   Goiânia, Brasil,
Faculdade de Ciências Econômicas, Universidade
Católica de Goiás, 1970.
209 p.   32 cm.
Bibliography: pp. 196-209.

18348   Araújo, Hilton Carlos de.
Teatro integrado.   Experiências.   Rio de Janeiro,
Serviço Nacional de Teatro, 1976.
123 p.   21 cm.   (Cartilhas de teatro, 8)

18349   Araújo, Iaperi, 1950-
José Leite & outros cantos.   Prefacio de Edgar
Barbosa.   Xilogravuras: Irani.   Natal, Imp. Univer-

61

sitária, 1968.
66 p.   plates.   23 cm.

18350 Araújo, Nancy de Queiroz.
Problemas da fermentação alcoólica industrial. Rio
de Janeiro, Instituto Nacional de Tecnología, Ministério
da Industria e Comércio, 1969.
79 p.   graphs, tables.   22 cm.

18351 Araújo, Vivaldo Campbell de.
Sôbre a germinação de Aniba (Lauraceae) [por]
V. Campbell de Araújo. [Manaus] Conselho Nacional de
Pesquisas, Instituto Nacional de Pesquisas da Amazônia,
1967.
v.   illus.   23 cm.   (Instituto Nacional de
Pesquisas da Amazônia. Botanica. Publicação, no. 23)
Summary in Portuguese and English.
Bibliography: p. 14.
Contents. - 1. Aniba duckei Kostermans (Pau-rosa
Itauba)

18352 Araújo Filho, José Ribeiro de.
0 porto de Vitória. São Paulo, Universidade de São
Paulo, Instituto de Geografia, 1974.
300 p.   7 pl., maps (1 fold.), tables, diagrs.
(Série teses e monografias, no. 9)
p. 145-6 repeated in an insert.
"Bibliografia": p. 269-300.

18353 Araujo Sánchez, Francisco.
Los dos últimas leyes ecuatorianas de régimen muni-
cipal; comparación descriptiva. Vol. 1. Quito,
Instituto de Estudios Administrativos, Universidad
Central, 1966.
169 p.   21 x 32 cm.

18354 Araujo Villegas, Arturo.
Guía del procedimiento criminal. 2. ed. corregida
y aumentada. Potosí, Bolivia, 1960.
229 p.   19 cm.   (Manuales de procedimiento)

18355 Aravena Arredondo, Leonardo.
Naturaleza jurídica del arbitraje. [Santiago de
Chile] Editorial Jurídica de Chile, 1969.
137 p.   23 cm.
Bibliography: p. 131-133.

18356 Araya, Carlomagno.
La gruta iluminada, poemas. [San José, Costa Rica,

Imprenta Metropolitana, 1962]
118 p.   port.   21 cm.

18357   Araya, Guillermo.
Atlas lingüístico-etnográfico del sur de Chile
(Alesuch) (preliminares y cuestionario). Valdivia,
Chile, Instituto de Filología, Facultad de Filosofía
y Letras, Universidad Austral de Chile, 1968.
76 p.   tables, illus., map.   23 cm.   (Anejos
de Estudios Filosóficos, 1)

18358   Araya, José Francisco.
La cartografía de los procesos morfogenéticos actuales
en Chile transicional. Santiago, Instituto de Geografía,
Universidad de Chile, 1965.
23 p.   illus., maps.   27 cm.
Includes bibliography.

18359   Arbeláez, Fernando, comp.
Panorama de la nueva poesía colombiana. [1. ed.
Bogotá] Ministerio de Educación, Imprenta Nacional,
1964.
548 p.   22 cm.

18360   Arbeláez Camacho, Carlos, 1916-
De arquitectura e historia (estudios) Medellín,
Universidad Pontificia Bolivariana, 1968.
62 p.   16 cm.   (Colección "Rojo y negro," 59)
Includes bibliographical references.

18361   Arbeláez Lema, Federico.
Orientación universitaria y profesional. [Bogotá]
Librería Voluntad [1970]
144 p.   20½ cm.   (Biblioteca del Ecuador, 9)

18362   Arboleda, José Rafael.
Las ciencias sociales en Colombia. Rio de Janeiro,
1959.
74 p.   25 cm.   (Centro Latino-Americano de
Pesquisas en Ciencias Sociais. Publicação no. 7)

18363   Arboleda, José Rafael.
Histoire et anthropologie du noir en Colombie.
Trad. de l'espagnol par Marie-Christine Chazelle et
André Ahandagbe. Dakar, Senegal, Centre de Hautes
Études Afro-Ibéro-Américaines, Université de Dakar,
1968.
32 p.   27 cm.   (Pub. 4)
Bibliography: pp. 30-31)

18364   Arce, José, 1881-
El congreso de Belgrano. Buenos Aires, Ministerio
de Educación y Justicia, 1965.
182 p.   illus.   25 cm.   (Publicaciones del
Museo Roca. Estúdios, 8, p. [213]-390)

18365   Arce, José, 1881-
La Constitución argentina en la teoría y en la
práctica. En apéndice: I. Los problemas de la cultura
en la Constitución. II. La Constitución en su primer
centenario. III. Naturaleza y atribuciones de los
cuerpos políticos del estado. Buenos Aires, De Palma,
1961.
xiv, 260 p.   21 cm.

18366   Arce, Luis A   de.
El Real Hospital Nuestra Señora del Pilar en el siglo
XVIII (un hospital para los esclavos del Rey) 1764-1793
[por] Luis A. de Arce. La Habana, [Consejo Científico,
Ministerio de Salud Pública] 1969.
99, [8] p.   ports., facsims.   23 cm.   (Cuadernos
de Historia de la Salud Pública, 41)

18367   Arce de Vásquez, Margot.
La obra literaria de José de Diego. San Juan,
Puerto Rico, Instituto de Cultura Puertorriqueña, 1967.
xvi, 673 p.   22 cm.
Bibliography: p. [667]-673.

18368   Archangelsky, Sergio.
... Fundamentos de paleobotánica... La Plata,
Argentina, 1970.
348 p., 22 pl.   25 cm.
At head of title: Universidad Nacional de La Plata,
Facultad de Ciencias Naturales y Museo. Serie técnica
y didáctica, no. 11.

18369   Archer, Maria, 1905-
Brasil, fronteira da Africa. São Paulo, Editôra
Felman-Rêgo [1963]
176 p.   21 cm.

18370   Archila, Ricardo, ed.
Bibliografía médica venezolana, 1959-1961. Caracas,
Ministerio de Sanidad y Asistencia Social, 1967.
391 p.   21 cm.

18371   Archila, Ricardo, ed.
Bibliografía médica venezolana, 1962-1964. Editor

responsable: Ricardo Archila. Autores natos: los médicos venezolanos. Obra auspiciada y editada por cuenta del Ministerio de Sanidad y Asistencia Social. Caracas, 1968.
383 p.   23 cm.

18372   Archiveros de Argentina, Jornadas, 2nd, Córdoba, 1969.
Trabajo preparatorio. Resoluciones y recomendaciones aprobadas en distintas reuniones archivísticas y afines. Córdoba, 1969.
[39] p.   35 cm.

18373   Arcila Farias, Eduardo.
Historia de la ingeniería en Venezuela. Caracas, Colegio de Ingenieros de Venezuela, 1961.
2 v.   illus.   24 cm.
"Año centenario, 1861-1961."

18374   Arciniegas, Germán, 1900-
El estudiante de la mesa redonda. Buenos Aires, Editorial Sudamericana [1971]
231 p.   18 cm.   ("Colección Piragua," 151)
"Edición actualizada y aumentada."

18375   Arciniegas, Germán, 1900-
Nueva imagen del Caribe. Buenos Aires, Editorial Sudamericana [1970]
464 p.   illus.   21 cm.

18376   Arcos, Juan.
El sindicalismo en América Latina. Fribourg, Switzerland [etc., etc.] Oficina Internacional de Investigaciones Sociales de FERES, 1964.
192 p.   22 cm.   (Estudios sociológicos latino-americanos, 12)

18377   Ardao, Arturo.
Filosofía de lengua española; ensayos. [Montevideo] Alfa [1963]
176 p.   19 cm.   (Colección Carabela, 16)

18378   Ardao, Arturo.
Racionalismo y liberalismo en el Uruguay. Montevideo, 1962.
398 p.   20 cm.   (Montevideo. Universidad. Publicaciones. Historia y cultura, 1)

18379   Ardón, Víctor M
Bibliografía para el desarrollo de los programas

65

de matemáticas en la educación media. Guatemala,
Instituto de Investigaciones y Mejoramiento Educativo,
Universidad de San Carlos de Guatemala, 1971.
25 p.   29 cm.

18380 Ardón, Víctor M
Bibliografía y notas para el desarrollo de los
programas del idioma inglés en la educación media.
Guatemala, Instituto de Investigaciones y Mejoramiento Educativo, Universidad de San Carlos de
Guatemala, 1971.
34 p.   29 cm.

18381 Ardón, Víctor M
La educación industria, en Centro América. Guatemala,
Instituto de Investigaciones y Mejoramiento Educativo,
1965.
61 p.   23 cm.   (Estudios de la educación media
en Centro América)
Bibliography: p. 99-100.

18382 Arduini, Juvenal.
Homem-libertação. Uberaba, Gráf. Zebu, 1968.
194 p.   21 cm.

18383 Arduz Caballero, Walter, 1934-
Canto a la ciudad de los cuatro nombres. Sucre,
Bolivia [Universidad Mayor de San Francisco Xavier,
1960]
43 p.   19 cm.   (Biblioteca "Universidad Mayor
de San Francisco Xavier." Serie poética, 3)

18384 Areão, João Steudel.
O velho e a môça. Capa de Jayro Silva. Rio de
Janeiro, Irmãos Pongetti Editôres, 1963.
254 p.   19 cm.

18385 Areas metropolitanas e desenvolvimento integrado no
Brasil. Rio de Janeiro, Ministério do Interior,
1967.
48 p.   23 cm.
Bibliographical references included in "Notas."
Contents. - O Serviço Federal de Habitação e
Urbanismo e o Fundo de Financiamento de Planos de
Desenvolvimento Local Integrado. - Desenvolvimento
metropolitano integrado no Brasil, por H. J. Cole. -
Instituição de regiões metropolitanos no Brasil, por
Eurico de Andrade Azevedo. - Anteprojeto de lei
complementar sôbre áreas metropolitanas.

66

18386 Arellano, Jesús.
          Palabra de hombre; poemas, 1956-1966. México,
       Universidad Nacional Autónoma de México, 1966.
          99 p.   20 cm.
          Contents. - Paso a la voz. - Limpia la madrugada. -
       Camino libre. - Nuevo dia.

18387 Arellano Jiménez, Guillermo.
          Cultivo de los trigos en el Ecuador; el mal y su
       remedio. El abono químico Trigol. Quito [Editorial
       "Santo Domingo," 1961]
          142 p.   ports.   22 cm.

18388 Arellano Moreno, Antonio, ed.
          Documentos para la historia económica de Venezuela.
       Caracas, Instituto de Antropología e Historia,
       Facultad de Humanidades y Educación, Universidad
       Central de Venezuela, 1961.
          420 p.   24 cm.   (Serie de fuentes históricas, 2)
          Continues the compilation of 16th century documents
       begun in the author's Fuentes para la historia económica
       de Venezuela, siglo XVI.
          Bibliography: p. 407-[412]

18389 Arellano Moreno, Antonio, ed.
          Relaciones geográficas de Venezuela; recopilación,
       estudio preliminar y notas de Antonio Arellano
       Moreno. Caracas, Academia Nacional de Historia,
       1964.
          lvi, 578 p.   facsims., maps.   23 cm.
       (Biblioteca de la Academia Nacional de la Historia,
       70)
          Fuentes para la historia colonial de Venezuela.
          Includes bibliographical references.

18390 Arenas, Antonio Vicente.
          Derecho penal colombiano; parte general. Bogotá,
       Universidad Nacional de Colombia, 1964.
          1 p.l., [5]-402 p.   25 cm.

18391 Ares Somoza, Paulino.
          Marxismo ortodoxo. Buenos Aires, 1964.
          207 p.   21 cm.
          Bibliography: p. 9-10.

18392 Aretz de Ramón y Rivera, Isabel.
          Cantos Navideños en el folklore venezolano.
       Transcripciones musicales de Isabel Aretz y Luis
       Felipe Ramón y Rivera. Caracas, Edición "Casa de

la Cultura Popular," Ministerio del Trabajo [1962]
129 p.   illus., music.   22 x 23 cm.   (Colección
del Instituto de Folklore del Ministerio de Educación)
Includes unaccompanied melodies.

18393   Aretz-Thiele, Isabel.
Manual de folklore venezolano. Segunda edición,
revisada. Caracas, Instituto Nacional de Cultura
y Bellas Artes [1969]
263 p.   illus.   17½ cm.   (Biblioteca popular
venezolano, v. 120)

18394   Arévalo Martínez, Rafael, 1884-
Honduras; novela. Guatemala, Editorial del
Ministerio de Educación Pública "José de Pineda
Ibarra," 1959.
254 p.   illus.   21 cm.   (Colección Contempo-
ráneos, 48)

18395   Argentina: 1930-1960. Buenos Aires, Sur [1961]
446 p.   illus., ports.   22 cm.

18396   Argentine Republic.
Lotería de Beneficencia Nacional y Casinos;
manual oficial descriptivo (una institución al
servicio del país) Notas sobre el origen... de la
Lotería de Beneficencia Nacional y Casinos con
motivo del septuagesimo primer aniversario de su
fundación. Buenos Aires, 1965.
154 p.   illus., ports.   24 cm.
Cover title.

18397   Argentine Republic. Archivo General.
Política lusitana en el Río de la Plata; colección
Lavradio. Buenos Aires, 1961-
v.   facsims., fold. map, ports.   27 cm.
"Homenaje del Archivo General de la Nación a la
Revolución de Mayo en su 150° aniversario."
Contents. - 1. 1808-1809. - 2. 1810-1811. -
3. 1812-1815.
Library has v. 1-3.

18398   Argentine Republic. Caja Nacional de Ahorro Postal.
La Revolución de Mayo; material para uso de educa-
dores y estudiantes existente en la Biblioteca
"Domingo F. Sarmiento" de la Caja Nacional de Ahorro
Postal. Buenos Aires, 1960.
24 p.   26 cm.

18399 Argentine Republic. Caja Nacional de Ahorro Postal.
Biblioteca.
General José de San Martín; material para uso de
educadores y estudiantes existente en la Biblioteca
"Domingo F. Sarmiento" de la Caja Nacional de Ahorro
Postal; homenaje al libertador, 1850-1961. Buenos
Aires, 1961.
15 ℓ.   23 cm.

18400 Argentine Republic. Centro de Documentación Científica.
Guía de escuelas y cursos de bibliotecología en
la República Argentina. Buenos Aires, Consejo
Nacional de Investigaciones Científicas y Técnicas,
1965.
31 p.   charts.   26 cm.

18401 Argentine Republic. Centro Nacional de Documentación
e Información Educativa.
Bases para el curriculum de primer ciclo de las
escuelas de nivel intermedio. Buenos Aires, 1971.
519 p.   30 cm.

18402 Argentine Republic. Comisión de Integración Eléctrica.
Operación de sistemas eléctricos en los paises
miembros de la CIER. Informe del coordinador técnico
Ing. Leo Sudak. Buenos Aires, 1968.
3 v.   illus., graphs (part fold.), tables (part
fold.), maps (part fold.)   28½ cm.

18403 Argentine Republic. Comisión Nacional de Administración
del Fondo de Apoyo al Desarrollo Económico.
Alimentación con suplemento proteico en terneros
destetados temprano. Resultados de un ensayo
realizado en La Pampa. [Buenos Aires, 1961]
15 p.   26 cm.
"Operación carnes."

18404 Argentine Republic. Comisión Nacional de Administración
del Fondo de Apoyo al Desarrollo Económico.
CAFADE: 2 años de labor, 1959-1961. [Buenos
Aires] Presidencia de la Nación, 1961.
114 p.   illus.   26 cm.

18405 Argentine Republic. Comisión Nacional de Administración
del Fondo de Apoyo al Desarrollo Económico.
CAFADE: progress report, 1959-1961. [Buenos Aires]
Office of the President, 1961.
108 p.   illus.   26 cm.

18406   Argentine Republic. Comisión Nacional de Energía
        Atómica.
        Informe sobre el RA-3 reactor nuclear de experimen-
        tación y producción. Buenos Aires [1967]
        17 p.   illus., map.   29 cm.

18407   Argentine Republic. Comisión Nacional de Energía
        Atómica. Departamento de Metalurgia.
        Reseña de la tarea realizada por el Departamento de
        Metalurgia de la Comisión Nacional de Energía Atómica,
        al cumplirse el séptimo aniversario de la inauguración
        de sus laboratorios de investigación. Buenos Aires,
        1967.
        65 p.   illus.   22 cm.

18408   Argentine Republic. Comisión Nacional Ejecutiva de
        Homenaje al Sesquicentenario del Nacimiento de
        Domingo F. Sarmiento.
        La educación y el desarrollo social y económico.
        Recomendaciones del Congreso de Educación realizado
        en San Juan, República Argentina, del 5 al 11 de
        septiembre de 1961. [n.p., 1961?]
        [67] p.   23 cm.

18409   Argentine Republic. Congreso. Biblioteca.
        Abastecimiento, precios, monopolio, bibliografía.
        Buenos Aires, 1964.
        26 p.   28 cm.   (Argentine Republic. Congreso.
        Biblioteca. Serie Asuntos económicos, 4)

18410   Argentine Republic. Congreso. Biblioteca.
        Bibliografía sobre la vivienda. Buenos Aires,
        1964.
        113 p.   29 cm.   (Antecedentes para la docu-
        mentación parlamentaria, no. 7)

18411   Argentine Republic. Congreso. Biblioteca.
        Inmigración. Buenos Aires, 1967.
        44 ℓ.   28 cm.   (Serie Antecedentes para la
        documentación legislativa, no. 17)
        Cover title.

18412   Argentine Republic. Congreso. Biblioteca.
        Ley de control de precios para promover la defensa
        y seguridad nacionales, contener la especulación,
        el excesivo aumento de precios y las tendencias
        inflacionarias y otros propósitos. Buenos Aires,
        1964.

14 p.   29 cm.   (Serie Antecedentes extranjeros
[para la documentación parlamentaria])

18413   Argentine Republic. Congreso. Biblioteca.
Vivienda. Buenos Aires, 1966.
60 p.   28 cm.   (Serie Antecedentes para la
documentación legislativa, no. 16)

18414   Argentine Republic. Congreso. Biblioteca. Departamento
de Legislación Comparada.
Fomento industrial. [Buenos Aires] 1966.
43 l.   28 cm.   (Serie Antecedentes para la
documentación legislativa, no. 12)

18415   Argentine Republic. Congreso. Biblioteca. Servicio
de Referencia.
Bancos centrales. Buenos Aires, 1964.
40 l.   28 cm.   (Serie asuntos económicos, 2)
Cover title.
Contents. - Carta orgánica del Banco Central de la
República Argentina, actualizada a octubre de 1963. -
Bibliografía (leaves 27-40)

18416   Argentine Republic. Congreso. Biblioteca. Servicio
de Referencia.
Delitos contra la seguridad del estado. Buenos
Aires, 1960.
vi, 236 p.   28 cm.   (Serie Antecedentes para
la documentación parlamentaria, no. 2)

18417   Argentine Republic. Congreso. Biblioteca. Servicio
de Referencia.
Sucesión presidencial. Buenos Aires, 1962.
23 p.   29 cm.   (Serie Antecedentes extranjeros,
no. 2)
Acefalia presidencial en la Constitución y en la
ley (7 l.) by N. Costa Vici, issued as "Anexo".

18418   Argentine Republic. Congreso. Cámara de Senadores.
Reglamento de la Cámara de Senadores de la nación.
Buenos Aires [Impr. del Congreso de la nación] 1960.
viii, 104 p.   23 cm.

18419   Argentine Republic. Congreso. Cámara de Senadores.
Retornó Monseñor Cagliero. Repatriación de sus
restos. Roma, 1926 - Viedma, 1964. Buenos Aires,
Imprenta del Congreso de la nación, 1966.
312 p.   illus.   28 cm.

18420   Argentine Republic. Consejo de Investigaciones
        Científicas y Técnicas.
        Calendario de reuniones científicas y técnicas
        a realizarse en la República Argentina 1970. Buenos
        Aires [1970?]
        195 p.   23 cm.

18421   Argentine Republic. Consejo Federal de Inversiones.
        Analfabetismo en la Argentina: evolución y
        tendencias actuales. [Buenos Aires, 1963]
        61 p.   tables (part fold.)   29 cm.

18422   Argentine Republic. Consejo Federal de Inversiones.
        Bases para una política nacional de vivienda.
        [Buenos Aires] Consejo Federal de Inversiones, 1964.
        357 p.   illus.   28 cm.
        "Versión preliminar para crítica y comentario."

18423   Argentine Republic. Consejo Federal de Inversiones.
        Costo estructural de obras de aprovechamiento
        hidráulico. [Buenos Aires] 1963.
        422 p.   illus., diagrs., fold. map.   28 cm.

18424   Argentine Republic. Consejo Federal de Inversiones.
        Importancia y proyección del riego en la economía
        agraria de la región árida y semiárida de la
        Argentina. [Buenos Aires] Consejo Federal de
        Inversiones, 1964.
        x, 370 p.   illus., maps, tables (part fold.)
        27 cm.
        "Versión preliminar para crítica y comentario."

18425   Argentine Republic. Consejo Federal de Inversiones.
        Matriz interregional e intersectorial de confi-
        cientes de insumos nacionales e importados.
        Buenos Aires [n.d.]
        1 v.   (fold., unpaged)   18 x 26 cm.

18426   Argentine Republic. Consejo Federal de Inversiones.
        Política fiscal en la Argentina. Buenos Aires,
        1963.
        3 v.   tables (part fold.)   28-34 x 44 cm.

18427   Argentine Republic. Consejo Federal de Inversiones.
        Programa conjunto para el desarrollo agropecuario
        e industrial: 1. informe (semestre 15-5-62 al
        15-11-62) [publicado por el] Consejo Federal de
        Inversiones [y el] Instituto de Investigaciones

y Financieras de la C. G. E. Buenos Aires, 1962.
4 v.   graphs, tables (part fold.)   27 cm.

18428   Argentine Republic. Consejo Federal de Inversiones.
Recursos acuáticos vivos. Buenos Aires, 1963.
347 p.   illus., maps.   28 cm.

18429   Argentine Republic. Consejo Federal de Inversiones.
Sistema tributario de la minería en la República
Argentina. Buenos Aires, 1962.
40 p.   23 cm.

18430   Argentine Republic. Consejo Nacional de Desarrollo.
Plan nacional de desarrollo, 1965-1969. Buenos
Aires, 1965.
459 p.   illus. maps (part fold. col.)   30 cm.
Errata slip inserted.

18431   Argentine Republic. Consejo Nacional de Desarrollo.
Junta Nacional de Carnes.
Análisis y factibilidad de desarrollo económico
y técnico de las plantas faenadoras, industrializa-
doras y frigoríficas de carnes, subproductos y deri-
vados en la República Argentina. Objetivos y
metodología de su estudio. [Buenos Aires] 1963.
unpaged.   maps.   35 cm.

18432   Argentine Republic. Consejo Nacional de Desarrollo.
Secretaría.
Encuesta de consumo de alimentos en la Capital
Federal y gran Buenos Aires. Buenos Aires, 1968.
203 p.   29 cm.   (Serie C, no. 72)
Summary in English and French.

18433   Argentine Republic. Consejo Nacional de Desarrollo.
Sector Educación.
Educación, recursos humanos y desarrollo económico-
social; situación presente y necesidades futuras.
Buenos Aires, Secretaría del Consejo Nacional de
Desarrollo, 1968.
2 v.   tables.   30 cm.   (Serie C, 73)

18434   Argentine Republic. Consejo Nacional de Investigaciones Científicas y Técnicas.
Guía de las carreras que se cursan en universidades nacionales y otros institutos de enseñanza
superior. Segunda edición. [Buenos Aires] 1960.
217 p.   illus.   24 cm.

18435   Argentine Republic. Consejo Nacional de Investiga-
        ciones Científicas y Técnicas.
        Organización y funciones; disposiciones legales,
        reglamentos internos. Buenos Aires, 1959.
        88 p.   diagrs.   24 cm.

18436   Argentine Republic. Consejo Nacional de Investiga-
        ciones Científicas y Técnicas.
        Política científica y organización de investiga-
        ción científica en la Argentina. Paris, Unesco,
        1970.
        136 p.   28½ cm.   (Estudios y documentos de
        política científica, 20)

18437   Argentine Republic. Constitution.
        Constitución de la Nación Argentina. Buenos Aires
        [Secretaría de la Honorable Cámara de Diputados de
        la Nación] 1952.
        75 p.   23 cm.

18438   Argentine Republic. Constitution.
        Constitución de la Nación Argentina. Buenos Aires,
        Imprenta del Congreso de la Nación, 1964.
        59 p.   27 cm.

18439   Argentine Republic. Departamento de Estadística.
        Retención y desgranamiento, cohorte 1969-1975.
        Educación primaria, edad escolar. [Buenos Aires,
        1976]
        121 p.   maps, tables.   14½ x 20 cm.

18440   Argentine Republic. Dirección General de Investiga-
        ciones Agrícolas.
        Utilización y conservación del suelo en Argentina
        (Informe de la Comisión de Utilización y Conservación
        del Suelo del Grupo Mixto Gobierno Argentino-Naciones
        Unidas. Noviembre 1956) [Buenos Aires, 1958]
        47 p.   illus.   cm.   (Argentine Republic.
        Instituto Nacional de Tecnología Agropecuaria.
        Instituto de Suelos y Agrotecnia. Publicación,
        no. 56)
        "De "IDIA" no. 114, junio de 1957."

18441   Argentine Republic. Dirección General de Parques
        Nacionales.
        Curso interamericano de parques nacionales y
        protección y conservación de los recursos naturales
        renovables. Buenos Aires, 1966.
        24 p.   illus., map.   26 cm.

18442 Argentine Republic. Dirección General de Parques
Nacionales.
Parques nacionales argentinos. [Texto preparado
por la Dirección de Protección de la Naturaleza.
Colaboraron: M. J. Dimitri, H. Correa Luna y J.
Liebermann. Buenos Aires, 1959]
unpaged.   illus.   23 cm.

18443 Argentine Republic. Dirección Nacional de Energía y
Combustibles.
Evolución de la producción y consumo de energía
eléctrica y combustibles;   período 1955-1966.
Buenos Aires, 1967.
unpaged.   22 x 30 cm.

18444 Argentine Republic. Dirección Nacional de Estadística
y Censos.
Boletín de estadística. Suplemento de actualización
de principales series. [Buenos Aires] 1963.
23 p.   29 cm.
Cover title.

18445 Argentine Republic. Dirección Nacional de Estadística
y Censos.
Censo de población, 1960; resultados provisionales
por departamentos y/o partidos, suministrados por los
comités censales provinciales [n.p., 1961?]
various pagings.   33 cm.

18446 Argentine Republic. Dirección Nacional de Estadística
y Censos.
Censo industrial, 1954. Buenos Aires, 1960.
xiii, 383 p.   map.   29 cm.

18447 Argentine Republic. Dirección Nacional de Estadística
y Censos.
Censo nacional de 1960, población; resultados
provisionales. Buenos Aires, 1961.
187 p.   illus.   28 cm.

18448 Argentine Republic. Dirección Nacional de Estadística
y Censos.
Censo nacional, 1960; características principales
de la población obtenidas por muestro. [Buenos
Aires, 1963]
xii, 200 p.   tables.   30 cm.

18449 Argentine Republic. Dirección Nacional de Fiscalización y Comercialización Ganadera. Area de Trabajo

y Lechería.
Reseña estadística. Buenos Aires.
v. 30 cm. annual.
Library has 1974, 1975.

18450 Argentine Republic. Dirección Nacional de Geología
y Minería.
Catálogo de publicaciones de la Dirección Nacional
de Geología y Minería, incluyendo los informes
inéditos. Ordenado y clasificado por Antonio Amato.
Buenos Aires, 1960.
113 p. 27 cm.

18451 Argentine Republic. Estación Experimental Agropecuaria
Anguil.
Catálogo de publicaciones editadas por la Estación
Experimental Agropecuaria Anguil, La Pampa. [Anguil,
Argentina, 1968]
12 ℓ. 35 cm.

18452 Argentine Republic. Fuerza Aérea Argentina.
Libro de oro, 1912-1962. [Buenos Aires, 1963]
409 p. illus., maps, ports. 23 x 33 cm.
Caption title: Libro de oro de la Fuerza Aérea
Argentina.
Errata slip inserted.

18453 Argentine Republic. Instituto de Biología Marina.
... La reproducción de la merluza en el Mar
Argentino (Merluciidae, Merlucius merlucius hubbsi)
1. Descripción histológica del ciclo del ovario de
merluza, por Haraldo E. Christiansen. 2. La reproducción de la merluza y su relación con otros
aspectos biológicos de la especie, por Haraldo E.
Christiansen y María B. Cousseau. Mar del Plata,
1971.
75 p. illus. 26½ cm.

18454 Argentine Republic. Instituto Experimental del
Mogólico.
Mogolismo (Instituto Experimental del Mogólico)
[Buenos Aires, 1964]
476 p. illus. (part fold.) 25 cm.
Includes bibliographies.

18455 Argentine Republic. Instituto Geográfico Militar.
Atlas de la República Argentina. Segunda edición.
[Buenos Aires] Ejército Argentino, Instituto Geo-

gráfico Militar, 1959.
20 p. (chiefly maps)   29 x 40 cm.

18456   Argentine Republic.   Instituto Nacional de Previsión
Social. Biblioteca.
Ediciones bibliográficas.   año 1, no. 1-4, 1947-
1948. Buenos Aires.
1 v.   22 cm.
No more published?

18457   Argentine Republic.   Instituto Nacional de Vitivini-
cultura.
El ácido sórbico y su aplicación en enología.
[Mendoza, 1967?]
12 p.   23 cm.   (Cartilla de divulgación)

18458   Argentine Republic.   Instituto Nacional de Vitivini-
cultura.
Poda de la vid.   [Mendoza, 1964]
23 p.   illus.   23 cm.   (Cartilla de divulgación)
Cover title.

18459   Argentine Republic.   Instituto Nacional de Vitivini-
cultura.
Síntesis de estadística vitivinícola.   [Mendoza]
1967 [i.e. 1968]
119 ℓ.   col. illus.   27 cm.
Cover title.

18460   Argentine Republic.   Laws, statutes, etc.
Arrendamientos y aparcerías rurales; leyes 13.246
y 14.451, actualizadas.   Ordenación y comentarios
por Humberto A. Wernli.   Buenos Aires, Forum
Ediciones, 1962.
xii, 147 p.   maps (part fold.)   24 cm.
(Cuaderno de legislación ordenada no. 3)
Bibliography: p. 142.

18461   Argentine Republic.   Laws, statutes, etc.
Código civil de la República Argentina (con las
notas de Vélez Sarsfield) y leyes complementarias.
Buenos Aires, Lajouane, 1960 [cover 1961]
983 p.   24 cm.   (Códigos y leyes usuales de
la República Argentina)

18462   Argentine Republic.   Laws, statutes, etc.
Código civil de la República Argentina, con las
notas de Vélez Sarsfield, y leyes y decretos com-

plementarios. Buenos Aires, V. P. de Zavalía
[1960]
1129 p.   20 cm.

18463   Argentine Republic. Laws, statutes, etc.
Código civil; legislación complementaria, guía
índice alfabética, nueva ley de alquileres.
[17] edición actualizada hasta 1961.   Buenos Aires,
Editorial Claridad [1961]
533 p.   23 cm.   (Biblioteca jurídica, v. 2)

18464   Argentine Republic. Laws, statutes, etc.
Código de comercio. 30. edición, revisada y
puesta al día, 1960. Buenos Aires, Editorial
Claridad [1960]
352 p.   21 cm.   (Biblioteca jurídica, v. 3)

18465   Argentine Republic. Laws, statutes, etc.
Código de procedimientos en materia penal y
leyes complementarias, concordado y comentado [por]
Luis A. Barberis. Buenos Aires, R. Depalma,
1956-59.
2 v.   23 cm.   (Legislación argentina vigente)

18466   Argentine Republic. Laws, statutes, etc.
Código penal; códigos de procedimientos en lo
criminal de la Nación y Provincia de Buenos Aires,
leyes complementarios de ambos Códigos y Código
municipal de faltas. 16. edición puesta al día,
1960. Buenos Aires, Editorial Claridad [1960]
349 p.   21 cm.   (Biblioteca jurídica, v. 4)

18467   Argentine Republic. Laws, statutes, etc.
Código penal; códigos de procedimientos en lo
criminal de la nación y provincia de Buenos Aires;
leyes complementarias de ambos códigos, código
municipal de faltas. Edición especial. [Buenos
Aires] Editorial Trazo, 1962.
360 p.   20 cm.

18468   Argentine Republic. Laws, statutes, etc.
Código procesal civil y comercial de la Nación,
Ley 17.454. Buenos Aires, Poder Ejecutivo Nacional,
Secretaría de Justicia, 1967.
294 p.   24 cm.

18469   Argentine Republic. Laws, statutes, etc.
Compendio de sociedades anónimas; manual práctico
para el fundador, accionista, presidente, director,

78

síndico, gerente, contador, auditor, abogado, escribano, profesor, estudiante. Buenos Aires, El Accionista, 1960.
804 p.   forms.   27 cm.

18470   Argentine Republic. Laws, statutes, etc.
Legal system governing foreign investment.
[Buenos Aires] Ministry of Economy [1976]
27 p.   28 cm.

18471   Argentine Republic. Laws, statutes, etc.
Ley penitenciaría nacional, complementaria del Código penal (Decreto ley no. 412.58) Antecedentes y texto. [Buenos Aires, Taller Gráfico de la Penitenciaría Nacional, 1958]
64 p.   24 cm.

18472   Argentine Republic. Laws, statutes, etc.
Leyes del trabajo, comentadas, anotadas y concordadas [por] Manuel Ossorio y Florit. Buenos Aires, Bibliográfica Omeba [1961]
759 p.   24 cm.   (Libros científicos)

18473   Argentine Republic. Laws, statutes, etc.
Leyes impositivas; los últimos textos ordenados de las leyes de impuesto y su reglamentación: reditos, ventas, eventuales, beneficios extraordinarios, herencias, sustitutivo identificado, aprendizaje, lucrativas, ley 11.683, revaluación activos. Buenos Aires, Editorial Bregna, 1961.
cover-title, 255, [1] p.   tables, forms.
18 cm.

18474   Argentine Republic. Ministerio de Agricultura y Ganadería. Servicio Nacional de Fiscalización Ganadera. Departamento de Lechería.
Reseña estadística, año 1970. [Buenos Aires? 1971?]
42 p.   tables.   30½ cm.

18475   Argentine Republic. Ministerio de Asistencia Social y Salud Pública.
Leyes de medicamentos. Informe del Ministro de Asistencia Social y Salud Pública, Arturo Oñativia, en la Comisión de Asistencia Social y Salud Pública de la honorable Cámara de Diputados de la Nación, producido el 22 de julio de 1965. Buenos Aires, 1965.
91 p.   table.   23 cm.

18476   Argentine Republic. Ministerio de Cultura y Educación.
        Departamento de Estadística Educativa.
        La educación en cifras. Buenos Aires, 1971.
        301 p.   graphs, maps.   22 x 30 cm.

18477   Argentine Republic. Ministerio de Cultura y Educación.
        Departamento de Estadística Educativa.
        La educación en cifras, 1958-1967. Buenos Aires,
        1972.
        iii, 115 p.   23 x 36 cm.

18478   Argentine Republic. Ministerio de Cultura y Educación.
        Departamento de Estadística Educativa.
        La educación en cifras. Tomo II. 1963-1972.
        Buenos Aires, 1973.
        543 p.   maps, tables, diagrs.   22 x 31 cm.

18479   Argentine Republic. Ministerio de Cultura y Educación.
        Departamento de Estadística Educativa.
        La educación en la República Argentina, año 1973.
        Buenos Aires, 1974.
        26 p.   22½ x 30 cm.

18480   Argentine Republic. Ministerio de Cultura y Educación.
        Departamento de Estadística Educativa.
        Estadística educativa. Síntesis 1967-1971.
        Buenos Aires, 1972.
        150 p.   tables, graphs, fold. tables in pocket
        at end.   11½ x 15½ cm.

18481   Argentine Republic. Ministerio de Cultura y Educación.
        Departamento de Estadística Educativa.
        Estadística educativa. Síntesis 1969-1973.
        Buenos Aires [1974?]
        152 p.   9 x 14½ cm.

18482   Argentine Republic. Ministerio de Cultura y Educación.
        Departamento de Estadística Educativa.
        Estadística educativa: síntesis, 1970-1974.
        Buenos Aires, Ministerio de Cultura y Educación,
        1975.
        iv, 158 p.   11 x 15½ cm.

18483   Argentine Republic. Ministerio de Cultura y Educación.
        Departamento de Estadística Educativa.
        Estadística educativa, 1970. Buenos Aires, 1970.
        304 p.   tables, graphs.   34 cm.

18484 Argentine Republic. Ministerio de Cultura y Educación.
Departamento de Estadística Educativa.
Estadística educativa, 1973. (Cifras provisionales
al 30 de junio) Buenos Aires, 1974.
395 p.   maps, tables, diagrs.   30 cm.

18485 Argentine Republic. Ministerio de Cultura y Educación.
Departamento de Estadística Educativa.
Estadísticas de la educación, 1964-1973. Buenos
Aires [1974?]
228 p.   22 x 30 cm.
Tables.

18486 Argentine Republic. Ministerio de Cultura y Educación.
Departamento de Estadística Educativa.
Estadísticas de la educación, 1974. Buenos Aires,
1974.
403 p.   maps, tables.   29 cm.

18487 Argentine Republic. Ministerio de Cultura y Educación.
Departamento de Estadística Educativa.
Estadísticas de la educación; establecimientos -
alumnos y docentes por dependencia, repartición y
jurisdicción, 1965-1974. Buenos Aires, 1974.
212 p.   14½ x 20½ cm.

18488 Argentine Republic. Ministerio de Cultura y Educación.
Departamento de Estadística Educativa.
Estadísticas de la educación comunicados para la
prensa, año 1974. Buenos Aires, 1974.
148 p.   tables, diagrs.   20½ x 29cm.

18489 Argentine Republic. Ministerio de Cultura y Educación.
Departamento de Estadística Educativa.
Estadísticas de la educación comunicados para la
prensa, año 1975. Buenos Aires, 1975.
162 p.   maps, tables.   20½ x 29 cm.

18490 Argentine Republic. Ministerio de Cultura y Educación.
Departamento de Estadística Educativa.
Estadísticas de la educación. Buenos Aires,
1975.
21 p.   tables.   21 cm.

18491 Argentine Republic. Ministerio de Educación y Justicia.
Educational development in the Argentine Republic
during the year 1960. [Buenos Aires, 1961]
19 p.   tables.   25 cm.

18492 Argentine Republic. Ministerio de Educación y
Justicia. Departamento de Documentación e
Información Educativa.
Experiencias y contribuciones para la enseñanza
de la lengua oral y escrita. [Buenos Aires, 1961]
186 p.   25 cm.   (Serie Didáctica, 1)

18493 Argentine Republic. Ministerio de Obras y Servicios
Públicos. Subsecretaría de Energía.
Energía eléctrica. Anuario estadístico, 1969.
[Buenos Aires, 1970?]
65 p.   tables.   23 x 29½ cm.

18494 Argentine Republic. Ministerio de Trabajo y Seguridad
Social. Dirección General de Estudios e Investigaciones.
Conflictos del trabajo [Buenos Aires] 1961.
108 p.   diagrs., tables.   26 cm.   (Cuadernos
de investigación social)
Bibliography: p. 107-108.

18495 Argentine Republic. Policía Federal. Museo.
Iconografía policial; colección Fortuny. [Buenos
Aires, 1965]
62 p.   illus. (part col.)   25 cm.   (Publicación no. 2)
"Esta publicación tiene el carácter de un homenaje
de la Policía Federal Argentina a la memoria del
pintor español don Francisco Fortuny en el centenario
de su nacimiento."
Bibliography: p. [61]-62.

18496 Argentine Republic. Presidencia de la Nación.
La política económica argentina. [Buenos Aires]
1967.
41 p.   31 cm.

18497 Argentine Republic. Presidencia de la Nación.
Secretaría General.
Boletín informativo. Exposiciones de los señores
secretarios de estado efectuadas por radio y tele-
visión. [Buenos Aires] 1968.
2 v.   graphs, tables.   27 cm.

18498 Argentine Republic. Presidente, 1958-   (Frondizi)
La Argentina ante los problemas mundiales:
definición de una política exterior al servicio de
la nación. Buenos Aires, 1961.
25 p.   21 cm.

18499   Argentine Republic. Secretaría de Agricultura y
        Ganadería. Dirección Nacional de Fiscalización y
        Comercialización Ganadera. Area de Trabajo Lechería.
        Reseña estadística. Año 1972. [Buenos Aires?
        1973?]
        42 l.   39 cm.

18500   Argentine Republic. Secretaría de Estado de Vivienda.
        Imágenes de vivienda. Buenos Aires, 1969.
        [95] p.   illus.   19 x 28 cm.

18501   Argentine Republic. Secretaría de Estado de Vivienda.
        Banco Hipotecario Nacional.
        Recuerdos del viejo congreso. [Buenos Aires]
        Banco Hipotecario Nacional [n.d.]
        [159] p.   20½ cm.

18502   Argentine Republic. Secretaría de Prensa.
        La República Argentina; aspectos de su realidad
        económica. [Buenos Aires] 1960 [cover 1961]
        176 p.   maps (1 col.)   diagrs., tables.   28 cm.

18503   Argentine Republic. Servicio de Hidrografía Naval.
        Departamento de Meteorología.
        Resumen de sondeos aerológicos: Orcadas y Ushuaia.
        Año Geofísico Internacional, 1957-58. Buenos Aires,
        1959.
        40 p.   illus.   25 cm.   (Argentine Republic.
        Servicio de Hidrografía Naval. Público, H. 406)
        Spanish and English.

18504   Arguedas, Alcides, 1879-1946.
        Etapas de la vida de un escritor. Prólogo y notas
        de Moisés Alcázar. La Paz, 1963-
        v.   port.   20 cm.

18505   Arguedas, José María.
        Los ríos profundos. Santiago, Chile, Editorial
        Universitaria, 1967.
        261 p.   18 cm.   (Letras de América, 1)

18506   Argueta, Manlio.
        El valle de las hamacas. Buenos Aires, Editorial
        Sudamericana [1968]
        159 p.   19 cm.

18507   Arias, Abelardo.
        De tales cuales. Buenos Aires, Editorial Sud-

americana [1973]
255 p.   19 cm.

18508 Arias, Abelardo.
       Límite de clase.   Buenos Aires, Editorial Sud-
       americana [1964]
       285 p.   18 cm.   (Colección Novelistas latino-
       americanos)

18509 Arias, Abelardo.
       Polvo y espanto.   Buenos Aires, Editorial Sud-
       americana [1971]
       320 p.   19 cm.

18510 Arias, Abelardo.
       Ubicación de la escultura argentina en el siglo XX.
       [Buenos Aires] Ediciones Culturales Argentinas,
       Ministerio de Educación y Justicia, Dirección General
       de Cultura [1962]
       39 p.   plates.   25 cm.   (Biblioteca del
       sesquicentenario.   Cuadernos culturales [18, 026 EP])

18511 Arias, Abelardo.
       La viña estéril.   Buenos Aires, Editorial Sud-
       americana [1968]
       253 p.   18 cm.   (Colección "El Espejo")

18512 Arias, Hermes Duarte.
       Uso do microscópio electrônico de varredura na
       observação de pelotas de minério de ferro. [Por]
       Hermes Duarte Arias e Walter A. Mannheimer. Rio de
       Janeiro, Coordenação dos Programas de Pós-Graduação
       de Engenharia, Universidade Federal do Rio de
       Janeiro, 1971.
       21 p.   illus.   29½ cm.   (Pub. 4.71)

18513 Arias B   , Jorge.
       La población de Centroamérica y sus perspectivas.
       Guatemala, Facultad de Ingeniería, Universidad de
       San Carlos de Guatemala, 1966.
       59 p.   23 cm.   (Temas de ingeniería, 2)

18514 Arias Ramírez, Javier, 1924-
       Razón de la vigilia.   [Bogotá, Editorial Guadalupe]
       1964.
       63 p.   18 cm.
       Poems.

18515   Arias Robalino, Augusto, 1903-
        Obras selectas [de] Augusto Arias. Quito,
        Editorial Casa de la Cultura Ecuatoriana, 1962.
        950 p.   19 cm.
        Contents. - Mariana de Jesús. - El cristal indígena. -
        Vida de Pedro Fermín Cevallos. - Luis A. Martínez. -
        Virgilio en castellano. - Pasión y certeza de Sor
        Juana Inés de la Cruz. - Goethe. - Mujeres de Quito. -
        El Quijote de Montalvo. - Jorge Isaacs y su María. -
        José Marti. - Tres ensayos. - España en los Andes. -
        España eterna. - Zorrilla de San Martín y el charrúa. -
        Escritores del noventa y ocho. - Rubén Darío,
        americano y universal. - Poeta de eternidades. -
        Almas y lugares.

18516   Arín Ormazábal, Angel de.
        Doctrina social católica. San Sebastián [España]
        Escuela Superior de Técnica Empresaria   [1961]
        648 p.   24 cm.
        Bibliography: p. [13]-24.

18517   Arinos, Afonso, 1868-1916.
        0 contratador dos diamantes. Peça brasileira.
        Rio de Janeiro, Serviço Nacional de Teatro, 1973.
        viii, 56 p.   21 cm.

18518   Aristotele.
        Política. Versión española, notas e introducción
        de Antonio Gómez Robledo. México, Ciudad Univer-
        sitaria, Universidad Nacional Autónoma de México,
        1963.
        250 p.   24 cm.   (Obras)

18519   Arita, Carlos Manuel.
        Cantos del trópico, dedicado a la niñez y a la
        juventud de Honduras. Tegucigalpa, Impr.
        Ariston, 1962.
        162, iii p.   illus.   21 cm.

18520   Arita, Carlos Manuel.
        Saludo lírico a Comayagua, con ocasión de haber
        sido declarada capital de la República, durante la
        visita que hiciera el ciudadano presidente,
        Dr. Ramón Villeda Morales. Septiembre 8 de 1962.
        [Comayagua? 1962]
        15 p.   19 cm.

18521   Ariza S   , Alberto E
        Los domínicos en Panamá, por Alberto E. Ariza S.

[1. ed.] Bogotá, Convento-Seminario de Santo
Domingo [1964]
95 p.   illus., maps, ports.   24 cm.
Bibliography: p. [4]

18522 Ariza S   , Alberto E
Los domínicos y la villa de Leiva. Nota prologal
de Carlos López Narváez. Bogotá, Convento-Seminario
de Santo Domingo [1963]
175 p.   illus., ports.   22 cm.
Bibliography: p. [4]

18523 Arlt, Mirta.
El teatro como fenómeno colectivo. Santa Fé,
Universidad Nacional del Litoral, Departamento de
Extensión Universitaria [1967]
79, [1] p.   20 cm.   (Colección Extensión
universitaria, no. 102)
Bibliography: p. [80]

18524 Armas, Luis F   de.
Anomalías en algunos Buthidae (Scorpionida) de
Cuba y Brasil [por] Luis F. de Armas. La Habana,
Instituto de Zoología, Academia de Ciencias, 1977.
6 p.   illus.   23 cm.   (Poeyana, 176)
"Literatura citada": p. 5-6.
Abstract in English: p. 1.

18525 Armas, Luis F   de.
Dos nuevas especies de Cryptocellus (Arachnida:
Ricinulei) de Cuba [por] Luis F. de Armas. La
Habana, Instituto de Zoología, Academia de Ciencias,
1977.
11 p.   illus.   23 cm.   (Poeyana, 164)
"Literatura citada": p. 10-11.
Abstract in English: p. 1.

18526 Armas, Luis F   de.
Dos nuevas especies de Schizomus Arachnida:
Schizomida de Cuba [por] Luis F. de Armas.
La Habana, Instituto de Zoología, Academia de
Ciencias, 1977.
8 p.   illus., maps, table.   23 cm.   (Poeyana,
166)
Abstract in English: p. 1.

18527 Armas, Luis F   de.
Escorpiones del archipiélago Cubano. I. Nuevo
género y nuevas especies de Buthidae (Arachnida:

scorpionida)   La Habana, Instituto de Zoología,
Academia de Ciencias de Cuba, 1973.
   23 p.   illus., tables.   24½ cm.   (Poeyana,
114)
Abstract in English.

18528 Armas, Luis F   de.
       Escorpiones del archipiélago cubano. V. Nuevas
especies de centruroides (Scorpionida; Buthidae)
La Habana, Instituto de Zoología, Academia de
Ciencias de Cuba, 1976.
   55 p.   illus., tables.   23 cm.   (Poeyana,
146)
Abstract in English.

18529 Armas, Luis F   de.
       Escorpiones del archipiélago cubano. VI. Familia
diplocentridae (Arachnida: Scorpionida)   La Habana,
Instituto de Zoología, Academia de Ciencias de
Cuba, 1976.
   35 p.   illus., tables.   23 cm.   (Poeyana,
147)
Abstract in English.

18530 Armas, Luis F   de.
       Notas sobre Mastigoproctus baracoensis Franganillo,
1931 (Arachnida: Uropygi)   La Habana, Instituto
de Zoología, Academia de Ciencias de Cuba, 1973.
   4 p.   illus.   24½ cm.   (Poeyana, 100)
Abstract in English.

18531 Armas, Luis F   de.
       Redescripción de Tityus obtusus (Karsch, 1879)
(Scorpionida: Buthidae) [por] Luis F. de Armas.
La Habana, Instituto de Zoología, Academia de
Ciencias, 1977.
   7 p.   illus., table.   23 cm.   (Poeyana,
178)
       "Literatura citada": p. 7.
       Abstract in English: p. 1.

18532 Armas, Luis F   de.
       Tipos de las colecciones escorpiológicas P.
Franganillo y Universidad de La Habana (Arachnida:
Scorpionida)   La Habana, Instituto de Zoología,
Academia de Ciencias de Cuba, 1973.
   18 p.   tables.   24½ cm.   (Poeyana, 101)
       Abstract in English.

18533   Armas, Luis F   de.
          Tricobotriotaxia de Alayotityus nanus Armas
          y Centruroides guanensis cubensis Moreno (Scor-
          pionidae: Buthidae) [por] Luis F. de Armas.
          La Habana, Instituto de Zoología, Academia de
          Ciencias de Cuba, 1977.
          9 p.   illus., diagrs.   23 cm.   (Poeyana,
          162)
          "Literatura citada":   p. 4.
          Abstract in English: p. 1.

18534   Armas Chitty, José Antonio de, 1908-
          Canto solar a Venezuela [por] J. A. de Armas
          Chitty. Dibujos: César Rengifo. [Caracas,
          Ediciones de la Biblioteca, Universidad Central
          de Venezuela, 1968]
          138 p.   illus.   24 cm.

18535   Armas Chitty, José Antonio de, 1908-
          Caracas; origen y trayectoria de una ciudad.
          Caracas, Fundación Creole, 1967.
          2 v.   23 cm.

18536   Armas Chitty, José Antonio de, 1908-   ed.
          Documentos para la historia colonial de los
          Andes venezolanos (siglos XVI al XVIII) Prólogo
          por J. A. de Armas Chitty. Caracas, Instituto
          de Antropología e Historia, Facultad de Humanidades
          y Educación, Universidad Central de Venezuela,
          1957.
          317 p.   22½ cm.   (Fuentes históricas, 1)

18537   Armas Chitty, José Antonio de, 1908-
          ... Influencia de algunas capitulaciones en la
          geografía de Venezuela. Serie de historia.
          Caracas, Instituto de Antropología e Historia,
          Facultade de Humanidades y Educación, Universidad
          Central de Venezuela, 1967.
          260 p.   23 cm.

18538   Armas Chitty, José Antonio de, 1908-   ed.
          Poetas guayaneses. Selección y explicación
          por J. A. de Armas Chitty. Edición conmemorativa
          del bicentenario de Ciudad Bolívar. Caracas,
          Ministerio de Educación, 1964.
          184 p.   22 cm.

18539   Armas Chitty, José Antonio de, 1908-   ed.
          Tucupido; formación de un pueblo del llano.

Caracas, Instituto de Antropología e Historia,
Facultad de Humanidades y Educación, Universidad
Central de Venezuela, 1961.
291 p.   col. map, facsim., tables.   24 cm.
(Serie de historia)
Bibliography: p. 249-256.

18540 Armas Chitty, José Antonio de, 1908-
Vida política de Caracas en el siglo XIX.
Caracas, Ministerio de Educación, Dirección Técnica,
Departamento de Publicaciones [1969]
[266] p.   22 cm.

18541 Armas Chitty, José Antonio de, 1980-
Vocabulario del hato. Caracas, Universidad
Central de Venezuela, 1966.
208 p.   20 cm.   (Colección Avance, 13)
Bibliography: pp. 203-[209].

18542 Armas Lara, Marcial.
El renacimiento de la danza guatemalteca y el
origen de la marimba. Guatemala, Centro Editorial
"José de Pineda Ibarra," Ministerio de Educación
Pública, 1964.
452 p.   illus. (part col.) facsims., music,
ports.   26 cm.
On cover: Folklore guatemalteco.

18543 Armellada, Cesáreo de, ed.
Por la Venezuela indígena de ayer y de hoy;
relatos de misioneros capuchinos en viaje por la
Venezuela indígena durante los siglos XVII, XVIII
y XX. Caracas, Sociedad de Ciencias Naturales
La Salle, 1960-
v.   illus., maps.   24 cm.   (Monografías
no. 5)
Contents. - t. 1. Siglos XVII y XVIII.

18544 Armenta C   , Santiago.
Fluctuación estacional de artrópodos en algodonero
en el Valle del Fuerte, Sin., [por] Santiago
Armenta C. [y] Joel Rodríguez V. Mexico, Sociedad
Mexicana de Entomología, 1974.
47-61 p.   diagrs.   24 cm.
Abstract in English.
Reprinted from Folia entomológica mexicana,
no. 28, April 1974.

18545 Arméstar V   , Miguel A
       La tierra y el hombre; visión panorámica del
       problema agrario-social del Perú y su estrecha
       relación con el capital. Lima, Imprenta y Litografía
       Salesiana, 1963.
       174 p.   22 cm.
       Bibliography: p. 169.

18546 Armesto, Alejandro.
       Tiempo de morir; [novela] Portada y dibujos de
       Villar Chao. Lugo, Ediciones "Celta," 1962.
       51 p.   19 cm.   (Colección "Aquí y ahora")

18547 Armijo, Roberto.
       Francisco Gavidia; la odisea de su genio. [Por]
       Roberto Armijo [y] José Napoleón Rodríguez Ruiz.
       Vol. 1. San Salvador, Dirección General de Publica-
       ciones, Ministerio de Educación, 1965.
       301 p.   21 cm.   (Colección Certamen Nacional
       de Cultura, 31)

18548 Armijo, Roberto.
       Francisco Gavidia. La odisea de su genio. [Por]
       Roberto Armijo y José Napoleón Rodríguez Ruiz.
       Primer premio. República de El Salvador. Certamen
       Nacional de Cultura, 1965. Tomo segundo. San Sal-
       vador, Ministerio de Educación, Dirección General
       de Publicaciones [1967]
       217 p.   illus., facsim.   21 cm.

18549 Armijo, Roberto.
       Jugando a la gallina ciega. Pieza en 2 actos...
       San Salvador, El Salvador, Ministerio de Educación,
       Dirección General de Cultura [1970]
       69 p.   19½ cm.

18550 Arnau Macías, Manuel.
       Dr. José H. Pazos y Caballero (gran entomólogo
       cubano), 1867-1928. La Habana, Consejo Científico,
       Ministerio de Salud Pública, 1968.
       144 p.   front., facsims., illus.   23 cm.
       (Cuadernos de historia de la salud pública, 39)
       Bibliography: p. [145].

18551 Arnaud, Expedito.
       Aspectos de legislação sobre os índios do Brasil.
       Belém, Museu Paraense Emílio Goeldi, 1973.
       45 p.   27 cm.   (Publicações avulsas, no. 22)

18552 Arnaud, Expedito.
       A extinção dos indios Kararaõ (Kayapó) - Baixo
       Xingu, Pará [por] Expedito Arnaud [e] Ana Rita Alves.
       Belém, Museu Paraense Emílio Goeldi, 1974.
       19 p.   23 cm.   (Boletim do Museu Paraense
       Emilio Goeldi. Nova série: Antropologia, no. 53)

18553 Arnaud, Expedito.
       Os índios Gaviões de oeste, pacificação e inte-
       gração [por] Expedito Arnaud. Belém, Museu Paraense
       Emílio Goeldi, 1975.
       86 p., 4 pl.   28 cm.   (Publicações avulsas, 28)

18554 Arnaud, Expedito.
       Os indios Munduruku e o Serviço de Proteção aos
       Indios [por] Expedito Arnaud. Belém, Museu Paraense
       Emílio Goeldi, 1974.
       60 p.   23 cm.   (Boletim do Museu Paraense
       Emílio Goeldi. Nova serie: Antropologia, no. 54)
       "Summary": p. 53-54.
       "Bibliografia citada": p. 54-60.

18555 Arnaud, Expedito.
       O parentesco entre os índios Galibí do rio
       Oiapoque. Belém, Museu Paraense Emílio Goeldi,
       1968.
       19 p.   illus. (part fold.)   23 cm.   (Boletim
       do Museu Paraense Emílio Goeldi. Nova série:
       Antropologia, no. 33)
       Caption title.
       Bibliography: p. 10-11.

18556 Arnedo Álvarez, Gerónimo.
       El papel del Partido en la lucha por la organiza-
       ción, consolidación y desarrollo de los movimientos
       de masas; informe rendido ante el XII Congreso [d]el
       Partido Comunista de la Argentina, realizado entre
       los días 22 de febrero y 3 de marzo 1963. Buenos
       Aires, Editorial Anteo, 1963.
       29 p.   30 cm.

18557 Arocho Rivera, Minerva.
       Sinfonía en negro; poemas. Ilustraciones de
       Aurelio Juan Ortiz. San Juan, P. R., 1964.
       79 ℓ.   illus., port.   22 cm.

18558 Arózqueta Rojano, Sadot.
       Nuevos aspectos del derecho de familia. [Mexico]
       Ciudad Universitaria, 1963.

104 p.   23 cm.
Tesis profesional - Universidad Nacional Autónoma
de México.
Bibliography: p. 103-104.

18559   Arraes, Miguel.
0 povo no poder.   [São Paulo] Editôra Fulgor
[1963]
31 p.   21 cm.   (Coleção Universidade do povo,
12)
"Discurso proferido pelo governador Miguel Arraes
em São Paulo 22-5-63."

18560   Arraes, Raymundo de Monte.
Decadência e redenção do Nordeste; a política dos
grandes estados. Rio de Janeiro, 1962.
183 p.   19 cm.

18561   Arrangoiz y Berzábal, Francisco de Paula de, d. 1889.
México desde 1808 hasta 1867. Prólogo de Martín
Quirarte. 2. ed. México, Editorial Porrúa, 1968.
li, 966 p.   22 cm.   (Colección "Sepan cuantos",
no. 82)
Bibliography: p. xiv-li.

18562   Arras, Mario S   , 1926-
Asido al viento. Ilustraciones de José Guadalupe
Guadiana. Monterrey, México, Ediciones Sierra
Madre [1966]
47 p.   illus.   25 cm.   (Poesía en el mundo,
12)

18563   Arras, Mario S   , 1926-
Canciones de viento. Monterrey, México,
Ediciones Sierra Madre, 1968.
24 p.   22 cm.   (Poesía en el mundo, 56)

18564   Arrate y Acosta, José Martín Félix de, d. 1766.
Llave del Nuevo Mundo; antemural de las Indias
Occidentales. La Habana descripta: noticias de su
fundación, aumentos y estados [por] José Martín
Félix de Arrate. [4. ed.] La Habana, Comisión
Nacional Cubana de la UNESCO, 1964.
270 p.   facsim.   23 cm.
Bibliography: p. [259]-266.

18565   Arreaza Calatrava, José Tadeo, 1885?-
Poesías [por] J. T. Arreaza Calatrava. Selección:
Oscar Sambrano Urdaneta. Prólogo: Fernando Paz-

Castillo. Caracas, Ediciones del Ministerio de
Educación, Dirección de Cultura y Bellas Artes,
Departamento de Publicaciones, 1964.
221 p.   18 cm.   (Biblioteca popular venezolana,
98)
Contents. - De "Odas. La triste e otros poemas." -
De "Cantos de la carne y del reino interior." -
Canto a la batalla de Carabobo. - Canto a Venezuela. -
El 19 de abril. - Canto al ingeniero de minas.

18566   Arredondo, Oscar.
Nueva especie de Mesocnus (Edentata: Megalonychidae)
del pleistoceno de Cuba [por] Oscar Arredondo.
La Habana, Instituto de Zoología, Academia de Ciencias,
1977.
10 p.   illus., table.   23 cm.   (Poeyana, 172)
"Literatura citada": p. 10.
Abstract in English: p. 1.

18567   Arredondo Andrade, Patricio.
La realidad del derecho; una reelaboración del
concepto derecho vigente. Santiago de Chile
[Editorial Universitaria] 1967.
126 p.   21 cm.
Memoria de prueba (licenciatura en ciencias
jurídicas y sociales) - Universidad de Chile,
Santiago.
Bibliography: p. 122-123.

18568   Arredondo Fernández, Jaime.
... El consejo de ministros en nuestra constitución. Tesis que para obtener el título de abogado
presenta Jaime Arredondo Fernández. México, 1968.
93 p.   23 cm.

18569   Arredondo y Miranda, Francisco de.
Recuerdos de las guerras de Cuba (Diario de
campaña, 1868-1871)   Introducción y notas de
Aleida Plasencia Mord. La Habana, 1962 [i.e. 1963]
192 p.   28 cm.
At head of title: Biblioteca Nacional "José Marti."

18570   Arreola, Juan José.
Cuentos. La Habana, Casa de las Américas, 1969.
185 p.   17 cm.   (Colección "La Honda")
18571   Arriaga, Eduardo.
Venezuela, proyección de la población económica-
mente activa, 1950-1975. Santiago, Chile, 1965.
38 p.   27 cm.   (Chile. Universidad, Santiago.

Centro Latinoamericano de Demografía. Series C, no. 26)

18572 Arriaga, Noël de, 1918-
Sol sobre o pecado. 3 atos. Rio de Janeiro, Serviço Nacional de Teatro, 1972.
118 p.   21 cm.

18573 Arriaga, Pablo José de, 1564-1622.
Extirpación de la idolatría del Pirv. Buenos Aires, 1910.
143 p. (on double leaves)   28 cm.
Reprint of the original edition of 1621.

18574 Arriaga Paz, Rafael.
La contrarrevolución agraria en México. México, 1963.
83 p.   23 cm.
Tesis (licenciatura en derecho) - Universidad Nacional Autónoma de México.
Bibliography: p. 81-83.

18575 Arrieta Chavarría, Omar.
Proyecto de Investigación: "Cambios recientes en la actividad agropecuaria de mercado y de subsistencia en la región central," por Omar Arrieta Chavarría. San José, Costa Rica, 1977.
25-27 p.   illus.   25 cm.
Reprinted from Costa Rica. Instituto Geográfico Nacional. Informe semestral. Jul.-Dec. 1976.

18576 Arrom, José Juan.
Esquema generacional de las letras hispano-americanas, ensayo de un método. Segunda edición. Bogotá, Instituto Caro y Cuervo, 1977.
263 p.   23 cm.   (Publicaciones del Instituto Caro y Cuervo, 39)

18577 Arroyo, Leonardo.
O tempo e o modo: [literatura infantil e outras notas] São Paulo, Conselho Estadual de Cultura, Comissão de Literatura [1963]
170 p.   22 cm.   (Coleção Ensaio, 25)

18578 Arroyo de Colón, Maria.
... La profesión del magisterio... Hotel Americana [San Juan de Puerto Rico] 19 de noviembre de 1963. [San Juan, 1963?]
53 p.   28 cm.

At head of title: Seminario de la Confederación
mundial de organizaciones de profesionales de la
enseñanza.

18579   Arroyo Llano, Rodolfo.
        Ygnacio Zaragoza, defensor de la libertad y la
        justicia. Monterrey, México, 1962.
        179 p.   illus.   24 cm.

18580   Arroyo Soto, Victor Manuel.
        El habla popular en la literatura costarricense.
        San José, Universidad de Costa Rica, 1971.
        320 p.   23½ cm.   (Serie tesis de grado, 18)

18581   Arrufat, Antón.
        Repaso final. La Habana, Ediciones Revolución,
        1964.
        157 p.   22 cm.

18582   Artaud, Antonin, 1896-1948.
        Les Tarahumaras. Décines (Isère) L'Arbalète
        [1963]
        217 p.   16 cm.
        "Trois conférences à l'Université de Mexico:
        Surréalisme & révolution; L'homme contre le destin;
        Le théâtre & les dieux": p. [167]-[208]

18583   Artecona de Thompson, Marialuisa.
        Grito en los Andes; [poemas] Prólogo de R.
        Antonio Ramos. Asunción, Sociedad Bolivariana
        del Paraguay, 1964.
        26 p.   22 cm.

18584   Artes de México.
        Arte popular de México. Introducción de Alfonso
        Caso. Textos de Daniel F. Rubín de la Borbolla
        [et al.] Directora del catálogo: Eugenia C. de
        Rius. Edición especial de la revista Artes de
        México por encargo del Instituto Nacional Indigenista.
        México, 1963.
        34, 29 p.   275 illus., 25 col. plates.   32 cm.
        Spanish, English, and French.

18585   Artese, Edla Monteiro.
        Reflexos da adolescência. Rio de Janeiro,
        Irmãos Pongetti, 1963.
        83 p.   19 cm.

18586　Asamblea Interuniversitaria de Filología y Literaturas
Hispánicas, 5th, Universidad Nacional del Sur, 1968.
Actas. [Bahía Blanca] Departamento de Humanidades,
Instituto de Humanidades, Universidad Nacional del
Sur, 1968.
263 p.　24 cm.

18587　Ascanio, Osvaldo.
Los suelos y su utilización agrícola en el Valle
de la Juventud. La Habana, Instituto de Suelos,
Academia de Ciencias de Cuba, 1970.
12 p.　map, tables.　28½ cm.　(Serie Pinar
del Rio, no. 26)

18588　Aschmann, Herman P
Castellano-totonaco, totonaco-castellano; dialecto
de la Sierra Norte de Puebla. [1. ed.] México,
Instituto Lingüistico de Verano, 1962.
v, 171 p.　illus.　21 cm.　(Serie de vocabularios indígenas Mariano Silva y Aceves, no. 7)
Cover title: Vocabulario totonaco de la Sierra.

18589　Ascoli, Carlos A　de.
Esquema histórico-económico de Venezuela (del
mito del Dorado a la economía del café) Caracas,
Banco Central de Venezuela, 1970.
402 p.　20 cm.

18590　Asenjo, Conrado, 1881-
Recuerdos y añoranzas de mi viejo San Juan;
[artículos. San Juan, P. R.]　1960 [i.e. 1961]
137 p.　illus.　24 cm.

18591　Asfura Prado, Jorge.
El delito de difamación. México, 1962.
133, [7] p.　24 cm.
Tesis profesional - Universidad Nacional Autónoma
de México.
Bibliography: p. [135]-[137]

18592　Asinari, Amanda.
... Aportes para realizar trabajos de investi-
gación acerca de historia rural. [n.p., 1969?]
[18] p.　35 cm.
At head of title:　Il jornadas de archiveros de
Argentina.

18593　Asociación Colombiana de Facultades de Medicina.
Medicina y desarrollo social; la contribución de

la educación médica a la tarea del desarrollo
económico-social. Bogotá, Ediciones Tercer Mundo
y el Comité Ejecutivo de la A.C.F.M., 1964.
301 p.   illus.   24 cm.
"Se incluyen... los trabajos y conclusiones presentados en las reuniones preparativas, durante la
Asamblea [General Extraordinaria] y en el XXVII
Consejo Directivo, que se reunió en mayo de Bogotá."
Includes bibliographies.

18594   Asociación de Amigos del País, Guatemala, C.A.
La realidad agraria en Guatemala. [Guatemala,
1970]
12 p.   map.   21 x 23 cm.
Cover title.

18595   Asociación de Bibliotecarios Graduados de la República
Argentina.
Tercera reunión nacional de bibliotecarios,
organizada por la Asociación de Bibliotecarios
Graduados de la República Argentina, celebrada en
la ciudad de La Plata, del 10 al 12 de septiembre
de 1964 en la sede de la biblioteca pública de la
universidad. La Plata, 1964.
103 p.   28 cm.

18596   Asociación Demográfica Costarricense.
Quinto seminario nacional de demografía. Informe...
Set. 24-25 de 1970. San José [n.d.]
503 p.   graphs, tables (part fold.)   28 cm.

18597   Asociación Interamericana de Bibliotecarios y Docu-
mentalistas Agrícolas.
Nómina geográfica de miembros de la Asociación
Interamericana de Bibliotecarios y Documentalistas
Agrícolas a 30 de junio de 1969. Turrialba, Costa
Rica, 1969.
32 p.   27 cm.   (Boletín técnico, 10)

18598   Asociación Nacional de Industriales.
La empresa y el desarrollo nacional. Desarrollo
nacional. Declaración de la XXVIII Asamblea,
Manizales, Octubre, 1972. [Bogotá? 1972?]
32 p.   22 cm.

18599   Asociación Nacional de Industriales.
Medellin and surrounding area; guide for the
industrial investor. Medellin, Colombia, 1961.
64 p.   23 cm.

18600   Asociación Obrera Minera Argentina.
         La política minera desde el punto de vista sindical.
         Buenos Aires, 1968.
         [14] p.   26 cm.
         Cover title.
         "Apartado de la Revista Minería, ediciones año 1967."

18601   Asociación Venezolana de Facultades (Escuelas) de
         Medicina.
         Tercer seminario nacional de educación médica y
         primera conferencia de la Asociación Venezolana de
         Facultades (Escuelas) de Medicina. Caracas [1967]
         224 p.   23 cm.

18602   Aspillaga H   , Gonzalo.
         La concesión de servicio público eléctrico [por]
         Gonzalo Aspillaga H. Santiago, Editorial Universitaria
         1965.
         152 p.   21 cm.
         Tesis (licenciatura en ciencias jurídicas y
         sociales) - Universidad de Chile, Santiago.
         Bibliography: p. 145-148.

18603   Associação Brasileira de Crédito e Assistencia Rural.
         O sistema brasileiro cooperativo de extensão
         rural. Rio de Janeiro, Abcar, 1964.
         40 p.   22½ cm.

18604   Association of Caribbean Universities and Research
         Institutes.
         Directory of institutes and centers devoted to
         research in the Caribbean. Prepared by Association
         of Caribbean Universities and Research Institutes
         and the Institute of Caribbean Studies, University
         of Puerto Rico. Rio Piedras, P. R., 1971.
         various pagination.   29 cm.
         - - - -. Supplement. 1972.
         various pagination.   29 cm.

18605   Assumpção, Rosely Maria Viegas.
         Usina piloto de breu e terebintina; primeiras
         observações [por] Rosely Maria V. Assumpção, Ennio
         Silva Lépage [e] Maria Celina Santana. São Paulo
         [Instituto de Pesquisas Tecnológicas] 1973.
         15 ℓ.   illus.   30 cm.   (Instituto de
         Pesquisas Tecnológicas. Publicação no. 999)
         Cover title.
         Bibliography: leaf 15.

18606 Assunção, Fernando 0
El gaucho. Con un prólogo crítico del profesor
Daniel D. Vidart. Montevideo, Imprimería Nacional,
1963.
556 p.   illus. facsims.   25 cm.
"Apartado del tomo XXIV de la Revista del Instituto
Histórico y Geográfico del Uruguay."
Bibliography: p. 543-550.

18607 Astey V   , Luis, 1921-   comp.
Dramas latinos medievales del ciclo de Navidad.
Edición, con traducción y notas, de Luis Astey V.
Monterrey, México, 1970.
x, 116 p.   24 cm.   (Publicaciones del Instituto
Tecnológico y de Estudios Superiores de Monterrey.
Serie: Letras, 4)
Latin and Spanish.
Bibliography: p. 113-116.

18608 Astey V   , Luis, 1921-
El poema de la creación, Enuma Elish. Traducción
y notas de Luis Astey V. ... Monterrey, México,
Ediciones Sierra Madre [1961]
73 p.   25½ cm.   (Poesía en el mundo, 9)

18609 Asti Vera, Armando.
George Boole; precursor de la lógica simbólica.
Buenos Aires, Departamento de Filosofía, Facultad
de Filosofía y Letras, Universidad de Buenos Aires,
1968.
193 p.   22½ cm.

18610 Astrada, Carlos, 1894-
Ensayos filosóficos. [Bahía Blanca] U[niversidad]
N[acional del] S[ur] 1963.
318 p.   21 cm.
"Aparecieron, en su mayoría en diversas publicaciones
académicas y revistas culturales argentinas."

18611 Astudillo, Rubén.
Este es El Pueblo. Cuenca, Núcleo del Azuay de
la Casa de la Cultura Ecuatoriana, 1973.
263 p.   illus.   21 cm.

18612 Astudillo Espinosa, Carlos T
El procedimiento en un juicio de trabajo:
proyecto de Código de procedimiento en juicios de
trabajo; recopilación de los artículos aplicables
del juicio civil en un juicio de trabajo, las leyes

99

y decretos que reglamentan al Código de trabajo
y la jurisprudencia dictada por la Excma. Corte
Suprema en estos mismos juicios, de la que ha sido
posible la redacción del articulado de este código
[por] Carlos Astudillo Espinosa. Quito, Editorial
Casa de la Cultura Ecuatoriana, 1961.
148 p.   22 cm.

18613   Astudillo Sandoval, Homero.
Inconstitucionalidad de los capitales constitutivos
en la Ley mexicana del seguro social. .México, 1963.
101 p.   23 cm.
Tesis (licenciatura en derecho) - Universidad
Nacional Autónoma de México.
Bibliography: p. 101.

18614   Atanasiú, Andrés Homero.
El retorno, y otros cuentos. [La Plata] Municipalidad de La Plata [1962]
81 p.   18 cm.
Contents. - El retorno. - Las voces. - El anti-
cuario. - Rosalía y el cielo. - El ladrón. - Destino.

18615   Atcon, Rudolph P
Manual sôbre o planejamento integral do campus
universitaria. Florianópolis, Brasil, Imprensa da
Universidade Federal de Santa Catarina, 1970.
107 p.   illus.   24 cm.

18616   Ateneo de la Juventud.
Conferencias del Ateneo de la Juventud. [Por]
Antonio Caso [et al] Prólogo, notas y recopilación
de apéndices de Juan Hernández Luna [1. ed.]
México, Centro de Estudios Filosóficos, Universidad
Nacional Autónoma de México, 1962.
215 p.   23 cm.   (Nueva biblioteca mexicana, 5)

18617   Athanásio, I   Emílio.
Os adolescentes de hoje e de amanhã por I. Emílio
Athanásio. Introdução do Pe. Huylo Ribeiro Quinta-
nilha, S.J. Petrópolis, Edición Voces, 1967.
83 p.   18 cm.
Bibliography: p. 79-81.

18618   Atkinson, L   Jay, 1913-
Agricultural productivity in Colombia [by L. Jay
Atkinson. Washington] U.S. Dept. of Agriculture,
Economic Research Service [1970]
vi, 101 p.   illus., map.   27 cm.   (Foreign

agricultural economic report no. 66)
Cover title.
"[Issued] in cooperation with the Ministry of
Agriculture and the National Department of Planning
of Colombia."
Bibliography: p. 99-101.

18619 Atkinson, L   Jay, 1913-
Changes in agricultural production and technology
in Colombia. [Washington, D.C.] U.S. Department of
Agriculture, Economic Research Service, in cooperation
with the Ministry of Agriculture and Central Planning
Agency of Colombia [1969]
84 p.   maps, graphs, tables.   27 cm.   (U.S.
Department of Agriculture. Economic Research Service.
Foreign agricultural economic report, no. 52)

18620 Atlántico, 50 [i.e. cincuenta] años [1910-1960]; un
homenaje al Departamento del Atlántico en el primer
cincuentenario de su fundación. [Texto económico
por José Raimundo Sojo; texto histórico por Leopoldo
Pinzón; reportajes industriales: Juan Goenaga,
Max Cadena y Porthos Campo P. Medellín, Talleres
de Interprint] 1960.
59, [39] p.   illus., maps, ports.   32 cm.
"Edición auspiciada por la Corporación Cívica de
Barranquilla."

18621 Aub, Max, 1903-
La calle de Valverde; [novela] Xalapa, Universidad
Veracruzana, 1961.
396 p.   20 cm.   (Universidad Veracruzana.
Ficción, 26)

18622 Audrin, José M   , 1879-
Os sertanejos que eu conheci [por] José M. Audrin.
Prefácio de Alceu Amoroso Lima. Rio de Janeiro,
Livraria J. Olympio, 1963.
xiv, 205 p.   map, port.   23 cm.   (Coleção
Documentos brasileiros, 117)

18623 Aufricht, Hans, 1902-
Legislación comparada de banca central. [1. ed.]
México, Centro de Estudios Monetarios Latinoamericanos,
1964.
xviii, 307 p.   22 cm.   (C.E.M.L.A. Estudios)
Bibliographical footnotes.

18624   Auguste, Carlet R
        L'économique n'est qu'un aspect du social. Port-
        au-Prince, Haïti, Impr. de l'État, 1948.
        31 p.   22 cm.

18625   Aura, Alejandro, 1944-
        Varios desnudos y dos docenas de naturalezas
        muertas. Monterrey, México, Ediciones Sierra Madre,
        1971.
        44 p.   22 cm.   (Poesía en el mundo, 92)

18626   Austral, Antonio G
        Prehistoria de la región pampeana sur [por] Antonio
        G. Austral. Bahía Blanca, Universidad Nacional
        del Sur, Extensión Cultural [1968]
        22 p.   21 cm.   (Serie: Las Raíces)

18627   Austria, José de, 1791-1863.
        Bosquejo de la historia militar de Venezuela.
        Estudio preliminar por Héctor García Chuecos.
        Caracas, Academia Nacional de la Historia, 1960.
        2 v.   23 cm.   (Biblioteca de la Academia
        Nacional de la Historia, 29-30)

18628   Auto de Vicente Anes Joeira. [Reprodução fac-similar
        das duas edições quinhentistas, introdução, leitura
        crítica anotada e índices de palavras. Edição
        preparada pela professôra Cleonice Berardinelli.
        [Rio de Janeiro] Instituto Nacional do Livro,
        Ministério da Educação e Cultura, 1963.
        154 p.   illus., facsims.   24 cm.   (Dicionário
        da língua portuguêsa. Textos e vocabulários, 1)

18629   Automovil Club de Chile.
        Carretera panamericana. [Santiago, n.d.]
        6 ℓ.   28½ cm.

18630   Automovil Club de Chile.
        Conozca Chile. Santiago and Concepción [n.d.]
        16 p.   illus., maps (part fold.)   20 cm.

18631   Auxier, George Washington, 1905-
        The Cuban question as reflected in the editorial
        columns of middle western newspapers (1895-1898)
        Columbus, Ohio State University, 1938.
        9 p.l., 328 numb. ℓ.   map.   28 cm.
        Ph.D. dissertation - Ohio State University.

18632 Auza, Néstor Tomás.
Estudio e índice general de "El Plata Científico
y Literario", 1854-1855 y "Atlántida", 1911-1913.
Buenos Aires, Instituto de Historia Argentina y
Americana, Facultad de Historia y Letras, Universidad
del Salvador, 1968.
85 p.   20 cm.   (Colección índices y bibliografías, 3)

18633 Avalos Ansieta, Benigno.
El arte popular en la América Latina. [Santiago,
Chile, 1962]
124 p.   19 cm.

18634 Aveleyra Arroyo de Anda, Luis.
Antigüedad del hombre en México y Centroamérica;
catálogo razonado de localidades y bibliografía
selecta, 1867-1961. Contribución al XXXV Congreso
Internacional de Americanistas, Ciudad de México,
agosto de 1962. [1. ed.] México, Universidad
Nacional Autónoma de México, 1962.
72 p.   fold. maps.   24 cm.   (Publicaciones
del Instituto de Historia, 1. ser., no. 70. Cuadernos:
Serie antropológica, no. 14)
Bibliography: p. 57-58.

18635 Aveleyra Arroyo de Anda, Luis.
Los cazadores primitivos en Mesoamérica. México,
Universidad Nacional Autónoma de México, 1967.
81 p.   19 cm.   (Instituto de Investigaciones
Históricas. Cuadernos: Serie antropológica, 21)

18636 Avellaneda, Manuel O
Toxicidad salina en álamo y sauce álamo. Saline
toxicity in poplar and white willow. Mendoza,
Instituto de Suelos y Riego, Facultad de Ciencias
Agrarias, Universidad Nacional de Cuyo, 1961.
[26] p.   (Experimenta)
English summary.

18637 Avila, Federico, 1904-
Los valles interandinos. [Tarija, Bolivia]
Universidad Autónoma "J. M. Saracho," Biblioteca
de Estudios Socio-Económicos, 1960.
102 p.   21 cm.

18638 Ávila, Fernando Bastos de.
Neo-capitalismo, socialismo, solidarismo. Capa

de Milton Ribeiro. Rio de Janeiro, 1963.
176 p. 20 cm. (Temas atuais, 18)

18639 Avila, Francisco J
Aprendizaje y psicagogía de atrasados mentales
[por] Francisco J. Avila. Prólogo del doctor
Jerónimo de Moragas. Caracas [Impr. Nacional] 1961.
104 p. illus. 23 cm.
Revised edition of the author's thesis, Barcelona,
presented under title Contribución al estudio del
aprendizaje viso-motor en niños deficientes mentales.
Bibliography: p. 101-104.

18640 Avila Franco, Julio César, ed.
Compendio de legislación agropecuaria y organismos
agrícolas de Colombia, por Julio César Avila Franco
[et al.] Bogotá, 1962.
157 ℓ. 27 cm.
At head of title: Servicio Técnico Agrícola
Colombiano Americano, "STACA."
"Apéndice: Decretos reglamentarios de la Ley
reforma agraria": [2] ℓ. inserted.

18641 Avila Garrón, José.
Sinfonía tropical; novela. Sucre [Bolivia] 1962.
100 p. 19 cm.

18642 Ayala, Francisco.
El cine; arte y espectáculo. Xalapa, México,
Facultad de Filosofía, Letras y Ciencias, Universidad
Veracruzana, 1966.
164 p. (Cuadernos de la Facultad de Filosofía,
Letras y Ciencias, 34)

18643 Ayala, Walmir, 1933-
Um animal de Deus. Romance. [Rio de Janeiro]
Lidador [1967]
182 p. 22 cm.

18644 Ayala, Walmir, 1933-
Auto representada na festa de São Lourenço [por]
José de Anchieta. (Livre adaptação de Walmir Ayala)
Rio de Janeiro, Serviço Nacional de Teatro, 1973.
viii, 41 p. 21 cm. (Coleção Dramaturgia
brasileira)

18645 Ayala, Walmir, 1933-
A beira do corpo [romance] Rio de Janeiro,

Editôra Letras e Artes, 1964.
125 p.   22 cm.

18646 Ayala Anguiano, Armando.
La aventura de México. Realizada bajo la
dirección de Armando Ayala Anguiano. [1. ed.]
México, Publicaciones AAA [1968-
2 v.   illus. (part col.)   maps (part col.),
ports. (part col.)   31 cm.
Includes bibliographies.
Contents: v. 2. Conquistados y conquistadores.
Library has vol. 2.

18647 Ayala-Castañares, Agustín.
Ecología y distribución de los foraminíferos
recientes de la Laguna Madre Tamaulipas. México...
por Agustín Ayala-Castañares y Luis R. Segura.
México, Instituto de Geología, Universidad Nacional
Autónoma de México, 1968.
89 p.   illus., fold. tables, maps.   24½ cm.
(Boletín 87)

18648 Ayala Echavarri, Rafael.
Bibliografía histórica y geográfica de Queretaro.
México, Secretaría de Relaciones Exteriores,
Departamento de Información para el Extranjero,
1949.
xiii, 389 p.   24 cm.

18649 Ayala Mercado, Manuel.
El crédito agrícola y el plan de desarrollo agropecuario de Bolivia. La Paz [Taller Gráfica Bolivianos]
1963.
128 p.   map.   19 cm.
"El trabajo... presentado en calidad de tesis al
Primer Curso Internacional de Crédito Agrícola, que
se llevó a cabo en la ciudad de México de mayo a
diciembre de 1962. Con algunas ampliaciones y
pequeñas modificaciones de forma, se ha mantenido
el texto original."
Bibliography: p. 125-128.

18650 Ayala Queirolo, Victor.
Historia de la cultura en el Paraguay.
[Asunción, Impr. Zamphirópolos, 1966]
241, [7] p.   20 cm.
Bibliography: p. [243]

18651 Ayon de Messner, Digna E
Trayectoría histórica y cultural de la Universidad
de Guayaquil 1867-1967. Segunda edición...
[Guayaquil] Departamento de Publicaciones, 1967.
359 p.   illus., facsims.   22 cm.

18652 Ayres, Lula Cardoso.
Lula Cardoso Ayres. [Introdução de Gilberto
Freyre. São Paulo] Museo de Arte de São Paulo, 1960.
[22] p., 20 plates.   illus., port.   21 cm.

18653 Ayub M   , Alejandro R
Minerales de manganeso en los Estados de Sonora,
Durango, Zacatecas y San Luis Potosí. México, 1960.
136 p.   illus., maps (part fold.)   profiles,
tables.   23 cm.   (Consejo de Recursos Naturales
no Renovables. Boletín 49)

18654 Azevedo, Antonio Carlos Thyse de.
Modelo de código de obras para pequeños e médios
municipios [por] Antonio Carlos Thyse de Azevedo.
[Rio de Janeiro] Ministério do Interior, Serviço
Federal de Habitação e Urbanismo, 1973 [1972?]
32 p.   22 cm.

18655 Azevedo, Aroldo de, 1910-   ed.
Brasil, a terra e o homem. Por um grupo de
geógrafos sobre a direção de Aroldo de Azevedo.
São Paulo, Companhia Editora Nacional [1964-   ]
v.   illus., maps (part fold., part col.)
profiles.   27 cm.   (Brasiliana (formato especial)
v. 1-   )
Includes bibliographies.
Contents. - v. 1. As bases físicas.

18656 Azevedo, Arthur, 1855-1908.
A Capital federal, comédia-opereta de costumes
brasileiros, em 3 atos e 12 quadros. Rio de Janeiro,
Serviço Nacional de Teatro, 1972.
vi, 112 p.   21 cm.

18657 Azevedo, Hélio Carvalho Antunes de.
Recursos minerais do Sul da Bahia (primeiros
resultados) [por] Hélio Carvalho Antunes de Azevedo
[e] Paulo Ganem Souto. Bahía, Brazil, CEPEC-CEPLAC,
1971.
31 p.   tables, 4 fold. maps in pocket at end.
24 cm.   (CEPLAC. Boletim tecnico, 10)

18658   [Azevedo, João Ferreira de] 1945-   ed.
         Documentário da comemorações do cinqüentenário
         do Grêmio Literário Guimarães Passos... Maceió,
         Universidade Federal de Alagoas, 1979.
         153 p.   illus. (1 fold.)   30 cm.

18659   Azevedo, Manoel Antônio Álvares de, 1831-
         Cartas de Álvares de Azevedo. Comentários de
         Vicente de Azevedo. [São Paulo] Academia Paulista
         de Letras, 1976.
         253 p.   ports.   22 cm.   (Academia Paulista
         de Letras, Biblioteca, vol. 1)

18660   Azevedo, Marcello Casado d', ed.
         Atenção, signos, graus de informação. Pôrto
         Alegre, Universidade Federal do Rio Grande do Sul,
         1973.
         83 p.   23 cm.   (Cadernos universitários, 4)

18661   Azevedo, Marcello Casado d'.
         Comunicação, linguagem, automação. Pôrto Alegre,
         Brasil, Comissão Central de Publicações, Universidade
         Federal do Rio Grande do Sul, 1970.
         105 p.   23 cm.   (Cadernos universitários, 1)

18662   Azevedo, Marcello Casado d', ed.
         Pensamento, código, informação. Pôrto Alegre,
         Universidade Federal do Rio Grande do Sul, 1972.
         95 p.   23 cm.   (Cadernos universitários, 3)

18663   Azevedo, Murillo Nunes de.
         Transportes sem rumo; o problema dos transportes
         no Brasil. Rio de Janeiro, Editôra Civilização
         Brasileira [1964]
         141 p.   22 cm.   (Retratos do Brasil, v. 25)

18664   Azevedo, Thales de.
         Antecedentes do homem. [Salvador] 1961.
         76 p.   19 cm.   (Publicações da Universidade
         da Bahía, III, 13)

18665   Azevedo, Thales de.
         Ensaios de antropologia social. [Salvador] 1959.
         182 p.   illus.   23 cm.   (Publicações da
         Universidade da Bahía, IV-5)
         Includes bibliography.

18666   Azevedo, Victor de.
         Manuel Prêto, "O herói de Guairá". São Paulo,

107

Conselho Estadual de Cultura [1971]
111 p.   24 cm.   (Coleção historia, 12)

18667   Azevedo do Amaral, Ignacio M
Ensaio sôbre a revolução brasileira; contribuição
para o estudo dos problemas da brasilidade. 1931-1934.
Rio de Janeiro, Imprensa Naval, 1963.
331 p.   23 cm.

18668   Azeves, Ángel Héctor.
La elaboración literaria del Martín Fierro.
La Plata, Universidad Nacional de La Plata, Facultad
de Humanidades y Ciencias de la Educación [1960]
138 p.   23 cm.   (Universidad Nacional de
La Plata. Departamento de Letras. Monografías y
tesis, 4)
"La Revue de littérature comparée, Paris, 1956, y
la Revista de Educación La Plata, 1957 y 1958,
anticiparon algunos fragmentos de este libro."

18669   Azofeifa, Isaac Felipe.
Vigilia en pie de muerte; poesía. Primer Premio
República de El Salvador, Certamen Nacional de
Cultura, 1961. San Salvador, Ministerio de Educación,
1961.
108 p.   (Colección Certamen Nacional de Cultura,
19)

18670   Azopardo, Mercedes G
Coronel de marina Juan Bautista Azopardo, por
Mercedes G. Azopardo. Buenos Aires, 1961.
76, [27] p.   illus., facsims., maps.   25 cm.
(Departamento de Estudios Históricos Navales.
Serie C: Biografías navales argentinas, no. 3)
Bibliography: p. [99]

18671   Azopardo, Mercedes G
Lugar del primer combate naval argentino, por
Mercedes G. Azopardo. Buenos Aires, 1966.
xii, 70 p.   illus., facsims., maps.   25 cm.
(Departamento de Estudios Históricos Navales.
Serie B: Historia naval argentina, no. 9)
"Apéndice no. 3: Documentos que figuran en el
sumario instruido en Buenos Aires a raíz de la
pérdida del combate de San Nicolás": p. [53]-62.
Bibliography: p. 64-67.

B

18672 Baa, Enid M
Doctoral dissertations and selected theses on
Caribbean topics accepted by universities of Canada,
United States and Europe, from 1778-1968...
St. Thomas, V. I., Bureau of Public Libraries &
Museums, Department of Conservation & Cultural
Affairs, 1969.
91 p.   29 cm.

18673 Bacha, Magdala Lisboa.
0 ensino de leitura da 2a à 6a série primária.
Prefacio de Abgar Renault. Belo Horizonte, Centro
Regional de Pesquisas Educacionais João Pinheiro,
1966.
228 p.   illus., map, tables.   22 cm.
Bibliography: p. 224-225.

18674 Bache Halsey Stuart, Inc., New York.
Tax exempt bonds of the Commonwealth of Puerto
Rico: Investor problem or investor opportunity?
[New York] 1976.
7 p.   28 cm.

18675 Bachini, Epimenio.
La transformación agraria. Cololó, Uruguay,
Secretaría de Relaciones y Cultura de la Unidad
Cooperaria no. 1, Cooperativa Agropecuaria de
Producción Integral [1963]
27 p.   illus.   22 cm.

18676 Bacigalupo Bottazzi, Virgilio.
Proyecto de automación del Banco del Estado de
Chile [por] Virgilio Bacigalupo Bottazzi, Mario
Pumarino Valenzuela, José Dekovič Torres. Santiago,
Chile, Ediciones del Banco del Estado de Chile,
1969.
87 p.   diagrs. (part fold.), fold. col. map.
27½ cm.
Bibliography: p. 85-86.

18677 Badano, Ariel H
50 [i.e. Cincuenta] mentiras y 50 verdades sobre
Cuba. Montevideo, Ediciones "Estrella" [1961]
78 p.   20 cm.

18678   Baena, Antônio Ladislau Monteiro.
         ... Compêndio das eras da província do Pará.
         [Rio de Janeiro, Oficinas da Companhia Gráfica LUX,
         para a Universidade do Pará] Universidade Federal
         do Pará, 1969.
         395 p.   24 cm.   (Coleção amazônica. Série
         José Verissimo)

18679   Baer, Werner, 1931-
         The Puerto Rican economy and United States
         economic fluctuations. Río Piedras, Social Science
         Research Center, University of Puerto Rico [1962]
         xvi, 155 p.   diagrs., tables.   22 cm.
         Bibliography: p. 153-155.

18680   Baerresen, Donald W
         Latin American trade patterns. Washington,
         Brookings Institution, 1965.
         xiv, 329 p.   24 cm.
         Bibliography: p. 325-329.

18681   Baers, Johannes, d. 1653.
         ... Olinda conquistada; narrativa do padre João
         Baers, capellão do C. Theodoro de Waerdenburch;
         traduzida do hollandez por Alfredo de Carvalho...
         Recife, Laemmert & c., 1898.
         1 p.l., [v]-xiv, 54 p.   port.   19 cm.
         (Para a historia de Pernambuco, II)

18682   Baethgen, Raúl E   , 1894-
         La ronda de los nietos; [poemas de] Raúl E.
         Baethgen. Montevideo, Impresora Uruguaya, 1964.
         61 p.   24 cm.
         Contents. - Silvana cumplió un año. - Torta con
         una velita. - Epístola a Luis Raúl. - El rostro de
         mi madre redivivo ha vuelto. - Bruno. - Raúl
         Eduardo. - Sandro. - Elogio de una antigua canción
         infantil. - Malhumor de abuelo. - Los quince años
         de Silvana. - Mi mesa de trabajo.

18683   Báez, Buenaventura, 1812-1884.
         Papeles de Buenaventura Báez [editada por]
         Emilio Rodríguez Demorizi. Santo Domingo, Editora
         Montalvo, 1969.
         362 p.   24 cm.   (Academia Dominicana de la
         Historia. Publicaciones, XXI)

18684   Báez Ortiz, Bolivar.
         "New approaches to public finance," speech

delivered by Dr. Bolivar Báez Ortiz, secretary of
state for finance, Santo Domingo's Executive Club,
Inc. Santo Domingo, D.R., May 31st, 1979. Santo
Domingo, 1979.
[4] p. 28 cm.
At head of title: Secretariat of State for Finance.

18685   Baeza Flores, Alberto, 1914-
Hombre peregrino. Carátula: composición foto-
gráfica del artista Juan Pi. Mendoza, Argentina,
Brigadas Líricas Lanzadas desde San Rafael, 1962.
[48] p. 28 cm. (Radicaciones poéticas, 5)

18686   Baeza Gajardo, Mario.
Veinte canciones chilenas en versiones corales
de diversos autores. Seleccionadas y editadas por
Mario Baeza G. [2. ed.] Santiago de Chile,
Editorial del Pacífico [1962]
87 p. 25 cm. (Federación de Coros de Chile.
Publicaciones. Serie A, v. 1)
Includes music.

18687   Baeza González, Oliva.
El delito de portación de arma de fuego sin
licencia; estudio dogmático. México, 1963.
112 p. 24 cm.
At head of title: Universidad Nacional Autónoma
de México. Facultad de Derecho y Ciencias Sociales.
Bibliography: p. 111-112.

18688   Bagú, Sergio.
Estratificación y movilidad social en Argentina.
Rio de Janeiro [Centro Latino-Americano de Pesquisas
em Ciencias Sociais] 1959.
46 p. 20 cm. (Publicación no. 6)

18689   Bagú, Sergio.
Evolución histórica de la estratificación social
en la Argentina. Buenos Aires, Instituto de Investigaciones Económicas y Sociales, 1969.
145 p. 22½ cm. (Esquema)

18690   Bahamonde N   , Nibaldo.
Dos nuevos Munidopsis en aguas chilenas
(Crustacea decapoda, Anomura) Santiago, Museo
Nacional de Historia Natural, 1963.
157-170 p. illus. 26 cm.
Reprinted from Boletín del Museo Nacional de

Historia Natural, t. XXVIII, no. 2.
"Referencias bibliográficas": p. 169-170.

18691 Bahía, Brazil (State) Arquivo Público.
Os documentos árabes do Arquivo do Estado da Bahía.
Editados, transcritos e comentados por Rolf Reichert.
Salvador, Centro de Estudos Afro-Orientais, Universidade Federal da Bahía, 1970.
1 v. (unpaged)   25 cm.   (Publicações do Centro
de Estudos Afro-Orientais, 9. Serie Documentos)

18692 Bahía, Brazil (State) Comissão de Planejamento
Econômico.
Pesquisa sôbre a consumo de produtos industriais
[pela] Fundação Comissão de Planejamento Econômico.
Salvador, 1967.
182 p.   diagrs., map, tables.   28 cm.

18693 Bahía, Brazil (State) Departamento de Estradas de
Rodagem. Serviço de Pesquisas Tecnológicas.
O Serviço de Pesquisas Tecnológicas do Departamento
de Estradas de Rodagem da Bahia. Salvador, 1967.
[9] l.   illus.   30 cm.

18694 Bahía, Brazil (State) Departamento Estadual de
Estatística.
Divisão territorial da Bahía. Salvador, 1968.
37 l.   tables.   31 cm.
Cover title.

18695 Bahía, Brazil (State) Secretaria das Minas e Energia.
Coordenação da Produção Mineral.
Anuario da mineração. Salvador, 1979.
v.   maps, tables, diagrs.   27½ cm.
Library has 1977, 1978.

18696 Bahía, Brazil (State) Secretaria das Minas e Energia.
Coordenação da Produção Mineral.
Inventário dos recursos minerais, 1978.
Salvador, 1979.
539 p.   maps, tables (1 fold.), diagrs. 27½ cm.

18697 Bahía, Brazil (State) Secretaria do Trabalho e Bem
Estar Social.
... Operário-industrial na Bahia. [Salvador,
Bahía? n.d.]
2 v.   fold. tables.   30 cm.
At head of title: Mão de obra.

112

18698   Bahía, Brazil.   Universidade Federal.
        Afro-Asia, no. 12   [Special number in honor of
        Roger Bastide]   Bahía, 1974.
        257 p.   port.   24½ cm.   (No. 12, 1976)

18699   Bahía Blanca, Argentine Republic.   Universidad Nacional
        del Sur.
        Catálogo de publicaciones 1948-1974.   Bahía
        Blanca, Biblioteca Central, 1976.
        xi, 260 p.   23 cm.

18700   Bahía Blanca, Argentine Republic.   Universidad
        Nacional del Sur.
        Estatuto de la Universidad Nacional del Sur.
        Buenos Aires, 1968.
        53 p.   23 cm.
        At head of title: Secretaría de Estado de Cultura
        y Educación.

18701   Bahía Blanca, Argentine Republic.   Universidad
        Nacional del Sur.   Centro de Documentación Biblio-
        tecológica.
        Documentación - Bibliotecológica.   No. 1.
        Bahía Blanca, 1970.
        66, 165 p.   26 cm.

18702   Bahía, Juarez.
        Três fases da imprensa brasileira.   Santos,
        Editôra Presença, 1960.
        124 p.   23 cm.
        Bibliography: p. 123-124.

18703   Baigts Romani, Luis.
        El salvamento marítimo y su diferencia con otras
        figuras jurídicas.   México, 1963.
        174 p.   24 cm.
        Tesis (licenciatura en derecho) - Universidad
        Nacional Autónoma de México.
        Bibliography: p. 173-174.

18704   Bailey, John J
        Presidential control of the extended state:
        emerging trends in Latin America [by] John J. Bailey.
        Austin, Office of Public Sector Studies, Institute
        of Latin American Studies, University of Texas at
        Austin, 1977.
        iii, 21 p.   28 cm.   (ILAS Technical papers
        series, no. 11)

113

18705   Baisre, Juan.
        Caracterización química de tres tipos de suelos
        de Cuba. La Habana, Instituto de Suelos, Academia
        de Ciencias de Cuba, 1972.
        23 p.   illus., tables, diagrs.   28½ cm.
        (Serie suelos, no. 15)

18706   Bajarlía, Juan Jacobo.
        Monteagudo, drama en tres actos. Buenos Aires,
        Talía [1962]
        51 p.   20 cm.

18707   Baker, Robert J
        A new subspecies of Uroderma bilobatum (Chiroptera:
        phyllostomatidae) from Middle America, by Robert J.
        Baker and V. Rick McDaniel. [Lubbock, Tex.] 1972.
        4 p.   22½ cm.   (Texas Tech University. Museum.
        Occasional papers, no. 7)

18708   Balanzat, Manuel.
        El número natural y sus generalizaciones. San
        Luis, 1953.
        190 p.   24 cm.   (Universidad Nacional de Cuyo.
        Facultad de Ciencias de la Educación. Publicaciones
        de matemáticas y física, fasc. 1)

18709   Balassa, Bela A
        Industrial protection in developing countries.
        Washington, International Bank for Reconstruction
        and Development, 1970.
        54 p.   29 cm.   (Report EC-175)

18710   Balderrama Hugues, Alejandro.
        Fundamentación de la Ley de la propiedad industrial
        y estudio de los derechos del inventor. México
        [1963?]
        115 p.   22 cm.
        Tesis profesional - Universidad Nacional Autónoma
        de México.
        Bibliography: p. 115.

18711   Balech, Enrique.
        Cuatro especies de Gonyaulax, sensu lato, y
        consideraciones sobre el género (dinoflagellata)
        por Enrique Balech. Buenos Aires, 1977.
        115-136 p., 3 pl.   27 cm.
        Reprinted from Revista del Museo Argentino de
        Ciencias Naturales, Hidrobiología, tomo V, no. 6.
        Abstract in English: p. 134.

18712   Balech, Enrique.
        La familia Podolampacea (Dinoflagellata). Mar de
        Plata [Argentina] 1963.
        33 p.   illus.   25 cm.   (Instituto de Biología
        Marina. Boletín no. 2)
        Bibliography: p. [27]

18713   Balech, Enrique.
        Fitoplancton marino [por] Enrique Balech [y] Hugo J.
        Ferrando. [Buenos Aires] Editorial Universitaria
        de Buenos Aires [1964]
        viii, 157 p.   illus.   23 cm.   (Manuales de
        EUDEBA/ciencias naturales)
        Bibliography: p. 147-155.

18714   Balech, Enrique.
        El plancton de Mar del Plata durante el período
        1961-1962 (Buenos Aires) Mar del Plata, 1964.
        49 p.   illus.   26 cm.   (Instituto de Biología
        Marina. Boletín no. 4)
        Summary in English.
        Bibliography: p. [48]-49.

18715   Baleeiro, Aliomar.
        Cinco aulas de finanças e política fiscal.
        [Salvador] 1959.
        106 p.   22 cm.   (Salvador, Brazil. Universidade.
        Publicações, IX: Econômica, 3)
        Bibliography: p. [101]-102.

18716   Balke, Judith.
        Coercive pronatalism and American population
        policy. Berkeley, International Population and Urban
        Research, Institute of International Studies,
        University of California [1973?]
        85-109 p.   28 cm.   (Reprint no. 434)
        Reprinted from Commission on Population Growth and
        the American Future, Research reports, vol. VI,
        Aspects of population growth and policy, edited by
        Robert Parke, Jr. and Charles F. Westoff.

18717   Ballesteros Gaibrois, Manuel.
        La idea colonial de Ponce de León; un ensayo de
        interpretación. San Juan, P. R., Instituto de
        Cultura Puertorriqueña, 1960.
        292 p.   22 cm.
        Bibliography: p. [245]-246.

115

18718   Ballivían Calderón, René.
        Principios de economía minera. [Buenos Aires]
        Universidad de Buenos Aires, Facultad de Ciencias
        Exactas y Naturales, Departamento de Ciencias
        Geológicas, 1960.
        117 ℓ.   33 cm.

18719   Balogh, Thomas.
        Obstáculos al desarrollo económico. [1. ed.]
        México, Centro de Estudios Monetarios Latino-
        americanos, 1963.
        244 p.   22 cm.

18720   Balseiro, José Agustín, 1900-
        Expresión de Hispanoamérica, segunda serie. San
        Juan de Puerto Rico, Instituto de Cultura Puerto-
        riqueña, 1963.
        207 p.   22 cm.
        Primera serie published 1960.
        Bibliographical references.

18721   Baltra Cortés, Alberto.
        Problemas del subdesarrollo económico latino-
        americano. [Buenos Aires] Eudeba, Editorial Univer-
        sitaria de Buenos Aires [1966]
        94 p.   18 cm.   (Biblioteca de América. Libros
        del tiempo nuevo, 41)

18722   Banco Agrícola y Pecuario, Caracas.
        El BAP y su gente. [Caracas, 1962]
        273 p.   illus.   24 cm.
        Includes brief biographical sketches of the
        officials of BAP.
        "Ley del Banco Agrícola y Pecuario": p. 229-251.
        "Decreto no. 318: Reglamento de la Ley del Banco
        Agrícola y Pecuario": p. 252-264.

18723   Banco Argentino del Atlántico.
        Memoria y balance general. [Mar del Plata]
        v.   26 cm.   annual.
        Report year ends June 30.
        Library has 1968/69 (12° ejercicio)

18724   Banco Central de Chile.
        Estudios monetarios. Santiago, Chile, 1968.
        180 p.   25 cm.
        Contents - Prefacio, by C. Massad. Introducción,
        by J. Marshall. Fase de transición: economía y
        finanzas de Chile, 1964-1966, by F. Garcés G.

El programa monetario y la emisión, by R. French-Davis M. Línea de crédito según presupuesto de caja, by M. E. Ovalle de Vigneaux. Una estructura analítica del proceso financiero; aplicación a la situación chilena, by J. Espinosa C. Algunos comentarios sobre el proceso de ajuste de la balanza de pagos, by C. Massad.

18725   Banco Central de Costa Rica.
Estadísticas económicas 1956 a 1961. [San José]
1962.
25 ℓ. (chiefly tables)   28 cm.
At head of title: Banco Central de Costa Rica.
Departamento de Estudios Económicos.

18726   Banco Central de Honduras. Departamento de Estudios
Económicos.
Honduras en chifras, 1971-1973. [Tegucigalpa?
1973?]
27 p.   18 cm.

18727   Banco Central de la República Argentina, Buenos Aires.
Billetes y monedas en circulación. Año 1968.
[Buenos Aires? 1968?]
[8] p.   facsimiles of bank notes and coins.
14½ x 19½ cm.

18728   Banco Central de la República Argentina, Buenos Aires.
Disposiciones legales sobre bancos y moneda.
Buenos Aires, 1960.
202 p.   tables.   22 cm.

18729   Banco Central de la República Argentina, Buenos Aires.
Transacciones intersectoriales de la economía
argentina. Buenos Aires, 1964.
51 p.   28½ cm.   (Suplemento del Boletín
estadístico, no. 4, abril de 1964)

18730   Banco Central de Nicaragua.
Boletín nicaraguense de bibliografía y documentación.
Managua.
nos.   illus., facsims.   27½ cm.
Library has nos. 14 (1976) - 21 (1978); and
nos. 27 - 28 (1979).

18731   Banco Central de Reserva de El Salvador, San Salvador.
El Banco Central de Reserva de El Salvador;
sus funciones y objetivos. San Salvador, 1961.
27 p.   20 cm.

117

18732　Banco Central de Reserva del Perú.
　　　　Actividades productivas del Perú; programación
　　　　del desarrollo. Lima, 1963.
　　　　1 v.　　20 cm.

18733　Banco Central de Reserva del Perú.
　　　　Plan nacional de desarrollo económico y social
　　　　del Perú, 1962-1971. Lima, 1962.
　　　　1 v.　　graphs, tables.　　20 cm.

18734　Banco Central de Venezuela, Caracas.
　　　　El Banco Central y la economía nacional; organización
　　　　y funcionamiento. Caracas, Gráfica Americana,
　　　　1961.
　　　　26 p.　　23 cm.

18735　Banco Central de Venezuela, Caracas.
　　　　Estudio sobre presupuestos familiares e índices
　　　　de costo de vida para las ciudades de Mérida, Valera,
　　　　San Cristóbal y Barinas. Caracas, 1969.
　　　　81 p.　　forms.　　23 cm.
　　　　At head of title:　Banco Central de Venezuela.
　　　　Universidad de los Andes.

18736　Banco Central de Venezuela, Caracas.
　　　　Estudio sobre presupuestos familiares en el area
　　　　metropolitana de Caracas, para la elaboración de un
　　　　índice de costo de vida. Caracas, 1968.
　　　　165 p.　　forms, fold. plan.　　22 cm.

18737　Banco Central de Venezuela, Caracas.
　　　　Herrajes. Catálogo general. Colección, Banco
　　　　Central de Venezuela. Herrajes de puerta. Candados
　　　　y cerrojos. Herrajes de arcones, petacas, cofres,
　　　　etc. Utensilios. Objetos diversos. Caracas [n.d.]
　　　　127 p.　　illus.　　32 cm.

18738　Banco Centroamericano de Integración Económica.
　　　　Institución Financiera International. [Tegucigalpa,
　　　　Editorial Diseños Offset, 1977]
　　　　69 p.　　19½ cm.

18739　Banco Centroamericano de Integración Económica.
　　　　Origen, políticas y gestión. Tegucigalpa, 1969.
　　　　51 p.　　28 cm.

18740　Banco Centroamericano de Integración Económica.
　　　　Departamento de Investigaciones y Promoción Económica.
　　　　Oportunidades de integración económica en el

Mercado común centroamericano. Tegucigalpa, 1967.
65 p.   27 cm.
Also available in Spanish edition.

18741   Banco da Amazônia.
Amazônia: legislação desenvolvimentista.
Belém, Pará, Departamento de Estudos Econômicos,
Banco da Amazônia, 1969.
380 p.   23 cm.

18742   Banco da Amazônia. Departamento de Estudos Econômicos.
Amazônia: instrumentos para o desenvolvimento.
Belém, 1969.
215 p.   col. illus., maps (part col., part fold.)
25 cm.
Bibliography: p. 212-215.

18743   Banco da Amazônia. Departamento de Estudos Econômicos.
O BASA e o desenvolvimento da Amazônia. Belém,
DESEC, 1968.
49 p.   22 cm.   (Documento no. 5)

18744   Banco da Amazônia. Departamento de Estudos Econômicos.
Diagnóstico econômico preliminar das áreas urbanas
do Acre, Amapá, Roraima e Rondônia. Belém, 1969.
61 p. [62] ℓ.   24½ cm.   (Documento no. 9)

18745   Banco de Crédito del Perú.
Platería virreynal. [Lima, 1974]
200 p.   illus. (part col.)   30 cm.
"Colección arte y tesoros del Perú creada y
dirigida por José Antonio de Lavalle [y] Werner
Lang. Banco de Crédito del Perú en la Cultura."

18746   Banco de Desenvolvimento de Espírito Santo.
Alguns indicadores econômicos e sociais do
Espírito Santo 1950/68. [Vitória? 1969?]
various pagination.   28 cm.

18747   Banco de Desenvolvimento de Espírito Santo.
Aspectos fundamentais da política econômica do
Espírito Santo. Vitória, Brasil, 1971.
87 ℓ.   30 cm.

18748   Banco de Desenvolvimento de Minas Gerais, Belo
Horizonte.
Diagnóstico da economia mineira. Belo Horizonte
[1969]
6 v. in 7.   diagrs. (part fold.), maps (part

119

fold.), tables. 27 cm.
Vol. 2 (anexo) consists of fold. maps.
Bibliography: v. 2, p. 241.
Contents. - 1. Diagnóstico. - 2. O espaço natural.
O espaço natural (anexo) 2. v. - 3. População e
infraestrutura. - 4. Agropecuária. - 5. Indústria. -
6. Serviços e setor público.

18749 Banco de Desenvolvimento de Minas Gerais, Belo Horizonte.
Leste: Mata, Mucuri, Rio Doce. [Belo Horizonte,
1968?]
1 v. (unpaged)   illus., maps.   31 cm.
(Estudos regionais, 2)

18750 Banco de Desenvolvimento de Minas Gerais, Belo Horizonte.
Programa de desenvolvimento da pecuária de corte.
[Belo Horizonte] 1970.
2 v.   illus., maps (part fold.) diags.   32 cm.

18751 Banco de Desenvolvimento de Minas Gerais, Belo Horizonte.
Departamento de Desenvolvimento Mineral. Gerência
do Setor II.
Programa pedra preciosas; [um novo enfoque ao
setor. Belo Horizonte] 1973.
32 ℓ.   29 cm.

18752 Banco de Desenvolvimento do Estado de Pernambuco.
Como obter financiamento, Carteira de Crédito
Industrial. Recife [1968]
28 p.   diagrs.   21 cm.

18753 Banco de Guatemala. Departamento de Investigaciones
Agropecuarias e Industriales.
Indice de estudios técnicos del Departamento de
Investigaciones Agropecuarias e Industriales,
1963-1967. Guatemala, 1968.
76 p.   21½ cm.

18754 Banco de la Provincia de Río Negro. Departamento de
Promoción, Crédito Agrario, Cooperativismo y
Colonización.
Boletín de divulgación. [Viedma]
v.   illus.   28 cm.
Library has nos. 1-4.

18755 Banco de la República, Bogotá.
Catálogo general de la Biblioteca Luis-Angel
Arango. [Bogotá] Talleres Gráficos del Banco de la
República [197-?]

9 v.   28 cm.
Library has v. 2 - 9.
----- ----- Supplemento no. 1. Bogotá [197-?]
9 v.   28 cm.
----- ----- Fondo colombiano. Bogotá [197-?]
Library has v. 3, 4, and Supplemento no. 1,
v. 1, 2.

18756 Banco de la República, Bogotá.
       Próceres, 1810, en el sesquicentenario de la
       independencia, 1960. Bogotá [1960?]
       225 p.   col. illus., col. ports.   26 cm.

18757 Banco de la República, Bogotá.
       Series estadísticas y gráficos. Diciembre de 1966.
       [Bogotá] Departamento de Investigaciones Económicas,
       Banco de la República, 1966.
       101 p.   map, tables.   19 x 28 cm.

18758 Banco de la República, Bogotá. Comisión de Estudios.
       Conclusiones. Bogotá, 1965.
       184 p.   fold. table.   28½ cm.

18759 Banco de la República, Bogotá. Departamento de
       Investigaciones Económicas.
       Atlas de Economía Colombiana. Primera Entrega.
       Aspectos Físico y Geográfico, 1959-
          v.   illus. (part col.), maps (part fold.,
       part col.), diagrs. (part col.), tables.   40 cm.
       At head of title: Banco de la República.
       Departamento de Investigaciones Económicas.
       Contents. - 1. Entrega. Aspectos físico y geo-
       gráfico.

18760 Banco de la República, Bogotá. Departamento de
       Investigaciones Económicas.
       Colombia. The investor's guide. [Bogota? 1970?]
       151 p.   illus., maps (part fold.)   12½ cm.

18761 Banco de la República, Bogotá. Museo de Oro.
       [Museo de Oro] Bogotá, 1965.
       unpaged.   illus.   23½ cm.

18762 Banco de la República Oriental del Uruguay.
       Primera exposición, Premio Blanes: pintura,
       agosto 1961 [Montevideo, 1961]
       unpaged.   illus.   17 x 23 cm.
       Text by Felipe Gil.

121

18763 Banco de México.
Bibliografía monetaria y bancaria de México,
1943-1958. México, Departamento de Estudios
Económicos, Banco de México, 1965.
64 p.   23 cm.

18764 Banco de México. Biblioteca.
Comercio exterior de México, 1943-1967. México,
1968.
89 p.   21 cm.   (Serie de bibliografías especiales, 8)

18765 Banco de México. Biblioteca.
Inversiones extranjeras, 1940-1961. México,
1962.
41 p.   22 cm.   (Serie de bibliografías especiales, 4)

18766 Banco de México. Biblioteca.
Inversiones extranjeras en México, 1940-1967.
México, 1968.
28 p.   21 cm.   (Serie de bibliografías especiales, 7)

18767 Banco de México. Departamento de Estudios Económicos.
Biblioteca.
La bibliografía económica de México en 1956 y
1957. México, 1960.
141 p.   21 cm.

18768 Banco de México. Departamento de Investigaciones
Industriales.
Directorio de empresas industriales beneficiadas
con extensiones fiscales, 1940-1960. [Recopiladas
y sistematizadas por Mario Velarde Maass. México,
1961]
383 p.   22 cm.

18769 Banco de México. Departamento de Investigaciones
Industriales.
Índice de monografías e informes técnicos del
Departamento de Investigaciones Industriales,
1943-1962. [México] Banco de México [1963]
95 p.   22 cm.

18770 Banco de México. Departamento de Investigaciones
Industriales.
Información del mercado común y bibliografía
preliminar sobre actividades económicas de los

122

países latinoamericanos. [México] 1960.
86 l.   30 cm.

18771   Banco de México. Departamento de Investigaciones
        Industriales. Servicio Bibliográfico y Archivo
        Técnico.
        Bibliografía industrial de México, 1967 -
            v.   20 cm.   annual.
        Library has 1967, 1968, 1970, 1971, 1972.

18772   Banco de México. Subdirección de Investigación
        Económica y Bancaria.
        Bibliografía económica de México, 1975. México,
        1976.
        410 p.   21 cm.

18773   Banco de Previsión Social, Mendoza, Argentine Republic.
        Memoria y balance general. Mendoza.
            v.   27 cm.   annual.

18774   Banco de Previsión Social, Montevideo.
        Regimen policial. Elaboración y redacción:
        Roberto Ferreria Badaro [y] Washington Plada
        Suárez. Montevideo, 1972.
        20 p.   18½ x 20 cm.

18775   Banco del Caribe, Caracas.
        Venezuela; su economía en hechos y cifras, 1960-
        1963. [Caracas, Ediciones Banco del Caribe, 1965]
        222 p.   illus., maps.   24 cm.
        Errata slip inserted.
        Bibliography: p. 213-214.

18776   Banco do Estado de São Paulo.
        Relatório da Diretoria: 1926-1966, 40 anos de
        desenvolvimento! [São Paulo, 1967]
        68 p.   col. illus.   29 cm.
        Cover title.

18777   Banco do Nordeste do Brasil, Fortaleza.
        Aspectos econômicos da cultura do feijáo no
        nordeste. Fortaleza, 1969.
        77 l.   tables, graphs.   29 cm.

18778   Banco do Nordeste do Brasil, Fortaleza.
        Relatório; exercício de 1967... [Fortaleza?
        1968?]
        165 p.   tables.   23 cm.

18779   Banco do Nordeste do Brasil, Fortaleza. Departamento
de Estudos Econômicos do Nordeste.
A agro-indústria do caju no Nordeste: situação
atual e perspectivas. Fortaleza, 1973.
220 p.   illus., fold. maps.   23 cm.
Summary in English.
Bibliography: p. 191-193.

18780   Banco do Nordeste do Brasil, Fortaleza. Departamento
de Estudos Econômicos do Nordeste.
Consumo de produtos industriais na Cídade de
Arapiraca. Fortaleza, 1972.
122 p.   illus.   22 cm.   (Banco do Nordeste
do Brasil, S. A. PCublicações] 221)
Cover title: Cidade de Ârapiraca: consumo de
produtos industriais.

18781   Banco do Nordeste do Brasil, Fortaleza. Departamento
de Estudos Econômicos do Nordeste.
Consumo de produtos industriais na cidade de
Fortaleza. Fortaleza, 1972.
127 p.   illus.   22 cm.   (Banco do Nordeste
do Brasil, S. A. PCublicações] 142)
At head of title: ETENE.

18782   Banco do Nordeste do Brasil, Fortaleza. Departamento
de Estudos Econômicos do Nordeste.
Consumo de produtos industriais na Cidade de
Mossoró (RN). Fortaleza, 1972.
116 p.   24 cm.   (Banco do Nordeste do Brasil,
S. A. PCublicações] 215)
At head of title: ETENE.
Cover title: Cidade de Mossoró; consumo de
produtos industriais.

18783   Banco do Nordeste do Brasil, Fortaleza. Departamento
de Estudos Econômicos do Nordeste.
Consumo de produtos industriais na cidade de
Propría. Fortaleza, 1972.
118 p.   illus.   21 cm.   (Banco do Nordeste
do Brasil, S. A. PCublicações] 211)

18784   Banco do Nordeste do Brasil, Fortaleza. Departamento
de Estudos Econômicos do Nordeste.
Consumo de produtos industriais na cidade de
Recife (PE). Fortaleza [1968]
119 p.   illus., forms.   23 cm.   (Banco do
Nordeste do Brasil. PubClicações] no. 171)
At head of title: ETNE.

124

18785 Banco do Nordeste do Brasil, Fortaleza. Departamento
Industrial e de Investimentos.
Financiamento industrial. Fortaleza, 1970.
60 p. map, tables. 24 cm.

18786 Banco do Nordeste do Brasil, Fortaleza. Divisão de
Agricultura.
Mercado consumidor de aves e ovos em Maceió.
Fortaleza, 1972.
77 p. illus. 22 cm. (Banco do Nordeste
do Brasil, S. A. [Publicações] 214)
Cover title: Consumo de aves e ovos na cidade de
Maceió.

18787 Banco do Nordeste do Brasil, Fortaleza. Divisão de
Agricultura.
Mercado consumidor de aves e ovos em Parnaíba.
Fortaleza, 1973.
57 p. 22 cm. (Banco do Nordeste do Brasil,
S. A. [Publicações] 219)
Cover title: Consumo de aves e ovos na cidade de
Parnaíba.

18788 Banco do Nordeste do Brasil, Fortaleza. Escritório
Técnico de Estudos Econômicos do Nordeste.
Efeitos da sêca sôbre a economia agropecuária do
Nordeste, 1958. Fortaleza, 1959.
22 p. illus., map, graphs. 22 cm.
(Publicações, 72)

18789 Banco do Nordeste do Brasil, Fortaleza. Escritório
Técnico de Estudos Econômicos do Nordeste.
Sisal. [Fortaleza] 1957-59.
2 v. illus., fold. maps, tables (part fold.)
25 cm.
Contents. - v. 1. Problemas econômicas. - v. 2.
Problemas técnicos.

18790 Banco Econômico da Bahia.
Catálogo das medalhas da república. Contribuição
aos festejos do 4.º centenário do Rio de Janeiro.
[Bahía, n.d.]
211 p. illus. 29 cm.

18791 Banco Español del Río de la Plata, Buenos Aires.
Memoria y balance general. [Buenos Aires]
v. 25 cm. annual.
Library has 1969.

125

18792 Banco Ganadero Argentino, Buenos Aires. Servicio de
Investigaciones Económicas.
La producción rural argentina en 1964. Buenos
Aires, 1965.
61 ℓ.   maps, graphs, tables.   28 cm.

18793 Banco Ganadero Argentino, Buenos Aires. Servicio de
Investigaciones Económicas.
La producción rural argentina. Primer semestre
de 1965. Contenido: I. La producción y los precios.
II. Márgenes de comercialización. III. Sección estadística. Buenos Aires, 1965.
60 p.   28 cm.

18794 Banco Ganadero Argentino, Buenos Aires. Servicio de
Investigaciones Económicas.
La producción rural argentina en 1968. Buenos
Aires, 1969.
61 p.   tables, maps.   28 cm.

18795 Banco Industrial de Jalisco, Guadalajara, México.
Jalisco, datos y números, 1934-1959. Guadalajara,
1959 [i.e. 1960]
201 p.   illus.   21 cm.

18796 Banco Industrial de la República Argentina.
La industria del vidrio plano... por E. Osvaldo
Spinelli. [Buenos Aires?] 1965.
[17] p.   tables.   34 cm.

18797 Banco Industrial de la República Argentina.
Memoria y balance. 1.- ejercicio; 1944-
Buenos Aires.
v.   diagrs.   24-30 cm.   annual.
Reports for 1944-   issued by the bank under
its earlier name: Banco de Crédito Industrial
Argentino.

18798 Banco Industrial de la República Argentina. Departamento de Economía.
Estudio de la industria de harina de pescado, por
el contador público nacional Hector Horacio
Bagnasco. Buenos Aires, 1969.
15 p.   illus.   33 cm.

18799 Banco Industrial de la República Argentina. Dirección
de Promoción y Desarrollo Industrial.
Industria petroquímica. Consideraciones generales
sobre desarrollo en la República Argentina. [Buenos

126

Aires, 1960]
43 p.   29 cm.

18800   Banco Industrial de la República Argentina. Dirección
de Promoción y Desarrollo Industrial.
La mecanización agrícola en la Argentina;
análisis de mercado sobre las principales máquinas
agrícolas, por Jorge R. I. Fullaondo. [Buenos
Aires] 1959.
53 p.   29 cm.

18801   Banco Industrial de la República Argentina. División
Económica.
Estudio y plan de promoción de la industria
quesera en la República Argentina. Buenos Aires,
1964.
39 p.   illus., tables.   34 cm.

18802   Banco Industrial de la República Argentina. División
Económica.
La industria de la preservación de la madera por
impregnación. Estudio preliminar sobre las perspectivas de su desarrollo en la Argentina.
Buenos Aires, 1962.
49 p.   illus., tables.   34 cm.

18803   Banco Nacional de Comercio Exterior, S. A., México.
Historia de un esfuerzo. [México, 1962]
unpaged.   illus.   29 cm.

18804   Banco Nacional de Comercio Exterior, S. A., México.
La integración económica latino-americana.
Mexico, 1963.
xxxi, 967 p.   23 cm.

18805   Banco Nacional de Comercio Exterior, S. A., México.
México, 1960: facts, figures, trends. México,
1960.
366 p.   col. illus., col. maps, charts,
tables.   23 cm.

18806   Banco Nacional de Comercio Exterior, S. A., México.
Misión mexicana a Sudamérica; informe sobre las
posibilidades de fomento al comercio inter-
latinoamericana. 2. ed. [México, 1958]
282 p.   23 cm.

18807   Banco Nacional de Costa Rica, San José.
Memoria de la celebración del cincuentenario,

127

1914-1964. [San José, 1965]
245 p. illus. 27 cm.

18808 Banco Obrero, Caracas.
Análisis del problema de la vivienda en Maracaibo.
Caracas, 1963.
282 p. illus., col. plans, tables. 32 cm.
Prepared by the bank's Oficina de Programación y
Presupuesto.

18809 Banco Obrero, Caracas.
Con motivo de la inauguración del puente sobre
el Lago, el Banco Obrero expone su gestión en el
Estado Zulia. [Caracas, 1962]
[16] p. illus. 22 cm.

18810 Banco Obrero, Caracas.
Plan nacional de vivienda 1965-1968, segundo año.
[Caracas] Banco Obrero, Oficina de Programación y
Presupuesto, Unidad de Estadística [1967]
97 p. illus. (part col.), plans, col. port.
30 cm.
Cover title.

18811 Bancroft, Hubert Howe, 1832-1918.
History of Mexico, being a popular history of
the Mexican people from the earliest primitive
civilization to the present time, by Hubert Howe
Bancroft; maps and illustrations. New York, The
Bancroft company, 1914.
vii, 581 p. illus. (incl. ports., maps)
20½ cm.
"This volume was written and printed, in part,
in 1887 under title of 'A popular history of the
people'."-Pref.
"Chronological table of the rulers of Mexico,
and dates upon which they assumed office":
p. [569]-574.

18812 Bandeira, Antônio Rangel.
Diálogos no espelho. São Paulo, Comissão de
Literatura, Conselho Estadual de Cultura, 1968.
123 p. 22 cm. (Coleção ensaio, 54)

18813 Bandeira, Manuel, 1886-
3 [i.e. Três] conferências sôbre cultura hispanoamericana [por] Manuel Bandeira, Augusto Tamayo
Vargas [e] Cecília Meireles. [Rio de Janeiro]
Ministério da Educação e Cultura, Serviço de

128

Documentação [1959]
105 p.   20 cm.   (Cadernos de cultura, 120)
Contents. - Em louvor das letras hispano-
americanas, por M. Bandeira. - Tres poetas de
América, por A. T. Vargas. - Expressão femininia
da poesia na América, por C. Meireles.
Full name: Manuel Carneiro de Sousa Bandeira
Filho.

18814 Bangou, Henri.
       La Guadeloupe, 1492-1848. [Aurillac, 1962]
       350 p.   22 cm.

18815 Baptista, Priscilla.
       ... Fonemas del Baure con atención especial a la
       supresión de la vocal, por Priscilla Baptista y
       Ruth Wallin. Traducción de Carlos Villaroel.
       Publicado por el Instituto Lingüístico de Verano
       en colaboración con el Ministerio de Educación y
       Bellas Artes, Oficialia Mayor de Cultura, Dirección
       Nacional de Antropología. Cochabamba, Bolivia,
       1964.
       21 p.   21½ cm.
       At head of title: Notas lingüísticas de Bolivia,
       no. 7.

18816 Baptista Filho, Olavo.
       População e desenvolvimento; interpretação da
       dinâmica demografía [por] Olavo Baptista Filho.
       São Paulo, Livraria Pioneira Editôra [1965]
       xiv, 137 p.   22 cm.   (Biblioteca pioneira de
       estudos brasileiros)
       Bibliography: p. [135]-137.

18817 Baptista Quevedo, Alfredo, 1867-1944.
       Pequeño libro de sonetos. Compilación de los
       hijos del autor. Prólogo de Joaquín Gabaldón
       Márquez. Trujillo [Venezuela] Impr. Oficial,
       1961.
       103 p.   illus.   20 cm.   (Publicaciones del
       Gobierno del Estado Trujillo)
       Biblioteca trujillana de cultura.

18818 Baralt, Rafael María, 1810-1860.
       Rafael María Baralt. Prólogo de Rafael Yepes
       Trujillo. Caracas, 1963.
       xxxiv, 340 p.   port.   23 cm.   (Colección
       clásicos venezolanos de la Academia Venezolana de
       la Lengua, 7)

18819   Baranyai, Leopold.
        International commodity agreements [by] L.
        Baranyai and J. C. Mills. [1st English ed.,
        rev. and updated, by J. C. Mills] Mexico,
        Centro de Estudios Monetarios Latinoamericanos,
        1963.
        190 p.   22 cm.   (Studies C. E. M. L. A.)
        Translation of Convenios de estabilización de las
        materias primas.
        Issued without the text of the international
        agreements.
        Biography: p. 181-185.

18820   Barata, Manoel, ed.
        Formação histórica do Pará... Belém, Universidade
        Federal do Pará, 1973.
        376 p.   port.   24 cm.   (Coleção amazônica.
        Série José Veríssimo)

18821   Baratta, María de.
        Cuzcatlán típico. Ensayo sobre etnofonía de
        El Salvador, folklore, folkwisa y folkway. Por
        María de Baratta. San Salvador, El Salvador,
        Publicaciones del Ministerio de Cultura [1951?-52?]
        2 v. (740 p.)   illus. (part. col.) ports.,
        music.   22 cm.
        "Páginas históricas de la raza lenca de la
        República de El Salvador, estudio arqueológico,
        etnológico, filológico y geográfico, por Jeremías
        Mendoza" (v. 1, p. [363]-404) has special t. p.)
        Bibliography: v. 1, p. [405]-[406]

18822   Baraya, José María, 1828-1878.
        Biografías militares. [Bogotá] Librería del
        Ejército, 1962.
        542 p.   24 cm.   (Ejército de Colombia.
        Biblioteca del Ejército, V, no. 11)

18823   Barbados. Commissioner of Police.
        Annual report. [Bridgetown? 1966?]
        20 p., [18] ℓ.   34½ cm.   annual.

18824   Barbados. Prime Minister.
        Financial statement and budget proposals made by
        the honourable the prime minister on 30th June,
        1967. [Bridgetown? 1967?]
        22 p.   24 cm.

                            130

18825   Barbados. Public Library, Bridgetown.
        Barbadiana; a list of works pertaining to the
        history of the island of Barbados, prepared in the
        Public Library to mark the attainment of indepen-
        dence. Bridgetown, 1966.
        44 p.   22 cm.

18826   Barbados. Registration Office.
        Report on vital statistics and registrations for
        the year 1966. [Bridgetown, 1966?]
        6 p., [13] ℓ.   tables.   32½ cm.

18827   Barbados. Statistical Service.
        Balance of payments of Barbados, 1964-1966.
        Garrison, St. Michael, Statistical Service [1968]
        24 p.   tables.   32½ cm.

18828   Barbados. Supervisor of Elections.
        General election, 1966 (held on 3rd November, 1966)
        Administrative report. [Bridgetown? 1966?]
        6 p., [20] ℓ.   tables.   33 cm.

18829   Barberena, Santiago Ignacio.
        Historia de El Salvador, época antigua y dela
        conquista. Tomo II. San Salvador, Dirección
        General de Publicaciones, Ministerio de Educación,
        1969.
        324 p.   25½ cm.   (Colección Historia, 11)

18830   Barbieri, Vicente, 1903-1967.
        Obra poética. Anotación preliminar de Carlos
        Mastronardi; epílogo por Juan Carlos Ghiano.
        Buenos Aires, Emecé Editores [1961]
        427 p.   port.   23 cm.   (Selección Emecé de
        obras contemporáneas)
        Bibliography: p. 405-424.

18831   Barbieri, Vicente, 1903-1967.
        ... Prosas dispersas de Vicente Barbieri.
        Selección, advertencia preliminar, cronología bio-
        bibliográfica, contribución a la bibliografía de
        Vicente Barbieri y notas de Aurelia C. Garat y
        Ana María Lorenzo. La Plata, Universidad Nacional
        de La Plata, Facultad de Humanidades y Ciencias de
        la Educación [1970]
        313 p.   illus.   24½ cm.
        At head of title: Departamento de Letras. Insti-
        tuto de Literatura Argentina e Iberoamericana.
        Textos, documentos y bibliografías, IV.

131

18832 Barbosa, José Expedicto.
       Liderança de reuniões. Brasília, Banco Regional
       [1968]
       15 l.   22 cm.

18833 Barbosa, Maria Dorothéa.
       Indice comentado as publicações do Museu Para-
       naense. Curitiba, 1965.
       86 p.   23 cm.   (Curitiba, Brazil. Museu Para-
       naense. Arquivos. Nova série. Documentaçao, no. 1)
       English summary: p. [1]

18834 Barbosa, Ruy, 1849-
       ... Finanças e politica da republica. Discursos e
       escriptos. Capital federal, Companhia impressora,
       1892.
       x p., 1 l., 475 p., 1 l.   23½ cm.

18835 Barbosa, Waldemar de Almeida.
       A capitania de Minas Gerais. [Belo Horizonte,
       1970?]
       35 p.   19 cm.

18836 Barboza, Onédia Célia de Carvalho.
       Imprensa academica paulista: descoberta de Byron.
       [São Paulo, 1973]
       183-191 p.   24½ cm.
       Reprinted from Lingua e literatura, revista dos
       Departamentos de Letras da Faculdade de Filosofia,
       Letras e Ciências Humanas da Universidade de São
       Paulo, ano II, no. 2, 1973.

18837 Barboza de la Torre, Pedro A
       El bibliotecario universitario, un docente...
       Tucumán, Universidad Nacional de Tucumán, Biblio-
       teca Central, 1969.
       31 p.   24 cm.   (Ciencia de la documentación.
       Serie II: La biblioteca, no. 7)

18838 Barceló Sifontes, Lyll.
       Indice de repertorios hemerográficos venezolanos
       (siglo XX, tomo 1) [por] Lyll Barceló Sifontes.
       Caracas, Universidad Católica Andrés Bello, 1977.
       119 p.   illus.   19 cm.   (Colección Manda)

18839 Barcelona. Biblioteca Central.
       Catálogo de la Exposición de El Libro en España
       e Hispanoamérica. Barcelona, Instituto Nacional
       del Libro Español, 1962.

132

233 p.   illus. (part col.)   ports., facsims.,
21 cm.
At head of title: Unión Internacional de Editores,
XVI Congresso.
Cover title: El libro en España e Hispanoamérica.
Bibliography: p. 219-221.

18840   Barcelona. Cámara Oficial de Comercio y Navegación.
Catálogo de la exposición bibliográfica, cartográfica y de grabados y litografías marítimas,
celebrada en el vestíbulo de la Casa Lonja del Mar,
con motivo del LXXXV aniversario de la constitución
de la Cámara Oficial de Comercio y Navegación de
Barcelona, 24 octubre - 5 noviembre 1961.
[Barcelona, 1961?]
51 p.   21 cm.

18841   Bardella, Gianfranco.
Setenta y cinco años de vida económica del Perú,
1889-1964. Editado por el Banco de Crédito del Perú
en ocasión del septuagésimo quinto aniversario de su
fundación. [Lima, 1964]
217 p.   illus., facsims., ports.   28cm.
Bibliography: p. 215-217.

18842   Bardem, Juan Antonio.
Muerte de un ciclista [film] Xalapa, Mexico,
Universidad Veracruzana, 1962.
128 p.   20 cm.   (Universidad Veracruzana.
Ficción, 40)

18843   Bardem, Juan Antonio.
Los sogadores; guión [cinematográfico] Xalapa,
Mexico, 1962.
259 p.   20 cm.   (Universidad Veracruzana.
Ficción, 37)
"El film se exhibe con el nombre de La Venganza."

18844   Barnes, Ben.
O sítio de Aratu e a geologia de Recôncavo [por]
Ben Barnes e Dirceu Cezar Leito. São Paulo,
Instituto de Geografia, Universidade de São Paulo,
1972.
14 p.   fold. map.   24½ cm.   (Geomorfologia,
24)

18845   Barnola, Pedro Pablo.
Al encuentro de Bolívar. Caracas, 1970.
305 p.   23 cm.   (Archivo General de la Nación, 8)

133

18846   Barnola, Pedro Pablo, ed.
        Textos oficiales de la primera república de
        Venezuela. I. Pórtico por Cristóbal L. Mendoza.
        Estudio preliminar por el P. Pedro Pablo Barnola,
        S. J. Caracas, Academia Nacional de la Historia,
        1959.
        2 v. fold. facsims. 23 cm. (Biblioteca de
        la Academia Nacional de Historia, 1, 2)

18847   Barón Castro, Rodolfo.
        José Matías Delgado y el movimiento insurgente de
        1811. [l. ed.] San Salvador, Ministerio de
        Educación, Dirección General de Publicaciones [1962]
        239 p. 21 cm. (Biblioteca José Matías
        Delgado, 3)
        Includes bibliography.

18848   Barraclough, Solon.
        The state of Chilean agriculture before the coup,
        by Solon Barraclough. [Madison, Wis., Land Tenure
        Center, University of Wisconsin, 1974]
        11-13 p. 28 cm.
        Reprinted from LTC Newsletter, no. 43, Jan. - Mar.
        1974.

18849   Barral e da Pedra Branca, Luisa Margarida Portugal de
        Barros, condessa de, 1816-1881.
        Cartas a Suas Majestades 1859-1890. Rio de
        Janeiro, Ministério da Justiça, Arquivo Nacional,
        1977.
        504 p. facsims. 22½ cm. (Publicações
        históricas, 1.a série, 83)
        Bibliography: p. 430-433.

18850   Barrán, José Pedro, 1934-
        Bases económicas de la revolución artiguista [por]
        José P. Barrán y Benjamín Nahum. [Montevideo]
        Ediciones de la Banda Oriental [1964]
        145 p. 17 cm. (Ediciones de la Banda
        Oriental, 9)
        Bibliography: p. 145.

18851   Barrantes Ferrero, Mario.
        Apuntamientos sobre geografía histórica. [San José,
        Costa Rica, 1971]
        37-42 p. 26 cm.
        In Instituto Geográfico Nacional, Informe semestral,
        enero a junio, 1971.

18852 Barrantes Ferrero, Mario.
       Ensayo geográfico histórico de la primera expe-
       dición de Juan Vázquez de Coronado al sur del país,
       enero 27 - abril 18, 1563. [San José] 1961.
       46 p.   maps (1 fold.) table.   25 cm.
       Fold. col. map inserted.
       At head of title: Instituto Geográfico de Costa
       Rica.

18853 Barreda, Pedro F
       Geografía e historia de correos y telecomunicaciones
       de Guatemala; sus estudios. Guatemala, Dirección
       General de Correos y Telecomunicaciones, 1960
       [i.e., 1961]
       439 p.   illus.   22 cm.

18854 Barreda Avila, Rubén.
       El clamor del desterrado. [Guatemala? 1964]
       35 p.   22 cm.
       Cover title.
       Contents. - El clamor del desterrado. - Perfiles
       de angustia. - Las caricias del diablo verde. -
       Los hombres espectros.

18855 Barreda Fernández, Salvador.
       El derecho processal agrario como uno de los
       medios para realizar mejor la reforma agraria.
       México, 1962.
       165 p.   23 cm.
       Tesis (licenciatura en derecho) - Universidad
       Nacional Autónoma de México.
       Bibliography: p. 165.

18856 Barreda y Laos, Felipe, 1888-
       Punta del Este, Conferencia de la O.E.A.; VIII
       Reunión de Consulta de Ministros de Relaciones
       Exteriores: expulsión de Cuba. Lima, 1962.
       32 p.   18 cm.

18857 Barrera, Manuel.
       El sindicato industrial: anhelos, métodos de
       lucha, relaciones de la empresa. 2.a edición.
       Santiago, Chile, INSORA, Instituto de Administración,
       1969.
       79 p.   22 cm.   (Publicaciones INSORA, no. 48)

18858 Barrera Graf, Jorge.
       El derecho mercantil en la América Latina;
       [conferencias. 1. ed.] México, Universidad Nacional

Autónoma de México, 1963.
90 p.   24 cm.   (Publicaciones del Instituto
de Derecho Comparado. Serie D. Cuadernos de
derecho comparado, no. 4)

18859 Barrera Parra, Jaime, d. 1935.
Prosas de Jaime Barrera Parra. 1. ed. Bogotá,
Empresa Colombiana de Petróleos, Ediciones Continente,
1969.
347 p.   col. illus.   22 cm.
Recopilado y seleccionado por Ricardo Serpa Cuesto.
Contents. - Epistolario. - Notas del week-end. -
Gentes y tierras. - Panorama antioqueño.

18860 Barrera Sánchez, Ramón.
El delito de ataques a las vías de comunicación;
estudio dogmático. México, Universidad Nacional
Autónoma de México, 1963.
108 p.   24 cm.
Bibliography: p. 107-108.

18861 Barreto, Abílio.
Bello Horizonte; memória histórica e descriptiva.
2. ed., rev. e augmentada. Bello Horizonte, Edições
da Livraria Rex, 1936.
2 v. in 1.   illus. (part fold.), facsims., maps
(part fold., part col.), plans, ports.   24 cm.
Includes bibliographies.
Contents. - 1. História antiga. - 2. História
média. Planejamento, estudo, construcção, e inaugu-
ração da nova Capital (1893-1898)

18862 Barreto, Livio.
Dolentes. 2.a edição. Organização de Braga Montenegro. Apresentação e notas de Sanzio de Azevedo.
Em apéndice: "Livio Barreto" - prefácio à 1.a
edição - Waldemiro Cavalcanti. Fortaleza, Publicação
da Secretaria de Cultura do Ceará, 1970.
241 p.   front. (port.)   22½ cm.

18863 Barreto, Luiz Muniz.
Jupiter em 1959, por Luiz Muniz Barreto e Ronaldo
Rogério de Freitas Mourão. Rio de Janeiro [Sociedade
Editôra e Gráfica] 1960.
27 p.   illus.   23 cm.   (Observatorio Nacional.
Publicações do Serviço Astronômico, no. 11)
Bibliography: p. [23]

18864 [Barreto, Paulo] 1881-1921.
A bela Madame Vargas. Peça em 3 atos de João do
Rio [pseud.] Rio de Janeiro, Serviço Nacional de
Teatro, 1973.
viii, 68 p.   21 cm.

18865 Barreto de Menezes, Tobias, 1839-1889.
Obras completas. [Rio de Janeiro] Instituto
Nacional do Livro, 196-
v.   24 cm.
Bibliographical footnotes.
Contents. -   v. 2-3.   Estudos de filosofia.

18866 Barreto Soulier, Jorge.
Peces Ostraciidae del Atlántico colombiano, por
Jorge Barreto Soulier. Bogotá, Universidad de Bogotá
Jorge Tadeo Lozano, Facultad de Ciencias del Mar,
1971.
15 p., 5 pl.   24 cm.   (Boletín del Museo del
Mar, no. 3)
Summary in English: p. 5.

18867 Barretto, Vicente.
A ideologia liberal no processo da independência
do Brasil (1789-1824) Brasília, Câmara dos Deputados,
Centro de Documentação e Informação, Divisão de
Publicações, 1973.
160 p.   21 cm.
Bibliography: p. [153]-160.

18868 Barría Serón, Jorge.
Las relaciones colectivas del trabajo en Chile...
Santiago, INSORA, Instituto de Administración, 1967.
89 p.   22 cm.

18869 Barrientos O   , René.
Significado de la revolución de noviembre; decla-
raciones del Gral. René Barrientos, presidente de la
Excma. Junta Militar de Bolivia. [La Paz] Dirección
Nacional de Informaciones, 1964.
17 p.   illus.   21 cm.

18870 Barrientos Restrepo, Samuel.
Delitos contra la vida y la integridad personal
(comentarios al título XV del libro 2º del código
penal colombiano [Medellín] Editorial Bedout [1965]
430 p.   25 cm.

18871 Barrientos Restrepo, Samuel.
       Los hombres y las ideas; estudios. Medellín,
       Universidad Pontificia Bolivariana, 1965.
       63 p.   16 cm.   (Colección "Rojo y negro")
       Contents. - Estampa de un prelado. - Suárez y la
       educación. - Las escuelas penales. - El problema de
       la alegría.

18872 Barriga Vallalba, Antonio M
       Historia de la Casa de Moneda. Bogotá, Taller
       Gráficos del Banco de la República, 1969.
       3 v.   illus.   24 cm.   (Archivo de la
       economía nacional, 30)

18873 Barrios, Gilberto.
       Tres almas, [versos y prosas. León, Nicaragua,
       1964]
       30 p.   ports.   22 cm.

18874 Barroco. Belo Horizonte, Universidade Federal de
       Minas Gerais, 1, 1969-
              v.   22 x 22½ cm.
       Library has v. 1 and 2.

18875 Barrón Angeles, Pablo.
       Derechos reales no comprendidos en el código
       civil. [México] 1962.
       151 p.   diagrs.   23 cm.
       Tesis (licenciatura en derecho) - Universidad
       Nacional Autónoma de México.
       Bibliographical footnotes.

18876 Barros, Ivan de Queiroz.
       Elementos de añalise numérica. São Paulo,
       Instituto de Pesquisas Mathemáticas,Universidade de
       São Paulo, 1969.
       iv, 139 p.   27½ cm.   ("7º Colóquie Brasileira
       de Matemática")

18877 Barros, Maria Nazareth M   M   de.
       Introdução aos estudos históricos e sociais;
       planos de aula [por] Ma. Nazareth M. M. de Barros.
       Belém, Curso de Biblioteconomia, 1967.
       47 p.   27 cm.   (Documentos didáticos, 1)
       At head of title: Universidade Federal do Pará.
       Curso de Biblioteconomia.

18878 Barros, Raquel.
       El romancero chileno [por] Raquel Barros y Manuel

138

Dannemann. Santiago, Ediciones de la Universidad
de Chile, 1970.
119 p.   fold. tables, music.   24 cm.

18879   Barros Coêlho, Raimundo de, 1908-
Anatomia patológica das afecções hepáticas.
Recife, Universidade Federal de Pernambuco, 1971.
265 p.   illus.   24½ cm.

18880   Barroso, Gustavo.
História do Palácio Itamaraty. [Rio de Janeiro]
Ministério das Relações Exteriores, Museu Histórico
e Diplomático do Itamaraty, Seção de Publicações,
1968.
171 p.   illus.   28½ cm.

18881   Barroso, Jorge Alberto.
On the bounded sets of holomorphic mappings, by
Jorge Alberto Barroso, Mario C. Matos and Leopoldo
Nachbin. Rio de Janeiro, Centro Brasileiro de
Pesquisas Físicas, 1974.
291-310 p.   29 cm.   (Notas de física, v. 21,
no. 15)

18882   Barroso, Maria Alice.
Um simple afeto recíproco. Rio de Janeiro,
Edições GRD, 1963.
268 p.   22 cm.

18833   [Barrow, Errol Walton]
[Address] [Bridgetown, Barbados? 1967?]
4 p.   33 cm.

18884   Barrow, Errol Walton.
Address by the prime minister, Hon. E. W. Barrow.
[Bridgetown, Barbados? 1967?]
5 p.   33 cm.

18885   Barrow, Errol Walton.
... Text of admittance speech... on the occasion
of the admission of Barbados to the United Nations.
Friday, December 9th, 1966. [Bridgetown, Barbados?
1966?]
6 p.   26½ cm.
18886   Bartlett, John Russell, 1805-1886.
Personal narrative of explorations and incidents
in Texas, New Mexico, California, Sonora, Chihuahua,
connected with the United States and Mexican
boundary commission, during the years 1850, '51, '52,

and '53. By John Russell Bartlett, United States
commissioner during that period... New York &
London, D. Appleton & company, 1854.
2 v.   fold. fronts., illus., plates.   23 cm.

18887 Barton, Wayne.
The Mayan calendar; light on the past, key to the
future. [Houston, Baroid/NL Industries, 1978]
4-10 p.   illus.   23 cm.
Reprinted from Baroid news bulletin, v. 29, no. 2,
fall 1978.

18888 Bartos, Robert E
The Soviet penetration of Cuba. [Oberammergau?
Germany] 1962.
59 ℓ.   31 cm.
At head of title: U. S. Army Field Detachment "R",
Office of the Assistant Chief of Staff, Intelligence,
Dept. of the Army, "The Army's Institute of Advanced
Russian Studies."
"Foreign Area Specialist Training Program (Russian)"
Includes bibliography.

18889 Barus, Vlastimil.
Nemátodos de la familia Tropisuridae Yamaguti, 1961,
parásitos de aves de Cuba. La Habana, Instituto de
Biología, Academia de Ciencias de la República de
Cuba, 1966.
22 p.   24½ cm.   (Poeyana, serie A, 20)

18890 Barus, Vlastimil.
Nemátodos, parásitos de aves en Cuba. La Habana,
Instituto de Biología, Academia de Ciencias de la
República de Cuba, 1966.
37 p.   illus.   25 cm.   (Poeyana, no. 22)

18891 Barus, Vlastimil.
Nemátodos, parásitos de aves en Cuba. Parte II.
Por Vlastimil Barus y Nerly Lorenzo Hernández.
La Habana, Instituto de Biología, Academia de
Ciencias de Cuba, 1970.
26 p.   illus., fold. table.   23½ cm.
(Poeyana, serie A, no. 71)

18892 Barus, Vlastimil.
Nota sobre la helmintofauna de ofidios en Cuba:
descripciones de tres especies nuevas de nemátodos,
por Vlastimil Barus y Alberto Coy Otero. La Habana,

140

Instituto de Biología, 1966.
16 p.   illus.   25 cm.   (Poeyana, no. 23)

18893   Barus, Vlastimil.
Nuevos registros de nemátodos que parasitan en
caballos (Equus caballus Linné) de Cuba, por
Vlastimil Barus y María Teresa del Valle. La Habana,
Instituto de Biología, Academia de Ciencias de la
República de Cuba, 1966.
10 p.   illus.   25 cm.   (Poeyana, no. 27)

18894   Basadre, Jorge.
Report on sources for national history of Perú.
Washington, Library of Congress, 1960.
23 ℓ.   28 cm.   (Hispanic Foundation consultant
reports)

18895   Basava Fernández del Valle, Agustín, 1923-
Ideario filosófico, 1953-1961. Presentación del
Dr. Fritz J. von Rintelen. [Nuevo León] Centro de
Estudios Humanísticos, Universidad de Nuevo León,
1961.
209 p.   20 cm.

18896   Basava Fernández del Valle, Agustín, 1923-
La imagen del hombre en Alfonso Reyes. [Discurso
de recepción como individuo de número de la Academia
Mexicana; contestación: Antonio Gómez Robledo]
Monterrey, Universidad de Nuevo León, 1964.
70 p.   20 cm.

18897   Bascón Carvajal, Federico, 1905-
7 [i.e. Siete] capítulos en la vida del gran
mariscal Andrés Santa Cruz. La Paz, Bolivia, 1965.
39 p.   port.   21 cm.

18898   Bascuñán Valdés, Antonio.
El delito de abusos deshonestos. Santiago,
Editorial Jurídica de Chile, 1961.
154 p.   18 cm.   (Universidad de Chile. Facultad
de Ciencias Jurídicas y Sociales. Seminario de
Derecho Penal y Medicina Legal, 2)

18899   Basile, David Giovanni.
Tillers of the Andes; farmers and farming in the
Quito basin [by] David Giovanni Basile. Chapel
Hill, N. C., Department of Geography, University of
North Carolina at Chapel Hill [1974]

141

[8], 174 p.   illus., maps, tables.   (Studies
in geography, no. 8)

18900 Basílico, Ernesto.
La controversia sobre el Canal Beagle; justificación
del derecho argentino a la soberanía sobre las islas
Picton y Nueva e islotes adyacentes, conforme al
Tratado de 1881. Buenos Aires, Colombo, 1963.
215 p.   illus., maps (part fold.)   facsims.
23 cm.
Bibliography: p. 213-215.

18901 Bassels Batalla, Angel.
Bibliografía geográfica de México. México,
Secretaría de Agricultura y Ganadería, Dirección
General de Geografía y Meteorología [1955]
ix, 562 p.   21 cm.

18902 Bastidas Aguirre, Jacinto.
Psicometría escolar; pruebas mentales y de rendi-
miento y estudios aplicados al educando ecuatoriano.
Texto recomendado para los colegios normales y pro-
fesores. 3. ed. oficial. Quito, Departamento
Editorial de Educación, 1960.
158 p.   illus., diagrs.   22 cm.
Bibliography: p. 154-156.

18903 Bastide, Roger.
As religiões africanas no Brasil; contribuição a
uma sociologia das interpretações de civilizações.
Trad. de Maria Eloisa Capellato e Olívia Frähenbühl.
São Paulo, Livraria Pioneira Editôra, Editôra da
Universidad de São Paulo, 1971.
2 v.   22 cm.   (Bibliotéca pioneira de ciências
sociais. Sociologia)
Original title: Les religions africaines au Brésil;
vers une sociologie des interpénétrations des
civilisations.

18904 Bastide, Roger, ed.
Usos e sentidos do têrmo "estrutura" nas ciências
humanas e sociais. Editôra Herder, Editôra da Uni-
versidade de São Paulo, São Paulo, R. Bastide,
E. Wolff, E. Beneveniste, C. Lévi-Strauss, P.
Francastel, F. Perroux, A. Marchal, J. Weiller,
J. Carbonnier, A. Mathiot, D. Lagache, R. Pagès,
H. Lefebvre, R. Aron, P. Vilar, M. Ch. Morazé,
L. Goldman. Roger Bastide, coordenador. Tradução
de Maria Heloiza Schabs Capellato. São Paulo,

142

Editôra Herder, Editôra da Universidade de São
Paulo, 1971.
197 p.   22 cm.
Original title: Sens et usage du terme structure
dans les sciences humaines et sociales.

18905   Bastos, Jairo Martins.
Orpheo; poesia. [Fortaleza] Imprensa Universitária
do Ceará, 1961.
44 p.   27 cm.

18906   Basurto, Jorge.
La influencia de la economía y del estado en las
huelgas; el caso de México. [México] Escuela Nacional
de Ciencias Políticas y Sociales, U.N.A.M., 1962.
iv, 146 p.   tables.   24 cm.
Cover title.
Bibliography: p. 144-146.

18907   Basurto Escalera, Francisco.
El estado-nación y su forma de poder. [México]
1963.
96 ℓ.   24 cm.
Tesis (licenciatura en derecho) - Universidad
Nacional Autónoma de México.
Bibliography: leaves 92-96.

18908   Batalha, Wilson de Souza Compos.
Tratado elementar de direito internacional privado.
São Paulo, Editôra Revista dos Tribunais, 1961.
2 v.   22 cm.

18909   Batalla del Pantano de Vargas, 1819. [Bogotá] 1969.
[40] p.   map, ports.   17 x 25 cm.
Cover title.
"Nota" (leaf at end) signed: Sección de Historia
y Publicaciones del Ejército de Colombia.
Contents. - Introducción, por O. Gutiérrez Ospina. -
Comandantes patriotas. - Comandantes realistas. -
Pantano de Vargas, por C. Cortés Vargas.

18910   Batis Martínez, Agustín Huberto.
Indices de El Renacimiento, semanario literario
mexicano (1869) Con un estudio preliminar.
México, 1963.
328 p.   illus.   24 cm.
Tesis (maestro en letras españolas) - Universidad
Nacional Autónoma de México.
Published also as Universidad Nacional Autónoma de

Mexico. Centro de Estudios Literarios. Publicaciones, 9.
Bibliography: p. 157-161.

18911 Batista, Sebastião Nunes.
... Bibliografia prévia de Leandro Gomes de
Barros [por] Sebastião Nunes Batista. Colaboração
de Hugolino de Sena Batista. Rio de Janeiro,
Divisão de Publicações e Divulgação, Biblioteca
Nacional, 1971.
3 p.l., 7-95, [5] p.   facsims.   21 cm.
At head of title: Biblioteca Nacional. Coleção
Rudolfo Garcia.

18912 Batista Ballesteros, Isaías.
El drama de Panamá y América. [Panamá, Impr.
Panamá, 1961]-65.
2 v.   illus., ports.   23 cm.
Vol. 1. Cover title.
Vol. 2 has imprint: Panamá, Ministerio de Educación,
Dirección Nacional de Cultura.
"Texto de documentos seleccionados": v. 1,
p. 125-157. "Apéndice documental": v. 1, p. 159-167;
v. 2, p. [245]-323.
Includes bibliographies.
Contents. - [t. 1] Nuestras relaciones con los
E. E. U. U. - t. 2. Visión de conjunto sobre el
problema canalero y de los cruentos sucesos de enero
de 1964.

18913 Batista Villarreal, Teresita.
... Catálogo de publicaciones periódicas cubanas
de los siglos xviii y xix, por Teresita Batista
Villarreal, Josefina García Carranza, Miguelina Ponte.
La Habana, Departamento Colección Cubana, Biblioteca
Nacional José Martí, 1965.
256 p.   29 cm.
At head of title: Biblioteca Nacional José Martí.

18914 Batres de Zea, Dolores.
Evolución de la música vocal a través de la
historia. Guatemala, Centro Editorial "José de
Pineda Ibarra," Ministerio de Educación Pública,
1962.
253 p.   illus.   21 cm.   (Colección Científico-
pedagógica, 18)

18915 Batres y Montúfar, José de, 1809-1844.
Poesías. San Salvador, Ministerio de Educación,

144

1961.
191 p.   18 cm.   (Biblioteca popular, v. 28)

18916 Batres y Montúfar, José de, 1809-1844.
Poesías de José Batres Montúfar; edición del
sesquicentenario de su nacimiento. Introducción y
notas de Adrían Recinos. [3. ed.] Guatemala,
Centro Editorial "José de Pineda Ibarra," Ministerio
de Educación Pública, 1962.
xxvi, 187 p.   21 cm.   (Colección Contemporáneos, 62)

18917 Batres y Montúfar, José de, 1809-1844.
El reloj; leyenda inconclusa del inmortal Pepe
Batres y terminada por S. B. Tomada de la 1. ed.
de 1881. Guatemala, La República Impr., 1965.
85 p.   1 col. illus.   21 cm.   (Leyendas de
Guatemala)

18918 Battistessa, Ángel J
Oir con los ojos, Shakespeare en algunos de sus
textos. La Plata, Universidad Nacional de La Plata,
Facultad de Humanidades y Ciencias de la Educación
[1969]
88 p.   23 cm.   (La Plata. Universidad Nacional.
Instituto de Letras. Sección de literatura argentina
e iberoamericana. Monografías y tesis, IX)

18919 Baucke, Oswaldo.
A inseto-fauna da acácia negra no Rio Grande do
Sul; biologia e controle às pragas mais importantes.
Porto Alegre, Secretaria da Agricultura, Secção de
Informações e Publicidade Agrícola, 1962.
32 p.   20 cm.

18920 Baudelaire, Charles, 1821-1867.
Algunos aspectos del mal en la poesía de Baudelaire.
Selección de Luis Astey V. Monterrey, México,
Ediciones Sierra Madre, 1967.
23 p.   22 cm.   (Poesía en el mundo, 49)

18921 Baudelaire, Charles, 1821-1867.
El perfume de la mujer y el dandismo en la
poesía de Baudelaire, por Luis Durango. Monterrey,
México, Ediciones Sierra Madre, 1967.
23 p.   22 cm.   (Poesía en el mundo, 48)
Parallel French and Spanish text.
Introduction by Luis Durango; no translator
indicated.

18922 Baudou, Alejandro C
A cincuenta años de la primera aplicación de la
vacuna antituberculoso B. C. G. en el hombre;
homenaje a la memoria del ex académico de número
Dr. Andrés R. Arena. Conferencia del señor académico
de número Dr. Alejandro C. Baudou en la Academia
Nacional de Medicina, sesión pública del 1° de julio
de 1971. Buenos Aires, Academia Nacional de Agronomía y Veterinaria, 1971.
43 p.   27 cm.   (Academia Nacional de Agronomía
y Veterinaria. [Actas] t. 25, no. 2)

18923 Bayardo Bengoa, Fernando.
La tutela penal del secreto. Montevideo, Facultad
de Derecho, 1961.
379 p.   25 cm.   (Biblioteca de publicaciones
oficiales de la Facultad de Derecho y Ciencias Sociales
de la Universidad de la República, sección 3, 117)
Includes bibliography.

18924 Bayne, David R
Progress report on fisheries development in
El Salvador [by] David R. Bayne. Auburn, Ala.,
International Center for Aquaculture, Auburn University, 1974.
11 p.   illus., tables.   28 cm.   (Research
and development series, no. 7)

18925 Bayona Posada, Nicolás, 1899-
Sabanera. Bogotá, 1963.
46 p.   21 cm.
Poems.

18926 Bazán, F   Mario.
El coronel José Balta, primer mandatario civilista
del Perú. Lima, 1962.
151 p.   21 cm.

18927 Bazán, Rogelio.
Las estaciones, y otros poemas. [Buenos Aires]
Cuadernos del Siroco [1960]
59 p.   20 cm.   (Colección "Cuadernos del
siroco")

18928 Bazant, Jan.
Los bienes de la Iglesia en México (1856-1875);
aspectos económico y sociales de la revolución
liberal. [1. ed. México] El Colegio de México
[1971]

146

xiii, 364 p. 22 cm. (Centro de estudios históricos. Nueva serie, 13)
Bibliography: p. [349]-356.

18929 Bazzanella, Waldemiro.
Problemas de urbanização na América Latina; fontes bibliográficas. Rio de Janeiro, 1960.
123 p. 24 cm. (Centro Latino-americano de Pesquisas em Ciências Sociais. Publicação no. 2)

18930 Beaujón, Oscar.
El Libertador enfermo. Caracas, 1963.
142 p. 19 cm.
"Trabajo presentado a la Reunión sobre la Enfermedad Causal de la Muerte del Libertador, realizada bajo los auspicios de la Sociedad Venezolana de Historia de la Medicina, el 27 de junio de 1963.
Bibliography: p. [121]-142.

18931 Becco, Horacio Jorge, 1924- comp.
Antología de la poesía gauchesca, con introducción, vocabulario y bibliografía. [Madrid] Aguilar [1972]
1778 p. plates. 19 cm. (Colección Obras eternas)
Contains selections from Juan Baltasar Maziel, Bartolomé Hidalgo, Juan Gualberto Godoy, Hilario Acasubi, Manuel de Araucho, Estanislao del Campo, Antonio D. Lussich, José Hernández, Esteban Echeverría, Juan María Gutiérrez, Bartolomé Mitre, Rafael Obligado.

18932 Becco, Horacio Jorge, 1924- ed.
Cuentistas argentinos. Selección, prólogo y notas de Horacio Jorge Becco. [Buenos Aires] Ediciones Culturales Argentinas, Ministerio de Educación y Justicia, Dirección General de Cultura [1961]
381 p. 20 cm. (Biblioteca del sesquicentenario. Colección antologías)

18933 Becco, Horacio Jorge, 1924-
Ricardo Güiraldes. [Buenos Aires] Universidad de Buenos Aires, Facultad de Filosofía y Letras, Instituto de Literatura Argentina "Ricardo Rojas," 1959.
35 p. 23 cm. (Guías bibliográficas, 1)

18934 Becerra F , Jesús María.
Educación y código cooperativo para uso de cooperativas, colegios y universidades [por] Jesús María Becerra F. 1. ed. Bogotá, Librería

Stella, 1962.
236 p.   23 cm.   (Colección La Salle)
Bibliography: p. 30.

18935   Becerra López, José Luis.
La organización de los estudios en la Nueva
España. [l. ed.] México, 1963.
379 p.   24 cm.
Bibliography: p. 341-360.

18936   Becker, F
On the scattering of heavy ions at low energy in
the framework of molecular orbitals, by F. Becker,
S. Joffily, C. Beccaria and G. Baron. Rio de Janeiro,
Centro Brasileiro de Pesquisas Físicas, 1974.
63 p.   28 cm.   (Notas de física, v. XXXII,
no. 1)

18937   Becker, Klaus.
Alemães e descendentes do Rio Grande do Sul na
guerra do Paraguai. Canoas, Ed. Hilgert, 1968.
204 p.   illus., maps, ports.   23 cm.
Bibliography: p. 197-199.

18938   Becker, Maxwell E
Análisis forestal de Chile. [n.p., USAID/Chile,
Publication Service, 1962]
29 ℓ.   26 cm.

18939   Bécquer, Gustavo Adolfo, 1836-1870.
Rimas. [San Salvador, Departamento Editorial del
Ministerio de Educación, 1961]
23 p.   20 cm.   (Colección Azor, 10)

18940   Becu, Teodoro, 1890-
... La Colección de documentos de Pedro de Angelis
y el Diario de Diego de Alvear, por Teodoro Becu y
José Torre Revello; con ilustraciones y apéndice
documental. Buenos Aires, Talleres s.a. Casa
Jacobo Peuser, ltda., 1941.
144, liv, 19 p., 2 ℓ. xxix (i.e. 30) pl. (part
fold., incl. port., facsims., maps) on 29 ℓ., 6 fold.
plans, fold. tab.   28 cm.   (Buenos Aires.
Universidad Nacional. Publicaciones del Instituto
de Investigaciones Históricas, num. LXXV)
At head of title: Facultad de Filosofía y Letras.
Plans and table in pocket.

18941 Bedregal, Guillermo, 1926-
Algunos aspectos para la integración defensiva
de América Latina. Caracas, 1966.
43 p.   23 cm.   (Venezuela. Universidad
Central, Caracas. Instituto de Estudios Políticos.
Cuadernos, 9)

18942 Bedregal, Guillermo, 1926-
El convenio internacional del estaño [exposición
en el 1. Seminario de Comercialización de Metales y
Minerales en fecha 27 de oct. de 1961, por] Guillermo
Bedregal. Evolución y tendencia de los precios del
estaño; [análisis y programación del fomento a la
industria estañifera (exposición en el 1. Seminario
de Comercialización de Metales y Minerales en fecha
20 de octubre de 1961) por] Gossen Broersma. La Paz,
[Departamento de Relaciones Públicas de la Corporación
Minera de Bolivia, 1961?]
76 p.   illus.   19 cm.

18943 Bedregal, Guillermo, 1926-
Fundición de estaño en Bolivia; [conferencia]
La Paz [Centro de Estudios Políticos "Tupaj Amaru"]
1964.
43 p.   19 cm.

18944 Bedregal, Guillermo, 1926-
El plan nacional de desarrollo y la integración
de la industria estañifera de Bolivia. La Paz
[Departamento de Relaciones Públicas de la Corporación
Minera de Bolivia] 1962.
117 p.   19 cm.

18945 Bedregal, Guillermo, 1926-
Problemas de infraestructura, régimen monetario
y desarrollo económico en Bolivia. La Paz, 1962.
40 p.   19 cm.

18946 Bedregal, Guillermo, 1926-
La revolución boliviana, sus realidades y perspectivas dentro del ciclo de liberación de los pueblos
latino-americanos. [Exposición en el Foro Político-
Económico organizado por la Federación de Trabajadores
Fabriles de Bolivia] La Paz [Dirección Nacional de
Informaciones de la Presidencia de la República]
1962.
119 p.   19 cm.

18947   Bedrnik, Petr.
        Actividad de algunos coccidiostáticos contra
        especies intestinales de coccidia de conejos [por]
        Petr Bedrnik y Juan J. Martínez. La Habana,
        Instituto de Zoología, Academia de Ciencias de Cuba,
        1976.
        4, [4] p.   tables.   23 cm.   (Poeyana, 145)
        Abstract in English.

18948   Belaúnde Guinassi, César.
        La legislación pesquera en el Perú. [1. ed.]
        Lima [Editorial Universitaria] 1963.
        xxxix, 601 p.   22 cm.   (Biblioteca de derecho)

18949   Belfiore, Carlos J
        Industrialización del citrus. Buenos Aires,
        Banco Industrial de la República Argentina,
        Dirección General de Desarrollo Industrial, Departa-
        mento de Estudios Técnicos, 1960.
        128 p.   illus.   30 cm.
        Includes bibliography.

18950   Belize.
        Report on the goodwill tour of Mexico. [Belize
        City, Government printer, 1864?]
        24 p.   illus.   27 cm.

18951   Bell Escalona, Eduardo.
        Jurisprudencia tributaria de la Corte Suprema.
        Valparaiso, 1960-
        1 v. (loose-leaf)   27 cm.

18952   Bellegarde, Dantès, 1877-   ed.
        Au service d'Haiti; appreciations sur un Haitien
        et son oeuvre. Port-au-Prince, Impr. Théodore,
        1962.
        305 p.   24 cm.

18953   Belleza, Newton.
        Os amores de Gabriela. Rio de Janeiro, 1963.
        69 p.   20 cm.

18954   Belleza, Newton.
        Teatro grego e teatro romano. Rio de Janeiro,
        Irmãos Pongetti, 1961.
        88 p.   19 cm.
        Bibliography: p. [85]-88.

18955 Bellisio, Norberto Bernardo.
       Observaciones sobre el hallazgo de un pingüino
       albino en las Islas Orcadas del Sur. Espécimen
       obtenido durante la Campaña Naval Argentina del
       año 1963 al continente, islas y archipiélagos del
       Sector Antártico Argentino. Buenos Aires, Secretaría
       de Marina, Servicio de Hidrografía Naval, 1964.
       16 p.   illus.   26 cm.   ("H. 902")

18956 Bello, Andres, 1781-1865.
       Principios de derecho de jentes. Facsímile de la
       primera edición [1832] de la obra "Derecho de jentes"
       de don Andrés Bello, ordenada por el Congreso Nacional
       de Venezuela como homenaje en el centenario de la
       muerte del autor. Caracas, Dirección de Imprenta y
       Publicaciones del Congreso Nacional, 1965.
       267 p.   illus., facsims.   21 cm.
       Bibliographical footnotes.

18957 Bello, Luis Mario.
       Viaje argentino; apuntes para una biografía de
       nuestras ciudades y nuestros campos. [Buenos Aires]
       Ediciones Culturales Argentinas [1963, c1962]
       75 p.   illus.   25 cm.   (Biblioteca del
       sesquicentenario. Serie cuadernos)
       "Estas crónicas... fueron escritas para La Nación."

18958 Bello Hernández, Ernest.
       ... Las ciencias médicas en la filatelia cubana.
       La Habana, Consejo Científico, Ministerio de Salud
       Pública, 1970.
       [175] p.   24 cm.

18959 Bellolio, Walter.
       La sonrisa y la ira; relatos. Guayaquil, Núcleo
       del Guayas, Casa de la Cultura Ecuatoriana, 1968.
       140 p.   illus.   20 cm.

18960 Belmonte Román, Lucía, comp.
       Tesis existentes en la Biblioteca de la Facultad
       de Medicina. Bogotá, Ciudad Universitaria, Univer-
       sidad Nacional de Colombia, Centro de Bibliografía
       y Documentación, 1964.
       200 p.

18961 Belo Horizonte (prefeitura) Museu de Arte.
       XXII salão municipal de belas artes, Museu de Arte
       da prefeitura de Belo Horizonte. 12 de dezembro de
       1967 a 5 de fevreiro de 1968. [Belo Horizonte?

1968?]
18 ℓ.   illus.   24½ x 34 cm.

18962   Beltrán, Enrique.
Los museos de historia natural en México y la
Sociedad Mexicana de Historia Natural. México, Museo
de Historia Natural de la Ciudad de México, 1971.
12 p.   24½ cm.   (Acta Zoológica Mexicana, vol.
10, no. 4)

18963   Beltrán Avila, Marcos.
El tabú bolivarista, 1825-1828; comentario al margen
de los documentos que tratan de la fundación de
Bolivia. Oruro [Universidad Técnica de Oruro,
Departamento de Extensión Cultural, Sección Publi-
caciones] 1960.
236 p.   22 cm.   (Colección Cultura, no. 4)

18964   Beltrán Farrera, Carolina Elda.
La Constitución y el derecho administrativo
mexicano en relación con la planeación económica.
[Mexico] 1963.
88 p.   23 cm.
Tesis (licenciatura en derecho) - Universidad
Nacional Autónoma de México.
Includes legislation.
Bibliography: p. 85.

18965   Beltrán Farrera, María Elena.
Los problemas sociales y económicos de la coloni-
zación en México. México, 1963.
139 p.   23 cm.
Tesis (licenciatura en derecho) - Universidad
Nacional Autónoma de México.
Bibliography: p. 137-139.

18966   Beltrán Guerrero, Luis, 1914-
Perpetua heredad... Caracas, Biblioteca Venezolana
de Cultura, Ediciones del Ministerio de Educación,
1965.
317 p.   illus.   22 cm.

18967   Beltrán Heredia, B   Augusto.
El carnaval de Oruro y proceso ideológico e
historia de los grupos folklóricos. Oruro, Edición
del Comité Departamental de Folklore, 1962.
82 p.   illus.   19 cm.
Includes tunes.

152

18968   Bemis, Samuel Flagg, 1891-
        La crisis de los filibusteros: Abraham Lincoln
        y el projectado compromiso Crittendem [!] Trabalho
        leído por el académico correspondiente Dr. Samuel
        Flagg Bemis en la sesión pública celebrada del día
        12 de enero de 1956. Presentación del disertante,
        por el Dr. José Manuel Pérez Cabrera, secretario de
        la corporación. La Habana, Academia de la Historia
        de Cuba, 1956.
        24 p.   25½ cm.

18969   Benaím Pinto, Henrique.
        Análisis del estado actual de la educación médica
        en Venezuela, con observaciones sobre nuestra proble-
        mática universitaria. [Caracas] O[rganización de]
        B[ienestar] E[studiantil] Universidad Central de
        Venezuela [1969]
        283 p.   23 cm.
        "Correlato al tema Formación de profesionales de
        la medicina, presentado al VII Congreso Venezolano
        de Ciencias Médicas, Caracas, 23-30 de octubre, 1967,
        y actualizado para febrero de 1969."
        Includes bibliographies.

18970   Benasso, Eve.
        Días sin luz. Buenos Aires, 1956.
        174 p.   18 cm.

18971   Benatti, Felicio Padula.
        Perfil do mercado consumidor de Santo André e do
        "Grande São Paulo" [por] Felicio P. Benatti.
        Prólogo de José Wilson Saraiva. São Paulo, Fundação
        Santo André, 1969.
        217 p.   diagrs., tables.   23 cm.

18972   Benavides Lazo, Persio A
        Estudio comparativo de las legislaciones de
        seguridad social de Chile y Panamá. Santiago,
        Editorial Universitaria, 1959.
        147 p.   22 cm.
        Tesis (licenciatura en ciencias jurídicas y
        sociales) - Universidad de Chile.

18973   Benavides Pinho, Diva.
        ... Dicionário de cooperativismo (doutrina, fatos
        gerais e legislação cooperativo brasileira) 2.a
        edição ampliado é ilustrada. Prefácio do Prof. Paul
        Hugon. São Paulo, 1962.
        243 p.   23 cm.

153

18974 Benavides Ramírez, María Eva.
       Un título para trabajo en la Constitución de 1917.
       [Mexico] 1964.
       196 p.   23 cm.
       Tesis (licenciatura en derecho) - Universidad
       Iberoamericana.
       Includes bibliographies.

18975 Bendezú, Francisco.
       Arte menor. Dibujo de Ricardo Grau.   [Lima,
       Escuela Nacional de Bellas Artes, 1960]
       [16] p.   14 cm.   (Forma y poesía, 1)

18976 Benedetti, Adolfo Alberto.
       El pensamiento constitucional de Justo Arosemena.
       Prólogo del autor. Apéndice: Constitución del
       Estado Federal de Panamá, 1870. Panamá [Ediciones
       del Ministerio de Educación, Departamento de Bellas
       Artes y Publicaciones] 1962.
       174 p.   23 cm.
       Includes bibliography.

18977 Benedetti, Lúcia, 1914-   ed.
       Teatro infantil... III volume. Rio de Janeiro,
       Serviço Nacional de Teatro, 1974.
       194 p.   21 cm.
       Contents. - Anônimo. Bailes pastoris. - Anônimo.
       Reisado da borboleta. - Carlos Góis. Auto de natal.
       Dom Marcos Barbosa. Um menino nos foi dado. - Maria
       Clara Machado. O boi e o burro no caminho de Belém.
       Walmir Ayala. O galo de Belém. - Stella Leonardos.
       Auto da lapinha. - Zuleika Mello. De repente uma
       estrela... - Lúcia Benedetti. Sigamos a estrela.

18978 Benetti, Heloisa Domingues.
       A classificação de Colon. Pôrto Alegre, Departa-
       mento de Educação e Cultura, 1968.
       21 ℓ.   33 cm.
       At head of title: Universidade Federal do Rio
       Grande do Sul. Departamento de Educação e Cultura
       & Associação Rio-Grandense de Bibliotecários.
       "I Jornada Sul-Rio-Grandense de Biblioteconomia
       e Documentação... Tema 2: Processos técnicos."
       Bibliography: leaves 20-21.

18979 Benevides Pinho, Diva.
       ... Cooperativismo e problemas de desenvolvimento
       regional. Possibilidades de utilização do coopera-
       tivismo no desenvolvimento da região do Riveira.

                            154

[São Paulo, Faculdade de Filosofia, Ciencias e
Letras da Universidade de São Paulo, 1964]
316 p.   tables, graphs.   23½ cm.

18980 Bengoa, Juan León, 1895-
       La sandalia de madera; [pieza en tres actos]
       Buenos Aires, Argentores, Ediciones del Carro de
       Tespis [1964]
       54 p.   19 cm.   (Sociedad General de Autores
       de la Argentina (Argentores) [Publicación] no. 66)

18981 Benítez, José R
       Historia gráfica de la Nueva España, por el
       ingeniero José R. Benítez. Recopilada y redactada
       por iniciativa de la Cámara Oficial Española de
       Comercio de los Estados Unidos Mexicanos y editada
       por la misma. México, 1929.
       305 p., 2 ℓ.   plates (part col., part double)
       facsims., tables.   28½ cm.
       "Se acabo de imprimir la presente Historia gráfica
       de la Nueva España... en Barcelona, en los talleres
       del Instituto gráfico Oliva de Vilanova el día 26 de
       octubre de 1929..."

18982 Benítez, Luis G
       Historia cultural; reseña de su evolución en el
       Paraguay, de acuerdo al programa de la asignatura,
       para el 6. curso del bachillerato en humanidades y
       comercial [por] Luis G. Benítez [y] Jorge Báez.
       Asunción, El Arte, 1962.
       232 p.   20 cm.
       Includes bibliography.

18983 Benítez Cabrera, José A
       Africa, biografía del colonialismo. [La Habana]
       Ediciones Revolución [1964]
       454 p.   illus., maps.   21½ cm.

18984 Benítez Zenteno, Raúl.
       Proyecciones de la población de México, 1960-1980,
       por Raúl Benítez Zenteno y Gustavo Cabrera Acevedo.
       [México] Banco de México [Departamento de] Investi-
       gaciones Industriales, Oficina de Recursos Humanos
       [1966]
       245, [2] p.   23 cm.   (Estudio de los recursos
       humanos de México, 1)
       Bibliography: p. [247]

18985   [Benito, Miguel]
Publicaciones de Magnus Mörner, 31/3 1974, sobre
la historia de América Latina y demás. [Stockholm,
1974]
20 p.   21 cm.

18986   Benjamin, Harold Raymond Wayne, 1893-
A educação e o ideal democrático. Tradução de
Beatriz Osório. Rio de Janeiro, Centro Brasileiro
de Pesquisas Educacionais, 1960.
101 p.   22 cm.   (Rio de Janeiro. Centro
Brasileiro de Pesquisas Educacionais. Publicações.
Serie 7:   Cursos e conferências, v. 2)
Text in Portuguese and English.

18987   Benko, François.
La revolución industrial en el mundo; un ensayo de
síntesis de los hechos de desarrollo. Caracas
[Facultad de Arquitectura y Urbanismo, Universidad
Central de Venezuela] 1965.
181 p.   tables.   23 cm.
Bibliographical footnotes.

18988   Bennett, Gae A
Agricultural production and trade of Colombia.
Washington, Economic Research Service, U.S. Department of Agriculture, 1973.
109 p.   maps, tables.   27½ cm.

18989   Benson, Nettie Lee.
The Central American delegation to the first
constituent congress of Mexico, 1822-1823, by
Nettie Lee Benson and Charles R. Berry. [Austin
Institute of Latin American Studies, University of
Texas, 1969]
679-702 p.   23 cm.   (Offprint series, 95)
"Reprinted from The Hispanic American Historical
Review, vol. XLIX, No. 4, November 1969."

18990   Benson, Nettie Lee.
Latin American library history literature.
[n.p., 196-]
20 p.   29 cm.

18991   Benson, Nettie Lee.
Martín Fierro at the University of Texas [by]
Nettie Lee Benson. Austin, Institute of Latin
American Studies, University of Texas, 1968.
13-27 p.   23 cm.   (Offprint series, 63)

156

"Reprinted from The Library Chronicle, vol. VIII, no. 4, spring, 1968."

18992 Bento, Cláudio Moreira.
As batalhas dos Guararapes; descrição e analise militar. Recife, Universidade Federal de Pernambuco, 1971.
2 v. illus. 24½ cm.
Vol. 2 is a folio of maps.

18993 Bento, Cláudio Moreira.
A grande festa dos lanceiros (Parque histório Marechal Manuel Luiz Osório) Osório - RS - 10 maio - 1970. Preliminares de grande festa da nacionalidade (Parque Nacional dos Guararapes, Jaboatão, Pernambuco) Recife, Universidade Federal de Pernambuco, 1971.
129 p. illus. 23 cm.

18994 Benzoni, Girolamo, b. 1519.
La historia del mundo nuevo. Traducción y notas de María Vannini de Gerulewicz. Estudio preliminar de León Croizat. Caracas, Academia Nacional de la Historia, 1967.
xciv, 297 p. map. 23 cm. (Biblioteca de la Academia Nacional de la Historia, 86)

18995 Berckenhagen, Ernesto.
Glossário alemão-portugues; engenharia rodoviária. Rio de Janeiro, Instituto de Pesquisas Rodoviárias, 1969.
104 p. 23 cm. (Publicação 427)

18996 Berdiales, Germán, comp.
Exposición de la poesía española e hispanoamericana. Buenos Aires, Editorial Schapire [1968-
v. 21 cm. ([Colección Letras del Plata])
Contents. - t. 1. Coplas y romances.

18997 Berdichewsky, Bernardo.
Fases culturales en la prehistoria de los araucanos de Chile. [Santiago de Chile, 1971]
105-112 p. 24½ cm.
Reprinted from Revista chilena de historia y geografía, no. 139, 1971.

18998 Berenstein, C   A
... Some remarks on convolution equations, by C. A. Berenstein and M. A. Dostal. Recife, 1972.
28 p. 28 cm.

At head of title: Universidade Federal de
Pernambuco, Instituto de Matemática, Notas e
comunicações de matemática, no. 47.

18999 Berg, George H
Manual entomológico para inspectores de cuarentena
vegetal. [Managua, Nicaragua, 1959-   ]
v.   20 cm.

19000 Bergamín, José, 1895-
La decadencia del analfebetismo. La importancia
del demonio. Santiago de Chile, Cruz del Sur [1961]
97 p.   17 cm.   (Renuevos de cruz y raya, 2)

19001 Bergel Olivares, Reynaldo.
La Carretera Panamericana norte; descripción física
y cultural del marco regional entre cuesta El Melón
y cuesta Guayacán. Santiago, Instituto de Geografía,
Facultad de Filosofía y Educación, Universidad de
Chile, 1965.
52 p.   illus. (part fold.), maps (part fold.,
part col.)   26½ cm.
Summary in Spanish, English and French.

19002 Berger, Carlos Roberto.
Condições microbiológicas dos cones de gutapercha.
Ponta Grossa, Universidade Estadual de Ponta Grossa,
1973.
36 p.   22 cm.   (Cadernos universitários, 6)

19003 Bergés Chupani, Manuel D
Jurisprudencia dominicana, 1962-1966. Santo
Domingo, Secretaría de Educación, 1967.
liv, 343 p.   24½ cm.

19004 Bergoeing Guida, Jean Pierre.
Aspectos geomorfológicos de Isla de Chira, Costa
Rica. San José, Costa Rica, Instituto Geográfico
Nacional, 1978.
45-52 p.   illus., maps (1 fold.)   25½ cm.

19005 Bergoeing Guida, Jean Pierre.
Geomorfología de Puerto Jiménez, Península de
Osa, Costa Rica. San José, Costa Rica, 1978.
23-26 p.   fold. pl., maps (1 fold.)   25½ cm.
Reprinted from Costa Rica. Instituto Geográfico
Nacional. Informe semestral, enero a junio 1978.
Bibliografía: p. 26.

19006   Bergoeing Guida, Jean Pierre.
         Investigaciones geográficas en el sector Puerto
         Quepos - Manuel Antonio, provincia de Puntarenas,
         Costa Rica [por] Jean Pierre Bergoeing [y] Rogelio
         Jiménez R. San José, Costa Rica, 1978.
         29-44 p.   illus., fold. maps.   25½ cm.
         Reprinted from Costa Rica. Instituto Geográfico
         Nacional. Informe semestral, enero a junio 1978.
         Bibliografía: p. 44.

19007   Bergoeing Guida, Jean Pierre.
         Laguna de Hule, una cadera volcánica, por Jean Pierre
         Bergoeing y Luis G. Brenes. San José, Costa Rica,
         Instituto Geográfico Nacional, 1978.
         59-63 p.   illus. (1 fold.), map.   25½ cm.
         Bibliografía: p. 63.
         Reprinted from Instituto Geográfico Nacional,
         Informe semestral, Julio a Diciembre 1977.

19008   Bergoeing Guida, Jean Pierre.
         Modelado glaciar en la cordillera de Talamanca,
         Costa Rica. San José, Costa Rica, Instituto Geo-
         gráfico Nacional, 1978.
         33-44 p.   illus., maps.   25½ cm.
         Reprinted from Instituto Geográfico Nacional,
         Informe semestral, Julio a Diciembre 1977.

19009   [Bergoeing Guida, Jean Pierre]
         Regiones morfográficas de Costa Rica [por Dr.
         Jean P. Bergoeing G. y Lic. Luis G. Brenes Q.]
         San José, Costa Rica, Instituto Geográfico Nacional,
         1978.
         53-57 p.   table.   25½ cm.
         Reprinted from Instituto Geográfico Nacional,
         Informe semestral, Julio a Diciembre 1977.

19010   Bergoeing Guida, Jean Pierre.
         Sensores remotos y geomorfología aplicada.
         San José, Costa Rica, Instituto Geográfico Nacional,
         1978.
         27-32 p.   illus., maps, diagr.   25½ cm.
         Reprinted from Instituto Geográfico Nacional,
         Informe semestra, Julio a Diciembre 1977.

19011   Bermann, Gregorio, 1894-
         La salud mental y la asistencia psiquiátrica en
         la Argentina. [1. ed.] Buenos Aires, Editorial
         Paidós [1965]
         206 p.   20 cm.   (Biblioteca de psiquiatría,

psicopatología y psicosomática. Serie menor,
v. 1)
Bibliography: p. [197]-206.

19012 Bermuda Islands.
Census of Bermuda, 23rd October, 1960; report of
census & statistical tables compiled in accordance
with the Census Act, 1950. [Hamilton, Government
printer] 1961.
134 p.   27 cm.

19013 Bermudez, Federico.
Los humildes. [Santiago, República Dominicana,
Universidad Católica Madre y Maestra, 1968]
107 p.   18½ cm.

19014 Bermúdez, Oscar.
Pica en el siglo XVIII. Estructura económica y
social. [Santiago de Chile, 1973]
6-56 p.   illus., map.   24½ cm.
Reprinted from Revista chilena de historia y
geografía, no. 141, 1973.

19015 Bermúdez, Pedro Joaquín, 1905-
Estudio sistemático de los foraminíferos quito-
nosos, microgranulares y aranáceos [por] Pedro
Joaquín Bermúdez [y] Francés Charlton de Rivero.
Caracas, Universidad Central de Venezuela, 1963.
397 p.   illus.   23 cm.   (Ediciones de la
Biblioteca, 14. Colección Ciencias biológicas, 1)
Bibliography: p. 376-381.

19016 Bermúdez, Pedro Joaquín, 1905-
Las formaciones geológicas de Cuba. La Habana,
Ministerio de Industrias, Instituto Cubano de
Recursos Minerales, 1961.
viii, 177 p.   fold. map (in pocket), tables.
22 cm.   (Geología cubana, no. 1)
"Datos biográficos del Dr. Pedro Joaquín Bermúdez"
[por] Agustín Ayala-Castañares: p. v-viii.
Bibliography: p. 161-174.

19017 Bermúdez de Belloso, Mercedes.
Ausencias y retornos; poemas. [Maracaibo]
Universidad del Zulia, Facultad de Humanidades
[1967]
99 p.   18 cm.   (Arte y letras, 28)

19018   Bermúdez Limón, C
        Las obras públicas y el desarrollo económico de
        México. México, 1960.
        236 ℓ.   28 cm.
        Tesis (licenciado en economía) - Universidad
        Nacional Autónoma de México.
        Bibliography: leaves 233-236.

19019   Bernal, Ignacio.
        Bibliografía de arqueología y etnografía: Meso-
        américa y Norte de México, 1514-1960. México,
        Instituto Nacional de Antropología e Historia, 1962.
        xvi, 634 p.   fold. col. map.   33 cm.
        (Instituto Nacional de Antropología e Historia.
        Memorias, 7)

19020   Bernal, Ignacio.
        Teotihuacán [descubrimientos, reconstrucciones]
        México, Instituto Nacional de Antropología e Historia,
        1963.
        52 p.   illus., fold. col. map, plans.   27 cm.

19021   Bernal, José María.
        Economía cristiana; conferencias. Medellín,
        Universidad Pontificia Bolivariana, 1965.
        62 p.   16 cm.   (Colección "Rojo y negro")
        Contents. - Economía cristiana. - La moral en los
        negocios. - El pontificado y la cuestión social. -
        Carta a un católico que no reza.

19022   Bernal Guardia, Targidio A
        Reglas comunes al procedimiento civil, por
        Targidio A. Bernal Guardia. Panamá, Universidad de
        Panamá, 1963.
        318 p.   23 cm.   (Publicaciones de la Facultad
        de Derecho y Ciencias Políticas. Serie D. Trabajos
        de graduación, v. 2)
        Bibliography: p. 317-318.

19023   Bernal Maya, Nazario.
        Los salmos; estudio [por] Nazario Bernal Maya.
        Medellín, Universidad Pontificia Bolivariana, 1964.
        63 p.   16 cm.   (Colección Rojo y negro)
        Contents. - Los salmos. - Aranzazu y su vértebra
        fatal. - Marco Fidel Suárez. - Los Isazas.

19024   Bernaschina González, Mario.
        Cartilla electoral, con un apéndice que contiene
        el texto refundido de la Ley general de elecciones

[por] Mario Bernaschina G. [1. ed. Santiago]
Editorial Jurídica de Chile, 1958.
311 p.   18 cm.   (Cartillas del Instituto
Histórico y Bibliográfico de Ciencias Jurídicas y
Sociales, no. 12)

19025   Bernasconi, Irene.
Equinodermos antárticos. III. Ofiuroideos.
2) Ofiuroideos de Georgia del Sur por Irene Bernas-
coni y María Marta d'Agostino. Buenos Aires,
Imprenta Coni, 1976.
23 p., 2 pl.   27 cm.
Reprinted from Revista del Museo Argentino de
Ciencias Naturales "Bernardina Rivadavia", Hidro-
biología, t. V, no. 1.
Abstract in English.

19026   Bernasconi, Irene.
Ofiuroideos del mar epicontinental argentino,
por Irene Bernasconi y María Marta d'Agostino.
Buenos Aires, 1977.
65-114 p., 11 pl.   27 cm.
Reprinted from Revista del Museo Argentino de
Ciencias Naturales, Hidrobiología, tomo V, no. 5.
Summary in English: p. 111.

19027   Bernhard, Guillermo.
La reforma agraria en los países latinoamericanos.
Montevideo, 1962.
197 p.   illus.   20 cm.

19028   Berrera V   , Humberto.
Detonación de bombas nucleares en el Pacífico
sur. [Santiago de Chile, 1971]
190-198 p.   24½ cm.
Reprinted from Revista chilena de historia y
geografía, no. 139, 1971.

19029   Berrettini, Célia.
Teatro francês. São Paulo, Commissão de Literatura,
Conselho Estadual de Cultura, 1970.
147 p.   22 cm.   (Coleção ensaio, 70)

19030   Berthet, Luiz Arthaud.
Sôbre as condições suficientes dos extremais
condicionados. São Paulo, 1959.
169 p.   24 cm.   (Facultade de Ciências
Econômicas e Administrativas, Universidade de São
Paulo. Boletin no. 11. Cadeira I, no. 1)
Includes bibliography.

162

19031   Bertram, Gordon W
        The contribution of education to economic growth.
        [Ottawa, R. Duhamel, Queen's printer] 1966.
        vii, 150 p.   25 cm.   (Economic Council of
        Canada. Staff study, no. 12)
        Bibliographical footnotes.

19032   Bertrand, André, 1913-
        Las técnicas del trabajo gubernamental en el estado
        moderno; estudio de ciencias políticas y administra-
        tivas y de derecho constitucional comparado. Versión
        al castellano de Catalina Sierra. Bruselas, Instituto
        Internacional de Ciencias Administrativas, 1954.
        92 p.   24 cm.   (Publicaciones del Instituto
        de Administración Pública de México)
        "Estudio... realizado por el Instituto Interna-
        cional de Ciencias Administrativas bajo los auspicios
        de las Naciones Unidas."

19033   Berutti, Maria José.
        0 ar que nos envolve. Belo Horizonte, Centro
        Regional de Pesquisas Educacionais João Pinheiro,
        1967.
        9 p.   illus.   24 cm.   (Cadernos de educação, 1)

19034   Betancourt, José Ramón de, 1823-1890.
        Discursos y manifiestos políticos de J. R. de
        Betancourt, diputado á Cortés por las islas de Puerto
        Rico y Cuba... Madrid, Est. tip. de F. Pinto, 1887.
        2 p.l., 370 p., 1 ℓ.   front. (port.)   22½ cm.
        "Biografía" por el Sr. D. Calixto Bernal (signed:
        J. C. Bernal): p. [i]-xvii.

19035   Betancourt, Rómulo, Pres. Venezuela, 1908-
        Ante las perspectivas de un nuevo año; visión
        realista en el mensaje presidencial, 31 de diciembre
        de 1959. Apéndice económico. Caracas, Impr.
        Nacional, 1960.
        46 p.   illus.   23 cm.   (Publicaciones de la
        Secretaría General de la Presidencia de la República)

19036   Betancourt, Rómulo, Pres. Venezuela, 1908-
        Con voz de sinceridad ante el país; alocución del
        presidente Betancourt el 26 de abril de 1960.
        Caracas, Impr. Nacional, 1960.
        13 p.   port.   23 cm.   (Publicaciones de la
        Secretaría General de la Presidencia de la República)

19037   Betancourt, Rómulo, Pres. Venezuela, 1908-
        Discurso de San Cristóbal, en la celebración
        del cuatri-centenario de la ciudad, el 7 de abril
        de 1961. Caracas, Imprenta Nacional, 1961.
        15 p.   illus.   23 cm.   (Publicaciones de la
        Secretaría General de la Presidencia de la República)

19038   Betancourt, Rómulo, Pres. Venezuela, 1908-
        Dos años de gobierno democrático, 1959-1961.
        Caracas, Imprenta Nacional, 1961.
        537 p.   24 cm.

19039   Betancourt, Rómulo, Pres. Venezuela, 1908-
        En el Lara industrial. Caracas, Impr. Nacional,
        1960.
        68 p.   illus., map.   23 cm.   (His En la
        entraña de Venezuela, giras presidenciales, 3)

19040   Betancourt, Rómulo, Pres. Venezuela, 1908-
        En franco diálogo con los industriales; palabras
        del presidente Betancourt en la clausura de la
        Convención de Industriales, en Caracas, el 31 de
        enero de 1961. Caracas, Imprenta Nacional, 1961.
        7 p.   front.   23 cm.   (Publicaciones de la
        Secretaría General de la Presidencia de la República)

19041   Betancourt, Rómulo, Pres. Venezuela, 1908-
        Inabatible espíritu de servicio público; mensaje
        del presidente Betancourt después del atentado
        contra su persona el 24 de Junio de 1960. Caracas,
        Imprenta Nacional, 1960.
        8 p.   23 cm.   (Publicaciones de la Secretaría
        General de la Presidencia de la República)

19042   Betancourt, Rómulo, Pres. Venezuela, 1908-
        Por buen camino hacia la recuperación económica
        del país; alocución el 13 de septiembre de 1960.
        Caracas, Imprenta Nacional, 1960.
        19 p.   port.   22 cm.   (Publicaciones de la
        Secretaría General de la Presidencia de la República)

19043   Betancourt, Rómulo, Pres. Venezuela, 1908-
        Que debiera hacer Estados Unidos por América
        Latina; francas opiniones del Presidente Betancourt
        en declaraciones a la revista "Life." Caracas,
        Imprenta Nacional, 1960.
        11 p.   22 cm.   (Publicaciones de la Secretaría
        General de la Presidencia de la República)

19044   Betancourt Díaz, Jesús.
        La filosofía de la historia de Arnold J. Toynbee.
        Montevideo [Imp. Cordón] 1961.
        68 p.   24 cm.
        Bibliography: p. 67-68.

19045   Betencourt, José de Souza.
        Aspecto demográfico-social da Amazônia brasileira.
        Rio [de Janeiro] S[uperintendência do] P[lano de]
        V[alorizaçao] E[conômica da] A[mazônia] 1960.
        77 p.   illus.   22 cm.   (Coleção Araujo Lima.
        Nova série, 2)
        Includes bibliography.

19046   Bettarello, Ítalo.
        A poesia italiana atual; tradução, notas, e
        apresentação. São Paulo, Universidade de São Paulo,
        Faculdade de Filosofia, Letras e Ciências Humanas,
        1977.
        137 p.   23 cm.   (Boletim, no. 15 [nova série]
        Departamento de Letras Modernas, no. 3, Curso de
        italiano, no. 1)
        At bottom of t.-p.:   Elvira Rina Malerbi Ricci.
        "Lembrança do Ítalo Bettarello" [por] Alfredo Bosi:
        p. 135-137.

19047   Beuchat Reichardt, Cecilia, 1947-
        Psicoanálisis y Argentina en una novela de Ernesto
        Sábato. Santiago, Chile, Departamento de Castellano,
        Universidad Católica de Chile, 1970.
        19 p.   27 cm.   (Literatura Hispanoamérica,
        CA, 4)
        Resumé in English.

19048   Beveraggi Allende, Walter Manuel.
        El ocaso del patrón oro [por] Walter Beveraggi
        Allende. [Buenos Aires] Editorial Universitaria
        de Buenos Aires [1969]
        140 p.   19 cm.   (Colección Ensayos)
        Bibliographical footnotes.

19049   Bianchi Gundián, Manuel, 1895-
        Misión cumplida; la Comisión de Derechos Humanos
        en la República Dominicana (relatorio y documentos)
        1960-1966 [por] Manuel Bianchi. [Santiago de Chile]
        Editorial A. Bello, 1967.
        80, [49] p.   illus., ports.   23 cm.

19050 Biart, Lucien, 1828-1897.
Adventures of a young naturalist, by Lucien Biart;
edited and adapted by Parker Gillmore... with one
hundred and seventeen illustrations. New York,
Harper & brothers [187-?]
491 p. incl. front., illus. 19 cm.
Translation of Aventures d'un jeune naturaliste.

19051 Bible. O. T. Psalms. Spanish.
Once salmos. Monterrey, Mexico, Ediciones Sierra
Madre, 1969.
51 p. 22 cm. (Poesía en el mundo, 67)
Parallel Hebrew and Spanish text.
"Selección y dos notas de Asher Shamir y Luis
Astey V."

19052 Bible. N. T. Mark. Mundurukú. 1967.
O evangelho segundo São Marcos na lingua Mundurukú.
Tradução portuguesa de Mons. Alvaro Negromonte,
reproduzida, com a devida autorização do volume
"Novo Testamento," da Libraria AGIR editôra. Rio
de Janeiro, Sociedad Biblica do Brasil, 1967.
161 p. illus., map. 23½ cm.
In Mundurukú and Portuguese.

19053 Bible. N. T. Acts. Mundurukú.
Atos dos apóstolos na lingua Mundurukú. Rio de
Janeiro, 1968.
264 p. illus., maps. 22 cm.
"Edição experimental."

19054 Bibliografía de Daniel Valcárcel. Lima, 1961.
278-286 p. 25 cm.

19055 Bibliografia gonçalvina, centenário de Antônio
Gonçalves Dias, 1864-1964. [São Luís, Brasil]
Departamento de Cultura do Estado, 1964.
45 p. 24 cm.

19056 Biblioteca Lincoln, Buenos Aires.
Notas bibliotecológicas. Buenos Aires, Servicio
Cultural e Informativo de los Estados Unidos de
América, 1966.
278 p. illus. 20 cm.

19057 Biblioteca Municipal Mário de Andrade, São Paulo.
Catálogo de obras raras da Biblioteca Municipal
Mário de Andrade. [São Paulo] Prefeitura do
Município de São Paulo, Secretaria de Educação e

Cultura, Departamento de Cultura, 1969.
viii, 537 p.   facsims.   23 cm.

19058   Bidart Campos, German José.
Filosofía del derecho constitucional [por] Germán
J. Bidart Campos. [Buenos Aires] Ediar Sociedad
Anónima Editora Comercial, Industrial y Financiera
[1969]
319 p.   20 cm.
Includes bibliographical references.

19059   Biesanz, John.
La vida en Costa Rica.   [Por] John y Mavis Biesanz.
Traducción de Carlos Francisco Echeverria.   San José,
Ministerio de Cultura, Juventud y Deportes, Departa-
mento de Publicaciones, 1975.
413 p.   19 cm.   (Serie Nos ven, no. 5)

19060   Bilak, León, 1903-
1er [i.e. Primer] centenario de los primeros sellos
postales de Centro América, 1° de diciembre de 1862-
1962.   Guatemala, 1963.
47 p.   illus., facsims., ports.   23 cm.
Cover title.
Articles previously published in El Imparcial.

19061   Bilharinho, José Soares.
Elogio de Clementino Fraga.   Uberaba, Brasil,
Academia de Letras do Triângulo Mineiro, 1971.
56 p.   front. (port.)   24 cm.   (Caderno, 13)

19062   Bimbi, Gerardo A
Bases para la formación y funcionamiento de una
cooperativa, por Gerardo A. Bimbi.   [1. ed.]   Viedma,
1967.
116 p.   forms.   22 cm.
At head of title: Provincia de Río Negro. Ministerio de Obras y Servicios Públicos. Dirección de
Energía.
"Disposiciones que reglamentan el funcionamiento
de las sociedades cooperatives: A. De la Provincia
de Río Negro. B. Nacionales": p. [71]-111.
Bibliography: p. 113.

19063   Bird, Mark Baker, 1807-1880.
The black man, or Haytian independence.   Deduced
from historical notes, and dedicated to the govern-
ment and people of Hayti, by M. B. Bird...   New
York, The author, trade supplied by the American
News Company, 1869.

167

xxxii, [31]-461 p.   front. (port.)   18½ cm.
Originally published under title: The Republic
of Hayti, and its struggles.

19064 Birová, A
Nuevos hospederos intermediarios para Dispharynx
nasuta y Tropisurus confusus (Nematoda: Spirurata)
[por] A. Birová, A. Calvo, D. Ovies, A. Valdés.
La Habana, Instituto de Zoología, Academia de Ciencias,
1977.
    8 p.   tables.   23 cm.   (Poeyana, 175)
    "Literatura citada": p. 5.
    Abstract in English: p. 1.

19065 Bisch, P   M
Model calculations for the density of states in
actinide metals, by P. M. Bisch, M. A. Continentino,
L. C. Lopes and A. A. Gomes. Rio de Janeiro, Centro
Brasileiro de Pesquisas Físicas, 1973.
    101-134 p.   diagrs.   29 cm.   (Notas de física,
v. 21, no. 6)

19066 Bisch, P   M
Remarks on the effect of localized perturbations
on the spin polarization, by P. M. Bisch and A. A.
Gomes. Rio de Janeiro, Centro Brasileiro de Pesquisas
Físicas, 1974.
    25 p.   28 cm.   (Notas de física, v. XXIII,
no. 1)

19067 Bisch, P   M
Variational calculations of the spin polarization
induced by a local moment in s-d hybridized metals,
by P. M. Bisch and A. A. Gomes. Rio de Janeiro,
Centro Brasileiro de Pesquisas Físicas, 1974.
    327-373 p.   28 cm.   (Notas de física, v. XXI,
no. 17)
    Includes index to vol. XXI.

19068 Bischoff, Efraín U
Tres siglos de teatro en Córdoba, 1600-1900.
Córdoba, R. A., Dirección General de Publicidad,
1961.
    382 p.   illus.   24 cm.   (Universidad Nacional
de Córdoba. Facultad de Filosofía y Humanidades.
Instituto de Estudios Americanistas. Serie histórica,
no. 31)

168

19069 Bitar Letayf, Marcelo.
       La vida económica de México de 1824 a 1867 y sus
       proyecciones. México, 1964.
       363 p.   23 cm.
       Tesis (licenciatura en economía) - Universidad
       Nacional Autónoma de México.
       Bibliography: p. 354-363.

19070 Bittencourt, Edgard de Moura.
       O concubinato no direito. Rio de Janeiro,
       Editôra Alba, 1961.
       2 v.   24 cm.
       Bibliography: v. 2, p. [477]-483.

19071 Blahutiak, Alojz.
       Evaluación de la selectividad ecológica de tres
       insecticidas en Lysiphlebus testaceipes (Cresson),
       parásito del afido del maíz Rhopalosiphum maidis
       (Fitch) por A. Blahutiak, J. Krecek y Z. Ruzicka.
       La Habana, Instituto de Zoología, Academia de
       Ciencias de Cuba, 1973.
       18 p.   tables, graph. $24\frac{1}{2}$ cm.   (Poeyana,
       no. 113, 23 August 1973)
       Abstract in English.

19072 Blahutiak, Alojz.
       Factores que condicionan la regulación de las
       poblaciones de insectos. La Habana, Instituto de
       Zoología, Academia de Ciencias de Cuba, 1976.
       11 p.   23 cm.   (Poeyana, 152)
       Abstract in English.

19073 Blairet, Louis.
       Espagne et Cuba. Situation politique, financière,
       industrielle et commerciale, abolition de l'esclavage,
       conversión de la dette publique espagnole, projet
       d'expropriation du territoire de l'Espagne, par
       Louis Blairet, 2. éd. rev. et augm. de nouvelles
       considérations politiques... Paris [Impr. de C.
       Schiller, 1870]
       39 p. $21\frac{1}{2}$ cm.

19074 Blanch y Blanco, Celestino.
       Bibliografía Martiana, 1954-1963... La Habana,
       Biblioteca Nacional José Martí, Departamento de
       Colección Cubana, 1965.
       112 p.   29 cm.

19075 Blanco, Andrés Eloy, 1898-1955.
Andrés Eloy Blanco: parlamentario. Compilación
y selección: Luis Pastori. Prólogo: Luis B. Prieto
F. [Caracas] Congreso de la República [1967]
2 v. 23 cm.
"Intervenciones parlamentarias... a lo largo de
las sesiones legislativas comprendidas entre 1939
y 1947."

19076 Blanco, Andrés Eloy, 1898-1955.
Canto a los hijos. Monterrey, México, Ediciones
Sierra Madre, 1968.
24 p. 22 cm. (Poesía en el mundo, 60)
"Nota introductoria," p. 1-3, by Jorge Eugenio
Ortiz.

19077 Blanco, Eduardo, 1839-1912.
Carabobo, tus hijos, patria mía, superior batallar...
Prólogo de Augusto Mijares y epílogo de Cristobal L.
Mendoza. Edición conmemorativa del sesquicentenario
de la Batalla de Carabobo. Caracas, Presidencia de
la República de Venezuela, 1971.
145 p. illus., facsims. 30 cm.

19078 Blanco, Enrique José.
De Playa Girón a Punta del Este. Buenos Aires,
1962.
94 p. 20 cm.

19079 Blanco, José Félix, 1782-1872.
Bosquejo histórico de la Revolución de Venezuela.
Estudio preliminar por Lino Iribarren-Celis.
Caracas, Academia Nacional de la Historia, 1960.
277 p. 23 cm. (Biblioteca de la Academia
Nacional de la Historia, 28)
"La obra... que ahora se edita había quedada
dispersa, impresa en distintas publicaciones."

19080 Blanco, Ricardo Román.
O salteão, uma importantíssima instituçāo bélico-
escravadora do Brasil desconhecida: subsídios para
sua identificaçāo. 2. ed., corr. e aumen. São
Paulo, 1962.
71 p. 23 cm. (Instituções bélicas do Brasil
[1])
"Bibliografía": p. 171.

19081 Blanco Moreno, Roberto.
Historia de dos curas revolucionarios: Hidalgo y

170

Morelos. [1. ed.] Mexico, Diana [1973]
295 p.   22 cm.   (Serie: La otra historia de
México)

19082   Blanco Segura, Ricardo.
Monseñor Sanabria; apuntes biográficos. San José,
Editorial Costa Rica, 1962.
315 p.   illus.   21 cm.   (Biblioteca de
autores costarricenses, t. 7)
"Apéndices" p. [246]-305): 1. Pensamientos de
monseñor Sanabria escogidos de sus más notables
escritos pastorales, documentos, decretos, sermones,
discursos, cartas personales, etc., y de sus principales obras de investigación histórica. - 2. Documentos y apuntes diversos.

19083   Blandón H   , Aldemar.
Mercadeo del algodón en Colombia, por Aldemar
Blandón H. Bogotá, Instituto de Fomento Algodonero,
1968.
v, 122 p.   map.   25 cm.
Bibliography: p. 119-121.

19084   Blankstein, Charles S
Agrarian reform in Ecuador, by Charles S. Blankstein
and Clarence Zuvekas, jr. Madison, Land Tenure
Center, University of Wisconsin, 1974.
34 p.   tables.   28 cm.   (LTC no. 100)

19085   Blásquez López, Luis, 1900-
Bibliografía hidrogeológica de la República
Mexicana, recopilada por Luis Blásquez L. y Alfredo
Löehnberg. México, 1961.
101 p.   23 cm.   (Universidad Nacional Autónoma
de México. Instituto de Geología. Anales del
Instituto de Geología, t. 17)

19086   Blaug, Mark.
A cost-benefit approach to educational planning
in developing countries. Washington, International
Bank for Reconstruction and Development, International
Development Association, 1967.
41 p.   graphs.   29 cm.   (Report EC-157)

19087   Bletzer, Keith V
Transition to cooperativism in a panamanian rural
community. Madison, Land Tenure Center, University
of Wisconsin, 1977.
3-9 p.   28 cm.

Reprinted from Land Tenure Center, Newsletter, no. 55, January-March 1977.

19088 Bleznick, Donald W   ed.
Directions of literary criticism in the seventies, edited by Donald W. Bleznick and John F. Winter. Cincinnati, Ohio, Department of Romance Languages and Literatures, University of Cincinnati, 1972.
102 p.   22½ cm.

19089 Bliss Institute, Belize, British Honduras. Library.
A bibliography of the National collection in the Central Library, Bliss Institute, Belize. [Belize] British Honduras Library Service, 1960.
52 ℓ.   28 cm.

19090 Blixen, Hyalmar.
La guerra de los dioses [leyendas de la América precolombiana] Montevideo, 1947.
208 p.   21 cm.   (Biblioteca Alfar)
Inscribed by author.

19091 Bloch, Pedro, 1914-
Dona Xepa. Comédia em 3 atos. Rio de Janeiro, Serviço Nacional de Teatro, 1973.
viii, 60 p.   21 cm.

19092 Bloch, Pedro, 1914-
Problemas da voz e da fala. Para professores de jardim de infancia para professores dos cursos primario, secondario, e superior, para professionais da voz, para pais e educadores, atualização de foniatria para médicos. [Rio de Janeiro, 1963]
214 p.   illus.   22 cm.

19093 Blutstein, Howard I
Area handbook for Costa Rica, by Howard I. Blutstein et al. Washington, Government Printing Office, 1970.
xiv, 323 p.   illus., tables.   24 cm.

19094 Bobadilla G   , Patricio A
Estudio crítico de la legislación sindical chilena desde el punto de vista de la libertad sindical [por] Patricio A. Bobadilla G. Santiago [Editorial Universitaria] 1967.
110 p.   21 cm.
Memoria de prueba (licenciatura en ciencias jurídicas

172

y sociales) - Universidad de Chile, Santiago.
Bibliography: p. 105-106.

19095 Bock, Carl Heinz.
The negotiation and breakdown of the Tripartite
Convention of London of 31 October 1861; a diplomatic
prelude to the establishment of Maximilian in Mexico,
with special reference to Great Britain and France.
By Carl Heinz Bock. Marburg, 1961.
2 v. (609 p.)   21 cm.
Thesis - Marburg.
Vita.
Bibliography: v. 2, p. 575-609.

19096 Bogotá. Escuela Superior de Administración Pública.
Instituto de Administración General.
¿Que representa Ecopetrol para Colombia? [Bogotá,
1963]
64 p.   22 cm.

19097 Bogotá. Universidad de Los Andes. Centro de Estudios
sobre Desarrollo Económico.
Available publications. [Bogotá, 1977]
8 p.   27½ cm.

19098 Bogotá. Universidad de Los Andes. Centro de Estudios
sobre Desarrollo Económico.
Opinión pública acerca de la reforma agraria.
Bogotá, 1965.
ii, 94 p.   28 cm.
"Investigación... realizada... a solicitud del
Instituto Colombiano de la Reforma Agraria."

19099 Bogotá. Universidad Javeriana.
Education and progress of Colombia. Bogotá [1963]
72 p.   plan.   27 cm.
Cover title.

19100 Bogotá. Universidad Nacional de Colombia. Centro de
Investigaciones para el Desarrollo.
Alternativas para el desarrollo urbano de Bogotá,
D. E. Bogotá, 1969.
xi, 231 p.   tables, graphs, col. maps.   31 cm.

19101 Bogotá. Universidad Nacional de Colombia. Centro de
Investigaciones para el Desarrollo.
[Centro de investigación para el desarrollo]
Bogotá, 1969.
55 p.   24 cm.

173

19102   Bogotá. Universidad Nacional de Colombia. Facultad
de Ingeniería e Ingeniería Química. Biblioteca.
Catálogo general de la Biblioteca A. García Bonus,
1939-1949. Bogotá, 1959.
123 p.   24 cm.   (Boletín Bibliográfico, año 1,
no. 1)

19103   Bogotá. Universidad Nacional de Colombia. Instituto
de Ciencias Naturales.
Catálogo ilustrado de las plantas de Cundinamarca.
Gramineae, por P. Pinto-Escobar. Juncaceae,
Cyperaceae, por Luis Eduardo Mora-Osejo. Vol. 1.
Bogotá, Imprenta Nacional, 1966.
133 p.   illus.   22 cm.

19104   Bogotá. Universidad Nacional de Colombia. Oficina de
Planeación.
Estructura administrativa y docente. Bogotá, 1971.
75 p.   diagrs.   28 cm.

19105   Bogrand, Ricardo, 1930-
La espuma nace sola. San Salvador, Ministerio
de Educación, Dirección de Publicaciones, 1969.
40 p.   21 cm.   (Colección Caballito de mar, 26)

19106   Bohorquez C   , José Ignacio.
Índice del Boletín de la Asociación Colombiana de
Bibliotecarios 1957-1967. [Bogotá? 1968?]
[36] p.   illus.   25 cm.

19107   Boissonnade, Prosper, 1862-1935.
Saint-Domingue à la veille de la révolution et la
question de la représentation coloniale aux Etats
Généraux (janvier 1788-7 juillet 1789) par P.
Boissonnade... Paris, J. Geuthner; New York,
G. E. Stechert & co., 1906.
1 p.l., 299, [1] p.   25½ cm.
"Extrait du volume des Mémoires de la Société des
antiquaires de l'ouest, tome XXIX, année 1905."

19108   Boiteux, Lucas Alexandre.
A província de Santa-Catarina nas guerras do
Uruguai e do Paraguai (notas e apontamentos)...
Supervisão editorial do Prof. Walter F. Piazza.
[Florianópolis, Universidade Federal de Santa
Catarina, 1972]
199 p.   illus., facsims. (part fold.)   24½ cm.

174

19109   Boldori, Rosa.
        Mario Vargas Llosa y la literatura en el Perú de
        hoy. Santa Fé, Argentina, Ediciones Colmegna
        [1969]
            84 p.   18 cm.   (Colección Hispanoamérica)
        Bibliography: p. [79]-84.

19110   Bolet Peraza, Nicanor, 1838-1906.
        Nicanor Bolet Peraza. Estudio preliminar de
        Augusto Germán Orihuela. Caracas, 1963.
            xxxi, 341 p.   port.   23 cm.   (Colección
        clásicos venezolanos de la Academia Venezolana de
        la Lengua, 4)
            Includes bibliographies.

19111   Boletín bibliográfico pernambucano, v. 1-   1964-
        Recife, Academia Pernambucana de Letras e Universidade
        Federal de Pernambuco, 1965-
            v.   28 cm.
        Library has v. 4, 1967.

19112   Boletín de geología, no. 1-   1958-
        Bucaramanga.
            no. in   v.   illus., maps (part col.)   25 cm.
        irregular.
            Issues for 1958-61 published as Publicaciones
        científicas of the Universidad Industrial de Santander.
            Published by the Departamento de Geología, Univer-
        sidad Industrial de Santander (the department's
        official publication)
            Chiefly in Spanish; some articles in English or
        French.
            Summaries in English, French, and Spanish.
        Library has no. 1.

19113   Boletín de precios de productos agropecuarios.
        Caracas.
            no. in   v.   33 cm.   monthly.   (Serie III:
        Monografía de precios)
            Earlier volumes published by Venezuela. Dirección
        de Planificación Agropecuaria. División de Estadís-
        tica. Later volumes by the Dirección de Economía y
        Estadística Agropecuaria, División de Estadística.

19114   Bolívar, Rafael.
            Guasa pura. Caracas [Fondo de publicaciones de
        la Fundación Shell] 1967.
            134 p.   16 cm.   (Colección distinta, 4)

175

19115 Bolívar, Simón, 1783-1830.
       Carta de Jamaica. Caracas, Ediciones de la
       Presidencia de la República, 1972.
       176 p., 60 p. in facsim., 7 p.

19116 Bolivia. Comisión Nacional de Estudio de la Caña y del
       Azucar.
       Desarrollo de la industria azucarera en el Departa-
       mento de Santa Cruz. Informe, con una introducción
       sobre sus proyecciones en el planeamiento de la
       economía nacional. La Paz, Ministerio de Economía
       Nacional, Comisión Nacional de Estudio de la Caña y
       del Azucar, 1959.
       54 p.

19117 Bolivia. Comité Nacional de Inversiones.
       Perspectivas que ofrece Bolivia al inversionista.
       [Traducciones por cortesía de las Embajadas de Estados
       Unidos, República Federal Alemana, Francia, Japón.
       La Paz] 1962.
       115 p.   illus., maps.   20 cm.
       Cover title: Fomento a las inversiones: Bolivia.
       Contents. - Camino al crecimiento. - Road to
       progress. - Ley de fomento y estímulo a las inver-
       siones; original en español, traducciones al inglés,
       alemán, francés y japonés. - Guía del inversionista. -
       Guide for investors.

19118 Bolivia. Constitution.
       Constitución política del estado... Edición parti-
       cular autorizada. [La Paz, Editorial Fénix] 1965.
       74 p.   18 cm.

19119 Bolivia. Dirección Nacional de Estadística y Censos.
       Boletín estadístico. [La Paz] 1962.
       141 p.   illus.   32 cm.

19120 Bolivia. Dirección Nacional de Estadísticas y Censos.
       Proyección de la población, 1950-1962. [La Paz?
       Departamento de Publicaciones, 1963?]
       74 p.   illus., map.   24 cm.

19121 Bolivia. Dirección Nacional de Informaciones.
       Bolivia: 10 años de revolución. La Paz, 1962.
       263 p.   illus.   22 cm.

19122 Bolivia. Dirección Nacional de Informaciones.
       3 [i.e. Tres] exposiciones sobre el desarrollo.
       La Paz, Bolivia, 1963.
       116 p.   19 cm.

19123 Bolivia. Laws, statutes, etc.
       Código de minería. La Paz, Ministerio de Minas
       y Petróleo [1965]
       134 p. 19 cm.

19124 Bolivia. Laws, statutes, etc.
       Código mercantil y disposiciones conexas, concordado
       y anotado por Juan Valdivia Altamirano. La Paz
       [1961]
       xvi, 230, ix p.   21 cm.

19125 Bolivia. Ministerio de Relaciones Exteriores.
       La desviación del rio Lauca; antecedentes y docu-
       mentos. La Paz, 1962.
       303 p.   fold. map.   22 cm.

19126 Bolivia. Servicio Agrícola Interamericano.
       Estadísticas estimativas de la producción agro-
       pecuaria en Cochabamba. La Paz, 1960.
       8 p.   22 cm.

19127 Bolivia. Servicio Agrícola Interamericano.
       Estadísticas estimativas de la producción agro-
       pecuaria en Oruro. La Paz, 1960.
       10 p.   22 cm.

19128 Bolivia. Servicio Agrícola Interamericano.
       Estadísticas estimativas de la producción agro-
       pecuaria en Santa Cruz. La Paz, 1960.
       22 p.   22 cm.

19129 Bolivia. Servicio Agrícola Interamericano. División
       de Economía Agrícola.
       Principales enfermedades de plantas en Bolivia.
       La Paz, 1959.
       20 ℓ.   28 cm.

19130 Bollo, Sarah.
       Diana transfigurada. [Montevideo, Imp. Rosgal-
       Hilario Rosillo] 1964.
       30 p.   20 cm.
       Poems.
       Contents. - Despertar. - Encuentro y transfigu-
       ración.

19131 Bolsi, Alfredo S
       Estudio antropogeográfico del Valle de Santa María,
       Catamarca. Resistencia, Argentina, Departamento de
       Extensión Universitaria y Ampliación de Estudios,

177

Universidad Nacional del Nordeste, 1967.
xiv, 149 p.   fold. map, illus., photos.   22 cm.
(Serie humanidades, 3)

19132   Boltovskoy, Esteban.
Diccionario de la terminología del plancton marino
en cinco idiomas: inglés, español, alemán, francés
y ruso. Buenos Aires [República Argentina, Secretaría
de Marina, Servicio de Hidrografía Naval] 1963 [i.e.
1964]
114 p.   30 cm.   (República Argentina.   Secretarí‌a
de Marina.   Servicio de Hidrografía Naval.   Público H.
1019)
Title also in English on cover: Planktological
dictionary.

19133   Boltovskoy, Esteban.
Ejemplares patológicos en los foraminíferos
planctónicos por Esteban Boltovskoy.   Buenos Aires,
Imprenta Coni, 1976.
25-29 p., 1 pl.   27 cm.
Reprinted from Revista del Museo Argentino de
Ciencias Naturales "Bernardino Rivadavia", Hidro-
biología, T. V, no. 2.

19134   Boltovskoy, Esteban.
Foraminíferos   calcáreos uniloculares de profun-
didades grandes del Atlántico Sur y el Índico
(neogeno-reciente) por E. Boltovskoy y S. Watanabe.
Buenos Aires, 1977.
41-64 p., 6 pl.   27 cm.
Reprinted from Revista del Museo Argentino de
Ciencias Naturales, Hidrobiología, tomo V, no. 4.
Summary in English: p. 63.

19135   Boltovskoy, Esteban.
Foraminíferos de la zona de manglar de Guayaquil
(Ecuador) por Esteban Boltovskoy y Luis Muñiz
Vidarte.   Buenos Aires, 1977.
31-40 p., 4 pl.   27 cm.
Reprinted from Revista del Museo Argentino de
Ciencias Naturales, Hidrobiología, tomo V, no. 3.
Summary in English: p. 40.

19136   Boltshauser, João.
História da arquitetura.   Ilustraciones do autor.
Vol. 1.   Belo Horizonte, Escola de Arquitetura,
Universidade de Minas Gerais, 1963.

294 p.   22 cm.
No more published?

19137   Bombal, Susana.
Tres domingos.   Prólogo de Jorge Luis Borges.
[2. ed.]   Buenos Aires [Emecé Editores] 1960.
99 p.   19 cm.

19138   Bombino Matienzo, Juan P
El financiamiento de la vivienda propia en Vene-
zuela [por] Juan P. Bombino Matienzo.   [Cumana]
Universidad de Oriente [1966]
119 p.   24 cm.
Bibliography: 117-119 p.

19139   Bomfim, Paulo.
Tempo reverso; [versos.   São Paulo] Martins [1964]
87 p.   21 cm.

19140   Bonafina Dorrego, Andrés.
¿Comunismo en la Universidad de Buenos Aires?
Buenos Aires, 1962.
45 p.   20 cm.

19141   Bonavia, Duccio B   comp.
Arqueología peruana; precursores.   Selección,
introducción, comentario y notas de Duccio Bonavia y
Rogger Ravines.   Lima, Casa de la Cultura del Perú,
1970.
240 p.   illus.   18 cm.

19142   Bonazzi, Augusto.
Agricultura en el desierto; estudio sobre el
cultivo de las regiones desérticas de la cuenca
mediterránea: Israel, Grecia, y Tripolitania [por]
Augusto Bonazzi y M. V. Bonazzi.   [Caracas] Ediciones
de la Biblioteca, Universidad Central de Venezuela,
[1969]
140 p.   illus., maps.   23 cm.   (Colección
Temas)
Bibliography: p. 73-[75]

19143   Bond, Samuel Start.
... Poesías latinas, seguidas de sus cartas a
Miguel Antonio Caro.   Edición crítica preparada por
Manuel Briceño Jáuregui y Jorge Páramo Pomareda.
Bogotá, Instituto Caro y Cuervo, 1974.
233 p.   illus., facsims.   24½ cm.   (Publica-
ciones del Instituto Caro y Cuervo, XXXII)

19144 Bonet de Sotillo, Dolores.
Ramón Díaz Sánchez. Caracas, Escuela de Biblioteconomía y Archivos, Facultad de Humanidades y
Educación, Universidad Central de Venezuela, 1967.
71 p.   port.   17½ cm.   (Serie bibliográfica, 5)

19145 Bonfanti, Celestino.
La investigación bibliográfica y la comunicación
técnica; manual para los estudiantes de ingeniería
agronómica. Maracay, Universidad Central de Venezuela, 1965.
281 p.   illus.   21 cm.   (Revista de la
Facultad de Agronomía. Alcance no. 8)

19146 Bonfanti, Enrique.
El problema económico social argentino. La Plata,
Ministerio de Economía y Hacienda de la Provincia de
Buenos Aires, Dirección de Cultura y Capacitación
Administrativa, Departamento de Cultura, 1961.
51 p.   25 cm.
Includes bibliography.

19147 Bonifacio, José (0 Moço)
Poesías. Texto organizado e apresentado por
Alfredo Bosi e Nilo Scalzo. São Paulo, Conselho
Estadual de Cultura, 1962.
317 p.   20 cm.   (Coleção Poesía, 5)

19148 Bonifaz Ezeta, Angel.
Contribución del derecho del trabajo a la reforma
agraria mexicana. Mexico, 1963.
161 p.   23 cm.
Tesis (licenciatura en derecho) - Universidad
Nacional Autónoma de México.
Bibliographical footnotes.

19149 Bonifaz Nuño, Alberto.
El derecho del señor; comedia en tres actos.
[1. ed.] Mexico, Universidad Nacional Autónoma de
México, 1960.
185 p.   18 cm.

19150 Bonilla, Sonia.
La moral de trabajo y su relación con las
funciones técnicas de personal [by] Sonia Bonilla,
María Angelica Rovella, Raul Fernández Tuneu.
Montevideo, Instituto de Administración, Facultad
de Ciencias Económicas y de Administración, Univer-

sidad de la República, 1967.
49 p.   24 cm.   (Cuaderno no. 49)

19151 Bonilla Echeverri, Oscar.
Código de justicia penal militar y consejos de
guerra verbales. [Bogotá] Voluntad [1971]
257 p.   23 cm.

19152 Bonilla Gómez, Hermenegildo.
Ciencia jurídico-penal contemporánea. [Popayán,
Colombia, Taller Editoriales del Departamento] 1967
[i.e. 1968]
479 p.   illus.   25 cm.

19153 Bonnet, Edmond, 1848-
Souvenirs historiques de Guy-Joseph Bonnet,
général de division des armées de la république
d'Haiti... documents relatifs à toutes les phases
de la révolution de Saint-Domingue, recueillis et mis
en ordre par Edmond Bonnet... Paris, A. Durand,
1864.
xxiii, 502 p., 1 ℓ.   front. (port.)   21½ cm.

19154 Bonomi, Maria.
Elaboração e cancelamento de "Balada do terror e
8 variações". Rio de Janeiro, Museu de Arte Moderna,
1971.
unpaged.   illus.   17 cm.
Photographic documentation by Aldo Simoncini.
Text in English and Portuguese. Translation into
English by Vera Beltrão do Valle.
Commentary by Jayme Maurício.

19155 Bonomi, Maria.
Xilografias de Maria Bonomi. Rio de Janeiro,
Museu de Arte Moderna, 1971.
unpaged.   illus.   21½ cm.

19156 Bonzon, Alfred.
La nouvelle critique et Racine. São Paulo,
Faculdade de Filosofia, Letras e Ciências Humanas,
Universidade de São Paulo, 1971.
125 p.   24 cm.   (Boletim 350. Lingua e
literatura francesa, 7)

19157 Boole, George, 1815-1864.
Investigación de las leyes del pensamiento sobre
las que se fundamentan las teorías matemáticas de
la lógica y las probabilidades. (Selección)

181

Esbozo introductor, selección, traducción y notas
de Ernesto H. Battistella. [Maracaibo] Universidad
del Zulia, 1972.

19158 Boquady, Jesus Barros.
Romanceiro goiano (poemas)   Goiânia, Brasil,
Departamento Estadual de Cultura, 1971.
150 p.   20½ cm.

19159 Borba, Hermilo.
História do espetáculo [por] Hermilo Borba Filho.
Ed. rev. e atual. Rio de Janeiro, Ed. 0. Cruzeiro,
1968.
280 p.   21 cm.   (Coleção Pontos cardeais, v. 2)
Published in 1953 under title: História do teatro.
Bibliography: p. 279-286.

19160 Borba de Moraes, Rubens.
Bibliografia brasileira do período colonial;
catálogo comentado das obras dos autores nascidos no
Brasil e publicadas antes de 1808. São Paulo,
Instituto de Estudos Brasileiros, Universidade de
São Paulo, 1969.
xxii, 437 p.   facsims.   24 cm.   (Pub. do
Instituto de Estudos Brasileiros, 9)

19161 Borba Filho, Hermilo, 1917-
Cerámica popular do nordeste. Pesquisa de campo
realizada sob a patrocinio do Instituto Joaquim
Nabuco de pesquisas sociais Recife, em convênio com
a Campanha de defesa do folkclore brasileiro. Rio
de Janeiro, Ministerio da educação e cultura,
Campanha de defesa do folkclore brasileiro, 1969.
204 p., 25 pl.   21½ cm.

19162 Borba Filho, Hermilo, 1917-
0 general está pintando; novelas. Pôrto Alegre,
Editôra Globo, 1973.
136 p.   22½ cm.

19163 Bordón, F   Arturo.
Verdades del barquero; misión política del Partido
Liberal del Paraguay, campaña periodística de re-
vindicación de la verdad historia. Asunción, 1962.
1 v.   20 cm.
"La serie de artículos histórico-políticos apare-
cidos en 'Tribuna liberal' bajo el título de
'Verdades del barquero.'

19164 Borges, Jorge Luís, 1899–
Libro del cielo y del infierno [por] Jorge Luis
Borges [y] Adolfo Bioy Casares. Buenos Aires,
Sur [1970]
134 p. 18½ cm.

19165 Borges, José Carlos Cavalcanti.
A flor e o fruto; drama. (Segundo o romance "Dom
Camurro" de Machado de Assis) Recife, Imprensa
universitaria, 1971.
101 p. 23 cm.
"Prêmio Cláudio de Souza, 1970, da Academia Brasileira de Letras."

19166 Borges, José Carlos Cavalcanti.
Mão de mosa, pé de verso; três atos. Recife,
Imprensa Universitária, 1965.
101 p. 20 cm. (Comédia municipal, no. 3)

19167 Borges, Pedro.
Análisis del conquistador espiritual en América.
Sevilla, 1961.
189 p. 20 cm. (Publicaciones de la Escuela
de Estudios Hispano-Americanos de Sevilla, 132)
Seminario de Historia del Pensamiento. Colección
"Mar adentro," 15.
Cover title: Los conquistadores espirituales de
América.

19168 Borges, Wilson Alvarenga.
Revelação de homem. [n.p., 1963]
75 p. 20 cm.

19169 Borges R   , Julio Cesar.
Debajo del sol; turismo trujillano. Mérida,
Venezuela, Corporación de los Andes, 1967.
141 p. 22 cm.

19170 Borgo Derpich, José Luis.
La pesquería marítima peruana durante 1966. José
Luis Burgo Derpich. Isaac Vásquez Aguirre. Augusto
Paz Torres. Chucuito, Callao, Instituto del Mar del
Perú, 1967.
118 p. tables (part fold.) 28 cm.

19171 Borgonovi, Arnaldo.
Estudo comparativo sôbre a fiação da sêda com
emprêgo de água subterrânea e da água tratada de
Campinas. Campinas, Serviço de Sericicultura, 1968.

183

10 p.   tables.   23 cm.   (Boletim técnico de
sericicultura, no. 50)
Summary in English.
Bibliography: p. 10.

19172   Borgonovi, Arnaldo.
Influência das raças sôbre a pureza de sêda "grège"
[por] Arnaldo Borgonovi [e] João Rodrigues Pedro.
Campinas, Serviço de Sericicultura, 1966 [i.e. 1968]
13 p.   illus., tables.   23 cm.   (Boletim
técnico de sericicultura, no. 48)
Summary in English.
Bibliography: p. 13.

19173   Borja y Borja, Ramiro.
Constitución quiteña de 1812. Quito, Editorial
Casa de la Cultura Ecuatoriana, 1962.
110 p.   22 cm.

19174   Borja y Borja, Ramiro.
Reforma de la Constitución. Quito, Editorial Casa
de la Cultura Ecuatoriana, 1963.
409 p.   20 cm.

19175   Borjas Sánchez, José A
Andrés Bello, in memoriam. [Maracaibo] Facultad
de Humanidades y Educación, Universidad del Zulia
[1972]
76 p.   front. (port.)   24 cm.

19176   Borrero Moscoso, Alfonso María, 1866-1926.
Ayacucho. Cuenca, Casa de la Cultura Ecuatoriana,
Núcleo del Azuay, 1974.
628 p.   22½ cm.

19177   Borrero Moscoso, Alfonso María, 1866-1926.
Cuenca en Pichincha. Cuenca, Ecuador, Núcleo
del Azuay de la Casa de la Cultura Ecuatoriana, 1972.
2 v.   illus.   22½ cm.

19178   Bortoluzzi, Carlos Alfredo.
Estudo químico e petrográfico de amostras dos
carvões catarinenses das minas da Forquilha e do
Patrimônio, por Carlos Alfredo Bortoluzzi, Benour
C. Bittencourt e Joanna Nahuys. [Pôrto Alegre,
Instituto Tecnológico do Rio Grande do Sul] 1971.
49 p.   illus.   24 cm.   (Instituto Tecnológico
do Rio Grande do Sul. Boletim no. 58)

Summaries in Portuguese and French.
Bibliography: p. 47.

19179 Boscán F   , Luís A
Contaminación salina del lago de Maracaibo;
efectos en la calidad y aplicación de sus aguas
[por] Luís A. Boscán F., Fausto Capote F. [y]
José Farías. Maracaibo, Universidad del Zulia,
Centro de Investigaciones Biológicas, 1973.
37 p.   tables, diagrs.   27 cm.   (Boletín, 9)

19180 Bosch, Carlos.
Principios físicos del transistor de juntura.
[Edición revisada por el autor] Buenos Aires,
Editorial Universitaria de Buenos Aires [1963]
119 p.   illus.   23 cm.   (Manuales de Eudeba/
Física)
Bibliography: p. 115.

19181 Bosch, Jorge.
Introducción al simbolismo lógico. [3. ed.
Buenos Aires] Editorial Universitaria de Buenos
Aires [1967, c1965]
86 p.   illus.   23 cm.   (Ediciones previas.
Lógica)

19182 Bosch, Juan, Pres. Dominican Republic, 1909-
Más cuentos escritos en el exilio. Santo Domingo,
Editorial Librería Dominicana, 1964.
285 p.   port.   19 cm.   (Colección Pensamiento
dominicano, 32)

19183 Bosch, Juan, Pres. Dominican Republic, 1909-
El pentagonismo. Sustituto del imperialismo.
Un suplemento de la revista Ahora. [Santo Domingo,
1967]
56 p.   illus.   28 cm.

19184 Bosch, Juan, Pres. Dominican Republic, 1909-
Teoría del cuento; tres ensayos. Mérida, Venezuela, Centro de Investigaciones Literarias, Escuela
de Letras, Facultad de Humanidades y Educación,
Universidad de los Andes, 1967.
28 p.   20 cm.

19185 Bosch García, Carlos.
Historia de las relaciones entre México y los
Estados Unidos, 1819-1848. México, Escuela Nacional
de Ciencias Políticas y Sociales, 1961.

185

297 p.   23 cm.
Includes bibliography.

19186 Boschi, Enrique E
Los camarones comerciales de la familia Penaeidae
de la costa atlántica de América del Sur; clave para
el reconocimiento de las especies y datos bioecológicos
por Enrique E. Boschi. Mar del Plata [Argentina]
1963.
39 p.   illus., map.   25 cm.   (Instituto de
Biología Marina. Boletín no. 3)
Bibliography: p. 38-39.

19187 Boschi, Enrique E
Desarrollo larval de dos especies de crustáceos
decapodos en el laboratorio. Pachycheles baigae
Rodrigues da Costa (Porcellanidae) y Chasmagnathus
granulata Dana (Graspsidae). Mar del Plata, Instituto
de Biología Marina, Universidades Nacionales de
Buenos Aires, 1967.
46 p.   25 cm.   (Boletín, 12)

19188 Boschi, Enrique E
Estudio biológico pesquero del camarón Artemesia
longinaris Bate de Mar del Plata. Mar del Plata,
Universidades Nacionales de Buenos Aires, La Plata
y del Sur, P. E. de la Provincia de Buenos Aires,
Instituto de Biología, 1969.
[52] p.   illus., map, tables (part fold.)
35 cm.   (Boletín, no. 18)

19189 Boson, Gerson de Britto Mello.
A problemática universitária. Belo Horizonte,
Brasil, Serviço de Relações Universitárias da
Reitoria da Universidade Federal de Minas Gerais,
1968-1969.
2 v.   22 cm.   (Pub. 475, 486)

19190 Boson, Gerson de Britto Mello.
A problemática universitária. Belo Horizonte,
Serviço de Relações Universitárias da Reitoria,
Universidade Federal de Minas Gerais, 1968.
138 p.   21½ cm.   (Publicação, 45)

19191 Botafogo, A   J   S
O balanço da dynastia... Offerecido ao governo
provisorio dos Estados Unidos do Brazil, por A. J. S.
Botafogo. Rio de Janeiro, Imprensa Nacional, 1890.
151, iv p.   25 cm.

Contents. - 1. pte. Despezas da casa e familial
imperial desde o anno de 1808 até o dia 15 de
novembro de 1889. - 2. pte. Documentos históricos,
de caracter político e administrativo, contractos
de casamento, etc.

19192 Botelho, Pero de.
Poética; antologia da obra de arte. São Paulo,
Comissão de Literatura, Conselho Estadual de Cultura,
1970.
123 p.   21½ cm.   (Coleção ensaio, 75)

19193 Botelho de Oliveira, Manuel, 1636-1711.
Hay amigo para amigo; comedia famosa y nueva.
Rio de Janeiro, Serviço Nacional de Teatro, 1973.
viii, 57 p.   21 cm.   (Coleção Dramaturgia
brasileira)

19194 Botello de Flores, Conselo.
Charles Baudelaire. Monterrey, México, Ediciones
Sierra Madre, 1967.
20 p.   22 cm.   (Poesía en el mundo, 47)

19195 Botero, Ebel, 1928-
Cinco poetas colombianos; estudios sobre Silva,
Valencia, Luis Carlos López, Rivera y Maya.
Manizales, Imprenta Departamental, 1964.
270 p.   illus.   18 cm.   (Biblioteca de
escritores caldenses, 3. época, v. no. 19)
Includes bibliographical references.

19196 Botero Ramos, Emilio.
Lecciones de ortodoxia; estudios. Medellín,
Universidad Pontificia Bolivariana, 1964.
63 p.   16 cm.   (Colección Rojo y negro)
Contents. - La igualidad y la fraternidad humanas
ante la Iglesia. - La resurrección de Cristo. -
El transformismo.

19197 Botero Salazar, Tulio, 1904-
La libertad religiosa (cartas pastorales)
Medellín, Universidad Pontificia Bolivariana, 1967.
66 p.   16 cm.   (Colección Rojo y negro, 56)
Includes bibliographical references.

19198 Boulton, Alfredo.
Primera exposición del profesor del arte de
pintor, escultor y dorador Juan Pedro López,
1724-1787. [Museo de Bellas Artes de Caracas,

187

agosto 1963] Caracas [Dirección de Cultura, Ministerio de Educación] 1963.
68 p., 31 pl.   24 cm.
Cover title: Juan Pedro López. "Catálogo de las obras conocidas hasta ahora de Juan Pedro López": p. 60-68. "Testamento [de Juan Pedro López]": p. 21-24.

19199   Bourgois, François.
El Instituto Nacional de Pesca y el resultado de sus labores. Guayaquil, 1966.
40 p.   illus., fold. diags.   23 cm.   (Boletín informativo. vol. II, no. 3)

19200   Bouroncle Carreón, Alfonso.
Teatro: Se ma ha perdido un día, comedia; El puente maldito, drama. Lima, 1963 [i.e. 1964]
150 p.   21 cm.

19201   Boy, Herbert.
Una historia con alas. Con la colaboración y un punto final de E. Caballero Calderón, 2 ed., adicionada. Bogotá, Editorial Igueima, 1963.
286 p.   illus., map, ports.   20 cm.

19202   Boyanov, I
Algunos nuevos datos sobre la geología de los complejos de anfibolitas y granitoides en la parte sur de Las Villas, por I. Boyanov, G. Goranov y R. Cabrera. La Habana, Instituto de Geología y Paleontología, Academia de Ciencias de Cuba, 1975.
14 p.   illus., tables.   27 cm.   (Serie geológica, no. 19)
Abstract in English.

19203   Boyd-Bowman, Peter.
El habla de Guanajuato. [1. ed.] México, Imprenta Universitaria, 1960.
411 p.   24 cm.   (Universidad Nacional Autónoma de México. Publicaciones del Centro de Estudios Literarios. Serie de lingüística)
Includes bibliography.

19204   Boyd-Bowman, Peter.
Indice geobiográfico de cuarenta mil pobladores españoles de América en el siglo XVI. Bogotá, Instituto Caro y Cuervo, 1964.
lxvii, 275 p.   illus., maps.
Contents. - t. I. 1493-1519.

19205 Bracho Valle, Felipe.
       Yacimientos de estaño en La Ochoa, Dgo. y Juan
       Aldama, Zac. Vol. 2. México, Consejo de Recursos
       Naturales no Renovables, 1961.
       87 p.   p.l., maps.   23 cm.   (Boletín 60)

19206 Bracho Valle, Felipe.
       Yacimientos de estaño en la Sierra de Chapultepec,
       Zac., La Ochoa, Dgo. y Cosio, Ags. México,
       Consejo de Recursos no Renovables, 1960.
       116 p.   illus., maps (part fold., 3 in pocket)
       profiles (3 in pocket) tables.   23 cm.   (Consejo
       de Recursos Naturales no Renovables. Boletín 48)

19207 Bradshaw, Benjamin Spencer.
       Fertility differences in Peru: a reconsideration
       [by] Benjamin Spencer Bradshaw. [Austin, Institute
       of Latin American Studies, University of Texas, 1969]
       [15] p.   tables.   24½ cm.   (Offprint series,
       94)
       "Reprinted from Population Studies, vol. XXIII,
       no. 1, p. 5, March 1969."

19208 Brady, Eugene A
       The distribution of total personal income in Peru.
       Ames, Department of Economics, Iowa State University,
       1968.
       12 p.   29 cm.   (International studies in
       economics. Monograph, 6)

19209 Brady, Eugene A
       Production functions for the industrial sector of
       Peru. Ames, Department of Economics, Iowa State
       University, 1967.
       20 p.   28½ cm.   (International studies in
       economics. Monograph, 5)

19210 Braga, Virgínia Rayol, 1950-
       Espelho de três faces. São Luis [Brasil] Departa-
       mento de Cultura do Estado, 1973.
       97 p.   21 cm.

19211 Branda, Adolfo.
       La mitad de la luna, y otros cuentos. [La Plata]
       Municipalidad de La Plata [1962]
       180 p.   18 cm.
       Contents. - La mitad de la luna. - El histrion. -
       Villa sin nombre. - Agar. - La derrota. - Anodino.

189

19212 Brandão, Ademar Torres.
Utilização e custo da energia elétrica. [Salvador]
Universidade da Bahía, 1959.
114 p.   illus.   18 cm.   (Cadernos de textos,
cursos, mementos e sinopses)
Publicações da Universidade da Bahía, III, 11.
Bibliography: p. [113]-114.

19213 Brandão, Ambrosio Fernandes, fl. 1585-1613.
Diálogos das grandezas do Brasil. 2. ed. integral,
segundo o apógrafo de Leiden, aumentada por José
Gonsalves de Mello. Recife, Imprensa universitária,
1966.
xlvii, 216 p.   facsims.   23 cm.   (Documentos
para a historia do nordeste, 1)

19214 Braniff, Oscar.
La cuestión de la tierra, 1910-1911. México,
Instituto Mexicano de Investigaciones Económicas,
1960.
331 p.   20 cm.   (Colección de folletos para
la historia de la Revolución Mexicana, 1)

19215 Brannon de Samayoa, Carmen, 1899-
Fábula de una verdad [por] Claudia Lars [pseud.]
San Salvador, Ministerio de Cultura, Departamento
Editorial [1959]
92 p.   22 cm.   (Colección poesía, v. 11)

19216 Brasil/açucar. [Rio de Janeiro] Divulgação do M.I.C.,
Instituto do Açucar e do Alcool, Divisão Administrativa, Serviço de Documentação [1972]
243 p.   illus.   22 cm.   (Coleção Canavieira
no. 8)

19217 Brasil ano 2,000 [i.e. dois mil]; o futuro sem fantasia.
Plano, coordenação e texto: José Itamar de Freitas.
Rio de Janeiro, Artes Gráficas Gomes de Souza, 1968.
327 p.   illus., diagrs., tables.   22 cm.

19218 Brasil, Assis.
Beira rio, beira vida; romance [por] Assis Brasil.
[Rio de Janeiro] Edições O Cruzeiro [1965]
177 p.   22 cm.   (Tetralogia piauiense, 2)

19219 Brasil, Maria Auxiliadora de Souza.
Do Serviço de Estudos Pedagógicos (dezembro de
1960 - dezembro de 1967): supervisão de... Belo
Horizonte, Departamento de Educação, 1968.

35 ℓ.   32 cm.
Contents. - Dos estudos pedagógicos, por M. de L.
Rocha e M. A. de Souza Brasil. - Da documentação, por
Z. Bracarense Leite e M. A. de Souza Brasil. - Da
pesquisa e da medida em educação, por M. G. Damasceno,
N. Mahmud Láuar, M. de L. Rocha e M. A. de Souza
Brasil. - Da psicologia aplicada à educação, por M. J.
Barbosa Freitas e M. A. de Souza Brasil. - Dos progra-
mas de ensino e dos livros didáticos, por Y. Marques
Pereira, N. Carvalho e M. A. de Souza Brasil.

19220 Brasília. Fundação do Serviço Social do Distrito Federal.
       O desenvolvimento da comunidade em Brasília;
       uma estratégia de participação social. Informe
       preparado por José Lucena, Dantas, com a colaboração
       de Iraci Afonso de Moura, Mônica de Santa Luzia Reis
       e Leonilda Litran M. Andrade. Brasília, 1971.
       60 p.   28½ cm.

19221 Brasília. Universidade.
       Diagnóstico do desenvolvimento da Universidade de
       Brasília. 1962/1968. [Brasília] 1969.
       226 ℓ.   28 cm.

19222 Brasília. Universidade.
       Plano orientador da Universidade de Brasília.
       [Brasília] Editôra Universidade de Brasília, 1962.
       [46] p.   illus. (part col.)   maps (on lining
       papers) ports.   31 cm.

19223 Brasília. Universidade.
       Sistema estatístico para Universidade de Brasília.
       [Brasília] 1970.
       unpaged.   forms.   32 cm.

19224 Brasília. Universidade. Biblioteca Central.
       Guia da biblioteca central. Brasília, 1970.
       41 p.   illus.   22 cm.

19225 Brasília. Universidade. Instituto Central de Artes.
       Projeto Gráfica da UnB; ICA-FAU. Brasília,
       1969.
       3, 16 ℓ.   diagrs.   31 cm.
       Cover title.

19226 Brasília. Universidade. Instituto Central de Artes.
       Projeto Orquestra Sinfônica de Brasília; ICAFAU.
       Brasília, 1969.
       20 ℓ.   diagrs.   31 cm.

191

19227   Brau, Salvador.
        La colonización de Puerto Rico, desde el descu-
        brimiento de la isla hasta la reversión a la Corona
        española de los privilegios de Colón. Notas de
        Isabel Gutiérrez del Arroyo. San Juan, Puerto Rico,
        Instituto de Cultura Puertorriqueña, 1966.
        640 p.   20 cm.

19228   Braun, Kurt.
        Labor in Colombia. Washington, U. S. Department
        of Labor, Bureau of Labor Statistics, 1962.
        v, 54 p.   illus., map.   27 cm.   (BLS report
        no. 222)
        Cover title.

19229   Braun, Kurt.
        Labor law and practice in Colombia. [Washington]
        U. S. Department of Labor, Bureau of Labor Statistics
        [1962]
        iii, 41 p.   map, diagrs., tables.   26 cm.
        (BLS report no. 217)
        Cover title.

19230   Braun L   , Juan.
        Algunas características de la población inactiva
        en Chile y diseño de muestras empleadas para encuestas
        de ocupación y desocupación, por Juan Braun L. y
        José Luís Federic. Santiago, Chile, 1965.
        1 v.   various pagings.   tables.   27 cm.
        (Chile. Universidad, Santiago. Instituto de Economía,
        Publicaciones, no. 70)

19231   Bravo, Pedro, ed. and tr.
        Socialismo premarxista: Babeuf, Saint-Simon,
        Sismondi, Fourier, Owen, Leroux, Blanc, Blanqui,
        Proudhon, Weitling. Caracas, Instituto de Estudios
        Políticos, Universidad Central de Venezuela [1961]
        214 p.   port., facsim., plan.   24 cm.
        (Antología del pensamiento político, v. 1)

19232   Bravo Arauz, Bolivar.
        Quito monumental y pintoresco. Quito, Ecuador,
        Editorial Universitaria, 1961.
        307 p.   illus.   21 cm.

19233   Bravo B   , José María.
        Estudio sobre caminos vecinales en Colombia,
        Sur América, presentado a la IV Reunión Mundial de
        la Asociación Internacional de Carreteras, Madrid,

                              192

Octubre 14-20, 1962. [Bogotá, 1962]
77 ℓ.   illus.   22 x 29 cm.

19234   Bravo Covarrubias, Hipólito.
La reforma agraria y los tratados de Bucareli.
México, 1961.
101 p.   23 cm.
Tesis (licenciatura en derecho) - Universidad
Autónoma de México.

19235   Bravo Echeverría, Pablo R
Régimen jurídico administrativo de la aviación
civil no comercial en Chile. Santiago, Editorial
Universitaria, 1962.
93 p.   18 cm.

19236   Bravo G   , Luis R
El proceso didáctico de la lección. Cuenca, Casa
de la Cultura Ecuatoriana, Núcleo del Azuay, 1962.
72 p.   20 cm.

19237   Bravo Garzón, Roberto.
Viento sobre las aguas; pieza. Xalapa, México,
1962.
138 p.   18 cm.   (Universidad Veracruzana.
Ficción, 35)

19238   Bravo Lira, Bernardino.
Revolución e independencia en 1810. [Santiago
de Chile, 1969]
17-40 p.   24½ cm.
Reprinted from Revista chilena de historia y
geografía, no. 137, 1969.

19239   Brazil. Agencia Nacional.
Metas; realizações governamentais. [Rio de
Janeiro] Agência Nacional, Serviço de Documentação,
1958.
91 p.   16 cm.   (Publicação, no. 1)

19240   Brazil. Arquivo Nacional.
Catálogo de obras raras. Exposição e publicação
por motivo do Ano Internacional do Livro no Ses-
quicentenário da Independência do Brasil. Rio de
Janeiro, 1972.
140 p.   23 cm.

19241   Brazil. Arquivo Nacional.
Flora fluminensis de frei José Mariano da Conceisão

193

Vellozo: documentos.   Rio de Janeiro, 1961.
397 p.   ports., facsims.   28 cm.   (Publicações, v. 48)

19242   Brazil.   Arquivo Nacional.
... Registro de estrangeiros 1831-1839.   Rio de
Janeiro, 1962.
536 p.   24 cm.   (Publicações do Arquivo Nacional,
1.ª serie, v. 50)
At head of title: Ministério da justiça e negócios
interiores.   Arquivo nacional.

19243   Brazil.   Arquivo Nacional.
Relação de algumas cartas das sesmarias concedidas
em território da capitania do Rio de Janeiro,
1714-1800.   Rio de Janeiro, 1968.
74 p.   facsims.   (Publicações, 61)

19244   Brazil.   Arquivo Nacional.
Tombos das cartas das sesmarias do Rio de Janeiro,
1594-1595, 1602-1605.   Rio de Janeiro, 1967.
xxiv, 271 p.   23 cm.   (Publicações, 60)

19245   Brazil.   Arquivo Nacional.   Serviço de Registro e
Assistência.
Catálogo coletivo dos arquivos brasileiros;
contribuição preliminar de repertório referente
a independencia do Brasil.   Rio de Janeiro, 1972.
73 p.   22½ cm.   (Série instrumentos de
trabalho, 24)

19246   Brazil.   Campanha Nacional de Alimentação Escolar.
Programa de educação alimentar para o primário.
[Rio de Janeiro?   n.d.]
160 p.   illus., tables.   16 x 23 cm.

19247   Brazil.   Campanha Nacional de Merenda Escolar.
Campanha nacional de merenda escolar.   [Rio de
Janeiro, 1967]
[20] p.   illus.   20½ cm.

19248   Brazil.   Centro Brasileiro de Pesquisas Educacionais.
Brasil: bibliografia do ensino superior.   [Rio de
Janeiro, 1961]
64 ℓ.   33 cm.

19249   Brazil.   Centro Brasileiro de Pesquisas Educacionais.
Caracterização sócio-econômica do estudante
universitário.   Rio de Janeiro, 1968.

194

440 p.   22 cm.   (Publicações. Série VIII,
Pesquisas e monogra ias, vol. 3)

19250 Brazil. Comissão de Coordenação e Implementação de
Tecnicas Financeiras.
1° [Primeiro] ciclo de palestras. [Rio de Janeiro,
Departamento de Imprensa Nacional, 1974]
224 p.   tables (part fold.), diagrs.   22 cm.

19251 Brazil. Comissão Encarregada da Conservação dos
Portos e das Obras Publicas Geraes da Provincia de
Pernambuco.
Memoria descriptiva e justificativa do projecto de
melhoramento do porto do Recife apresentado ao exm.
sr. conselheiro Antonio da Silva Prado, ministro e
secretario de estado dos negocios da agricultura,
comercio e obras publicas por Alfredo Lisbôa,
engenheiro chefe da Comissão encarregada da conservação dos portos e das obras publicas geraes da
provincia de Pernambuco em 1887. Pernambuco, Typo-
graphia Apollo, 1887.
136 p.   fold. map, tables.   24½ cm.

19252 Brazil. Comissão Nacional de Energia Nuclear.
Directoria Executiva da Área Mineral.
Boletim, 1-13. Rio de Janeiro, 1974.
13 nos.   illus.   24½ cm.

19253 Brazil. Companhía do Desenvolvimento do Plantalto
Central.
Estudos setoriais, 1972. Volume 3: Transporte,
energia elétrica, comunicações, turismo, instituições
financeiras. Brasília, 1972.
112 p.   tables, diagrs.   21 cm.

19254 Brazil. Confederação Nacional da Indústria.
II encontro de investidores no nordeste. Rio de
Janeiro, Edição do Serviço Social da Indústria,
Departamento Nacional, 1968.
247 p.   25 cm.

19255 Brazil. Congresso.
Emendas à Constituição de 1946; número 16:
reforma do Poder Judiciário. Brasília, Biblioteca
da Câmara dos Deputados, 1968.
189 p.   22 cm.   (Documentação constitucional)

19256 Brazil. Congresso.
Plano de valorização econômica do vale do São

Francisco. [Brasília?] 1963.
3 v.   23 cm.   (Câmara dos Deputados. Diretoria
de Documentação e Publicidade. Documentos parlamen-
tares, 113-116-117)
Includes legislation.

19257 Brazil. Congresso. Câmara dos Deputados.
Brasília. Brasília, 1972.
1078 p.   22½ cm.

19258 Brazil. Congresso. Câmara dos Deputados. Biblioteca.
Deputados brasileiros; repertório dos membros da
Câmara dos Deputados da sexta legislatura (1967-1971)
Brasília, 1968.
762 p.   illus.

19259 Brazil. Congresso. Câmara dos Deputados. Biblioteca.
Deputados brasileiros; repertório biográfico dos
membros da Câmara dos Deputados da Sétima Legislatura
(1971-1975)   Brasília, 1971.
630 p.   ports.

19260 Brazil. Congresso. Câmara dos Deputados. Biblioteca.
Deputados brasileiros; suplemento ao repertório
biográfico dos membros da Câmara dos Deputados da
Sétima Legislatura (1971-1975)   Brasília, 1971.
34 p.   ports.   22 cm.

19261 Brazil. Congresso. Câmara dos Deputados. Biblioteca.
John Fitzgerald Kennedy (bibliografia brasileira)
[Brasília, between 1963 and 1966]
692-700 p.   22 cm.
Separata do Boletim da Biblioteca da Câmara dos
Deputados, Brasília. 12(2): 691-700, jul./dez.
1963.

19262 Brazil. Congresso. Câmara dos Deputados. Biblioteca.
Reforma monetária international: bibliografia.
Brasília, Seção de Referência e Circulação, Biblioteca
da Câmara dos Deputados, 1967.
95 p.   22½ cm.

19263 Brazil. Congresso. Câmara dos Deputados. Comissão
de Ciência e Tecnologia.
Ciência, tecnologia e desenvolvimento. Brasília,
Coordenação de Publicações, Centro de Documentação
e Informação, 1973.
191 p.   22 cm.

19264 Brazil. Congresso. Câmara dos Deputados. Comissão
de Educação e Cultura.
Homenagem a Camões; conferências promovidas pela
Comissão de Educação e Cultura da Câmara dos
Deputados, no período de 18 a 23 de junho de 1972.
Brasília, 1973.
160 p.   22 cm.

19265 Brazil. Congresso. Câmara dos Deputados. Comissão
de Relações Exteriores.
28.º aniversário da organização das Nacões Unidas.
Pronunciamentos feitos na Comissão de Relações
Exteriores em 16/11/73. Brasília, Centro de
Documentação e Informação, Coordenação de Publicações,
1973.
63 p.   22 cm.

19266 Brazil. Congresso. Câmara dos Deputados. Comissão
Especial do Estatuto da Mulher.
... O trabalho feminino; a mulher na ordem economica
e social. Documentação organizada por Bertha Lutz,
presidente da Comissão. [Rio de Janeiro] Imprensa
Nacional, Industria do Jornal, 1937.
160, 3 p.   22 cm.
At head of title: Câmara dos deputados. Comissão
de [!] estatuto da mulher.
"Inclue-se aqui os textos legislativos brasileiros,
os documentos internacionaes e interamericanos que
mais interessam á mulher, as reivindicações por ella
mesma formuladas, etc." - Introd.
"Bibliographia consultada": p. [157]-160.

19267 Brazil. Congresso. Câmara dos Deputados. Comissão
Especial sôbre Poluição Ambiental.
I Simpósio sôbre Poluição Ambiental; documento-
síntese. Brasília, 1971.
129 p.   24 cm.

19268 Brazil. Congresso. Câmara dos Deputados. Diretoria
Legislativa.
Do processo legislativo. Ciclo de conferências
sobre prática legislativa (14 de abril a 28 de maio
de 1971). Brasília, 1972.
596 p.   diagrs.   22½ cm.

19269 Brazil. Congresso. Câmara dos Deputados. Secretaria
Geral da Presidência.
Legislação eleitoral e instruções baixadas pelo
tribunal superior (atualizadas) Julho de 1970.

197

Brasília, Departamento de Imprensa Nacional, 1970.
290 p.   24½ cm.

19270   Brazil. Congresso. Diretoria de Informação Legislativa.
Projeto de constituição; quadro comparativo,
projeto, constituição de 1946, emendas constitucionais
e atos institucionais. Brasília [1968]
141 ℓ.   22 x 32 cm.
Cover title.

19271   Brazil. Conselho do Desenvolvimento.
Program of targets. [Rio de Janeiro] 1958.
148 p.   diagrs., tables.   32 cm.

19272   Brazil. Conselho do Desenvolvimento.
Report on ports and dredging. [Rio de Janeiro]
1956.
130 ℓ.   illus.   33 cm.   (Document, no. 12)

19273   Brazil. Conselho de Desenvolvimento do Nordeste.
A policy for the economic development of the
Northeast. [Rio de Janeiro] 1959.
x, 97 ℓ.   tables.   28 cm.   (Document, no. 1)
Cover title.

19274   Brazil. Conselho de Desenvolvimento de Pernambuco.
Aspectos da economia pernambucanana. [Recife, 1968]
23 p.   29½ cm.
"Separata do Relatório do CONDEPE - 1968"

19275   Brazil. Conselho Nacional de Economia.
O problema dos capitais estrangeiros no Brasil
Apresentação do conselheiro Humberto Bastos. [Rio
de Janeiro, Lucas, I.B.G.E.] 1962.
21 p.   28 cm.
At head of title: Centro de Cultura Econômica.

19276   Brazil. Conselho Nacional de Estatística.
O Brasil em números. [Rio de Janeiro, 1960]
149 p.   illus. (part col.) map.   27 cm.
(Brazil. Instituto Brasileiro de Geografia e Estatística. Anuario estatístico do Brasil. Apêndice,
1960)

19277   Brazil. Conselho Nacional de Estatística.
O mundo em números. [Organizado pela Diretoria
de Documentação e Divulgação. Rio de Janeiro] 1957.
174 p.   27 cm.

19278 Brazil. Conselho Nacional de Geografía.
       Atlas do Brasil; geral e regional. Rio de Janeiro,
       Instituto Brasileiro de Geografía e Estatística,
       1959.
       xxii, 705 p.   illus., maps.   25 cm.

19279 Brazil. Conselho Nacional de Geografía.
       Curso de férias para aperfeiçõamento de professôres
       de geografía do ensino secundário, fevreiro de 1962.
       [Rio de Janeiro] I[nstituto] B[rasileiro de] G[eografía
       e] E[statística] 1963.
       246 p.   illus.   24 cm.

19280 Brazil. Conselho Nacional de Geografía.
       Curso de informações geograficas, 1961.   [Rio de
       Janeiro] 1962.
       81 p.   24 cm.

19281 Brazil. Conselho Nacional de Geografía.
       Geografía do Brasil. Roteiro de uma viagen,
       organizado por Antonio Teixeira Guerra e Eloisa de
       Carvalho. Rio de Janeiro, 1960.
       255 p.   illus., maps (part fold., part col.)
       24 cm.
       Includes bibliography.

19282 Brazil. Conselho Técnico de Economia e Finanças.
       Orçamentos dos estados e municipios para 1940.
       R[io] de Janeiro, Jornal do Comercio, 1941.
       2 v.   maps, diagrs., tables.   27 cm.
       (Finanças do Brasil, v. 11)
       At head of title: Secretaria do Conselho Técnico
       de Economia e Finanças.

19283 Brazil. Constitution.
       Constituição da república dos Estados Unidos do
       Brasil 1946. Acompanhada de um índice alfabético e
       remissivo de autoria do Dr. Arthur Malheiro. São
       Paulo, Saraiva, 1961.
       149 p.   16 cm.

19284 Brazil. Constitution.
       Constituição da República federativa do Brasil.
       Emenda constitucional no. 1, de 17 de octubro de
       1969. Contendo indice alphabetico e remissivo
       organizado pelo Dr. Carlos Eduardo Barreto. São
       Paulo, Edição Saraiva, 1970.
       312 p. $16\frac{1}{2}$ cm.

19285   Brazil. Constitution.
        Constituição do Brasil, promulgada em 24 de janeiro
        de 1967. [Rio de Janeiro] Departamento de Imprensa
        Nacional, 1967.
        86 p.   23½ cm.

19286   Brazil. Constitution.
        Constituição do Brasil promulgada em 24 de janeiro
        de 1967. 3.ª tiragem. Rio de Janeiro, Forense [n.d.]
        200 p.   16 cm.

19287   Brazil. Constitution.
        ... Constituições do Brasil, organização rev. e
        confecção dos índices por Fernando H. Méndes de
        Almeida... 3. ed. rev. e atualizada. São Paulo,
        Saraiva, 1961.
        4 p.l., 744 p., 1 l.   17 cm.   (Legislação
        brasileira)

19288   Brazil. Departamento Administrativo do Serviço Público.
        Documentação administrativa... Brasília, 1967.
        55 p.   23 cm.
        "Homenagem ao Ministro Alfredo Nasser. Conceito
        e Fins da Documentação Administrativa."

19289   Brazil. Departamento de Imprensa Nacional.
        25.ª mostra de livros. Comemoração do 158.º aniver-
        sário da fundação do Departamento de Imprensa Nacional.
        Edições de 1965. Rio de Janeiro, 1966.
        24 p.   23 cm.

19290   Brazil. Departamento de Imprensa Nacional.
        26.ª mostra de livros. Comemoração do 159.º aniver-
        sário da fundação do Departamento de Imprensa Nacional.
        Edições de 1966. Rio de Janeiro, 1967.
        28 p.   23 cm.

19291   Brazil. Departamento de Imprensa Nacional.
        27.ª mostra de livros. Comemoração do 160.º aniver-
        sario da fundação do Departamento de Imprensa Nacional.
        Edições de 1967. Rio de Janeiro, 1968.
        34 p.   23 cm.

19292   Brazil. Departamento Nacional da Produção Mineral.
        Esbôço geológico de quadrilátero ferrífero de
        Minas Gerais, Brasil. Preparado pela turma de campo
        constituída pelos geólogos do Departamento Nacional
        de Produção Mineral e do U. S. Geological Survey
        para o XII Congresso Anuál de Sociedade Brasileira

de Geología, setembro, 1958. [Rio de Janeiro, 1959?]
120 p.   fold. col. map (in pocket)   tables.
27 cm.   (Publicação especial, 1)

19293 Brazil. Departamento Nacional da Produção Mineral.
4o. Distrito - Nordeste.
Relatório preliminar sôbre as investigações
geológicas na Mina Brejuí - RN. [Equipe do projeto:
Frederico Lopes Meira Barbosa et al.] Recife, 1969.
53 ℓ.   illus., fold. maps (part in pocket)   30 cm.
Cover title.
"Projeto Tungstênio/Molibdênio."
Bibliography: leaves 51-53.

19294 Brazil. Departamento Nacional de Estradas de Rodagem.
Manual técnico de conservação. Rio de Janeiro,
1967.
1 v. (unpaged)   illus., tables.   24 cm.

19295 Brazil. Diretoria de Hidrografia e Navegação.
Lista de faróis, Brasil. Correta até 2 de janeiro
de 1962. [Rio de Janeiro] 1962.
366 p.   illus.   25 cm.   (DH 2-10)
"Correções à Lista de faróis, Brasil, 1962"
[correta até 30 jun 1962]: [12] ℓ. inserted.
Errata leaf inserted.

19296 Brazil. Diretoria de Hidrografia e Navegação.
Operação geomar, NOc "Almirante Saldanha". Rio de
Janeiro, 1972.
3 v.   maps (part fold.), diagrs., tables.
25½ cm.
Contents. - DG 20-VI (5/11/1958 a 15/1/1959; - VII
Comissão Oceanográfica) - DG 32-I (1/6 a 17/6/69;
XL Comissão Oceanográfica) - DG 32-II (10/9 a 27/10/70;
XLVI Comissão Oceanográfica)

19297 Brazil. Diretoria do Dominio da União.
... Relação geral dos bens da união registados
até 1941 pela Divisão de cadastro e registro;
organizada por ordem do eng. Ulpiano de Barros,
diretor. Rio de Janeiro, Imprensa Nacional, 1942.
466 p., 1 ℓ. incl. tables (part fold.)   fold.
diagr.   27 cm.
At head of title: Ministerio da fazenda. Tesouro
nacional. Directoria do domínio da união.
"Segunda edição." - p. [3]

201

19298   Brazil.   Diretoria do Patrimonio Historico e Artistico
        Nacional.
        Tricentenário de Parati; notícias históricas [por]
        J. S. A. Pizarro e Araujo e outros.   Rio de Janeiro,
        1960.
        85 p.   plates, fold. map.   26 cm.   (Publicações,
        no. 22)

19299   Brazil.   Directoria Geral de Estatística.
        ... Idades da população recenseada em 31 dezembro
        de 1890.   Rio de Janeiro, Officina de Estatistica,
        1901.
        2 p.l., 411 p., 1 ℓ.   29 cm.
        1 ℓ. of errata inserted.
        Portuguese and French in alternate lines.
        At head of title: Republica dos Estados Unidos
        do Brazil...   Ministerio da industria, viação e
        obras publicas...   Directoria geral de estatística.

19300   Brazil.   Directoria Geral de Estatística.
        Recenseamento da população do Imperio do Brazil
        a que se procedeu no dia 1.º de agosto de 1872.
        [Rio de Janeiro, 1873-76]
        21 v. in 22.   34 x 37 cm.
        Issued without title-pages, except "Cuadros geraes"
        which is bound with the vol. for São Paulo.
        The first census of Brazil, comp. by the Directoria
        Geral de Estatística.   cf. Statist. activ. Amer.
        nations, 1941, p. 72.
        Contents. - [1] Alagoas. - [2] Amazonas. -
        [3] Bahía. - [4] Ceará. - [5] Espirito Santo. -
        [6] Goyaz. - [7] Maranhão. - [8] Matto Grosso. -
        [9] Minas Geraes. 2 v. - [10] Pará. - [11] Para-
        hyba. - [12] Paraná. - [13] Pernambuco. - [14]
        Piauhy. - [15] Rio de Janeiro. - [16] Rio Grande do
        Norte. - [17] S. Pedro do Rio Grande do Sul. -
        [18] Santa Catharina. - [19] São Paulo. - [20]
        Sergipe. - [21] Municipio Neutro.

19301   Brazil.   Distrito Federal. Departamento de Turismo.
        Brasília. Carta turística. [Brasília? 1975?]
        map.   illus.   21½ x 58½ cm.

19302   Brazil.   Embassy, Washington.
        The Brazilian Northeast. [Washington, 1961]
        21 p.   maps, tables.   28 cm.

19303   Brazil.   Fundação Getúlio Vargas.
        Impacto da ação do govêrno sôbre as emprêsas

brasileiras [por Raimar] Richers [et al. Rio de
Janeiro] 1963.
xv, 222 p.   illus.   23 cm.
"Publicada em colaboração com a Missão Norte-
Americana de Cooperação Econômica e Tecnica-USAID-
Aliança para o Progresso.

19304   Brazil. Fundação Getúlio Vargas.
A integração da Amazônia e a ALAIC. Rio de
Janeiro, 1971.
46 p.   tables.   26 cm.

19305   Brazil. Instituto Brasileiro de Bibliografía e
Documentação.
Bibliografía brasileira de documentação. 1811-1960.
Vol. 1. Rio de Janeiro, 1960.
237 p.   24 cm.

19306   Brazil. Instituto Brasileiro de Bibliografía e
Documentação.
Bibliotécas especializadas brasilizadas brasileiras;
guia para intercâmbio bibliográfico.   Rio de Janeiro,
Conselho Nacional de Pesquisas, 1961.
174 ℓ.   24 cm.

19307   Brazil. Instituto Brasileiro de Bibliografía e
Documentação.
Bibliotécas especializadas brasileiras; guia para
intercâmbio bibliográfico, contendo plano para
aquisição planificada. Rio de Janeiro, 1962.
375 p.   illus.   23 cm.

19308   Brazil. Instituto Brasileiro de Bibliografía e
Documentação.
Guia de pesquisa bibliográfica em assuntos rodo-
viários. Rio de Janeiro, 1966.
122 p.   23 cm.
At head of title: Conselho Nacional de Pesquisas.
Instituto de Pesquisas Rodoviárias.
"Compilado por Célia R. Zaher, M. Esther Araujo e
Gilda M. Braga."
"Organizado pelo Instituto Brasileiro de Bibliografía
e Documentação, como contribuição ao 2.º Simpósio
sôbre Pesquisas Rodoviárias, realizado no Rio de
Janeiro, de 5 a 10 de setembro de 1966.

19309   Brazil. Instituto Brasileiro de Direito Financeiro.
Problemas de direito tributário; [curso de conferencias, por] Carlos da Rocha Guimarães, Eryma

203

Carneiro [e] Gilberto de Ulhôa Canto. [l. ed.]
Rio de Janeiro, Edições Financeiras [1962]
154 p.   24 cm.   (Publicação no. 10)
Contents. - Aspectos contábeis dos impostos, por
E. Carneiro. - Balanco fiscal, por E. Carneiro. -
Aspectos jurídicos de alguns impostos privativos
federais, por G. de Ulhôa Canto. - Tendências revi-
sionistas da Constituição em matéria tributária, por
G. de Ulhôa Canto. - O processo fiscal, por C. da
Rocha Guimarães.

19310   Brazil.   Instituto Brasileiro de Economía.   Centro de
Estudos Agrícolas.
Variações estacionais de preços, ao nível dos
agricultores, de alguns produtos selecionados, anos
de 1966 a 1969. Rio de Janeiro, 1971.
210 p.   tables, diags.   31 cm.

19311   Brazil.   Instituto Brasileiro de Estatística.
... Contribuições para o estudo da demografia no
Brasil (2.ª edição) [Rio de Janeiro] 1970.
458 p.   tables, graphs.   28 cm.
At head of title: Estudos de estatística teórica
e aplicada.

19312   Brazil.   Instituto Brasileiro de Geografía e Estatística.
Censo industrial. Guanabara. [Rio de Janeiro, n.d.]
xlix, 189 p.   3 fold. forms at end.   27 cm.
(VII Recenseamento geral - 1970. Série regional.
Volume IV - Tomo XVII)

19313   Brazil.   Instituto de Planejamento Econômico e Social.
Catálogo de edições 1975. Rio de Janeiro, 1975.
[20] p.   23 cm.

19314   Brazil.   Instituto de Planejamento Económico e Social.
Variações climáticas e fluctuações da oferta
agrícola no centro-sul do Brasil. Brasília, 1972.
2 v.   maps, tables, diagrs.   21 cm. (v. 1),
32 cm. (v. 2)
Contents. - v. 1. Relatório da pesquisa. - v. 2.
Zoneamento ecológico [maps]

19315   Brazil.   Instituto de Planejamento Econômico e Social.
Instituto de Planejamento. Setor de Agricultura.
Tecnologia moderna para a agricultura. Vol. 1 -
Defensivos vegetais. Trabalho básico: Miguel Martins
Chaves. Acompanhamento da execução: Mauricio
Rangel Reis. Revisão final e síntese: Eduardo

204

Martini, Theotonio Vasconcellos. Brasília, 1973.
136 p.   maps, tables, diagrs.   21 cm.
Bibliografia: p. 119-122.

19316   Brazil. Instituto do Açúcar e do Alcool.
Documentos para a história do açúcar. Rio de
Janeiro.
v.   24 cm.
Library has Vol. III: Engebo Sergipe do Conde;
espólio de Mem de Sá (1569-1579) 1963.

19317   Brazil. Instituto Histórico e Geográfico Brasileiro.
A Amazônia na era pombalina. Vol. I. Rio de
Janeiro, 1963.
431 p.

19318   Brazil. Instituto Histórico e Geográfico Brasileiro.
Revista. Tomo especial v. 1-13, 1956-1958. Rio
de Janeiro, Departamento de Imprensa Nacional,
1956-1959.
13 v.   24 cm.

19319   Brazil. Instituto Nacional de Colonização e Reforma
Agrária. Divisão de Cooperativismo e Sindicalismo.
Cooperativismo no Brasil. Brasília, 1973.
197 p.   tables, diagrs.   29 cm.

19320   Brazil. Instituto Nacional de Estudos Pedagogicos.
Conferências interamericanas de educação
[Rio de Janeiro] 1965.
vii, 150 p.   23 cm.

19321   Brazil. Instituto Nacional de Estudos Pedagogicos.
A educação em Minas Gerais e seus aspectos socio-
economicos. [Belo Horizonte] Centro Regional de
Pesquisas Educacionais de Minas Gerais [1964]
xiv, 32, [70] l.   illus., fold. maps, fold.
plans.   23 x 32 cm.

19322   Brazil. Instituto Nacional de Pesquisas da Amazônia.
National Research Institute of Amazonia (I.N.P.A.)
1954-1963. [Tradução da Prof. Marion R. Menezes.
Manaus, 1963]
53 p.   illus.   23 cm.
At head of title: Presidency of Republic.
National Research Council of Brazil.

19323   Brazil. Instituto Nacional de Pesquisas da Amazônia.
Museu Paraense Emílio Goeldi.

Museu Goeldi. [Belém, 197-]
folder.   illus., plan.   22 cm.

19324 Brazil. Instituto Nacional de Pesquisas da Amazônia.
Museu Paraense Emílio Goeldi.
... Programa nacional de pesquisas arqueológicas...
resultados preliminares do primeiro ano 1965-1966...
Belém, 1967.
158 p.   illus., maps.   27 cm.   (Publicações
avulsas no. 6)
At head of title: Conselho Nacional de Pesquisas.
Instituto Nacional de Pesquisas da Amazônia.

19325 Brazil. Instituto Nacional de Pesquisas da Amazônia.
Museu Paraense Emílio Goeldi.
Programa nacional de pesquisas arqueológicas. 4,
patrocinado pelo Conselho Nacional de Pesquisas e
Smithsonian Institution com a autorização e colaboração
do Patrimônio Histórico e Artístico Nacional.
Resultados preliminares do quarto ano 1968-1969.
Belém, 1971.
186 p.   illus.   28 cm.   (Publicações avulsas,
no. 15)
Summaries in English.

19326 Brazil. Instituto Nacional de Previdência Social.
Superintendência Regional no Estado do Rio de Janeiro.
Assessoria de Estatística.
Previdência social no Estado do Rio de Janeiro.
[Trabalho elaborado pela Assessoria de Estatística
da SRRJ em colaboração com o Departamento de Estatística do INPS. Niteroi?] 1970.
111 p.   27 cm.
"Editado pelo Departamento do Estatística do INPS,
como anexo do Mensario estatístico no. 206 - fevereiro
de 1970."

19327 Brazil. Instituto Nacional do Livro.
Bibliografía brasileira... por Aureo Ottoni &
outros. Rio de Janeiro, Ministério da Educação e
Cultura, Instituto Nacional do Livro.
v.   18 cm.
Library has: 1955, 1963, 1964, 1965.

19328 Brazil. Laws, statutes, etc.
Acidentes, segurança, higiene e medicina do
trabalho; coletânea de leis, decretos o portarias:
compilacão pelo Dr. Eduardo Gabriel Saad. 2.ª edição.
São Paulo, Fundação Central Nacional de Segurança,

Higiene e Medicina do Trabalho, 1972.
520 p.   21 cm.   (Serie Legislação, 1)

19329   Brazil. Laws, statutes, etc.
        Atos complementares 1 a 45. Brasília, Serviço
        Gráf. do Senado Federal, 1969.
        123 p.   19 cm.

19330   Brazil. Laws, statutes, etc.
        Atos complementares nos. 57 a 62. Ato institucional
        no. 11. [Brasília] Tribunal Superior Eleitoral,
        1969.
        11 p.   23 cm.
        Cover title.

19331   Brazil. Laws, statutes, etc.
        Atos institucionais 1 a 6. Brasília, Serviço Gráf.
        do Senado Federal [1969]
        41 p.   19 cm.

19332   Brazil. Laws, statutes, etc.
        The Brazilian income tax regulations (Decree no.
        47, 373 of 7th December 1959) incorporating all
        previous income tax legislation. An English trans-
        lation together with the original Portuguese text.
        Rio de Janeiro, British Chamber of Commerce in Brazil
        [1960]
        219 p.   tables.   24 cm.

19333   Brazil. Laws, statutes, etc.
        ... Código brasileiro de telecomunicações.
        [Rio de Janeiro] Departamento da Imprensa Nacional,
        1967.
        158 p.   maps, tables.   22 cm.

19334   Brazil. Laws, statutes, etc.
        Código da propriedade industrial; Decreto-lei no.
        1.005 de 21 de outubro 1969. São Paulo, Edição
        Saraiva, 1969.
        vi, 64 p.   23 cm.

19335   Brazil. Laws, statutes, etc.
        Código de processo civil (Decreto-lei no. 1.608 de
        18 de setembro de 1939)... Atual, notas remissivas
        e índice pelo dr... 4. ed. São Paulo, Ed. Saraiva,
        1968.
        xxiv, 831 p.   16 cm.   (Legislação brasileira)

207

19336   Brazil. Laws, statutes, etc.
        Código de processo civil. Quadro comparativo
        anotão... Autora: Leyla Castello Franco Rangel.
        Brasília, Senado Federal, Subsecretaria de Edições
        Técnicas, 1975.
        2 v.   26 cm.
        Contents. - v. 1. Quadro comparativo (Código vigente
        legislação anterior) - v. 2. Notas.

19337   Brazil. Laws, statutes, etc.
        Código de processo penal (decreto-lei no. 3.689,
        de 3 de outubro de 1941) e legislação complementar.
        Atualização e índices pelo dr. Floriano Aguiar Dias.
        [3. ed.] Rio [de Janeiro] Forense [1960]
        xvi, 566 p.   fold. form.   16 cm.

19338   Brazil. Laws, statutes, etc.
        Da compra e venda e da troca [1. ed.] Rio [de
        Janeiro] Forense [1961]
        294 p.   24 cm.
        Includes bibliography.
        Name of editor, Agostinho Alvim, at head of title.

19339   Brazil. Laws, statutes, etc.
        Os congressistas e a previdência social; legislação
        do Instituto de Previdência dos Congressistas.
        Brasília, 1966.
        30 p.   22 cm.
        Contents. - Lei no. 4.284, de 20 de novembro de
        1963. - Lei no. 4.937, de 18 de março de 1966. -
        Instituto de Previdência dos Congressistas; regula-
        mento.
        At head of title: Senado Federal. Serviço de
        Informação Legislativa.

19340   Brazil. Laws, statutes, etc.
        Consolidação das leis do trabalho; atualizada de
        acôrdo com as leis posteriores e contendo comentarios
        e notas explicativas e a jurisprudencia dos Tribunais
        do Trabalho; até outubro de 1961 [por] Victor Valerius.
        16. ed.   Rio de Janeiro, Gráfica Editôra Aurora, 1961.
        654 p.   19 cm.

19341   Brazil. Laws, statutes, etc.
        Consolidação das leis do trabalho e leis comple-
        mentares [por] Adriano Campanhole. 6. ed. rev.,
        anotada e atualizada. São Paulo, Editôra Atlas
        [1961]
        195, 343 p.   forms (1 inserted) tables.   24 cm.

19342 Brazil. Laws, statutes, etc.
Decreto-lei no. 288, de 28 de fevereiro de 1967.
Altera as disposições da Lei no. 3.173 de 6 de junho
de 1957 e regula a Zona Franca de Manaus. Manaus
[1968]
34 p.   18 cm.
At head of title: Presidência da República.
Superintendência da Zona Franca de Manaus. (SUFRAMA)
Manaus, Amazonas, Brasil.
Cover title.
Contents. - Decreto-lei no. 288 de 28 de fevereiro
de 1967. - Decreto no. 25, de 17 de março de 1967. -
Lei no. 569, de 7 de abril de 1967.

19343 Brazil. Laws, statutes, etc.
Decreto no. 61.244, de 28 de agôsto de 1967;
regulamentação da Zona Franca de Manaus. Manaus
[1968]
33 p.   18 cm.
At head of title: Ministério do Interior. Superintendência da Zona Franca de Manaus. (SUFRAMA)
Manaus, Amazonas, Brasil.
Cover title.

19344 Brazil. Laws, statutes, etc.
Direitos e obrigacões das estradas de ferro e de
seus servidores (doutrina, legislação, jurisprudência)
Rio de Janeiro, Freitas Bastos, 1960.
833 p.   23 cm.

19345 Brazil. Laws, statutes, etc.
Estatuto. Lei no. 4.215, de 27/4/63. Código,
de ética profissional. Tabela de honorários.
Cadastro geral dos profissionais inscritos, atuali-
zado até 31 de dezembro de 1967. [Pôrto Alegre]
Ordem Dos Advogados do Brasil, Seção do Rio Grande
do Sul [1969?]
164 p.   23 cm.

19346 Brazil. Laws, statutes, etc.
Estatuto da terra; lei no. 4.504, de 30 do novembro
de 1964 [Brasília?] Instituto Nacional do Desenvolvimento Agrario, 1965.
52 p.

19347 Brazil. Laws, statutes, etc.
Estatuto da terra; lei no. 4.504, de 30 de novembro
de 1964. Brasília, 1967.
58 p.   21 cm.

At head of title: Presidência da República.
Instituto Brasileiro de Reforma Agrária.
Cover title.

19348   Brazil. Laws, statutes, etc.
O estatuto dos funcionários [1. ed.] Rio [de
Janeiro] Forense [1962]
2 v. (837 p.)   24 cm.
Name of editor, J. Guimarães Menegale, at head of
title.
Bibliography: v. 2, p. [797]-801.

19349   Brazil. Laws, statutes, etc.
Estatuto dos funcionários públicos civis da união
e legislação regulamentadora (lei no. 711, de 28 de
outubro de 1952) [Rio de Janeiro] Serviço de
documentação do D.A.S.P., 1965.
250 p.   18 cm.

19350   Brazil. Laws, statutes, etc.
Imposto de renda. Rio de Janeiro, 1963.
112 p.   21 cm.

19351   Brazil. Laws, statutes, etc.
Imposto de renda, o seu é redistribuido em
beneficio do desenvolvimento do pais. [Brasília?]
Secretaria da Receita Federal, Ministério da
Fazenda, 1973.
42 p.   cover illus.   21½ cm.

19352   Brazil. Laws, statutes, etc.
... Imposto sôbre circulação de mercadorias...
impôsto de transmissão de bens imóveis... Paraíba,
1969.
122 p.   20 cm.

19353   Brazil. Laws, statutes, etc.
Legislação. [Rio de Janeiro] Secção de Publicações
do Serviço de Documentação [1961]
163 p.   22 cm.

19354   Brazil. Laws, statutes, etc.
Legislação civil remissiva, contendo o Código civil,
com índice alfabético remissivo, e os Códigos de
águas, caça, florestal, minas, pesca, bem assim a
legislação sôbre acidentes de trabalho, advogados,
direitos autorais, diversões, família, locação,
penhor, registros públicos, inclusive Registro
Torrens, seguros, terrenos de marinha, e tôdas as

leis civia, com remissões não só aos seus próprios
textos como as leis processuais e substantivas e
Regimentos dos tribunais. Rio de Janeiro, Freitas
Bastos, 1961.
822 p.   forms, tables.   23 cm.

19355   Brazil. Laws, statutes, etc.
Legislação comercial remissiva; contendo o Código
comercial, com índice alfabético remissivo, e os
Códigos brasileiros do an e da propriedade industrial,
com índices alfabéticos remissivos... Rio de Janeiro,
Freitas Bastos, 1962.
779 p.   illus., diagrs., forms.   23 cm.
Name of editor, J. Edvaldo Tavares, at head of title.

19356   Brazil. Laws, statutes, etc.
... Legislação cooperativista... Rio de Janeiro,
Seção de difusão e educação cooperativista, INCA,
1967.
55 p.   22 cm.
At head of title: Departamento de cooperativismo
e extensão rural. Divisão de cooperativismo.

19357   Brazil. Laws, statutes, etc.
Legislação tributária, ICM.   2d ed.   Recife,
Cia. Ed. de Pernambuco, 1968.
434 p.   tables.   22 cm.
Edited by Liberalino P. de Almeida and João
Bezerra de Alençar.

19358   Brazil. Laws, statutes, etc.
Lei de organização judiciária militar; Decreto-lei
no. 1.003 - de 21 de outubro de 1969. São Paulo,
Edição Saraiva, 1969.
vi, 50 p.   23 cm.

19359   Brazil. Laws, statutes, etc.
Lei orgânica da previdência social. Lei no.
3.807, de 26-8-60, com as alterações decorentes da
de no. 5.890, de 8-6-73, e de legislação anterior.
Rio de Janeiro, Instituto Nacional de Previdência
Social [1973?]
145 p.   25 cm.

19360   Brazil. Laws, statutes, etc.
Pequena coletánea da legislação brasileira de
educação (leis 4.024, 5.540 e 5.692) [ed. por]
Aderbal Jurema. Recife, Universidade Federal de

211

Pernambuco, 1972.
137 p.   24 cm.   (Cadernos de educação, 4)

19361 Brazil. Laws, statutes, etc.
Reforma agraria... Rio de Janeiro, Senado Federal,
Diretoria de Publicações, Serviço de Informação
Legislativa [1963]
245, 18 p.   23 cm.

19362 Brazil. Laws, statutes, etc.
Regras gerais da legislação penal em vigor: Código
penal, Lei das contravenções penais e tôdas as leis
especiais. Com o programa do Prof. Roberto Lyra
para conhecimento, interpretação e aplicação das
normas, explicações e dados. [Rio de Janeiro,
Distribuidora Record Editôra] 1961.
100 p.   16 cm.   (Manual de cultura forense,
direito penal, 2)

19363 Brazil. Laws, statutes, etc.
Renovatória de locação, com tôdas as alterações
havidas; jurisprudência do Supremo Tribunal Federal.
Rio de Janeiro, 1962.
203 p.   21 cm.
Name of editor, Ivan de Hugo Silva, at head of title.

19364 Brazil. Ministério de Educação e Cultura.
Semicom. Seminário Ibero-americano de Comunicação
e Mobilidade. Anais. De 3 a 19 de dezembro de 1972.
Assembléia Legislativa do Estado de São Paulo. [São
Paulo, 1972?]
457 p.   22 cm.

19365 Brazil. Ministério da Educação e Cultura. Campanha
de Defesa do Folklore Brasileiro.
Cadernos de folklore. no. 1-   Rio de Janeiro,
1968-
no.   23 cm.
Contents. 1. Maria de Lourdes Borges Ribeiro, Que é
folklore? 2. Oswald de Andrade Filho, A pintura
popular no Brasil. 3. Cecília Meirelles, Notas de
folklore gaúcho-acoriano. 4. Renato Almeida, Música
e dança folklóricas.

19366 Brazil. Ministério de Educação e Cultura. Instituto
Nacional de Estados Pedagógicos.
... Conferências interamericanas de educação.
[Rio de Janeiro] 1965.
150 p.   23 cm.

212

19367 Brazil. Ministério de Educação e Cultura. Instituto
Nacional de Estudos Pedagógicos.
Ensino superior. Coletânea de legislação básica.
Segunda tiragem do 1.ª edição. [Rio de Janeiro, n.d.]
454 p. 24 cm.

19368 Brazil. Ministério da Educação e Cultura. Movimento
Brasileiro de Alfabetização.
MOBRAL-seminario interamericano de educación de
adultos. Documento final. Original en español.
Versiones en inglés, francés y portugués. Rio de
Janeiro, Brazil, 9 a 18 de abril de 1973. [Rio de
Janeiro, 1973?]
93 p. 28 cm.

19369 Brazil. Ministério da Educação e Cultura. Movimento
Brasileiro de Alfabetização.
The MOBRAL system. [Rio de Janeiro? 197-?]
35 p. diagr. 34 cm.
In pocket at end: Appendix: Results for 1974
and perspectives for 1975 (8 p.), and broadside,
MOBRAL (95 x 65 cm.) with text on verso.

19370 Brazil. Ministério de Fazenda.
Proposta e relatorio. 1845/46-1890. Rio de
Janeiro, 1844-1889.
19 v. in 18. 24-36 cm.
Continued by its Relatorio.

19371 Brazil. Ministério da Fazenda. Comissão de Reforma.
Fundação Getulio Vargas.
Lei do impôsto de consumo. [Rio de Janeiro]
Guanabara [n.d.]
228 p. 23 cm. ([Publicações] Fundação Getulio
Vargas, 7)

19372 Brazil. Ministério da Fazenda. Contadoria Geral da
República.
[Textos das ordens expedidas em 1964] Rio de
Janeiro, 1968.
152 p. 28½ cm.

19373 Brazil. Ministério da Fazenda. Secretaria da Receita
Federal.
Impostos para o desenvolvimento do Brasil. Plano
geral de administração dos tributos federais
1969/70/71. [Rio de Janeiro? 1969?]
209 p. tables (part fold.) map in pocket at
end. 34 cm.

19374 Brazil. Ministério da Instrucção, Correios e
Telegraphos.
Relatorio. 1890/91-1891/92. Rio de Janeiro,
Imprensa Nacional, 1891-92.
2 v.   tables (part fold.)   fold. map.   24½ cm.
Report year ends in May.
Continued in the annual reports of the Ministério
da justiça e negocios interiores.

19375 Brazil. Ministério da Justiça. Arquivo Nacional.
Indice dos documentos relativos à América do Sul
existentes na Biblioteca da Ajuda. Rio de Janeiro,
1968.
153 p.   23 cm.

19376 Brazil. Ministério da Justiça. Arquivo Nacional.
Ofícios dos vice-reis do Brasil. Indice da corres-
pondência dirigida à Côrte de Portugal de 1763 a
1808. Volume 2 das publicações do Arquivo Nacional.
2.ª edição. Rio de Janeiro, 1970.
301 p.   24 cm.

19377 Brazil. Ministério da Saúde. Departamento Nacional
de Endemias Rurais.
Endemias rurais. Métodos de trabalho adotados
pelo DNERU. Rio de Janeiro, 1968.
278 p.   illus., tables, maps.   24 cm.

19378 Brazil. Ministério da Viação e Obras Publicas.
Aspectos econômicos da fabricação de automóveis
no Brasil. Rio de Janeiro, Serviço de Documentação,
1957.
50 p.   illus.   23 cm.   (Um piano em marcha,
no. 9)

19379 Brazil. Ministério das Minas e Energia. Comissão
Nacional de Energia Nuclear.
Ocorrências de urânio no Brasil... 6.º ciclo de
palestras para profesores do 2.º grau. [Brasília?]
1974.
24 p.   maps, diagrs.   31 cm.

19380 Brazil. Ministério das Minas e Energia. Comissão
Nacional de Energia Nuclear.
Uranio no Brasil, 1974. [Rio de Janeiro, 1974]
18 p.   illus., maps, diagrs.   29 cm.

19381 Brazil. Ministério das Relações Exteriores.
Arquivo diplomático da independencia. Ed. facsi-

214

milada da ed. de 1822. Brasília, 1972.
cxxxiii, 303 p.   23½ cm.

19382   Brazil. Ministério das Relações Exteriores.
Brasil-Argentina, 1961. [Rio de Janeiro,
Departamento de Imprenta Nacional] 1961.
93 p.   24 cm.

19383   Brazil. Ministério das Relações Exteriores.
Coleção das portarias (normativas) do Ministério
de Estado 1893 a 1960. [Rio de Janeiro] 1967.
502 p.   tables, diagr.   24½ cm.

19384   Brazil. Ministério das Relações Exteriores.
Documentos de política externa (de 15 de março a
15 de outubro de 1967) [Rio de Janeiro? 1967?]
122 p.   21 cm.

19385   Brazil. Ministério das Relações Exteriores.
Lista dos periódicos existentes na Biblioteca
do Itamaraty. Rio de Janeiro, 1966.
202 p.   33 cm.

19386   Brazil. Ministério das Relações Exteriores.
A politica exterior da Revolução brasileira.
Rio de Janeiro, Seção de Publicações, 1966-1967.
2 v.   28 cm.

19387   Brazil. Ministério das Relações Exteriores.
Testamento de relações diplomáticas entre o Brasil
e a União Sovietica, 1961. [Rio de Janeiro?] 1962.
78 p.   23 cm.

19388   Brazil. Ministério das Relações Exteriores.
Textos e declarações sôbre política externa, de
abril de 1964 a abril de 1965. [Rio de Janeiro]
Departamento Cultural e de Informações, 1964.
150 p.   23 cm.

19389   Brazil. Ministério das Relações Exteriores.
Viagem do presidente João Goulart aos Estados
Unidos da América e ao México. [Rio de Janeiro?]
Ministério das Relações Exteriores, Seção de
Publicações, 1962.
193 p.   23 cm.

19390   Brazil. Ministério das Relações Exteriores. Biblioteca.
Traduções de autores brasileiros, e livros sôbre o
Brasil escritos em idioma estrangeiro. [Rio de

215

Janeiro, 1960 or 61]
92 ℓ.   33 cm.

19391 Brazil. Ministério das Relações Exteriores. Comissão
de Estudos dos Textos da História do Brasil.
A Missão Bellegarde ao Paraguai (1849-1852)...
Exposição, antecedentes e notas por José Antônio
Soares de Souza. [Rio de Janeiro] Ministério das
Relações Exteriores,Divisão de Documentação, Seção
de Publicidade, 1966-1968.
2 v.   illus.   24½ cm.

19392 Brazil. Ministério das Relações Exteriores. Departamento
de Administração. Divisão de Pessoal.
Lista do pessoal. [Rio de Janeiro?]
v.   20 cm.   annual.

19393 Brazil. Ministério das Relacões Exteriores. Divisão
Cultural.
Brasília. [Rio de Janeiro, 1960]
26 p.   illus.   26 x 11 cm.

19394 Brazil. Ministério das Relações Exteriores. Mapoteca.
Mapas e planos manuscritos relativos ao Brasil
colonial conservados no Ministério das Relações
Exteriores e descritos por Isa Adonias para as comem-
orações do quinto centenário de morte do Infante
dom Henrique. [Rio de Janeiro] Ministério das
Relações Exteriores, Serviço de Documentação, 1960.
2 v.   fold. maps.   24 cm.

19395 Brazil. Ministério das Relações Exteriores. Serviço
de Documentação.
A politica exterior do Brasil. Brasília, Seção
de Publicações, Ministério das Relações Exteriores,
1967.
[48] p.   29 cm.

19396 Brazil. Ministério das Relações Exteriores. Serviço
de Publicações.
Anuario da divisão de atos, congressos e conferéncias
internacionais para 1942. Rio de Janeiro, 1941.
831 p.   21 cm.

19397 Brazil. Ministério de Fazenda. Secretaria da Receita
Federal.
Censo fiscal da união 1968. Plangef. 1969/70/71.
Objetivo no. 57. Rio de Janeiro, 1969.
162 p.   tables.   29 cm.

19398   Brazil. Ministério de Indústria e do Comércio.
        Instituto Brasileiro do Café.
        Anuario estatístico do café 1968/70.   [Rio de
        Janeiro?   1970?]
        137 p.   9 graphs.   31 cm.

19399   Brazil. Ministério de Indústria e do Comércio.
        Instituto Brasileiro do Café.
        Exportação brasileira de café. Rio de Janeiro,
        Divisão de Mercados, Departamento Econômico, 1968.
        1 v. (unpaged)   32 cm.   (Boletim do Departamento
        Econômico)

19400   Brazil. Ministério de Planejamento e Coordenação
        Econômica.
        Programa de ação econômica do Govêrno, 1964-1966;
        sintese. Com uma apresentação do Ministro Roberto
        Campos. Rio de Janeiro, 1964.
        240 p.   graphs, tables.   22 cm.   (Escritório
        de pesquisa econômica aplicada. Documentos, 1)

19401   Brazil. Ministério de Viação e Obras.
        Mapa rodoviário e turístico do Distrito Federal.
        [Brasília, 1975]
        map.   illus.   44½ x 59½ cm.

19402   Brazil. Ministério do Exército.
        Medalhística militar brasileira.   [Rio de Janeiro?]
        1968.
        unpaged.   illus.   24 cm.

19403   Brazil. Ministério do Interior.
        Relatório geral das atividades. Exercício de
        1968. [Rio de Janeiro, 1969]
        234 p.   24 cm.

19404   Brazil. Ministério do Interior. Coordenação de
        Comunicação Social.
        Nova sistematica dos incentivos fiscais.
        Brasília, 1975.
        16 p.   21 cm.
        Cover title.

19405   Brazil. Ministério do Interior. Superintendência
        da Região Sul.
        Informe geral da lavoura. Rio Grande do Sul.
        [Pôrto Alegre?   1968?]
        278 p.   tables, graphs.   33 cm.

217

19406   Brazil.   Ministério do Planejamento e Coordenação
        Econômica.
        Programa de investimentos públicos.   Distribuição
        regional, 1966.   [Rio de Janeiro?] 1966.
        251 p.   tables (part fold.)   33 cm.

19407   Brazil.   Ministério do Planejamento e Coordenação Geral.
        0 programa estratégico e os novos intrumentos de
        política econômica.   Brasília, 1969.
        254 p.   tables.   24 cm.

19408   Brazil.   Ministério do Planejamento e Coordenação Geral.
        Programa estratégico de desenvolvimento, 1968-1970:
        zoneamento agrícola e pecuário do Brasil; estudo
        especial.   Brasília, 1969.
        257 p.   maps, graphs, tables.   24 cm.

19409   Brazil.   Ministério Extraordinário para o Planejamento
        e Coordenação Econômica.
        0 Debate do programa de ação.   [Rio de Janeiro?
        1965]
        138 p.   34 cm.   (Documento de trabalho. no. 3)

19410   Brazil.   Polícia Criminal Internacional - Interpol.
        Das providências brasileiras no combate ao uso
        dos tóxicos.   Brazilian government measures in the
        fight against drugs.   Trabalho apresentado pela
        delegação do Brasil a XLI Assembleia Geral da
        OIPC - INTERPOL, em Viena, de 2 a 9 de outubro de
        1973.   [Brasília? Departamento de Imprensa Nacional,
        1973]
        89 p.   23 cm.
        Text in Portuguese and English.

19411   Brazil.   Presidência.
        Circulares de Secretaría da Presidência da
        República.   [Rio de Janeiro] D.A.S.P., Serviço de
        Documentação, 1959.
        194 p.   illus.   23 cm.

19412   Brazil.   Presidência.
        Plano trienal de desenvolvimento econômico e
        social, 1963-1965; síntese.   Rio de Janeiro, 1962.
        195 p.   22 cm.

19413   Brazil.   Presidência.   Serviço de Documentação.
        Programa de metas do presidente Juscelino Kubitschek
        Rio de Janeiro, 1958-
        v.   24 cm.

218

Vol. 1 is a summary of a work issued by the
Conselho do Desenvolvimento in 3 v. in 1958,
under title: Programa de metas.
Contents. - [v. 1] Estado do plano de desenvolvimento econômico em 30 de junho de 1958. -
v. 3. Estado do plano de desenvolvimento econômico
em 30 de setembro de 1959.

19414 Brazil. Presidente, 1961-   (Goulart)
Mensagem ao Congresso nacional apresentada pelo
presidente João Goulart por ocasião da abertura da
sessão legislativa de 1962. [Rio de Janeiro?]
1962.
47 p.   illus.   27 cm.

19415 Brazil. Presidente, 1961-   (Goulart)
Mensagem ao Congresso Nacional. Brasília [1963]
178 p.   27 cm.

19416 Brazil. Serviço de Economia Rural.
Contribuição ao estudo da estrutura da economia
agrária brasileira; segundo o censo de 1950. Rio de
Janeiro, 1960.
63 p.   22 cm.

19417 Brazil. Serviço de Estatística da Educação e Cultura.
Comentários sobre o ensino primário. Rio de Janeiro,
1961.
131 p.   diagrs., tables.   23 cm.

19418 Brazil. Serviço de Estatística Econômica e Finánceira.
Nomenclatura brasileira de mercadoria. 4. ed.
[Rio de Janeiro?] 1963.
208, 83 p.   25 cm.

19419 Brazil. Serviço de Informação Agrícola.
Agricultura em Brasília. Rio de Janeiro, 1960.
66 p.   illus.   19 cm.   (Série documentária,
no. 9)

19420 Brazil. Servico de Informacão Agricola.
Calendário agricola do Brasil: Estado de Santa
Catarina. Rio de Janeiro, 1960.
75 p.   19 cm.

19421 Brazil. Serviço Nacional de Aprendizagem Industrial.
Departamento Regional de São Paulo.
Obrigatoriedade escolar e trabalho dos menores
de 12 a 14 anos. São Paulo, 1968.

219

32 p.   22 cm.   (Série 1: Estudos e documentos,
v. 2)
Includes legislation.

19422   Brazil. Serviço Nacional de Aprendizagem Industrial.
Departamento Regional de São Paulo.
O SENAI em São Paulo, 1942-1967; ed. comemorativa
do jubileu de prata. São Paulo, 1968.
109 p.   illus.   23 x 29 cm.

19423   Brazil. Serviço Nacional de Aprendizagem Industrial.
Departamento Regional do Espírito Santo.
Cursos e programas. Vitória [1968]
32 p.   illus., diagrs.   30 cm.
Cover title.

19424   Brazil. Serviço Nacional de Recenseamento.
Atlas censitário industrial do Brasil. [Rio de
Janeiro, 1965]
ii, 104 p.   illus., maps (part col., part fold.)
32 x 42 cm.   (Série especial, v. 1)

19425   Brazil. Serviço Nacional de Recenseamento.
Censo agrícola de 1960: Brasil. [Rio de Janeiro,
1967-
v.   27 cm.   (VII recenseamento geral do
Brasil. Série nacional, v. 2)

19426   Brazil. Serviço Nacional de Recenseamento.
Censo demográfico. Resultados preliminares.
Série especial. Volume II. [Rio de Janeiro, 1960]
41 p.   graphs, tables.   23 x 35 cm. (VII
Recenseamento geral do Brasil - 1960)

19427   Brazil. Serviço Nacional de Recenseamento.
Censo demográfico de 1960; favelas do Estado da
Guanabara. [Rio de Janeiro, 1968]
xv, 97 p.   28 cm.   (VII recenseamento geral
do Brasil. Série especial, v. 4)

19428   Brazil. Serviço Nacional de Recenseamento.
Censo dos servidores públicos civis federais,
31 de maio de 1966; resultados preliminares.
[Rio de Janeiro] 1966-
v.   33 cm.

19429   Brazil. Serviço Nacional de Recenseamento.
Censo industrial de 1960: matérias-primas e
produtos. [Rio de Janeiro, 1968]

422 p.   28 cm.   (VII recensamento geral do
Brasil. Série especial, v. 5)

19430 Brazil. Serviço Nacional de Recenseamento.
Censos comércial e dos serviços de 1960:   Brasil.
[Rio de Janeiro, 1967?]
xxviii, 234 p.   27 cm.   (VII recenseamento
geral do Brasil. Série nacional, v. 4)

19431 Brazil. Serviço Nacional de Recenseamento.
Censos comércial e dos serviços de 1960.   Compra
e venda de mercadorias.   [Rio de Janeiro, 1967?]
xii, 212 p.   28 cm.   (VII recenseamento geral
do Brasil. Série especial, v. VI)

19432 Brazil. Serviço Nacional de Recenseamento.
Censos industrial de 1960.   [Rio de Janeiro, n.d.]
xxiv, 127 p.   28 cm.   (VII recenseamento
geral do Brasil. Série nacional, v. III)

19433 Brazil. Superintendência do Desenvolvimento da
Amazônia.
Amazônia; desenvolvimento e ocupação.   Belém,
Departamento Administrativo, Serviço de Documentação
e Divulgação, 1968.
102 p.   illus.   22½ cm.

19434 Brazil. Superintendência do Desenvolvimento da
Amazônia.
... Amazônia, modelo de integração.   The Amazon
region, a model of integration.   [Belém, 1973]
156 p.   illus.   29½ cm.
At head of title: SUDAM - 7; SUDAM year seventh.
Also published in French and Spanish.

19435 Brazil. Superintendencia do Desenvolvimento da
Amazônia. Divisão de Documentação.
Amazônia, modelo de integração.   The Amazon
Region, a model of integration.   [Belém, 1973]
1 v. (unpaged)   col. illus.   28 cm.
Portuguese and English.

19436 Brazil. Superintendência do Desenvolvimento da
Amazônia.
A Amazônia é o novo Brasil.   Amazonia is the new
Brazil. L'Amazonie est le nouveau Brésil.   [Belém,
Superintendência do Desenvolvimento da Amazônia,

221

```
                       1971-    ]
              unpaged.     illus.    29 cm.
```

19437 Brazil. Superintendência do Desenvolvimento da
       Amazônia.
       Amazônia legal. Manual do investidor. Belém,
       Assesoria de Programação e Coordenação, Divisão de
       Documentação, Superintendência do Desenvolvimento
       da Amazônia, 1972.
       77 p.   26 cm.

19438 Brazil. Superintendência do Desenvolvimento da
       Amazônia.
       Amazonie, modèle de integração. Amazônia, modelo
       de integração. [Belém, 1973]
       156 p.   illus.   27½ cm.   (SUDAM, ano 7)
       In Portuguese and French.

19439 Brazil. Superintendência do Desenvolvimento da
       Amazônia.
       ... Documentação amazônica; catálogo coletivo.
       Belém, 1974-76.
       2 v. in 4 pts.   28 cm.   (Documentação amazônica,
       v. 1, nos. 1 and 2)
       At head of title: Rede de Bibliotecas da Amazônia
       REBAM.
       "... repertoriando 630 referências de documentos
       oficiais da região": no. 1, pt. 1, p. 2.
       "O segundo fascículo da 'Documentação amazônica;
       catálogo coletivo' arrola 557 documentos sôbre a
       região, editados pelos orgãos participantes da REBAM.
       As informações contidas no catálogo abrangem dois
       períodos: na primeira parte, são relacionados os
       documentos publicados a partir de 1970, que atualizam
       o primeiro fascículo e na segunda parte, temos o
       levantamento retrospectivo, repertoriando documentos
       de 1965 a 1969": no. 1, pt. 2, p. [3]

19440 Brazil. Superintendência do Desenvolvimento da
       Amazônia.
       Estudos e pesquisas sôbre a castanha-do-Pará.
       Belém, 1976.
       100 p.   illus., tables, diagrs.   28 cm.

19441 Brazil. Superintendência do Desenvolvimento da
       Amazônia.
       ... Guia de ação comunitária para conservação da
       natureza e dos recursos naturais. [Rio de Janeiro?
       1971?]

345 p.   fold. table.   24 cm.
At head of title: Fundação Brasileira para a
conservação da natureza.
Title of original: Community action for environ-
mental quality, 1970. "Tradução autorizada pela
Citizens' Advisory Committee on Environmental
Quality."

19442   Brazil. Superintendência do Desenvolvimento da
Amazônia.
... Instituições, especialistas e pesquisadores
da Amazônia. [Belém, 1976]
282 p.   map.   28 cm.
At head of title: Rede de Bibliotecas da Amazônia -
REBAM. Sistema de Informações para Amazônia - SIAMA.

19443   Brazil. Superintendência do Desenvolvimento da
Amazônia.
Operação Amazônia (discursos). Belém, Pará,
Serviço de Documentação e Divulgação, 1968.
134 p.   24 cm.

19444   Brazil. Superintendência do Desenvolvimento da
Amazônia.
Perspectivas para o desenvolvimento do turismo na
Amazônia. Belém, 1976.
19, [9] p.   tables, diagrs.   28 cm.

19445   Brazil. Superintendência do Desenvolvimento da
Amazônia.
Pesquisa mineral no Iri/Curuá. Relatório
preliminar. Belém, Assessoria de Programação e
Coordenação, Divisão de Documentação, Superintendência
do Desenvolvimento da Amazônia, 1972.
62 p.   illus., fold. maps.   29 cm.

19446   Brazil. Superintendência do Desenvolvimento da
Amazônia.
Pesquisa mineral no Tapajós/Jamanxim. Relatório
preliminar. Belém, Assessoria de Programação e
Coordenação, Divisão de Documentação, Superintendência
do Desenvolvimento da Amazônia, 1972.
172 p.   illus., maps, tables (1 fold.)   28 cm.
- - - - Anexos. 18 fold. maps.

19447   Brazil. Superintendência do Desenvolvimento da
Amazônia.

223

Plano de desenvolvimento da Amazônia. 1972-1974.
[n.p.] 1971.
117 p.   fold. maps, tables.   24 cm.

19448 Brazil. Superintendência do Desenvolvimento da
Amazônia.
1. Plano quinquenal de desenvolvimento. Belém,
SUDAM, Serviço de Documentação e Divulgação, 1967.
380 p.   tables (part fold.)   23 cm.

19449 Brazil. Superintendência do Desenvolvimento da
Amazônia.
Os problemas e desafios da Amazônia brasileira.
[Belém] 1973.
27 p.   28½ cm.

19450 Brazil. Superintendência do Desenvolvimento da
Amazônia.
Relatorio geral, Fevereiro/69 a Agusto/72.
Belém, 1972.
29 p.   tables (part fold.)   26 cm.

19451 Brazil. Superintendência do Desenvolvimento da
Amazônia.
Subsídios ao plano regional de desenvolvimento
(1972/74)   Belém, 1971.
246 p.   fold. maps, tables.   24 cm.

19452 Brazil. Superintendência do Desenvolvimento da
Amazônia.
Zona nordeste da Amazônia legal; numeração e
denominação dos municipios.   [Rio de Janeiro?
197-?]
map.   53 x 75 cm.
Scale: 1:5,000,000.

19453 Brazil. Superintendência do Desenvolvimento do
Maranhão.
Pesquisa agrícola pilôto 1967/8. Região centro,
municipios de: Pedreiras e Dom Pedro. [n.p., 1968?]
108 p.   illus., tables, graphs, maps.
25 x 27½ cm.

19454 Brazil. Superintendência do Desenvolvimento do
Nordeste.
Bases de la politique de developement du Nord-Est
du Brésil et schema du plan quinqinenal de la
SUDENE (Superintendance du Développement du Nord-Est)

224

Recife, SUDENE-Divisão de Documentação, 1963.
28 l.   28 cm.   (Série: Planejamento)

19455   Brazil. Superintendência do Desenvolvimento do Nordeste.
The bases of development policy for the northeast
of Brazil and scheme of SUDENE's five-year plan.
[Recife] 1961.
11 l.   fold. map.   30 cm.
Cover title.

19456   Brazil. Superintendência do Desenvolvimento do Nordeste.
The Brazilian Northeast; SUDENE and its first
guiding plan. Recife, 1962.
30 l.   maps.   32 cm.

19457   Brazil. Superintendência do Desenvolvimento do Nordeste.
Catálogo das publicações editadas pelo DRH/SUDENE
1962-1970. Recife, 1970.
[187] p.   32 cm.

19458   Brazil. Superintendência do Desenvolvimento do Nordeste.
IV [i.e. Quarto] Plano diretor de desenvolvimento
econômico e social do Nordeste, 1969-1973 (anteprojeto)
Recife, 1968-
v.   maps, tables.   32 cm.

19459   Brazil. Superintendência do Desenvolvimento do Nordeste.
Series: Incentives. no. 1-   Recife,
Translations Center, Division of Documentation,
SUDENE [1966-   ]
no.   23 cm.
Issued by the agency under its English name:
Superintendency for the Development of Northeast
Brazil.
In English.

19460   Brazil. Superintendência do Desenvolvimento do Nordeste.
SUDENE; atividades em 1964. Recife, 1965.
37 l.   29 cm.

19461   Brazil. Superintendência do Desenvolvimento do Nordeste.
SUDENE des anos. Recife, 1969.
205 p.   illus., maps.   28 cm.
Summary in English and French.

19462   Brazil. Superintendência do Desenvolvimento do Nordeste.
Departamento de Recursos Humanos.
... Pesquisa sôbre o deficit habitacional na
cidade de Aracati. Fortaleza, Ceará, 1967.

225

39 p.   tables, fold. maps.   30 cm.
At head of title: SUDENE - Departamento de
Recursos Humanos; UFC - Instituto de Pesquisas
Econômicas.

19463 Brazil. Superintendência do Desenvolvimento do Nordeste.
Departamento de Recursos Naturais.
Bibliografia cartográfica do Nordeste. Recife,
Divisão de Documentação, 1965.
209 p.   23 cm.
At head of title: Superintendência do Desenvolvi-
mento do Nordeste, Departamento de Recursos Naturais,
Divisão de Cartografia.

19464 Brazil. Superintendência do Desenvolvimento do Nordeste.
Divisão de Pesquisa e Experimentação Agropecuária.
Experimento de fertilidade em solos de tabuleiros;
resultados dos efeitos de calagem e adubação com a
cultura do feijão mulatinho (Phaseolus vulgaris)
Recife, Divisão de Documentação, 1967.
16 p.   diagrs.   23 cm.   (Brasil. SUDENE.
Agricultura, 7)
Cover title: Experimentos de feijão-mulatinho em
tabuleiros.

19465 Brazil. Superintendência do Desenvolvimento da Região
Sul.
Dados gerais sôbre a pecuária de Santa Catarina.
Asininos e caprinos. [n.p., 196-]
unpaged.   33½ cm.

19466 Brazil. Superintendência do Desenvolvimento da Região
Sul.
Dados gerais sôbre a pecuária de Santa Catarina.
Bovinos. [n.p., 196-]
unpaged.   33½ cm.

19467 Brazil. Superintendência do Desenvolvimento da Região
Sul.
Dados gerais sôbre a pecuária de Santa Catarina.
Eqüinos e muares. [n.p., 196-]
unpaged.   33½ cm.

19468 Brazil. Superintendência do Desenvolvimento da Região
Sul.
Dados gerais sôbre a pecuária de Santa Catarina.
Ovinos. [n.p., 196-]
unpaged.   33½ cm.

19469 Brazil. Superintendência do Desenvolvimento da Região
       Sul.
       Dados gerais sôbre a pecuária de Santa Catarina.
       Suínos. [n.p., 1969?]
       unpaged. tables. 34 cm.

19470 Brazil. Superintendência do Desenvolvimento da Região
       Sul.
       Dados gerais sôbre a pecuária do Rio Grande do Sul.
       [n.p., 196-]
       3 v. 33½ cm.

19471 Brazil. Treaties, etc.
       Apontamentos para o direito internacional, ou
       coleção completa dos tratados celebrados pelo Brasil
       com differentes nações estrangeiras; acompanhada de
       uma noticia historica, e documentada sobre as
       convenções mais importantes por Antonio Pereira
       Pinto... Rio de Janeiro, F. L. Pinto & cª.,
       1864-66.
       3 v. 23 cm.

19472 Brazil 71 - Cultural aspects. Rio de Janeiro,
       Sindicato Nacional de Editores de Libros [1971?]
       [64] p. illus. 22½ cm.

19473 Brene, José R
       El gallo de San Isidro. La Habana, Ediciones
       Revolución, 1964.
       162 p. 20 cm.

19474 Brenes Mesen, Roberto, 1874-1947.
       Roberto Brenes Mesen. Presentado por María Eugenia
       Dengo de Vargas. San José, Costa Rica, Ministerio
       de Cultura, Juventud y Deportes, Departamento de
       Publicaciones, 1974.
       437 p. illus., facsim. 19½ cm. (Serie
       ¿Quién fué y qué hizo? no. 21)

19475 Brenes Quesada, Luís Guillermo.
       Cambios en el uso del suelo: Cuenca del río
       San Carlos en la zona de Providencia, por Luís G.
       Brenes Q. San José, Costa Rica, 1977.
       19-23 p. map. 25 cm.
       Reprinted from Costa Rica. Instituto Geográfico
       Nacional. Informe semestral, Jul.-Dec. 1976.

19476 Brenes Quesada, Luís Guillermo.
       Deterioro de los bosques y suelos en Costa Rica,

por Luís Guillermo Brenes Quesada. [San José,
Costa Rica, Instituto Geográfico Nacional, 1977]
18-35 p.   illus.   26 cm.
Reprinted from Costa Rica. Instituto Geográfico
Nacional. Informe semestral. Enero a junio 1977.

19477 Brennand, Deborah.
       0 cadeado negro... Recife, Universidade Federal
       de Pernambuco, 1971.
       66 p.   24½ cm.
       "Separata da Revista Estudos Universitários,
       v. 11, no. 1, Jan.-Mar. 1971."

19478 Bresolin, Antônio.
       Depoimento prestado na Comissão Parlamentar de
       Inquérito que investiga as atividades do IBRA e do
       INDA. Brasília, Câmara dos Deputados, 1968.
       15 p.   23 cm.

19479 Brewer, Forrest.
       Vocabulario mexicano de Tetelcingo, Morelos;
       castellano-mexicano, mexicano-castellano. Compilado
       por Forrest Brewer y Jean G. Brewer. [1. ed.]
       México, Instituto Lingüístico de Verano, 1962.
       vii, 274 p.   illus.   21 cm.   (Serie de voca-
       bularios indígenas Mariano Silva y Aceves, no. 8)

19480 Brewer Carías, Allan-Randolph.
       Las instituciones fundamentales del derecho
       administrativo y la jurisprudencia venezolana.
       Caracas, Facultad de Derecho, Universidad Central
       de Venezuela, 1964.
       494 p.   24 cm.   (Colección Tesis de doctorado,
       v. 4)
       Tesis - Universidad Central, Caracas.
       Bibliography: p. [465]-468.

19481 Brewer Carías, Allan-Randolph.
       Los problemas constitucionales de la integración
       económica latinoamericana. Caracas, Banco Central
       de Venezuela, 1968.
       131 p.   19 cm.
       Bibliographical footnotes.

19482 Brezieres, Maurice.
       Floreana, Paraiso infernal; un rincón de las
       Islas Encantadas. [Guayaquil, Empresa Publicitaria
       Amazonas] 1965.
       140 p.   illus., map, ports.   22 cm.

228

19483 Brice, Angel Francisco.
La sublevación de Maracaibo en 1799, manifestación de su lucha por la independencia; discurso de incorporación como individuo de número [de] Academia Nacional de la Historia; contestación del... Carlos Felice Cardot, Caracas, 4 de agosto de 1960. Caracas, Italgrafía S.A., 1960.
44 p.   25 cm.

19484 Briceño Perozo, Mario.
Archivos venezolanos.   Caracas, Italgráfica [1970]
12 p.   27 cm.

19485 Briceño Perozo, Mario.
Documentos para la historia de la fundación de Caracas existentes en el Archivo general de la nación.   Caracas, Archivo general de la nación, 1969.
761 p.   illus.   24 cm.   (Biblioteca venezolana de historia, VII)

19486 Briceño Perozo, Mario.
General en jefe Carlos Soublette.   Caracas, Italgráfica [1970]
14 p.   port.   27 cm.

19487 Briceño Perozo, Mario.
Historia bolivariana.   Caracas, Departamento de Publicaciones, Ministerio de Educación, 1970.
214 p.   illus.   24 cm.   (Colección Vigilia, 26)

19488 Briceño Perozo, Mario.
El verbo adherir.   Caracas, 1970.
7 p.   23 cm.

19489 Briceño-Picon, Mario, 1928-
Cartilla patriótica.   La infamia del Esequibo. Caracas, Ediciones Independencia, 1966.
79 p.   illus., maps.   24 cm.

19490 Briggs, Elinor.
Mitla Zapotec grammar.   [1. ed.] México, Instituto Lingüístico de Verano, 1961.
110 p.   24 cm.

19491 Briones, Guillermo.
El obrero industrial: aspectos sociales del desarrollo económico en el Perú [por] Guillermo

Briones y José Mejía Valera. [Lima] Instituto de
Investigaciones Sociológicas, Universidad Nacional
Mayor de San Marcos de Lima, 1964.
xiv, 109 p.   21 cm.

19492 Briscoe, C   B
Weather in the Luquillo Mountains of Puerto Rico.
Río Piedras, P. R., Institute of Tropical Forestry,
Forest Service, U. S. Dept. of Agriculture, 1966.
250 p.   19 cm.   (Forest Service, research
paper, ITF 3)

19493 Briseño Hermosillo, Rodolfo.
Impuestos sobre ventas; el impuesto federal sobre
ingresos mercantiles. México, 1963.
243, [5] p.   24 cm.
Tesis (licenciatura en derecho) - Universidad
Nacional Autónoma de México.
Bibliography: p. [245]-[248]

19494 British Honduras. Department of Agriculture.
Annual report... 1964. Belize City, 1964.
1 v.   tables, part fold.   32 cm.

19495 British Museum. Department of Oriental Antiquities
and Ethnography.
Guide to the Maudslay collection of Maya sculptures
(casts and originals) from Central America. [London]
1923.
95 p.   illus., maps.   23 cm.

19496 Brito, Ignacio Machado.
... Contribuição a paleontologia do Estado do
Pará. Sôbre um balanomorfo da formação Pirabas
(crustacea - Cirripodia) Belém, 1972.
3 p., 1 pl.   24½ cm.
At head of title: Boletím de Museu Paraense,
Emilio Goeldi, Nova série, Geología, no. 18,
24 abril 1972.

19497 Brito, Otario T
Aprenda analise... Rio de Janeiro e São Paulo,
Livraria Freitas Bastos S.A., 1965.
122 p.   18 cm.

19498 Brito Broca.
Letras francesas. Edicion organizada e prefaciada
por Francisco de Assis Barbosa. São Paulo, Conselho
Estadual de Cultura, 1969.

276 p.   24½ cm.   (Comissão Estadual de
Literatura. Coleção textos e documentos, 11)

19499   Brito Figueroa, Federico.
        La estructura económica de Venezuela colonial.
        Caracas, Instituto de Investigaciones, Facultad de
        Economía, Universidad Central de Venezuela, 1963.
        426 p.   illus., maps.   24 cm.
        Tesis - Universidad Central de Venezuela.
        Bibliography: p. 407-[421]

19500   Britto, Jomard Muniz de, 1937-
        Contradições do homen brasileiro [Rio de Janeiro]
        Tempo Brasileiro, 1964.
        103 p.   21 cm.   (Coleção Brasil hoje, 5)

19501   Britto, Rubens da Silva.
        ... A febre amarela no Pará [por] Rubens da
        Silveira Britto [e] Eleyson Cardoso. Belém,
        Assessoria de Programação e Coordenação, Divisão de
        Documentação, 1973.
        241 p.   illus., tables (2 fold.), facsims.
        23 cm.
        At head of title: Ministério do Interior. Superin-
        tendência do Desenvolvimento da Amazônia.

19502   Britto García, Luis.
        El presupuesto del Estado. Caracas, Publicación
        de la Contraloría General de la República de Venezuela,
        1968.
        609 p.   24½ cm.

19503   Broadbent, Sylvia M
        Los chibchas; organización socio-política [por]
        Sylvia M. Broadbent. [Bogotá] Facultad de Sociología,
        Universidad Nacional de Colombia, 1964.
        131 p.   20 cm.   (Serie latinoamericana, no. 5)
        "Extractos de documentos" p. 41-127.
        Bibliography: p. 129-131.

19504   Brodbeck, Sully.
        Problemática da bibliografía sul-rio-grandense.
        Pôrto Alegre, Departamento de Educação e Cultura,
        1968.
        9 l.   33 cm.
        At head of title: Universidade Federal do Rio
        Grande do Sul. Departamento de Educação e Cultura
        & Associação Rio-Grandense de Bibliotecários.
        "I Jornada Sul Riograndense de Biblioteconomia

e Documentação... Tema 3.1: Bibliotecas públicas
estaduais e municipais."

19505 Broide, Julio.
Banco Interamericano de Desarrollo; sus antecedentes
y creación. Washington [1961]
160 p.   23 cm.   (Publicaciones del Banco
Interamericano de Desarrollo)

19506 Brosch, Carlos Dias, 1920-
Aprovietamento dos finos de carvão vegetal [por]
Carlos Dias Brosch [e] José Kaoro Furuno. São Paulo,
Instituto de Pesquisas Tecnológicas, 1968.
369-371 p., diagrs., tables.   27 cm.   (Instituto
de Pesquisas Tecnológicas. Publicação no. 854)
Cover title.

19507 Brosch, Carlos Dias, 1920-
Caracterização de alguns minérios de ferro brasi-
leiros pelo ensaio de redutibilidade [por] Carlos
Dias Brosch [e] Henrique P. Rizzo. São Paulo,
Instituto de Pesquisas Tecnológicas, 1967.
687-692 p.   illus., tables.   27 cm.   (Instituto
de Pesquisas Tecnológicas. Publicação no. 838)
"Contribuição técnica no. 703, apresentada ao XXII
Congresso da ABM; Vitória, ES, julho de 1967."
Bibliography: p. 692.

19508 Brosch, Carlos Dias, 1920-
Pelotização de minério de manganês [por] Carlos
Dias Brosch, Roberto Pimentel de Souza, José Kaoro
Furuna. São Paulo, Instituto de Pesquisas Tecnoló-
gicas, 1967.
695-697 p.   diagrs.   27 cm.   (Instituto de
Pesquisas Tecnológicas. Publicação no. 843)
"Contribuição técnica no. 704, apresentada ao XXII
Congresso da ABM; Vitória, ES, julho de 1967."
Bibliography: p. 697.

19509 Brosch, Carlos Dias, 1920-
Possibilidades da utilização de carga pré-reduzida
nos altos-fornos para o caso brasileiro [por] Carlos
Dias Brosch [e] Henrique P. Rizzo. São Paulo,
Instituto de Pesquisas Tecnológicas, 1968.
81-91 p.   illus., tables.   27 cm.   (Instituto
de Pesquisas Tecnológicas. Publicação no. 847)
Bibliography: p. 91.
"Trabalho apresentado ao Simpósio de Redução,

232

realizado pela Comissão Técnica de Redução de Minérios
de Ferro da ABM; Ipatinga, MG, dezembro de 1966."

19510 Brovedani, Bruno.
Bases analíticas de la política monetaria. México,
Centro de Estudios Monetarios Latinoamericanos, 1961.
144 p.   graphs, tables.   21 cm.

19511 Brown, Lyle C
Latin America, a bibliography. Kingsville,
Texas College of Arts and Industries, 1962.
80 ℓ.   29 cm.

19512 Brown, Robert T
... Una política de transportes para Chile, por
Robert T. Brown y Carlos Hurtado R. T. Santiago,
1963.
xii, 99 p.   illus.   27 cm.   (Publicaciones
del I. de E., no. 59)
At head of title: Instituto de Economía. Universidad de Chile.
Bibliographical footnotes.

19513 Brown, William Lacy, 1913-
Races of maize in the West Indies. Washington,
National Academy of Sciences, National Research
Council, 1960.
vi, 60 p.   illus., map.   24 cm.   (National
Research Council. Publicacion 792)
Bibliography: p. 43-44.

19514 Brown University. John Carter Brown Library.
A collection's progress; two retrospective
exhibitions by the John Carter Brown Library, Brown
University. I. Illustrating the growth of the
Library in terms of those who have been responsible
for it. The Grolier Club, New York City, April 16
to June 1, 1968. II. A selection from the additions
made by the Associates since 1944 shown on the
occasion of their twenty-fifth Annual Meeting.
The Library, Providence, Rhode Island, April 5 to
September 1, 1968. Providence, R. I., The Associates
of the John Carter Brown Library, 1968.
79 p.   illus.   26 cm.

19515 Brown University. John Carter Brown Library.
Opportunities for research in the John Carter Brown
library. Providence, R. I., Brown University, 1968.

88 p.   facsims.   20½ cm.
Bibliography of writings about the Library:
p. 73-74.

19516 Browning, Clyde E
A bibliography of dissertations in geography,
1901 to 1969; American and Canadian universities.
Chapel Hill, Department of Geography, University of
North Carolina, 1970.
ix, 96 p.   24 cm.   (Studies in geography, 1)

19517 Browning, Harley L
Selectivity of migrants to a metropolis in a
developing country: a Mexican case study [by] Harley
L. Browning and Waltraut Feindt. [Austin, Institute
of Latin American Studies, University of Texas, 1969]
347-357 p.   tables.   24 cm.   (Offprint
series, 97)
Reprinted from Demography, vol. 6, no. 4, November,
1969."

19518 Browning, John.
La formación de un revolucionario: los años
juveniles de Antonio José de Irisarri. [Santiago de
Chile, 1971]
34-49 p.   24½ cm.
Reprinted from Revista chilena de historia y
geografía, no. 139, 1971.

19519 Brubacher, John S
A importância da teoria em educação. Tradução
de Beatriz Osorio. Rio de Janeiro, Centro Brasileiro
de Pesquisas Educacionais, Ministério da Educação
e Cultura, 1961.
210 p.   20 cm.   (Cursos e conferências,
ser. VII, vol. 3)

19520 Brughetti, Romualdo.
Alfredo Bigatti. [Buenos Aires] Ediciones Culturales
Argentinas, Ministerio de Educación y Justicia,
Dirección General do Cultura [1962]
35 p.   illus.   25 cm.   (Biblioteca del ses-
quicentenario. Argentinos en las artes)

19521 Bruni Celli, Blas.
Los secuestros en la guerra de independencia,
trabajo de incorporación del Dr. Blas Bruni Celli
como individuo de número de la Academia Nacional de
la Historia; discurso de contestación del individuo

234

de número Carlos Felice Cordol.   Caracas [Imp.
Nacional] 1965.
    197 p.   24 cm.
At head of title: Academia Nacional de la Historia.
"Apendice" (p. 107-183) contains documents.
Includes bibliographies.

19522   Buck, Wilbur Francis.
Agriculture and trade of the Caribbean region:
Bermuda, the Bahamas, the Guianas, and British
Honduras.   Washington, Economic Research Service,
U. S. Department of Agriculture, 1971.
    202 p.   tables.   27 cm.   (ERS-foreign, 309)

19523   Buck, Wilbur Francis.
Agriculture and trade of the Dominican Republic.
Washington, Economic Research Service, U. S. Depart-
ment of Agriculture, 1972.
    iv, 41 p.   illus., maps.   27½ cm.   (ERS-
foreign, 330)
"Supersedes and updates ERS-foreign 51. The
Dominican Republic - agriculture and trade,
published in August 1963."

19524   Buckle, D
Child guidance centers [by] D. Buckle [and]
S. Lebovici.   Geneva, World Health Organization,
1960.
    133 p.   24 cm.   (World Health Organization.
Monograph Series, no. 40)
Bibliography: p. 126-127.

19525   Buechner, Helmut K
The avifauna of northern Latin America. A symposium
held at the Smithsonian Institution, 13-15 April 1966.
Washington, Smithsonian Institution Press, 1970.
    119 p.   27½ cm.
At head of title: Smithsonian contributions to
zoology, number 26.   Helmut K. Buechner and Jimmie
H. Buechner, editors.

19526   Buenas Van Severn, J   Ricardo.
La invasión filibustera de Nicaragua y la guerra
nacional.   [2nd ed.] San Salvador, El Salvador,
Ministerio de Educación, Dirección General de
Publicaciones [1962]
    146 p.   24 cm.   (Colección Historia, v. 8)

19527   Buenaventura de Carrocera, Father.
        Misión de los capuchinos en Cumaná. Caracas,
        Academia Nacional de la Historia, 1968.
        3 v.   23 cm.   (Biblioteca de la Academia
        Nacional de la Historia, 88-90)
        Contents. - t. 1. Su historia. - t. 2. Documentos
        (1650-1730). - t. 3. Documentos (1735-1817)

19528   Bueno, Antônio Sylvio Cunha.
        Urgência para conclusão da Brasília-Acre; fronteira
        do Peru e outras rodovias [por] Cunha Bueno.
        Brasília, Câmara dos Deputados, 1967.
        9 p.   23 cm.
        "Discurso proferido na sessão de 20 de maio de 1967."

19529   Bueno, Francisco de Assis Vieira, 1816-1908.
        A cidade de São Paulo; recordações evocadas de
        memória; noticias históricas [por] Francisco de Assis
        Vieira Bueno. Explicação de Sergio Buarque de
        Holanda. [São Paulo] Academia Paulista de Letras,
        1976.
        60 p.   22 cm.   (Academia Paulista de Letras,
        Biblioteca, vol. 2)

19530   Bueno, Francisco da Silveira, 1898-   comp.
        Antologia arcaica; trechos, em prosa e verso,
        coligidos em obras do século VIII ao século XVI.
        2. ed. São Paulo, Ed. Saraiva, 1968.
        xiv, 215 p.   21 cm.
        Includes bibliographies.

19531   Bueno, Miguel.
        Principios de ética; teoría y práctica de la
        moralidad según las posturas éticas y filosóficas,
        integración del sistema normativo desde la univer-
        salidad axiológica hasta la singularidad casuística.
        México, Editorial Patria, 1961.
        276 p.   20 cm.   ([Obras] 10. Colección
        Principios, 6)

19532   Bueno, Salvador.
        Figuras cubanas; breves biografías de grandes
        cubanos del siglo XIX. La Habana, Comisión Nacional
        Cubana de la Unesco, 1964.
        390 p.   20½ cm.

19533   Bueno, Salvador.
        Historia de la literatura cubana. [La Habana]

Editora del Ministerio de Educación [1963]
464 p.   illus.   23½ cm.

19534   Buenos Aires. Biblioteca Lincoln.
La biblioteca pública. [Buenos Aires, 1968]
16 p.   28 cm.

19535   Buenos Aires. Biblioteca Lincoln.
... Futuras posibilidades de los servicios de
referencia en bibliotecas universitarias...
Buenos Aires, 1968.
10 p.   26 cm.
At head of title: Contribución de la Biblioteca
Lincoln al punto A del temario de la 6a. reunión
nacional de bibliotecarios, Bahía Blanca, 10-13
septiembre 1968.

19536   Buenos Aires. Bolsa de Comercio.
Contratos; compra-venta y locación de obras y
servicios. [Buenos Aires] 1970.
9 p.   23 cm.

19537   Buenos Aires. Universidad Católica Argentina "Santa
María de los Buenos Aires". Instituto de Cultura y
Extensión Universitaria.
Hacia la nueva universidad. Colaboradores: Derisi,
et al. Buenos Aires, Ediciones "Hombre-Vida", 1966.
153 p.   18 cm.   (Instituto de Cultura y
Extensión Universitaria de la Pontificia Universidad
Católica "Santa María de los Buenos Aires". Temas
Universitarios, 1)

19538   Buenos Aires. Universidad Nacional. Departamento de
Orientación Vocacional.
Actas de las Primeras Jornadas Argentinas de
orientación vocacional, Octubre 27-28-29-30, 1965.
[Buenos Aires? 1965?]
429 p.   29 cm.

19539   Buenos Aires. Universidad Nacional. Facultad de
Arquitectura y Urbanismo. Biblioteca.
Normas para la catalogación de diapositivas.
[Buenos Aires] 1967.
15 p.   illus.   23 cm.

19540   Buenos Aires. Universidad Nacional. Instituto
Bibliotecológico.
Catálogo de la biblioteca; obras. [Buenos Aires,

1964]
146 p.   26 cm.

19541   Buenos Aires. Universidad Nacional. Instituto Biblio-
        tecológico.
        Catálogo de la biblioteca; publicaciones periódicas.
        [Buenos Aires, 1967]
        xiii, 48 p.   26 cm.   (Publicación no. 24)

19542   Buenos Aires. Universidad Nacional. Instituto Biblio-
        tecológico.
        Guía de escuelas y cursos de bibliotecología y
        documentación en América Latina. Primera parte:
        Argentina. Buenos Aires, 1972.
        34 p.   31 cm.

19543   Buenos Aires. Universidad Nacional. Instituto Biblio-
        tecológico.
        Guía de las bibliotecas de la Universidad de Buenos
        Aires [Buenos Aires, Impr. de la Universidad, 1966]
        64 p.   22 cm.

19544   Buenos Aires. Universidad Nacional. Instituto Biblio-
        tecológico.
        Tesis presentadas a la Universidad de Buenos Aires,
        1963-64. Buenos Aires, 1968.
        67 p.   29 cm.

19545   Buenos Aires. Universidad Nacional. Instituto Biblio-
        tecológico.
        Tesis presentadas a la Universidad de Buenos Aires,
        1967-1968. Buenos Aires, 1972.
        63 p.   30 cm.

19546   Buenos Aires. Universidad Nacional. Servicio Univer-
        sitario de Salud. Departamento de Estadística.
        Informe anual. [Buenos Aires]
        v.   33 cm.
        Library has 1967.

19547   Buenos Aires (Province) Constitution.
        Constitución de la Provincia de Buenos Aires.
        Sancionada en el año 1934. Antecedentes, referencias
        generales y texto vigente anotado por José Abel
        Verzura... Buenos Aires, Ediciones Depalma, 1964.
        90 p.   illus.   17 cm.

19548   Buenos Aires (Province) Dirección de Cultura.
        1ª [i.e. Primera] muestra del libro bonaerense;

238

catálogo provisorio. La Plata, 1965.
25 p.   23 cm.

19549   Buenos Aires (Province) Dirección de Vialidad.
XIV concurso de trabajos sobre temas viales.
La Plata, 1972.
237 p.   tables (part fold.), diagrs.   28 cm.
(Publicación, 99)

19550   Buenos Aires (Province) Dirección de Vialidad.
La computadora en apoyo técnico. Diseño y computo
del camino. Plan de sistematización... La Plata,
1969.
40 p.   graphs, fold. tables.   (Publicación
no. 90)

19551   Buenos Aires (Province) Dirección de Vialidad.
Dia del camino, 5 de octubre 1960. [La Plata, 1961]
231 p.   illus., maps.   31 cm.

19552   Buenos Aires (Province) Dirección de Vialidad.
Biblioteca Técnica.
Catálogo de la Biblioteca Técnica. La Plata,
División Publicaciones y Biblioteca, 1963.
350 p.   27 cm.   (Publicación, no. 37)

19553   Buenos Aires (Province) Instituto Bibliográfico.
Índice analítico de la revista Archivos de
pedagogía y ciencias afines, 1906-1914 [y] Archivos
de ciencias de la educación, 1914-1919. La Plata
[1961]
99 p.   23 cm.

19554   Buenos Aires (Province) Laws, statutes, etc.
Normas legales vigentes. 1970. [La Plata?]
Asesoría general de gobierno [1971]
623 p.   22½ cm.

19555   Buenos Aires (Province) Laws, statutes, etc.
Normas legales vigentes. La Plata, 1974.
863 p.   22½ cm.
"Segunda edición."
At head of title: Provincia de Buenos Aires.
Asesoría General de Gobierno.

19556   Bufill, José Angel.
Manuel Guillot Castellano ¡presente! Bosquejo
biográfico de un héroe, de un mártir. [n.p.,
Movimiento de Recuperación Revolucionaria, Secretaría

239

de Información, 1964]
55 p.   illus.   18 cm.

19557   Buford, Nick.
The University of San Marcos of Lima in the
eighteenth century. Baton Rouge, La., Latin American
Studies Institute, Louisiana State University, 1969.
44 p.   29½ cm.   (Working paper no. 1, series 2)

19558   Buggenhagen, Erich Arnold von.
Pensamento filosófico brasileiro na atualidade;
respostas às perguntas apresentadas por Stanislavs
Ladusãns. São Paulo, 1968.
74 p.   24 cm.   (Faculdade de Filosofia, Ciências
e Letras de São Jose do Rio Prêto, Estado de São
Paulo. Publicação, no. 5)

19559   Buguelsky, Yuri Y
... Geoquímica e hidrogeoquímica de la corteza de
intemperismo ferroniquelifera de Cuba, por Y. Y.
Buguelsky y Francisco Formell Cortina. La Habana,
Academia de Ciencias de Cuba, Instituto de Geología,
1967.
[43] p.   tables.   27 cm.   (Serie geológica,
no. 3)

19560   Buguelsky, Yuri Y
La hidrogeoquímica y cuestiones de la génesis de
las cortezas de intemperismo niquelíferas de Cuba.
Por Y. Y. Buguelsky y F. Formell Cortina. La Habana,
Academia de Ciencias de Cuba, Instituto de Geología,
1973.
18 p.   tables.   28 cm.   (Serie geológica,
no. 12)

19561   Buguelsky, Yuri Y
Influencia del factor hidrogeoquímico en la
formación y distribución de las cortezas de intemperismo de Cuba. Por Yuri Y. Buguelsky y Francisco
Formell Cortina. La Habana, Academia de Ciencias
de Cuba, Instituto de Geología, 1973.
15 p.   map, diagrs., fold. table.   28½ cm.
(Serie geológica, no. 13)

19562   Buhler Lorca, Gustavo.
El factor demográfico en el desarrollo económico.
Santiago, Editorial Universitaria, 1962.
93 p.   19 cm.

240

19563   Buide, Mario S
        Reptiles de la península Hicacos.   La Habana,
        Instituto de Biología, Academia de Ciencias de
        Cuba, 1966.
        12 p.   26 cm.   (Poeyana, no. 21)
        Résumé in English.

19564   Bulhões, Octavio Couvea de.
        Función de los precios en el desarrollo [conferencias.
        1 ed.] México, Centro de Estudios Monetarios Latino-
        americanos, 1961.
        91 p.   22 cm.

19565   Bullaude, José.
        Enseñanza audiovisual y comunicación; teoría y
        crítica [por] José Bullaude con la colaboración de
        Lidia P. de Bosch y Lilia F. de Menegazzo.   Buenos
        Aires, Librería del Colegio [1968]
        182 p.   illus., facsim.   18 cm.
        Includes bibliographies.

19566   Bullrich, Silvina.
        Los monstruos sagrados.   Buenos Aires, Editorial
        Sudamericana [1971]
        211 p.   19 cm.

19567   Bulnes Cerda, Arturo.
        El seguro de crédito de exportación.   [Santiago]
        Editorial Jurídica de Chile, 1968.
        115 p.   23 cm.   (Universidad Católica de Chile.
        Facultad de Ciencias Jurídicas Políticas y Sociales.
        Memoria no. 22)
        Bibliography: p. 109.

19568   Bunse, Heinrich A
        Estudos de dialetologia no Rio Grande do Sul;
        problemas, métodos, resultados.   Colaboração de
        Mário S. Klassmann.   Pôrto Alegre, Comissão de
        Publicações, Faculdade de Filosofia, Universidade
        Federal do Rio Grande do Sul, 1969.
        47 p.   maps.   21 cm.

19569   Burbano, José Ignacio, ed.
        Poetas románticos y neoclásicos.   Estudio preli-
        minar de José Ignacio Burbano.   Selecciones.   Puebla,
        México, J. M. Cajica, Jr., 1960.
        640 p.   22 cm.   (Biblioteca ecuatoriana
        mínima.   La colonia y la república)

19570   Burcoa, Pedro Anibal.
        ... Determinación de los ácido orgánicos fijos
        del vino por cromatografía sobre papel. Por Dr.
        Pedro Anibal Burcoa, Ing. Agr. Srta. Sara M. Salva-
        tierra, Farm. Sra. Juana Navarro de Patiño.
        [Mendoza? n.d.]
        20 p.   tables.   26½ cm.

19571   Burgos, Juan Jacinto.
        Las heladas en la Argentina [por] Juan J. Burgos.
        Buenos Aires [Secretaría de Estado de Agricultura
        y Ganadería de la Nación, Instituto Nacional de
        Tecnología Agropecuaria] 1963.
        xxiv, 388 p.   illus., maps.   23 cm.   (Colección
        científica, v. 3)
        Bibliography: p. [347]-364.

19572   Burguess, Paul.
        ... Justo Rufino Barrios: una biografía. Traducción
        del inglés, documentación y nota preliminar:
        Francis Gall. [Guatemala] 1971.
        285 p.   port., facsims.   24 cm.
        At head of title: Comité pro festejos del centenario
        de la revolución de 1871. Publicación especial no. 17
        de la Sociedad de geografía e historia de Guatemala.

19573   Burk, Ignacio.
        Breve historia de la psicología; de los orígenes
        a Wundt. Caracas, Departamento de Pedagogía, Instituto
        Pedagógico, 1966.
        165 p.   23 cm.   (Ediciones Gaceta de Pedagogía, 1

19574   Burke, Joseph Henry, 1908-
        The citrus industry of Mexico. Washington, U.S.
        Department of Agriculture, Foreign Agricultural
        Service, 1962.
        68 p.   map, illus.   24½ cm.   (FAR, 121)

19575   Burke, Joseph Henry, 1908-
        The olive industry of Mexico. Rev. Washington,
        Department of Agriculture, Foreign Agricultural
        Service, 1961.
        iv, 23 p.   illus., map.   23 cm.   ([U.S.
        Foreign Agricultural Service] Report no. 85)
        "Supersedes an earlier study published in 1955...
        under title, Olive industry in Lower California,
        Mexico."

19576 Burke, Melvin.
Land reform in the Lake Titicaca region. Madison,
Land Tenure Center, University of Wisconsin, 1974.
301-339 p.   tables, graphs.   23 cm.   (LTC
reprint no. 110)
Reprinted from Beyond the revolution: Bolivia
since 1952. James M. Malloy and Richard S. Thorn,
editors.

19577 Burke, William.
Derechos de la América del Sur y México. Estudio
preliminar de Augusto Mijares. Caracas, Academia
Nacional de la Historia, 1959.
2 v.   23 cm.   (Biblioteca de la Academia
Nacional de la Historia, 10, 11)

19578 Burks, David D
Survey of the Alliance for Progress; insurgency
in Latin America. A study prepared at the request
of the Sub-committee on American Republics Affairs
of the Committee on Foreign Relations, United States
Senate. Washington, U.S. Government Printing Office,
1968.
29 p.   20 cm.

19579 Burnham, L   Forbes S
Breakthrough. Address by Prime Minister Forbes
Burnham, leader of the People's National Congress,
at the 16th annual delegates' congress, 6th May,
1973. [Georgetown, Guyana?] 1973.
36 p.   illus.   23½ cm.

19580 Burnham, L   Forbes S
Four talks to the nation. 1973 election radio
addresses to the nation by the Honourable L. F. S.
Burnham, O.E., S.C., prime minister, Guyana, South
America. Georgetown, Guyana, 1973.
31 p.   illus.   23 cm.

19581 Burnham, L   Forbes S
The survival of our nation, address to the nation
by Hon. L. F. S. Burnham, O.E., S.C., prime minister
of Guyana, on the occasion of the celebration of
the fourth anniversary of the Co-operative Republic
of Guyana, February 23, 1974, at the National Park,
Georgetown. [Georgetown, Guyana, 1974]
8 p.   illus.   22 cm.

19582 Burnham, L   Forbes S
       The year of break through. Address to the Nation
       by Prime Minister, L. F. S. Burnham, S.C., on the
       occasion of the third anniversary of the cooperative
       republic of Guyana, February 23, 1973, National Park.
       [Georgetown? Guyana] 1973.
       16 p.   illus.   20 cm.

19583 Bursztyn Dobry, Rosa.
       Estudio comparativo de las legislaciones de seguridad
       social de Chile y Perú. Santiago, Editorial Univer-
       sitaria, 1962.
       114 p.   20 cm.

19584 Burzaco, Raúl Horacio.
       Andrea; o, El amor, tragicomedia en 4 movimientos.
       Milena, monodrama. [Buenos Aires, Cuadernos del
       Siroco, 1963]
       62 p.   20 cm.   (Colección Arlequín; teatro, 6)

19585 Burzio, Humberto F
       Historia del torpedo y sus buques en la Armada
       Argentina, 1874-1900. Buenos Aires, Departamento
       de Estudios Históricos Navales, 1968.
       580 p.   illus.   26 cm.   (Serie B: Historia
       naval argentina, 12)

19586 Busaniche, José Luis, 1892-
       San Martín vivo. [Buenos Aires] Editorial Univer-
       sitaria de Buenos Aires [1964, c1963]
       197 p.   18 cm.   (Serie del siglo y medio, 57)

19587 Buse, Hermann.
       Perú, 10,000 años. Lima, 1962.
       273 p.   illus.   25 cm.   (Colección Nueva
       crónica)

19588 Bushnell, G   H   S
       L'art de l'Amérique precolombienne... Paris,
       Librairie Larousse [1966]
       288 p.   illus., maps.   22 cm.

19589 Bustamente, Carlos María de, 1774-1848.
       Tres estudios sobre don José María Morelos y Pavón.
       Edición facsimilar. México, 1963.
       125 p. (incl. facsims.: 32, 8, 40 p. 2 ports.
       1 col.)   24 cm.   (Biblioteca Nacional de México.
       Instituto Bibliográfico Mexicano. Publicaciones, 9)
       Contents. - Nota preliminar, por M. Alcala. -

Ed. Lic. don Carlos María de Bustamente y don José
María Morelos y Pavón, por A. Martínez Baez. -
Reseña bibliográfica, por J. I. Mantecón (p. 31-32) -
Elogio histórico del general don José María Morelos
y Pavón. - El Centzontli, núm.

19590 Bustamante Arellana, Carlos.
Entre luz y sombra; prosa de meditación y poesía.
San José, Costa Rica, 1962.
62 p.   16 cm.

19591 Bustamante Muñoz, A
Lista de los instrumentos internacionales con-
cluidos por el Ecuador. Quito, Editorial Casa de
la Cultura Ecuatoriana, 1960.
319 p.   21 cm.

19592 Bustos, Miguel Ángel.
El Himalaya o la moral de los pájaros. Tapa e
ilustraciones del autor. Buenos Aires, Editorial
Sudamericana [1970]
123 p.   19½ cm.

19593 Bustos Cerecedo, Miguel, 1912-
Memoria de tus pasos; poema. [1. ed.] México,
Metáfora, 1961.
57 p.   illus.   23 cm.

19594 Buteler, Patricio.
El régimen jurídico de los capitales extranjeros.
Córdoba, República Argentina, Universidad Nacional
de Córdoba, Dirección General de Publicaciones,
1964.
321-404 p.   24 cm.
"Del Boletín de la Facultad de Derecho y Ciencias
Sociales, año XXVII, no. 4-5, 1963."
Bibliography: p. 401-402.

19595 Butler, Charles Henry, 1859-1940.
The voice of the nation; the President is right;
a series of papers on our past and present relations
with Spain, by Charles Henry Butler... New York,
G. Munro's sons [1898]
2 p.l., [vii]-x, 11-124 p.   18½ cm.   (On cover:
"Cuba must be free series," no. 1)

19596 Butler, John Wesley, 1851-1918.
Sketches of Mexico. Cincinnati, Cranston & Curts

[c1894]
x, 316 p.   front.   19 cm.

19597   Butler, Joseph H
         Manufacturing in the Concepción Region of Chile:
         present position and prospects for future development.
         Washington, National Academy of Sciences, National
         Research Council, 1960.
         ix, 106 p.   maps, diagrs., tables.   28 cm.
         (Foreign field research program, report no. 7)
         Errata leaf inserted.
         Thesis - Colombia University.
         Bibliography: p. 99-103.

19598   Butt, Louise E
         Labor in Chile. Washington, Bureau of Labor
         Statistics in cooperation with the Agency for
         International Development, U.S. Department of Labor,
         1962.
         iv, 50 p.   map.   22 cm.   (BLS report, 224)

19599   Butterlin, Jacques.
         Microfauna del Eoceno inferior de la península
         de Yucatán, por Jacques Butterlin y Federico Bonet.
         México, Instituto de Geología, 1960.
         18 p.   illus., map, tables.   24 cm.   (Univer-
         sidad Nacional Autónoma de México. Instituto de
         Geología. Paleontología mexicana, no. 7)
         Bibliography: p. [17]

19600   Buxó, José Pascual.
         Góngora en la poesía novohispana. México, Imprenta
         Universitaria, 1960.
         114 p.   22 cm.   (Publicaciones del Centro de
         Estudios Literarios, 7)

19601   Buxó, José Pascual.
         Ungaretti, traductor de Góngora (un estudio de
         literatura comparada) Maracaibo, Facultad de
         Humanidades y Educación, Universidad del Zulia,
         1968.
         142 p.   24½ cm.   (Monografías y ensayos, 13)

                              C

19602   Caballero Deloya, Miguel.
         ... Pinetum del Instituto Nacional de Investi-

                             246

gaciones forestales. Primer reporte por Miguel
Caballero Deloya [y] Jaime Carillo Sánchez.
[México, Instituto Nacional de Investigaciones
Forestales] 1948.
21 p.   illus.   23 cm.   (México. Secretaría
de Agricultura y Ganadería. Subsecretaría Forestal
y de la fauna. Boletín divulgativo no. 14)

19603 Caballero León, Luis F
... Dr. Francisco Etchegoyen y Montane, padre de
la veterinaria cubana, 1870-1951. La Habana, 1971.
145 p.   illus.   24 cm.   (Cuadernos de
historia de la salud pública, 53)

19604 Cabral, Eunice de Manso, ed.
Escola brasileira de gravura; catálogo de estampas.
Organizado por Eunice de Manso Cabral, colaboração
de Cecilia Duprat de Britto Pereira. Rio de Janeiro,
Biblioteca Nacional, 1976.
[7]-122 p.   illus.   27 cm.
Reprinted from Anais da Biblioteca Nacional,
v. 96, 1976.

19605 Cabral, Octaviano.
Historias de uma região. Mato Grosso, fronteira
Brasil-Bolivia e Rondônia. 1. ed. Niterói, Editôra
Himalaya, 1963.
416, [2] p.   25 cm.
Bibliography: p. [418]

19606 Cabral, Plinio.
A Guerra depois da guerra; novela. Pôrto Alegre,
Ed. Globo, 1968.
97 p.   21 cm.

19607 Cabrera, Pancho.
Lucha y dolor del Paraguay; diálogo entre el
guerrillero paraguayo Ramón Silva y el poeta que
esto escribe. Rivera, Uruguay, Sine, 1961.
16 p.   illus.   19 cm.
Previously published in El Popular, Montevideo.

19608 Cáceres de Diaz, Lyda.
... Formas de retribución al maestro y su relación
con la escala de mérito... San Juan, P. R., 1963.
17 cm.   27 cm.
At head of title: Confederación mundial de
organizaciones de profesionales de la enseñanza.
Seminario sobre la profesión del magisterio con la

participación de un gran número de líderes
educativos de América Latina. Hotel Americana.
San Juan de Puerto Rico, 22 de noviembre de 1963.

19609 Cáceres Freyre, Julián Bernardo.
Diccionario de regionalismos de la Provincia de
La Rioja. Buenos Aires, Instituto Nacional de
Investigaciones Folklóricas, 1961.
203 p.   map.   20 cm.
Bibliography: p. 199-203.

19610 Cáceres Freyre, Julián Bernardo.
Juan B. Ambrosetti... [Buenos Aires] Ediciones
Culturales Argentinas, Dirección General de Difusión
Cultural, Subsecretaría de Cultura, Secretaría de
Estado de Cultura y Educación [1967]
149 p.   illus.   25 cm.

19611 Cademartori, José.
La economía chilena; un enfoque marxista.
[Santiago] Editorial Universitaria [1968]
293 p.   19 cm.   (Cormorán. Colección Imagen
de Chile, v. 3)
Bibliographical footnotes.

19612 Caeiro, Olívio.
Formas da "narrativa enquadrada" na novela alemã
do realismo poético. [São Paulo, 1973]
236-256 p.   24½ cm.
Reprinted from Língua e literatura, revista dos
departamentos de Letras da Faculdade de Filosofia,
Letras e Ciências Humanas da Universidade de São
Paulo, ano II, no. 2, 1973.

19613 Caffese, María Esther.
Mayo en la bibliografía. Buenos Aires, Universidad de Buenos Aires, Facultad de Filosofía y Letras,
1961 [i.e. 1962]
278 p.   24 cm.   (Publicaciones del Instituto
de Historia Argentina "Doctor Emilio Ravignani,"
102)

19614 Caillet-Bois, J
La novela de Benito Lynch, por J. Caillet-Bois.
Bibliografía de Benito Lynch, por A. Sonol. La
Plata, Universidad Nacional de La Plata, 1960.
140 p.   23 cm.   (Monografías y tesis, 3)

19615 Caillot, Severin.
       ... Cuba libre. Reims, Paillet et Godefroid
       [1896]
       3 p.l., 121 p., 2 ℓ. 24½ cm.

19616 El Caimán barbudo. Nos. 1-95. November 1971 -
       October 1975.
       v. illus. 32 cm.
       Library has nos. 1-95.

19617 Cajina-Vega, Mario, 1930-
       Familia de cuentos. Buenos Aires, Editorial
       Sudamericana [1969]
       155 p. 19 cm. (Colección El Espejo)

19618 Caldano, Julio.
       Proceso de industrialización de los vacunos en un
       establecimiento frigorífico. Buenos Aires, Junta
       Nacional de Carnes, Gerencia de Estudios e Investi-
       gaciones, 1958.
       82 p. 22 cm.

19619 Calcas, Celso.
       Três critérios. Teatro. Cena em un ato, versi-
       ficada. Rio de Janeiro, Serviço Nacional de Teatro,
       1972.
       viii, 14 p. 24 cm.

19620 Caldeira, Admardo Terra.
       Formação de preços - problemas. Belo Horizonte,
       Facultad de Ciencias Econômicas de Universidade de
       Minas Gerais, 1961.
       118 p. illus. 23 cm. (Estudos econômicos,
       politicos e sociais, 23)
       Includes bibliography.

19621 Caldeira, Clovis.
       Menores no meio rural; trabalho e escolarização.
       [Rio de Janeiro] Centro Brasileiro de Pesquisas
       Educacionais, I[nstituto] N[acional de] E[studos]
       P[edagogicos] Ministerio da Educação e Cultura,
       1960.
       190 p. illus., map. 22 cm. (Publicações
       do Centro Brasileiro de Pesquisas Educacionais.
       Série 6: Sociedade e educação, v. 4)
       Bibliography: p. 183-185.

19622 Caldera, Rafael.
       Discurso... en el acto de la toma de posesión

249

del cargo.   Caracas, 11 de Marzo de 1969. [Caracas,
1969]
[39] p.   illus.   24½ cm.

19623 Caldera, Rafael.
Discurso pronunciado... ante el cuerpo diplomático
12 de marzo de 1969. [Caracas, 1969]
31 p.   illus.   20½ cm.

19624 Calderón, Arturo.
Ebrio al límite del tiempo. México, Ediciones
Siglo 1-   Poesía, 1964.
36 p.   illus.   22 cm.

19625 Calderón, Félix Antonio, 1890-1923.
Lirio salvaje 2. [n.p.] Biblioteca de Autores y
Temas Monaguenses, 1963.
128 p.   front. (port.)   24½ cm.

19626 Calderón, Fernando, 1809-1845.
Muerte de Virginia por la libertad de Roma;
tragedia. Estudio preliminar de Francisco Monterde.
[1. ed.] México [Universidad Nacional Autónoma de
México, Dirección General de Publicaciones, Facultad
de Filosofía y Letras] 1960.
119 p.   18 cm.   (Ediciones Filosofía y letras,
50)

19627 Calderón, José B
Petroglifos prehistóricos de Colón del Tachira.
San Cristóbal, Venezuela, 1962.
108 p.   illus.   24 cm.   (Biblioteca de
autores y temas tachirenses, 27)
Bibliographical footnotes.

19628 Calderón Amaya, Luis Jesus.
Estudio geográfico del municipio de Ocotlán,
Jalisco. [México] Centro Universitario México,
1963.
81 p.   illus., maps (part fold.)   28 cm.
Tesis (maestro en geografía) - Universidad
Nacional Autónoma de México.
Bibliography: p. 81.

19629 Calderón de Muñoz, Alba Rosa.
Registro bibliográfico de publicaciones de
catedráticos de la Facultad de Humanidades [por]
Alba Rosa Calderón y Lourdes Bendfeldt Rojas.
[Guatemala] Universidad de San Carlos de Guatemala,

250

1962.
77 p.   23 cm.
"Fuentes":   p. [73]-77.

19630   Calderón de Nieto Caballero, María.
        La red; recetas de pescados y mariscos.   Bogotá
        [1964]
        120 p.   illus. (part col.)   22 cm.

19631   Calderón Otondo, Fernando.
        El control obrero en la empresa.   Potosí, Bolivia,
        1961.
        94, [2] p.   22 cm.   (Publicaciones del
        Departamento de Cultura de la Universidad Tomás Frías)
        Tesis (licenciatura en derecho) - Universidad Tomás
        Frías, Potosí.
        Bibliography: p. [95]

19632   Calderón Quijano, José Antonio.
        Guía de los documentos, mapas y planos sobre
        historia de América y España moderna en la Biblioteca
        Nacional de Paris, Museo Británico y Public Record
        Office de Londres [por] José Antonio Calderón
        Quijano con la colaboración de Luis Navarro García.
        Sevilla, 1962.
        70 p.   25 cm.   (Publicación de la Escuela de
        Estudios Hispano-Americanos de Sevilla, 144, no.
        general)

19633   Calderón Vega, Luis.
        Cuba 88 [i.e. ochenta y ocho]; memorias de la
        UNEC. México, 1959.
        192, 74 p.   ports.   21 cm.
        "Apéndice: Convocatoria y conclusiones de la
        Convención Iberoamericana de Estudiantes Católicos,
        12 al 22 de diciembre de 1931":   p. [1]-72 (2d
        group)

19634 Calderoni, A   V
        Micosis.   Tizón tardío de la papa y del tomate
        (Phytophthora infestans (Mont.) de Bary)   Buenos
        Aires, 1965.
        44 p.   23 cm.   (Argentine Republic.   Instituto
        Nacional de Tecnología Agropecuaria.   Curso de
        Fitopatología para Graduados.   Apuntes de clase no. 27)

19635   Calendario manual y guía universal de forasteros en
        Venezuela para el año 1810.   Estudio preliminar de
        Pedro Grases.   Caracas, Academia Nacional de la

Historia, 1959.
159 p.   facsim.   23 cm.   (Biblioteca de la
Academia Nacional de la Historia, 16)

19636   Calero, Orlando.
Introducción a la teoría de la relatividad;
física. San Salvador, Ministerio de Educación,
Departamento Editorial, 1961.
144 p.   21 cm.   (Colección Certamen nacional
de cultura, 15)
Includes bibliography.

19637   Cali, Colombia. Universidad del Valle. Departamento
de Bibliotecas.
Guía para consultar su biblioteca, elaborada por
Julialba Hurtado M. Cali, 1965.
35 p.   illus.   24 cm.

19638   Cali, Colombia. Universidad del Valle. Oficina de
Planeación Universitaria.
Universidad del Valle, Cali, Colombia. [Cali]
1965.
21 ℓ.   diagrs. (part col.)   plans.   34 cm.

19639   La calidad de la vida: el ambiente ecológico.
Caracas, Creole Petroleum Corporation, 1974.
44 p.   illus.   32 cm.   (El Farol, 1974)
Contents. - Eduardo Casanova, El hombre amenazado.
Octavio Jelambi, Evaluación y control de polución
atmosphérica en Caracas. Henry Cabello, T.E.M.A.
Una bella aventura en la naturaleza. Charles
Brewer Carias, En busca de los orígenes. A. Grajal,
P. López, C. Padial, T. Rojo, El ambiente: un
problema humano. José Joaquín Cabrera Malo, Un
bosque, una sabana, un hermoso paisaje.

19640   California. State College, San Francisco. Library.
The Frank V. DeBellis collection. [San Francisco]
1964.
30 p.   illus. (part col.)   26 cm.

19641   California. University, Los Angeles. Latin American
Center.
Latin American activities and resources [at the]
University of California, Los Angeles. Compiled
by Jane Treiman with the assistance of E. Toney Dixon
[and others] Los Angeles, 1970.
199 p.   tables.   29½ cm.

252

19642   Calmon, Pedro.
        A vida de D. Pedro II, o rei filósofo. Edição
        especial comemorativa do sesquicentenario de seu
        nascimento. Rio de Janeiro, Biblioteca do Exército,
        1975.
        [xiv], 3-316 p.   illus.   21 cm.   (Coleção
        General Benicio, v. 132, publ. 453)
        Title of 1938 ed.:   O rei filósofo.

19643   Calny, Eugenia, 1930-
        La madriguera. Teatro. Buenos Aires, Instituto
        Amigos del Libro Argentino [1967]
        79 p.   19 cm.

19644   Caloca Laurias, Ramiro.
        La reforma agraria y la enseñanza agrícola. México,
        1963.
        152 p.   24 cm.

19645   Calvache, Antonio.
        Bosquejo histórico del conocimiento de la geología
        de Cuba [por] A. Calvache. La Habana, Departamento
        de Geología, Academia de Ciencias de Cuba, 1965.
        107 p.   23 cm.
        Bibliography: p. 75-105.

19646   Calvento y Machuca, D   Mártires.
        Pétalos yertos [por] D. Mártires Calvento y
        Machuca. Montevideo, 1964.
        124 p.   20 cm.

19647   Calviello, Beatriz O
        Las especies argentinas de "Melanospora" Cda.
        por Beatriz C. Calviello. Buenos Aires, Imprenta
        Coni, 1976.
        93-103 p.   illus.   27 cm.
        Reprinted from Revista del Museo Argentino de
        Ciencias Naturales "Bernardino Rivadavia", Botánica,
        t. V, no. 4.
        Abstracts in English and Spanish.

19648   Calzada Bolandi, Jorge.
        Meditemos. [1. ed.] San José, Costa Rica, 1962.
        184 p.   19 cm.

19649   Calzada G   , José Jesús, 1950-
        Primeros sueños, primeros espejismos. Monterrey,
        México, Ediciones Sierra Madre, 1972.

253

54 p.   illus.   22 cm.   (Poesía en el mundo, 102)

19650   Calzadiaz Barrera, Alberto.
        Villa contra todo y ... En pos de la venganza
        sobre Columbus, N. M. México, 1960.
        2 v.   illus.   21 cm.
        Vol. 2, with title: Villa contra todo y contra
        todos, has imprint: México [Editores Unidos]

19651   Calzadilla, Juan.
        Pintores venezolanos. Caracas, Ministerio de
        Educación, Dirección Técnica, Departamento de Publi-
        caciones [1963]
        197 p.   illus.   19 cm.   (Colección Vigilia, 3)
        "Ensayos y artículos aparecidos en diarios y revistas
        de Caracas, entre 1956 y 1961."

19652   Calzadilla Núñez, Ramón.
        Nueva subespecie de Phoebis avellaneda (Merrich-
        Schäffer) (Lepidoptera: Pieridae) en Cuba. La Habana,
        Instituto de Zoología, Academia de Ciencias de Cuba,
        1973.
        2 p.   24½ cm.   (Poeyana, no. 110, 12 July 1973)
        Abstract in English.

19653   Camacho, Simón.
        A Lima. Caracas [Fondo de Publicaciones de la
        Fundación Shell] 1967.
        [167] p.   16½ cm.

19654   Camacho Camacho, Hipólito.
        Bases económicas para una nueva política azufrera
        en México. México, 1961.
        110 p.   23 cm.
        Tesis (licenciatura en economía) - Universidad
        Nacional Autonóma de México.
        Bibliography: p. 109-110.

19655   Camacho Guizado, Eduardo.
        Estudios sobre literatura colombiana, siglos
        xvi-xvii. [1. ed.] Bogotá, Ediciones Universidad
        de los Andes, 1965-
        v.   22 cm.
        Bibliography: v. 1, p. 105-107.

19656   Camacho Henríquez, Guillermo.
        Derecho del trabajo. Tomo I. Teoría general y
        relaciones individuales. Bogotá, Editorial Temis,

1961.
507 p.   21 cm.
No more published?

19657 Camacho Perea, Miguel.
El Valle del Cauca, constante socio-económica de
Colombia, estudio sobre el hombre vallecaucano:
su habitat, la tenencia de la tierra y su proceso
cultural. Cali, Imprenta Departamental [1962]
214 p.   illus., fold. maps.   25 cm.   (Biblioteca de autores vallecaucanos)
Stamped on t.p.: Librería Colombiana, Bogotá.
Bibliography: p. 213-214.

19658 Câmara, Arruda.
O direito da família e o projeto do Código civil.
Brasília, Câmara dos Deputados, 1968.
82 p.   23 cm.

19659 Câmara, J   Mattoso.
Introdução as línguas indígenas brasileiras. Com
um suplemento sôbre a técnica da pesquisa por Sarah
Gudschinsky, do Summer Institute of Linguistics.
Rio de Janeiro, Museu Nacional, 1965.
230 p.   illus., diagrs.   24 cm.

19660 Câmara, Jaime de Barros, Cardinal, 1894-
A Universidade Católica; 38. carta pastoral de
D. Jaime de Barros Câmara, Cardenal-Arcebispo do
Rio de Janeiro. Petrópolis, Editôra Vozes, 1963.
29 p.   24 cm.

19661 Câmara Cascudo, Luís da, 1899-
Gente viva. Recife, Universidade Federal de
Pernambuco, 1970.
189 p.   23 cm.

19662 Câmara Cascudo, Luís da, 1899-
Locuções tradicionais no Brasil. Recife, Universidade Federal de Pernambuco, 1970.
327 p.   23 cm.

19663 Camarero, Antonio.
Sócrates y las creencias demónicas griegas.
Bahía Blanca, Argentina, Instituto de Humanidades,
Universidad Nacional del Sur, 1968.
67 p.   23 cm.   (Cuadernos del Sur)

19664 (Entry on page 419)

255

19665 Camargo, Enaura Maria de Pádua.
Coleção dos catálogos de exposiciones de arte.
São Paulo, Escola de Comunicações e Artes, Universidade de São Paulo, 1974.
70 p.   21 cm.

19666 Camargo, Joracy, 1898-1973.
Deus lhe pague; peça em 3 atos. Rio de Janeiro,
Serviço Nacional de Teatro, 1973.
viii, 59 p.   21 cm.   (Coleção Dramaturgia
brasileira)

19667 Camargo, Joracy, 1898-1973.
Mania de grandeza. Comédia em tres atos. Rio de
Janeiro, Serviço Nacional de Teatro, 1974.
xii, 59 p.   21 cm.

19668 Camargo, Joracy, 1898-1973.
Maria Cachucha. Comédia em três atos e seis
quadros. Rio de Janeiro, Serviço Nacional de Teatro,
1974.
xii, 72 p.   21 cm.

19669 Camargo, José Francisco de.
A cidade e o campo; o êxodo rural no Brasil. Rio
de Janeiro, Ao Livro Técnico, Editôra da Universidade
de São Paulo, 1968.
115 p.   front., graphs, tables.   18 cm.
(Coleção Buriti, 20)

19670 Camargo, José Francisco de.
Niveis de desenvolvimento de uma economia e sua
abordagem política; considerações sôbre alguns
elementos relevantes para a formulação de uma
política de desenvolvimento econômico. São Paulo,
1962.
vii, 350 p.   23 cm.   (Faculdade de Ciências
Econômicas e Administrativas, Universidade de São
Paulo. Boletim no. 33. Cadeira 26)
Errata leaf inserted.
Bibliography: p. [337]-350.

19671 Camargo, Lenita Correa.
Política dos negócios. São Paulo, 1962.
177 p.   illus.   24 cm.   (Universidade de
São Paulo. Faculdade de Ciências Econômicas e
Administrativas. Boletim no. 27. Cadeira 17)
Includes bibliography.

19672 Camargo Piñuela, Sergio.
La industria cerillera en México; política indus-
trial. México, 1963.
136, [28] p.   illus., maps.   24 cm.
Tesis (licenciatura en economía) - Universidad
Nacional Autónoma de México.
Bibliography: p. [163]-[164]

19673 Camarlinghi Rosas, José.
Cara sucia; novela corta [par] Camarlinghi.
La Paz [Editorial Balsuaro, 1962]
73 p.   illus.   16 cm.

19674 Caminhos da evangelização; para o batismo, crisma e
Eucaristia [por] Albano Cavallin [et al. Petrópolis]
Vozes, 1970.
159 p.   21 cm.

19675 Caminos, Roberto.
Geología del sector noroccidental de la península
Hurd, Isla Livingston, Shetland del Sur, Antártica
Argentina. Por Roberto Caminos, Humberto G. Marchese,
Armando G. Massabie, Jorge R. Morelli, Carlos A.
Rinaldi, Juan P. Spikerman. Buenos Aires, Dirección
Nacional del Antártico, 1973.
32 p.   illus., fold. map, diagrs.   30 cm.

19676 Caminos de Artola, Aurora Rosa.
La acción del General Paz en el interior, 1829-1831.
Córdoba, R. A., Dirección General de Publicidad, 1962.
174 p.   illus.   28 cm.   (Universidad Nacional
de Córdoba. Facultad de Filosofía y Humanidades.
Instituto de Estudios Americanistas. Serie histórica,
no. 29)
Tesis - Universidad de Buenos Aires.
Includes bibliography.

19677 Camisa, Zulma C
Argentina; proyección de la población por sexo y
edad, 1960-1980 [por] Zulma C. Camisa. Santiago,
Chile [CELADE] 1965.
vi, 100 p.   illus.   28 cm.   (Naciones Unidas.
Centro Latinoamericano de Demografía. Serie C,
no. 62)

19678 Cammarota, Federico.
El dios del miedo; teatro. Buenos Aires, 1963.
31 p.   23 cm.

19679   Campaña Barrera, Aníbal.
Breve manual de consulta del afiliado al seguro
social ecuatoriano; preguntas y respuestas. Quito,
Imp. Caja del Seguro, 1962.
55 p.   22 cm.

19680   Campanha integrada de reflorestamento; manual 1966-1968.
Belo Horizonte, Imp. Oficial, 1968.
35 p.   maps, tables.   23 cm.

19681   Campello, Alberto José.
Padre Manoel da Nóbrega, um dos fundadores da
nação brasileira.   Recife, Brasil, Colégio Nóbrega,
1970.
39 p.   26 cm.

19682   Campinas, Brazil.   Instituto Agronômico do Estado de
São Paulo.
Indice bibliográfico do Instituto Agronômico.
Campinas, 1962.
122 p.   19 cm.
Contains a summary in English.

19683   Campinas, Brazil.   Instituto Agronômico do Estado de
São Paulo.
Solos da Bacia Paraná - Uruguai; [relatório apre-
sentado pela Secção de Agrogeologia do Instituto
Agronômico do Estado de São Paulo a Comissão Inter-
estadual da Bacia Paraná-Uruguai] São Paulo, 1961.
168 p.   illus., maps (part fold., part col.)
diagrs., tables.   33 cm.
At head of title: Comissão Interestadual da
Bacia Paraná-Uruguai.
Includes bibliographies.

19684   Campinas, Brazil.   Prefeitura Municipal.
Campinas, bicentenário e turismo, 1774-1974.
[Campinas?   1974?]
48 p.   illus.   21½ cm.

19685   Campino Vidal, José Miguel.
El salitre [por] José Miguel Campino Vidal [y]
Juan Herrera Riesco.   Santiago [de Chile]   Editorial
Universitaria, 1957.
100 p.   22 cm.
"Capítulo XXVI de la memoria... presentada para
optar al grado de licenciado [en ciencias jurídicas
y sociales, Universidad de Chile, Santiago]"

19686   Campisteguy, Juan, pres. Uruguay.
         Mensaje del Presidente de la República. Dr. Don
         Juan Campisteguy, a la H. Asamblea General al
         inaugurarse el segundo período de la XXX Legis-
         latura. 15 de marzo de 1930. Montevideo, 1930.
         46 p.   25 cm.

19687   Campo, Luis del.
         Aromita. Asunción [Paraguay] 1962.
         197 p.   24 cm.
         Poems.

19688   Campo del Pozo, Fernando.
         Historia documentada de los agustinos en Venezuela
         durante la época colonial. Caracas, Academia
         Nacional de la Historia, 1968.
         304 p.   23 cm.   (Biblioteca de la Academia
         Nacional de la Historia, 91)
         Bibliography: p. [275]-282.

19689   Campo Lacasa, Cristina.
         Notas generales sobre la historia eclesiástica
         de Puerto Rico en el siglo XVIII. [Sevilla] Escuela
         de Estudios Hispano-Americanos [1963]
         127 p.   illus., facsim., maps, plans.   25 cm.
         (Publicaciones de la Escuela de Estudios Hispano-
         Americanos de Sevilla, 137)
         Tesis - Universidad de Sevilla.
         Bibliographical footnotes.

19690   Campos, Alberto L
         La industria automotriz; análisis de mercado.
         [Buenos Aires?] 1960.
         42 p.   illus.   30 cm.
         At head of title: Banco Industrial de la
         República Argentina. Dirección de Promoción y
         Desarrollo Industrial. Gerencia de Investigaciones
         Técnicas.

19691   Campos, Asterio.
         O pensamento jurídico de Norberto Bobbio. São
         Paulo, Saraiva, 1966.
         134 p.   22 cm.   (Coleção "Direito e Cultura"
         [13])
         Bibliography: p. [127]-134.

19692   Campos, Dea Regina Bouret.
         ... Contribuição à paleontologia do Estado do
         Pará. Revisão da familia Arsidae, na formação

Pirabas (miocene inferior) XI - (Molusca, bivalvia)
Belém, 1974.
34 p., 4 p.l.   24½ cm.
At head of title: Boletim de Museu Paraense
Emílio Goeldi, Nova série, Geologia, no. 19,
3 janeiro 1974.

19693 Campos, Eduardo, 1923-
O abutre e outras estórias. Apresentação de Braga
Montenegro. Fortaleza, Imp. Universitária do Ceara,
1968.
189 p.   21 cm.
Contents. - O abutre - O casamento - Céu limpo -
Ela era seu A viagem definitiva - O tocador de
bombo - Menino de recado - A venda das mangas -
Visita para explicações - O episodio - Como um
gato sem gata.

19694 Campos, Fernando Arruda.
Tomismo e neotomismo no Brasil. Pref. de Luiz
Washington Vita. São Paulo, Ed. Grijalbo, 1968.
241 p.   21 cm.   (Estante do pensamento
brasileiro)
Bibliography: p. 226-233.

19695 Campos, Geir, 1924-
As sementes da independência. Rio de Janeiro,
Serviço Nacional de Teatro, 1972.
66 p.   21 cm.
Full name: Geir Naffer Campos.

19696 Campos, Geir, 1924-
O vestíbulo; contos escritos de 1948 a 1952.
Rio de Janeiro, Ministerio da Educação e Cultura,
Serviço de Documentação, 1960.
63 p.   23 cm.
Contents. - O vestíbulo - O amigo - O paude-sebo -
A faca - A estatua - A mina.

19697 Campos, Gerardo.
Estadística general (problemas y sus soluciones)
Caracas, Instituto de Investigaciones Económicas y
Sociales, 1969.
133 p.   23 cm.

19698 Campos, José Maria Moreira, 1914-
As vozes do morto. [São Paulo] Livraria F. Alves
[1963]
101 p.   24 cm.   (Coleção Alvorada, v. 9)

19699   Campos, Julieta.
La imagen en el espejo. México, Universidad
Nacional Autónoma de México, 1965.
171 p.   19 cm.   (Colección Poemas y ensayos)

19700   Campos, Martín.
Desde un vasto recuerdo; [poema. Buenos Aires]
Editorial Cuadernos del Siroco, 1961.
35 p.   20 cm.   (Colección "Cuadernos del
Siroco")

19701   Campos, Maximiano, 1941-
As emboscadas da sorte; contos. Recife, Universidade
Federal de Pernambuco, 1971.
235 p.   illus.   23½ cm.

19702   Campos, Maximiano, 1941-
Sem lei nem rei; romance, seguido de um ensaio
sôbre o Nôvo romance sertanejo, de Ariano Suassuna.
Rio de Janeiro, Ed. O Cruzeiro, 1968.
134 p.   21 cm.   (Novelas & romances da terra)

19703   Campos, Milton.
The production of I-131 in IPR-R1 reactor (Triga
Mark I Reactor) in Belo Horizonte, M. G., Brazil.
Belo Horizonte, 1963.
6 p.   24 cm.   (Publicação IPR-33)
"Paper presented to the 'Symposium on Pile Neutron
Research in Physics,' Vienna, Oct. 1961."
Summary in Portuguese and English.
Bibliography: p. 6.

19704   Campos, Noêmia Simões de.
E o vento acordara minha angustia... [São Paulo]
Martins [1963]
76 p.   22 cm.

19705   Campos, P   N
Guia dos noivos e dos esposos.   [São Paulo]
Ed. Paulinas [1970]
44 p.   16 cm.
3ª edição.

19706   Campos, P   N
Limitação responsável dos nascimentos, segundo a
encíclica Humanae vitae do Papa Paulo VI [por]
P. N. Campos. São Paulo, Ed. Paulinas, 1968.
127 p.   illus.   18 cm.   (Coleção Caminho,
Verdade e vida, 4)

19707　Campos, Paulo de Almeida.
　　　　A faculdade de educação na atual estrutura
　　　　universitária. Niterói, Brasil, Faculdade de
　　　　Educação da Universidade Federal Fluminense, 1971.
　　　　56 p.　　24 cm.

19708　Campos, Renato Carneiro.
　　　　Arte, sociedade e região. [Salvador, Brazil]
　　　　1960.
　　　　119 p.　　illus.　　19 cm.　　(Publicações da
　　　　Universidade da Bahía, II, 21)

19709　Campos, Renato Carneiro.
　　　　Ideologia dos poetas populares do Nordeste.
　　　　[Recife] MEC-INEP, Centro Regional de Pesquisas
　　　　Educacionais do Recife, 1959.
　　　　118 p.　　facsims.　　24 cm.　　(Instituto Nacional
　　　　de Estudos Pedagógicos-M. E. C. [e] Centro Regional
　　　　de Pesquisas Educacionais do Recife. Publicações.
　　　　Série Estudos e pesquisas, 1)
　　　　Bibliography: p. [117]-118.

19710　Campos, Renato Carneiro.
　　　　Ideologia dos poetas populares do nordeste.
　　　　Prefácio de Gilberto Freyre. Anotações de Mário
　　　　Souto Maior. 2a. edição. Recife, Instituto
　　　　Joaquim Nabuco de Pesquisas Sociais, 1977.
　　　　76 p.　　illus., facsim.　　23 cm.　　(Série
　　　　Estudos e pesquisas, 5)
　　　　"Bibliografia": p. 73-76.

19711　Campos, Sabino de, 1893-
　　　　Cantigas que o vento leva; memorial rimado
　　　　(1,400 trovas) Rio de Janeiro, Irmaos Pongetti,
　　　　1964.
　　　　225 p.　　port.　　22 cm.

19712　Campos, Theresa Catharina de Góes.
　　　　A TV nos tornou mais humanos? Princípios da
　　　　comunicação pela TV. Prefação de Ariano Suassuna.
　　　　Recife, Universidade Federal de Pernambuco, 1970.
　　　　305 p.　　illus.　　23 cm.

19713　Campos Andapia, Antonio.
　　　　Las sociedades financieras privadas en México.
　　　　México, Centro de Estudios Monetarios Latinoameri-
　　　　canos, 1963.
　　　　237 p.　　22 cm.　　(Estudios E.M.L.A.)
　　　　A revised and abridged edition of the author's

thesis (licenciatura en economía) Universidad
Nacional Autónoma de México, published in 1962
under title: Teoría de la intermediación
financiera y las sociedades financieras privadas
mexicanas.

19714 Campos Harriet, Fernando.
       Desarrollo educacional 1810-1960. [Santiago,
       Chile] A. Bello, 1960.
       210 p.   19 cm.
       Bibliography: p. 207-210.

19715 Campos Jiménez, Carlos María.
       Las ciencias sociales en Costa Rica. Rio de
       Janeiro, 1959.
       62 p.   22 cm.   (Centro Latino-Americano de
       Pesquisas em Ciências Sociais. Publicação, no. 8)

19716 [Campos Leão, José Joaquim de] 1829-1883.
       Mateus e Mateusa de Qorpo-Santo [pseud.] Rio de
       Janeiro, Serviço Nacional de Teatro, 1975.
       32-37 p.   21 x 33 cm.
       Reprinted from Cadernos de teatro, no. 65, Apr.-
       June 1975.

19717 Campos Leão, José Joaquim de, 1829-1883.
       ... As relações naturais. Comedia em quatro atos.
       Rio de Janeiro, Serviço Nacional de Teatro, 1972.
       vi, 18 p.   21 cm.
       At head of title: Qorpo Santo [pseud.]

19718 Campos Menéndez, Enrique, 1914-
       A generation of destiny [by] Enrique Campos
       Menéndez. Alberdi-Sarmiento Award Lecture series.
       Translated by Paul Wendell Allen, with an intro-
       duction by Yvonne Guillon Barrett. [Tempe, Center
       for Latin American Studies, Arizona State University,
       1975?]
       18 p.   23 cm.   (Alberdi-Sarmiento lecture
       series, 1974)

19719 Camprubí Alcázar, Carlos.
       Bancos de rescate, 1821-1832. Lima, 1963.
       46 p.   25 cm.

19720 Canale de Dotto, Isidora.
       La cocina moderna. Santa Fe, Argentina, Ediciones
       Colmegna [1962]
       188 p.   18 cm.

263

19721   Cancino, Luis A
La psique o personalidad del delincuente [por]
Luis A. Cancino. México, 1963.
180 p.   24 cm.
At head of title: Universidad Nacional Autónoma
de México. Facultad de Derecho.
Bibliography: p. 177-180.

19722   Candelas, José B
Some effects of the sugar programs on the sugar
industry of Puerto Rico. Rio Piedras, University of
Puerto Rico, 1959.
46 p.   23 cm.   (Puerto Rico. Agricultural
Experiment Station, Rio Piedras. Bulletin 151)
Includes bibliography.

19723   Cândido de Mello e Souza, Antônio, 1918-
Os parceiros do Rio Bonito, estudo sôbre o caipira
paulista e a transformação dos seus meios de vida.
Rio de Janeiro, Livraria José Olympio, 1964.
239 p.   port.   23 cm.   (Coleção documentos
brasileiros, dirigida por Alfonso Arinos de Melo
Franco, 118)

19724   Candioti, Alberto María, 1889-
El tratado antártico y nuestras fuerzas armadas.
Buenos Aires, 1960.
79 p.   illus.   20 cm.
Chiefly articles published in the newspaper
Crítica. "Tratado antártico; texto oficial":
p. 72-78.

19725   Canedo M   , Oscar Justiniano.
Tesis de nacionalización de los bienes de la
empresa Bolivian Gulf Oil Co. [por] Oscar Justiniano
Canedo M. [1. ed.] La Paz, Editorial y Librería
Difusión, 1969.
94 p.   19 cm.
Cover title: Gulf Oil: nacionalización de sus
bienes.

19726   Canfield, Delos Lincoln, 1903-
La pronunciación del español en América; ensayo
histórico-descriptivo. Prólogo de Tomás Navarro.
Bogotá, 1962 [i.e. 1963]
103 p.   fold. col. maps.   24 cm.   (Publicaciones del Instituto Caro y Cuervo, 17)
Bibliography: p. [31]-53.

19727 Cañizales Márquez, José.
       Formación social, moral y cívica. Texto aprobado
       por el Ministerio de Educación para el primer año
       (primer ciclo) de educación secundaria y recomendado
       como material de consulta para el sexto grado de
       educación primaria. 1. ed. Caracas, 1961.
       163, [4] p.   23 cm.
       Bibliography: p. [165]

19728 Canosa Capdeville, Yamandu.
       En torno a la axiología de Platón en su tensión
       perenne ético-religiosa. Montevideo, 1962.
       69 p.   25 cm.
       Includes bibliography.

19729 Canseco Vincourt, Jorge.
       La guerra sagrada. México, Instituto Nacional de
       Antropología e Historia, 1966.
       143 p.   22 cm.   (Serie historia, 14)

19730 Cantel, Raymond.
       Temas da atualidade na literatura de cordel;
       ensaios. São Paulo, Universidade de São Paulo,
       Escola de Comunicações e Artes [Departamento de
       Jornalismo e Editoração] 1972.
       74 l.   21 cm.   (Série Jornalismo, 26)
       Includes bibliographical references.

19731 Canton, Alfredo.
       Juventudes exhaustas; novela. Panamá [Ministerio
       de Educación, Departamento de Bellas Artes y
       Publicaciones] 1963.
       662 p.   22 cm.

19732 Caparroso, Carlos Arturo.
       Dos ciclos de lirismo colombiano. Bogotá, 1961.
       213 p.   21 cm.   (Publicaciones del Instituto
       Caro y Cuervo. Series menor, 6)
       Includes bibliography.

19733 Capistrán Garza, René.
       La iglesia católica y la revolución mexicana;
       prontuario de ideas políticas. México [Editorial
       Atisbos] 1964.
       202 p.   23 cm.

19734 Cappelletti, Ángel J
       Diógenes de Apolonia y la segunda filosofía
       jónica [por] Ángel J. Cappelletti. [Maracaibo]

265

Universidad del Zulia, 1974.
112 p.   21 cm.   (Biblioteca de textos filosóficos)

19735 Cappelletti, Angel J
       Introducción a Condillac [por] Angel J. Cappelletti.
       Maracaibo, Universidad del Zulia, 1973.
       431 p.   21 cm.   (Biblioteca de textos filosó-
       ficos)
       "Los textos": p. 229-428.
       Bibliography: p. 429-431.

19736 Cappelletti, Mauro.
       La jurisdicción constitucional de la libertad,
       con referencia a los ordenamientos alemán, suizo y
       austríaco. Traducción y estudio sobre la juris-
       dicción constitucional mexicana por Héctor Fix
       Zamudio. Prólogo del Dr. Mariano Azuela. México,
       Imprenta Universitaria, 1961.
       247 p.   (Publicaciones del Instituto de Derecho
       Comparado. Serie B: Estudios comparativos,
       b. Estudios especiales, no. 4)

19737 Caracas. Catedral. Cabildo.
       Actas del Cabildo Eclesiástico de Caracas;
       compendio cronológico. [Estudio preliminar por
       Manuel Pérez Vila] Caracas, Academia Nacional de
       la Historia, 1963.
       2 v.   2 facsims.   23 cm.   (Biblioteca de la
       Academia Nacional de la Historia, 65-65)
       Transcription of a calendar prepared by Juan
       Joseph Guzmán of the 25 volumes in manuscript of
       the Actas del Cabildo; the manuscript of the
       calendar is entitled: Yndice chronologico de los
       Acuerdos del MVS dean y cabildo de esta Santa
       Yglesia antes Cathedral, y ahora Metropolitana del
       Arzobispado de Caracas y Venezuela extendidos en
       ·sus respectivos Libros capitulares.
       Contents. - t. 1. 1580-1770. - t. 2. 1771-1806.

19738 Caracas. Cathedral. Cabildo.
       El Cabildo Metropolitano de Caracas y la guerra
       de emancipación; extractos del archivo capitular
       hechos con toda fidelidad por Nicolás Eugenio
       Navarro. Caracas, Academia Nacional de la Historia,
       1960.
       472 p.   facsims.   23 cm.   (Biblioteca de la
       Academia Nacional de la Historia, 34)

19739 Caracas. Museo Nacional de Bellas Artes.
Bienal Armando Reveron. Caracas, no. I-
1961-
20 x 23 cm.
Library has nos. 1-4, 1961-1967.

19740 Caracas. Museo Nacional de Bellas Artes.
Pintura venezolana, 1661-1961; exposición
organizada por el Museo de Bellas Artes de Caracas
como uno de los actos programados por el Ministerio
de Educación para celebrar el sequicentenario de
nuestra independencia. Caracas, 1961.
13 p.   297 illus. (part col.)   21 x 23 cm.
Bibliography: p. 13.

19741 Caracas. Universidad Central. Centro de Estudios
Literarios.
Bibliografía de la novela venezolana. [Caracas]
Universidad Central de Venezuela, Facultad de
Humanidades y Educación, Escuela de Letras [1963]
69 p.   24 cm.

19742 Caracas. Universidad Central. Consejo de Desarrollo
Científico y Humanístico.
Bibliografía de ciencia y tecnología del profesorado
de la U.C.V. Caracas, 1974.
264 p.   24 cm.   (Proyecto de investigación
no. CH-4)

19743 Caracas. Universidad Central. Consejo de Desarrollo
Científico y Humanístico.
Bibliografía de humanidades y ciencias sociales
del profesorado de la U.C.V. 1967-1970. Caracas,
1973.
101 p.   24 cm.

19744 Caracas. Universidad Central. Consejo de Desarrollo
Científico y Humanístico.
Bibliografía de humanidades y ciencias sociales
de la U.C.V. 1971-1974. Caracas, 1978.
136 p.   23 cm.

19745 Caracas. Universidad Central. Consejo de Desarrollo
Científico y Humanístico.
Catálogo de la investigación universitaria.
Caracas, 1963.
[184] p.   23 cm.

19746 Caracas. Universidad Central. Consejo de Desarrollo
Científico y Humanístico.
... Catálogo de la U.C.V. Investigación, trabajos
de catedra, trabajos de estensión. 1964/1966.
Caracas, 1969.
437 p. 24 cm.
At head of title: Universidad Central de Venezuela.
Consejo de Desarrollo Científico y Humanístico.
Proyecto de Investigación no. CH-4 a cargo de
Celestino Bonfanti, Facultad de Agronomía, Arabia
Teresa Cova, Facultad de Humanidades y Educación, con
la colaboración de Aledia de Acosta, Facultad de
Medicina.

19747 Caracas. Universidad Central, Caracas. Consejo de
Desarrollo Científico y Humanístico.
Materiales para el estudio de la cuestión agraria
en Venezuela (1800-1830). Estudio preliminar por
Germán Carrera Damas. Caracas, 1964-
v. 28 cm. (Publicación 2)
Contents. - v. 1. Sobre el significado socio-
económico de la acción histórica de Boves por G.
Carrera Dalmas. Bibliografía (p. [clix]-clxiv)
Documentos: no. 1-314, 1801-1830. Indices.

19748 Caracas. Universidad Central. Facultad de Arquitectura
y Urbanismo.
Boletín... Número especial dedicado a los problemas
de conservación y restauración de monumentos y sitios
históricos en América Latina. Caracas, 1973.
266 p. illus. 27 cm. (Boletín, no. 16)

19749 Caracas. Universidad Central. Facultad de Arquitectura
y Urbanismo.
Boletín. Caracas.
v. illus., maps, plans, facsims. 25½ cm.
Library has nos. 19 (Dec., 1974), 20 (June, 1975),
21 (Nov., 1975)

19750 Caracas. Universidad Central. Facultad de Derecho.
Documentos, no. 1, 1960- Caracas, 1960-
nos. 24½ cm.
Library has nos. 13-16, 19/20-27, 31-38, 41-43,
46-50.

19751 Caracas. Universidad Central. Instituto de Antropología e Historia.
Anuario. t. 1- 1964- Caracas.
v. illus., maps. 24 cm.

268

19752 Caracas. Universidad Central. Instituto de Estudios
Políticos.
Documentos. Caracas.
v. 22½ cm.
Library has no. 55, Oct.-Dec. 1973.

19753 Caracas. Universidad Central. Instituto de Investigaciones de Prensa.
Que publicó la prensa venezolana durante la
dictadura. [Caracas] Universidad Central de Venezuela,
Facultad de Humanidades y Educación, Escuela de
Periodismo, Instituto Venezolano de Investigaciones
de Prensa [1959]
20 p.

19754 Caracas à través de los tiempos. Caracas [Fondo de
publicaciones de la Fundación Shell] 1967.
363 p. 16½ cm. (Colección distinta, 8)

19755 Caram Mafud, Carlos.
Los fines y su efectividad en el regionalismo
de América. México, 1963.
226 p. 22 cm.
Tesis (licenciatura en derecho) - Universidad
Nacional Autónoma de México.
Bibliography: p. [223]-226.

19756 Carayon, Auguste, 1813-1874.
Bibliographie historique de la Compagnie de Jésus;
ou, Catalogue des ouvrages relatifs à l'histoire
des jésuites, depuis leur origine jusqu'à nos jours,
par le p. Auguste Carayon... Paris, A. Durand [etc.]
1864.
viii, 612 p. 27 x 21½ cm.
Contents. - 1. ptie. Généralités. - 2. ptie.
Histoire des cinq assistances de la Compagnie. -
3. ptie. Histoire des missions. - 4. ptie. Biographies
particulières. - 5. ptie. Satires, pamphlets,
apologies, etc.

19757 Carballido, Emilio, 1925-
Acapulco, los lunes, pieza en un acto. Monterrey,
Ediciones Sierra Madre, 1969.
65 p. 21 cm.

19758 Carballido, Emilio, 1925-
Almanaque de Juárez. Monterrey, Ediciones Sierra
Madre, 1972.

269

48 p.   front. (port.)   22 cm.   (Poesía en
el mundo, 100)

19759 Carballido, Emilio, 1925-
       D. F. (14 obras en un acto)   Xalapa, México,
       Universidad Veracruzana, 1962.
       197 p.   20 cm.   (Universidad Veracruzana,
       Ficción, 45)
       Contents. - Preámbulo. - Misa primera. - Selaginela.
       El censo. - Escribir, por ejemplo. - Tangentes. -
       El espejo. - La perfecta casada. - Paso de madrugada. -
       El solitario en octubre. - La medalla. - Un cuento
       de Navidad. - Parásitas. - Pastores de la ciudad,
       escrita en colaboración con L. J. Hernández. -
       Música de pastores de la ciudad, de R. Sanz.

19760 Carballo Hernández, Miguel Angel.
       La formación San Miguel (mioceno, Costa Rica) por
       Miguel Angel Carballo Hernández y Rudolf Fischer.
       San José, Costa Rica, 1978.
       45-144 p.   illus., tables (part fold.)   25½ cm.
       Reprinted from Costa Rica.   Instituto Geográfico
       Nacional.   Informe semestral, enero a junio 1978.
       Bibliografía: p. 93-101.

19761 Carbonell, Diego, 1884-1945.
       Psicopatología de Bolívar.   Introducción de María
       de Lourdes Carbonell.   Caracas, Universidad Central
       de Venezuela, 1965.
       xcv, [1], 456 p.   23 cm.   (Ediciones de la
       Biblioteca, 19.   Colección ciencias sociales, 10)
       Bibliography: p. xc-[xcvi]

19762 Carbonieri, José Fernando de Mafra.
       Os gringos; contos.   São Paulo, Conselho Estadual
       de Cultura, Secretaria de Cultura, Esportes e
       Turismo, 1973.
       188 p.   24 cm.   (Comissão Estadual de Litera-
       tura-Ficção, 2)

19763 Cárcamo Tercero, Hernán.
       Frases íntimas.   [Tegucigalpa? Tipo-Lito Suárez
       Romero] 1964.
       85 p.   22 cm.
       Includes poems.

19764 Cárcano, Miguel Angel, 1889-
       El estilo de vida argentino en Paz, Mansilla,
       González, Roca, Figueroa Alcorta y Sáenz Peña.

270

[Buenos Aires] Editorial Universitaria de Buenos
Aires [1969]
151 p.   18 cm.   (Colección Argentina. Siglo y
medio, 132)

19765 Cárcano, Miguel Angel, 1889-
Sáenz Peña; la revolución por los comicios. 1. ed.
Buenos Aires, 1963.
266 p.   port.   21 cm.
Bibliographical footnotes.

19766 Carciente, Jacob.
Estudio y proyecto de carreteras. Caracas, Universidad Central de Venezuela, Ediciones de la Biblioteca,
1965.
649 p.   illus., diagrs., charts, tables.   23 cm.
(Ediciones de la biblioteca, 22. Colección ingeniería,
1)

19767 Cárdenas C   , Antonio Luis.
Geografía física de Venezuela [por] Antonio Luis
Cárdenas C. Mérida, Taller Gráfico Universitarios,
1964.
283 p.   illus., maps.   24 cm.
Bibliography: p. 265-273.
Errata slip inserted.

19768 Cárdenas Valdez, Rigoberto.
La reforma agraria y el problema salino en el
Valle de Mexicali. México, 1962.
143 p.   illus.   23 cm.
Tesis (licenciatura en derecho) - Universidad
Nacional Autónoma de México.
Includes bibliography.

19769 Cardiel Reyes, Raúl, ed.
Los filósofos modernos en la independencia latino-
americana. [1. ed.] México, Escuela Nacional de
Ciencias Políticas y Sociales, Universidad Nacional
Autónoma de México, 1964.
306 p.   22 cm.
Includes bibliographies.
Contents. - Introducción. - La filosofía moderna:
Francisco Bacon. Renato Descartes. - El liberalismo
europeo: Juan Locke. Juan Jacobo Rousseau. - La
estructura del estado moderno: Montesquieu. Manuel
José Sieyes. - El ataque a la traducción: Voltaire.
Diderot. - Progreso y Utopía: Adán Smith.

271

19770   Cardona, Miguel, 1903-1964.
        Temas de folklore venezolano. Caracas, Ediciones
        del Ministerio de Educación, Dirección de Cultura
        y Bellas Artes, Departamento de Publicaciones, 1964.
        xxxiv, [2], 480 p.   illus.   22 cm.   (Biblio-
        teca venezolana de cultura)
        "Contribución a la bibliografía de Miguel Cardona":
        p. xxv-[xxxv]

19771   Cardona-Álvarez, Canuto, 1919-
        La caraota y otras leguminosas de grano en Venezuela;
        lineamientos de un plan para el fomento de la pro-
        ducción, 1967-1970 [por] Canuto Cardona Álvarez,
        Bernardo Herrera Klindt, y César Jiménez Escobar.
        Revisión final y edición: R. Gondelles A. y A.
        Pons C.; dibujos: J. Coll Mir. Caracas, Consejo de
        Bienestar Rural, Oficina de Estudios Especiales,
        1967.
        xviii, 266 p.   illus., maps.   28 cm.
        Bibliographical footnotes.

19772   Cardona Peña, Alfredo.
        Poema del retorno. México, Ecuador 0°0'0", 1962.
        unpaged.   illus.   17 cm.

19773   Cardoso, Fernando Henrique.
        Cuestiones de sociología del desarrollo en América
        Latina. [Santiago, Chile] Editorial Universitaria
        [1968]
        180 p.   19 cm.   (Colección Imagen de América
        Latina, v. 3)
        Bibliographical footnotes.

19774   Cardoso, Fernando Henrique.
        Empresário industrial e desenvolvimento econômico
        no Brasil. São Paulo, Difusão Européia do Livro,
        1964.
        196 p.   22 cm.   (Corpo e alma do Brasil, 13)
        "Apresentado em novembro de 1963 como tese de
        livre-docência de sociologia junto à Faculdade de
        Filosofia, Ciências y Letras da Universidade de
        São Paulo."
        Bibliography: p. 189-194.

19775   Cardoso, Lúcio, 1913-1968.
        O escravo. Peça em 3 atos. Rio de Janeiro,
        Serviço Nacional de Teatro, 1973.
        viii, 56 p.   21 cm.

19776 Cardoso, Ofélia Boisson.
       Problemas da adolescencia. 6.ª ediçao. [São
       Paulo] Ediçóes melhoramentos [n.d.]
       260 p.   24½ cm.

19777 Cardoso, Ofélia Boisson.
       Problemas da família. Pref. do prof. Lourenço
       Filho. São Paulo, Ed. Melhoramentos, 1968.
       184 p.   23 cm.   (Biblioteca de educaçao.
       Série "Grandes textos")
       Bibliographical footnotes.

19778 Cardoso, Ofélia Boisson.
       Problemas da infância. Crianças agressivas,
       crianças que não querem comer, crianças timidas,
       temas sexuais. 6.ª ediçao. São Paulo, Ediçóes
       Melhoramentos [1969]
       228 p.   24½ cm.

19779 Cardoso, Roberto N
       Sôbre a ocorrência no Brasil de Monolciolophinae
       e Afrograptidae, Conchostraçóes carenados. Rio de
       Janeiro, Serviço Gráfico do Instituto Brasileiro
       de Geografía e Estatística, 1965.
       35 p.   25 cm.   (Brasil. Departmento Nacional
       de Produçao Mineral. Divisão de Geología e Minera-
       logia. Boletím, no. 221)

19780 Cardot, Carlos Felice, ed.
       La libertad de cultos, polémica suscitada por
       William Burke. Caracas, Academia Nacional de la
       Historia, 1959.
       415 p.   facsims.   23 cm.   (Biblioteca de la
       Academia Nacional de la Historia, 12)
       Contents. - I. William Burke, La libertad de cultos.
       II. Apología de la intolerancia religiosa. Segunda
       parte. III. Antonio Gómez, Ensayo político contra
       las "Reflexiones" de William Burke. IV. Juan Nepo-
       muceno Quintana, La intolerancia político-religiosa
       vindicada. V. Juan Germán Roscio, Patriotismo de
       Nirgua y abuso de los reyes. VI. Los católicos de
       Irlanda.

19781 Cardot, Carlos Felice.
       Un maestro util y sabio. Caracas, 1960.
       13 p.   23 cm.

19782 Cardoza y Aragón, Luis, 1904-
       Nuevo Mundo. Xalapa, Universidad Veracruzana,

1960.
110 p.   20 cm.   (Universidad Veracruzana.
Ficción, 22)
Contents. - Nuevo Mundo. - Martirio de San Dionisio.
Dante en Nueva York. - Elogio de la embriaguez.

19783 Cardozo, Efraîm, 1906-
Afinidades entre el Paraguay y la Banda Oriental
en 1811. Montevideo, 1963.
57 p.   28 cm.
Cover title.

19784 Cardozo, Flávio José.
Singraduara. Contos. Pôrto Alegre, Editôra
Gloso [1969]
220 p.   22 cm.

19785 Cardozo, Lubio.
Bibliografía de la literatura merideña. Mérida,
Venezuela, Centro de Investigaciónes Literarias,
Facultad de Humanidades y Educación, Universidad de
Los Andes, 1967 (i.e. 1968)
91 p.   20 cm.

19786 Cardozo, Lubio.
Cuentos indígenas venezolanos (Baniba - Baré -
Piapoco - Puniabe) Mérida, Universidad de Los Andes,
Facultad de Humanidades y Educación, Centro de Inves-
tigaciones Literarias, 1968.
[54] p.   23½ cm.

19787 Cardozo, Lubio.
La poesía en Mérida de Venezuela. [Maracaibo]
Universidad del Zulia, Facultad de Humanidades y
Educación [1971]
221 p.   24 cm.   (Maracaibo. Universidad del
Zulia. Facultad de Humanidades y Educación. Mono-
grafías y ensayos, XV)
Bibliography: p. 163-215.

19788 Cardozo Gonzales, Armando.
Revistas agrícolas bolivianas; cronología y clasi-
ficación. La Paz, Bolivia, Sociedad de Ingenieros
Agrónomos de Bolivia, 1962.
69 ℓ.   facsims.   26 cm.   (Sociedad de
Ingenieros Agrónomos de Bolivia. Boletín biblio-
gráfico, no. 2)
An index to 10 periodicals.

19789   Caribbean Commission.
A bibliography of education in the Caribbean.
Bibliographie de l'enseignement dans la Caraibe.
Compiled by V. O. Alcalá, research secretary.
[Port-of-Spain?] Trinidad, Central Secretariat, 1959.
ix, 144 p.   27 cm.

19790   Caribbean Conference on Mental Health.
Children of the Caribbean: their mental health
needs; proceedings. [San Juan, P. R., Department
of Health, 1961]
179 p.

19791   Caribbean Organization.
Bibliography of development plans. Bibliographie
des plans de developpement. Hato Rey, P. R.,
Central Secretariat, 1963.
9 p.   28 cm.
Cover title.

19792   Caribbean Scholars' Conference, 10th, Rio Piedras,
P. R., 1961.
The Caribbean Scholars Conference, X. Institute
of Caribbean Studies, University of Puerto Rico.
[Rio Piedras] 1962.
26 ℓ.   36 cm.   (Caribbean studies special report)

19793   Carilla, Emilio.
El embajador Sarmiento; Sarmiento y los Estados
Unidos. [Rosario, Universidad Nacional del Litoral]
Facultad de Filosofía y Letras, Instituto de Letras
[1961?]
182 p.   illus.   23 cm.

19794   Carilla, Emilio.
Estudios de literatura argentina, siglo XIX.
Tucumán, Universidad Nacional de Tucumán, Facultad
de Filosofía y Letras, 1965 [i.e. 1966]
162 p.   illus., facsims., port.   24 cm.
(Cuadernos de Humanitas, no. 18)
Universidad Nacional de Tucumán. Publicación
no. 918.
Bibliographical footnotes.

19795   Carilla, Emilio.
Estudios de literatura hispanoamericana [por]
Emilio Carilla. Bogotá, Instituto Caro y Cuervo,
1977.

377 p.   23 cm.   (Publicaciones del Instituto
Caro y Cuervo, XLII)

19796 Carilla, Emilio.
Hispanoamérica y su expresión literaria; caminos
del americanismo. [Buenos Aires] Editorial Universitaria de Buenos Aires [1969]
115 p.   18 cm.   (Colección América. Temas)
Bibliographical footnotes.

19797 Carilla, Emilio.
Lengua y estilo en Sarmiento. La Plata, Universidad
Nacional de La Plata, Facultad de Humanidades y
Ciencias de la Educación, 1964.
110 p.   23 cm.   (Departamento de Letras.
Monografías y tesis, 7)

19798 Carilla, Emilio.
Literatura argentina; palabra e imagen. [Buenos
Aires] Editorial Universitaria de Buenos Aires
[1969-
v.   illus., facsims., ports.   23 cm.
(Colección Argentina)
Includes bibliographies.
Library has v. 1 only.

19799 Carilla, Emilio.
Ricardo Jaime Freyre. [Buenos Aires] Ediciones
Culturales Argentinas, Ministerio de Educación y
Justicia, Dirección General de Cultura [1962]
167 p.   front., illus.   (Biblioteca del
sesquicentenario. Serie: Biblioteca americana)

19800 Carli, Gileno de.
JQ, Brasília e a grande crise. Rio de Janeiro,
Irmãos Pongetti, 1961.
184 p.   20 cm.

19801 Carli, Gileno de.
Política de desenvolvimento do Nordeste (gênese
dos artigos 34/18) Recife, Brasil, Universidade
Federal de Pernambuco, 1971.
67 p.   23 cm.

19802 Carmagnani, Marcello.
El salariado minero en Chile colonial; su
desarrollo en una sociedad provincial: el Norte
Chico, 1690-1800. [Santiago] Universidad de Chile,
Centro de Historia Colonial, 1963.

276

114 p.   diagrs., tables.   23 cm.
Bibliography: p. 110-114.

19803   Carmichael, Elizabeth.
Informe preliminar de las investigaciones arqueológicas en el area de Minas, Rio Jubones, Ecuador
[por] Elizabeth Carmichael, Warwick Bray, John
Erickson. [Cuenca, Sección de Antropología e Arqueología del Núcleo del Azuay de la Casa de la Cultura
Ecuatoriana, 1979]
130-144 p.   plans.   21½ cm.
Reprinted from Revista de antropología, no. 6,
julio de 1979.

19804   Carneiro, André.
Introdução ao estudo da "science-fiction". São
Paulo, Comissão de Literatura, Conselho Estadual de
Cultura, 1968.
140 p.   22½ cm.   (Coleção ensaio, 53)

19805   Carneiro, Cyro de Athayde, 1899-
A fundação de Santos; o cemitério do Paquetá; a
estrada de ferro. Santos, Tip. da Santa Casa, 1968.
30 p.   illus.   24 cm.
Bibliography: p. 16.

19806   Carneiro, David, 1904-
Brasília e o problema da federação brasileira.
Curitiba, Brasil, Imprensa da Universidade Federal
de Paraná, 1970.
137 p.   graph.   24 cm.

19807   Carneiro, David, 1904-
Cicloeconomia [por] David Carneiro. Curitiba,
1958.
244 p.   illus.   23 cm.
Bibliography: p. 241-244.
On cover: Universidade do Paraná. Faculdade de
Ciências Econômicas.

19808   Carneiro, David, 1904-
Educação, universidade e história da primeira
universidade do Brasil. Curitiba, Imprensa da
Universidade Federal do Paraná, 1972.
204 p.   illus., tables (1 fold.)   24 cm.

19809   Carneiro, David, 1904-
Elite, liderança, e massas, e as nações subdesen-
volvidas; ensaio de interpretação sociológica [por]

277

David Carneiro. Curitiba [Imprensa da Universidade
do Paraná] 1964.
215 p.   16 cm.

19810   Carneiro, Edison.
        Capoeira. Rio de Janeiro, Campanha de Defesa do
        Folclore Brasileiro, 1971.
        8 p.   23 cm.   (Cuadernos de folclore, 14)

19811   Carneiro, Edison.
        Folklore in Brazil. Translations into English
        [by John Knox] French [by France Knox] and German
        [by Richard W. Brackmann. Rio de Janeiro] Ministry
        of Education and Culture of Brasil, Companha de Defesa
        do Folclore Brasileiro, 1963.
        48 p.   illus., port.   23 cm.
        "Contains the translations... of an article
        published in numbers 3 and 4 (1962) of the Revista
        Brasileira de Folclore."
        Errata slip inserted.

19812   Carneiro, Edison.
        Ladinos e crioulos; estudos sôbre o negro no
        Brazil. Rio de Janeiro, Editôra Civilização brasileira
        [1964]
        240 p.   illus.   21 cm.   (Retratos do Brasil,
        v. 28)
        Bibliography: p. 231-240.

19813   Carneiro, Octavio Augusto Dias, 1912-
        Dois ensaios sôbre economia internacional. Recife,
        Comissão de Desenvolvimento Econômico de Pernambuco,
        1961.
        114 p.   24 cm.
        Contents. - Noções fundamentais de economia inter-
        nacional. - Redimentos da teoria pura do comercio
        internacional.

19814   Carneiro, Victor Ribas.
        ABC do espiritismo. Curitiba, Federação Espírita
        do Paraná, 1972.
        233 p.   21 cm.

19815   Carnero Checa, Genaro.
        La acción escrita: José Carlos Mariátegui,
        periodista; ensayo. [1. ed.] Lima, 1964.
        221 p.   facsims., ports.   22 cm.
        Bibliographical footnotes.

278

19816 Caro, Miguel Antonio, 1843-1909.
El centenario de "El Tradicionista," datos para la
biografía de Miguel Antonio Caro. Edición, introducción y notas de Carlos Valderrama Andrade. Bogotá,
Instituto Caro y Cuervo, 1972.
141 p.   illus., facsims.   24 cm.   (Filólogos
colombianos, 7)

19817 Caro, Miguel Antonio, 1843-1909.
Gramática de la lengua latina para el uso de los
que hablan castellano, por M. A. Caro y R. J. Cuervo
... Décima edición, con estudio preliminar e índices
por Jorge Paramo Pomareda. Bogotá, Instituto Caro
y Cuervo, 1972.
ciii, 947 p.   23½ cm.

19818 Caroni, Italo.
L'ambigüité du point de vue dans Poil de carotte,
de Jules Renard. [São Paulo, 1973]
275-282 p.   24½ cm.
Reprinted from Língua e literatura, revista dos
departamentos de letras da Faculdade de Filosofia,
Letras e Ciências Humanas da Universidade de São Paulo,
ano II, no. 2, 1973.

19819 Carpeaux, Otto María, 1900-
Pequeña bibliografía crítica da literatura brasileira.
3. ed. revista e aumentada. [Rio de Janeiro] Editôra
Letras e Artes, 1964.
335 p.   21 cm.

19820 Carpentier, Alejo.
América Latina en su música. La Habana, UNESCO,
Oficina Regional de Cultura para América Latina y
el Caraibe, Centro de Documentación, 1975.
19 p.   28 cm.   (La cultura en América Latina.
Monografías, 3)

19821 Carpio, Adolfo P
Páginas de filosofía [por] Adolfo P. Carpio.
Rosario, [Argentina] Universidad Nacional del Litoral,
Facultad de Filosofía y Letras, 1967.
332 p.   18 cm.
Bibliographical footnotes.

19822 Carpio Castillo, Rubén.
México, Cuba y Venezuela [triángulo geopolítico
del Caribe] Caracas, 1961.

226 p.   illus.   21 cm.
Includes bibliography.

19823 Carranza, Luján.
Siesta y amarillo; cuentos.   Santa Fé, Ediciones
Colmegna [1968]
115 p.   18 cm.
Contents. - Mil doscientos grados de justicia. -
Un buen oficio. - Siesta y amarillo. - Celeste. -
El gato y el alambre. - Faustino. - Las voces. -
El llamado. - La mujer del paraguas. - Los ojos de
Aldo Coria. - El primer llanto. - Los dos baldíos.

19824 Carranza, Roque G
Aplicaciones del algebra moderna a la inferencia
estadística [por] Roque G. Carranza y Luis M. Frediani.
[Buenos Aires] Universidad de Buenos Aires, Facultad
de Ciencias Exactas y Naturales, Departamento de
Matemática, 1962.
125 p.   illus., diagrs.   28 cm.
Includes bibliography.

19825 Carrasco, Pedro.
El catolicismo popular de los tarascos [por]
Pedro Carrasco.   [México, Secretaría de Educación
Pública, Dirección General de Divulgación, 1976]
216 p.   17 cm.   (Sep-Setentas, 298)
"Bibliografía": p. 207-213.

19826 Carrasco Puente, Rafael, 1902-
Datos históricos e iconografía de la educación en
México.   México, Secretaría de Educación Pública,
1960.
284 p.   illus.   23 cm.

19827 Carrasco Puente, Rafael, 1902-
La prensa en México; datos históricos.   Prólogo
de María del Carmen Ruiz Castañeda.   [México]
Universidad Nacional Autónoma de México [1962]
300 p.   illus., facsims.   24 cm.

19828 Carrasquera, Susana Noemí.
Leyenda de los ríos Limay y Neuquén [por] Susana
Noemí Carrasquera [y] José Antonio Güemes.   Liminar
y prólogo de José Antonio Güemes.   Neuquén, Facultad
de Humanidades, 1965.
46 l.   26 cm.   (Universidad del Neuquén.
Facultad de Humanidades. Publicaciones. Mitología, 2)
Includes bibliographical references.

19829   Carrasquilla, Tomás.
        Frutos de mi tierra. Edición y estudio por
        Seymour Menton. Bogotá, Instituto Caro y Cuervo,
        1972.
        lxvii, 357 p.   23 cm.   (Biblioteca Colombiana, IV)

19830   Carrasquilla, Tomás.
        La Marquesa de Yolombó. Edición crítica de Kurt L.
        Levy. Bogotá, Instituto Caro y Cuervo, 1974.
        630 p.   front. (port.), geneal. tables.
        (Biblioteca Colombiana, X)

19831   Carrazedo, Renato Octavio.
        Os despojados; [romance] Glicinia desenhou a capa.
        Rio de Janeiro, Irmãos Pongetti, 1964.
        122 p.   19 cm.

19832   Carreño, Alberto María, 1875-
        La Real y Pontificia Universidad de México, 1536-
        1865. Mexico, Universidad Nacional Autónoma, 1961.
        502 p.   22 cm.   (Publicaciones de la Coordinación
        de Humanidades y del Instituto de Historia)

19833   Carreño, F   ed.
        30 [i.e. Treinta] cantos del oriente Venezolano
        [por] F. Carreño [y] A. Vallmitjana. [Caracas]
        Dirección del Cultura, Ediciones del Ministerio de
        Educación Nacional, Servicio de Investigaciones
        Folklóricas Nacionales, 1947.
        69 p.   16 x 24 cm.
        Unaccompanied melodies.

19834   Carreño Latorre, Héctor.
        Los días y (antes). Santiago, Chile, Ediciones
        de la I. Municipalidad de Santiago, 1967.
        199 p.   20 cm.
        "Juegos literarios 'Gabriela Mistral'".

19835   Carreño Luengas, Alfredo.
        Cooperativas agrícolas; administración, organización.
        [Bogotá] Ministerio de Agricultura, División de
        Extensión Agrícola [1962]
        22 p.   22 cm.   (Boletín de divulgación, no. 1)
        Cover title.

19836   Carrera, Daniel P
        Peculado (de bienes públicos y de trabajos o
        servicios, art. 261 del Código penal) [por] Daniel P.
        Carrera. Buenos Aires, Ediciones Depalma, 1968.

                        281

xv, 210 p.   23 cm.
Bibliographical footnotes.

19837   Carrera Andrade, Jorge, 1903-
        Interpretación de Rubén Darío. Managua, Secretaría
        de la Presidencia de la República, Ediciones "Cuaderno
        Darianos," 1964.
        21 p.   24 cm.   (Colección Ensayos, v. 2)

19838   Carrera Bascuñán, Helena.
        El secreto profesional del abogado; estudio teórico
        y práctico. [Santiago] Editorial Jurídica de Chile,
        1963.
        251 p.   19 cm.   (Abogacía)

19839   Carrera Damas, Germán.
        Boves: aspectos socio-económicos de su acción
        histórica. Caracas [Ministerio de Educación,
        Dirección Técnica] Departamento de Publicaciones,
        1968.
        263 p.   port.   22 cm.   (Colección Vigilia, 14)
        Bibliography: p. 255-263.

19840   Carrera Damas, Germán.
        Cuestiones de historiografía venezolana. [Caracas]
        Universidad Central de Venezuela [1964]
        185 p.   16 cm.   (Colección Avance, 7)

19841   Carrera Damas, Germán, ed.
        Historia de la historiografía venezolana; textos
        para su estudio. Selección, introducción e índices
        de Germán Carrera Damas. Caracas, Universidad
        Central de Venezuela, Ediciones de la Biblioteca,
        1961.
        lxxii, 650 p.   23 cm.   (Ediciones de la
        Biblioteca, 5. Colección Ciencias sociales, 4)
        Bibliographical footnotes.

19842   Carrera Damas, Germán.
        Temas de historia social y de las ideas; estudios
        y conferencias. Caracas, Biblioteca, Universidad
        Central de Venezuela, 1969.
        198 p.   22 cm.   (Colección temas)

19843   [Carrera Stampa, Manuel]
        Historia del correo en México. México, Secretaría
        de Comunicaciones y Transportes, 1970.
        xxiv, 304 p.   illus., maps.   29 x 30 cm.

282

19844 Carril, Bonifacio del.
Notas sobre la vida y la obra de San Martín;
conferencia pronunciada el 16 de agosto de 1960.
[Buenos Aires] Ministerio de Educación y Justicia,
Dirección General de Cultura, Comisión Nacional de
Museos, Monumentos y Lugares Históricos, 1960
[i.e. 1961]
45 p.   illus.   23 cm.   (Museo Histórico
Nacional, Publicaciones, Serie 2, no. 18)

19845 Carrillo Batalla, Tomás Enrique.
La economía del comercio internacional de Venezuela.
Apéndice: Disposiciones legales sobre control de
cambios. Caracas, Editorial "Mundo Económico," 1962.
235 p.   23 cm.

19846 Carrillo Batalla, Tomás Enrique.
Población y desarrollo económico. Caracas, Banco
Central de Venezuela, 1967.
168 p.   19 cm.
Bibliographical footnotes.

19847 Carrillo Blanco, Fidencio.
... Los modalidades de la reforma agraria y los
medios legales para la realización de sus fines...
presenta Fidencio Carrillo Blanco. México, D. F.
[Tipográfica Mercantil] 1961.
109 p., 1 ℓ.   23 cm.
Tesis (licenciatura en derecho) - Univ. de México.
"Bibliografía": p. 109.

19848 Carrillo E   , Francisco Eduardo, ed.
Las 100 [i.e. cien] mejores poesías peruanas con-
temporáneas [por] Francisco Carrillo. Lima, 1961.
153 p.   19 cm.   (Antologías de la rama florida)

19849 Carrillo E   , Francisco Eduardo, ed.
Cuento peruano; 1904-1966. [Prólogo, selección y
notas de Francisco Camillo] Lima, Biblioteca
Universitaria, 1966.
300 p.   22 cm.   (Narrativa peruana contemporánea)
Includes bio-bibliographical sketches of the authors.

19850 Carrillo Flores, Antonio.
... Address... 13 April 1970, in the Hall of the
Americas, Pan American Union building, Washington,
D. C. [Washington, 1970]
11 p.   28½ cm.

19851   Carrillo y Gabriel, Abelardo.
          Ixmiquilpan. México, Instituto Nacional de Antro-
          pología e Historia, 1961.
          49 p.   illus.   23 cm.   (México. Dirección
          de Monumentos Coloniales. Publicaciones, 13)

19852   [Carrió de la Vandera, Alonso] b. ca. 1706.
          El lazarillo de ciegos caminantes desde Buenos
          Aires hasta Lima [por] Concolorcorvo [pseud.]
          Paris, Desclée, 1938.
          352 p.   18 cm.   (Biblioteca de cultura peruana,
          1. ser., no. 6)
          "Nota preliminar" signed: V. G. C.

19853   Carrizo Inostroza, Mireya.
          La ley como fuente del derecho administrativo y
          su interpretación en el derecho chileno. Santiago,
          Editorial Universitaria, 1958.
          147 p.   22 cm.
          Chapter 3 of the author's thesis, Universidad de
          Chile, Santiago.
          Bibliography: p. 143-146.

19854   Carro Carro, Mario César.
          La prescripción extintiva y la caducidad. México,
          1961.
          83 p.   24 cm.
          Tesis (licenciatura en derecho) - Universidad
          Nacional Autónoma de México.
          Bibliography: p. 81-83.

19855   Carrocera, Buenaventura de, ed.
          Los primeros historiadores de las misiones
          capuchinas en Venezuela. Caracas, Academia Nacional
          de la Historia, 1964.
          495, [2] p.   23 cm.   (Biblioteca de la Academia
          Nacional de la Historia, 69)
          Includes reports by José de Carabantes, Agustín
          de Frías, Francisco de Tauste, Lorenzo de Zaragoza,
          Mateo de Anguiano.

19856   Carroll, Thomas F   , comp.
          Land tenure and land reform in Latin America;
          a selective annotated bibliography. Tenencia de la
          tierra y reforma agraria en America Latina; una
          bibliografía anotada de caracter selectivo. Washington
          Economic Development Division, Inter-American Deve-
          lopment Bank, 1965.
          474 p.   20 cm.

19857   Cartaginese, Martha S
        Revisión del género Doryopteris en Argentina por
        Martha S. Cartaginese. Buenos Aires, 1977.
        106-122 p., 8 pl.   27 cm.
        Reprinted from Revista del Museo Argentino de
        Ciencias Naturales, Botánica, tomo V, no. 5.
        Summary in English: p. 121.

19858   Carvajal, Mario, 1896-
        Estampas y apologías. Cali, 1963.
        311 p.   20 cm.   (Biblioteca de la Universidad
        del Valle, 8)
        "Algunos de los escritos que forman parte de este
        libro integraron otro que, bajo el mismo título, fué
        publicado hace varios años."

19859   Carvajal, Mario, 1896-
        Testimonio universitario. Cali, Colombia,
        Biblioteca de la Universidad del Valle, 1969.
        214 p.   21 cm.

19860   Carvajal de Arocha, Mercedes.
        Cinco cuentos del sur [por] Lucila Palacios [pseud.]
        Montevideo, Barreiro y Ramos, 1962.
        42 p.   16 cm.
        Cover title.

19861   Carvalho, Afranio de.
        Reforma agraria. Apresentação de Themistocles
        Cavalcanti. [Rio de Janeiro] Edições O Cruzeiro
        [1963]
        288 p.   23 cm.
        Contents. - Anteprojeto de lei agrária. - Apêndice:
        Análise de documentos relativos à reforma agrária.

19862   Carvalho, Arp Procopio de.
        Geopolitica do transporte aereo. [São José dos
        Campos, S. P., Brazil, Serviço das Publicações do
        CTA, 1963]
        xx, 407 p.   illus.   23 cm.
        Errata leaf inserted.
        Bibliography: p. 397-403.

19863   Carvalho, Benedito de.
        ... Manual do escrivão (Código de processo civil);
        um roteiro processual para os serventuarios da justiça,
        contendo formularios de atos e termos judiciais...
        Rio de Janeiro, Irmãos Pongetti, 1961.
        500 p.   forms.   22 cm.

19864   Carvalho, Cônego José Geraldo V   de.
Arte mensageira da esperança. Discurso proferido
na Academia Marianense de Letras ao receber o nôvo
acadêmico Prof. Dr. Edgar de Vasconcelos Barros.
Dia 6 de outubro de 1968. [Belo Horizonte?] Imprensa
oficial, 1970.
42 p.   front. (port.)   24 cm.

19865   Carvalho, Doris de Queiroz.
Bibliotecas de escolas técnicas industriais;
manual de organização e funcionamento. Rio de Janeiro,
Departamento de Ensino Médio, Ministério da Educação
e Cultura, 1970.
173 p.   illus., fold. diagrs.   24 cm.

19866   Carvalho, Elias Pessoa de.
Administração sindical. 3a. edição. Brasilia,
Instituto Nacional de Colonização e Reforma Agrária,
1973.
141 p.   22 cm.

19867   Carvalho, Hervasio Guimarães de.
Angular distribution of photofission fragments
from uranium, by H. G. de Carvalho, A. G. da Silva
and J. Goldemberg. Rio de Janeiro, Centro Brasileiro
de Pesquisas Físicas, 1960.
75-92 p.   illus.   28 cm.   (Notas de física,
v. 7, no. 5)

19868   Carvalho, Hervasio Guimarães de.
High-energy-proton fission cross-sections of U,
Th and Bi, by H. G. de Carvalho, R. A. M. A. Nazareth
and A. F. Stehney. Rio de Janeiro, Centro Brasileiro
de Pesquisas Físicas, 1972.
83-94 p.   diagrs.   29 cm.   (Notas de física,
v. 19, no. 2)

19869   Carvalho, Hervasio Guimaraes de.
On the photofission cross sections of 209_{Bi}, 232_{Th}
and 238_{U} at intermediate energies, by H. G. de
Carvalho, J. B. Martins, O. A. P. Tavares, V. di
Napoli, and M. L. Terranova. Rio de Janeiro,
Centro Brasileiro de Pesquisas Físicas, 1973.
67-97 p.   diagrs.   29 cm.   (Notas de física,
v. 21, no. 5)

19870   Carvalho, José Augusto.
Lampejos d'alma; [poesias] Vitória [Brasil] 1962.
123 p.   19 cm.

19871 Carvalho, Marcelino de.
Guía de boas maneiras. São Paulo, Companhia Editôra
Nacional, 1961.
217 p. 20 cm.

19872 Carvalho, Maria do Céu.
Gramática da lingua espanhola; antologia e excer-
cicios [por] Maria do Ceu Carvalho [and] Agostinho
Dias Carneiro. Rio de Janeiro, Fundação Nacional de
Material Escolar, Ministério da Educação e Cultura,
1969.
407 p. illus. 24 cm.

19873 Carvalho, Mercedes Cardozo Pessoa de.
"Contribuição sindical rural." 2.ª edição revista
e atualizada. Brasília, Instituto Nacional de
Colonização e Reforma Agrária, 1973.
101 p. 22 cm.

19874 Carvalho, Rodrigues de, 1905-
Aspéctos da influência africana na formação social
do Brasil. [Paraiba] Imprensa universitaria, 1967.
95 p. 21 cm.

19875 Carvalho, Rodrigues de, 1905-
Serrote prêto; Lampeão e seus sequazes. Prefácio
de Alberto Rangel. Rio de Janeiro, SEDEGRA, 1961.
377 p. illus., ports. 22 cm.

19876 Carvalho, Tito.
Vida salobra; romance. Florianopolis, Livraria
Acadêmica, 1963.
v, 200 p. 23 cm.

19877 Carvalho de Mendonça, José Xavier.
Novissima guia eleitoral, contendo todas as leis
e regulamentos eleitoraes vigentes, grande numero
de actos expedidos pelo governo para a boa e fiel
execução das disposições destas leis, a jurisprudencia seguida pelos juizes e tribunaes nos actos
relativos ao alistamento dos eleitores, os casos
mais importantes julgados pelas camaras legislativas
em materia de reconhecimento de poderes de seus
membros... por José Xavier Carvalho de Mendonça...
Rio de Janeiro, B. L. Garnier, 1888.
viii p., 1 ℓ., 550 p. 6 forms on fold. ℓ. 19 cm.

19878 Carvalho e Silva, Maximiano de.
0 centro de pesquisas da Casa de Rui Barbosa.

20 anos de atividades 1952-1972. Rio de Janeiro,
Fundação Casa de Rui Barbosa, 1972.
66 p.   illus., facsims.   25 cm.

19879 Carvalho Lopes, Octacílio de.
"Appasionata" (os amôres de Beethoven) São Paulo,
Comissão Estadual de Literatura, Conselho Estadual
de Cultura, 1970.
67 p.   24 cm.   (Coleção textos e documentos,
19)

19880 Carvalho Lopes, Octacílio de.
Pethion de Vilar. São Paulo, Comissão de Literatura,
Conselho Estadual de Cultura, 1967.
189 p.   22 cm.   (Coleção ensaio, 17)

19881 Carvalho Neto, Paulo de, 1923-   ed.
Cuentos folklóricos del Ecuador; 52 registros de
la tradición oral. Glosario: Miguel Sánchez
Astudillo; prólogos: Kurt Ranke [y] Stanley L. Robe.
[1. ed. Quito, Editorial Universitaria, 1966]
305 p.   illus.   20 cm.
Prologues in German and English.
"Fichas de investigación": p. [295]-299.

19882 Carvalho Neto, Paulo de, 1923-
Folklore del Paraguay; sistemática analítica.
Quito, Editorial Universitaria, 1961.
475 p.   22 cm.

19883 Carvalho Neto, Paulo de, 1923-
Folklore y educación. Quito, Editorial Casa de
la Cultura Ecuatoriana, 1961.
315 p.   21 cm.

19884 Carvalho Neto, Paulo de, 1923-
El negro uruguayo; hasta la abolición. Quito,
Editorial Universitaria [1965]
345 p.   illus.   22 cm.
"Cuadro esquemático de elementos culturales en el
area de Guatemala precolombina": fold. leaf inserted.
Bibliography: p. 181-184.

19885 Carvalho Neto, Paulo de, 1923-
Tratado del folklore ecuatoriano. Quito, Editorial
Casa de la Cultura Ecuatoriana, 1964-
v.   illus., maps, ports.   29 cm.
Bibliography: v. 1, p. 437-445.
Contents. - v. 1. Diccionario del folklore ecuatoriano

19886 Carvallo Concha, Adolfo.
Ley orgánica de la Caja Nacional de Empleados
Públicos y Periodistas. 2. ed. actualizada, concor-
dada, anotada y aumentada. Valparaiso, Editorial de
la Escuela de Derecho de la Universidad de Chile,
1968.
109 p. 21 cm.

19887 Carvallo Hederra, Sergio.
Recopilación y análisis de las modificaciones a
la legislación tributaria. 1.er semestre, año 1967.
[Santiago de Chile] Editorial Jurídica de Chile, 1967.
171 p. 23½ cm.

19888 Carvallo Salazar, José Leonardo.
Médicos jurídicos de impugnación en la Ley de vías
generales de comunicación. México [1963?]
64, [2] l. 24 cm.
Tesis (licenciatura en derecho) - Universidad
Nacional Autónoma de México.
Bibliography: leaves 64-[65]

19889 Casamiquela, Rodolfo M
Estudio del nillantún y la religión araucana [por]
Rodolfo M. Casamiquela. Bahía Blanca, 1964.
271 p. illus., map. 24 cm. (Universidad
Nacional del Sur. Instituto de Humanidades.
Cuadernos del Sur)
Bibliography: p. 253-257.

19890 Casamiquela, Rodolfo M
Geonomía de Río Negro [por] Rodolfo Casamiquela.
Viedma [Ministerio de Asuntos Sociales, Dirección
de Cultura] 1967.
49 p. 23 cm.

19891 Casamiquela, Rodolfo M
Sobre la significación mágica del arte rupestre
nord-patagónico. Bahía Blanca [República Argentina]
1960.
55 p. illus. 24 cm. (Universidad Nacional
del Sur. Instituto de Humanidades. Cuadernos del
Sur)

19892 Casas, Bartolomé de las, bp., 1474-1566.
Las exhortaciones que hacían en México los padres
a los hijos. Monterrey, México, Ediciones Sierra
Madre, 1972.
15 p. 22 cm. (Poesía en el mundo, 104)

19893 Casas, Bartolomé de las, bp., 1474-1566.
Los tesoros del Perú. Traducción y anotación de
Angel Losada. Madrid, Consejo Superior de Investi-
gaciones Científicas, Instituto "Gonzalo F. de Oviedo"
y "Francisco de Vitoria", 1958.
xxviii, 480 p.   facsims.   25 cm.
Transcription, with Spanish translation, of the
Latin manuscript in the Biblioteca de Palacio de
Madrid (Sig. Mss. 938)
"Breve nota bibliográfica": p. [457]

19894 Casas, Bartolomé de las, bp., 1474-1566.
Tratado de Indias y el Doctor Sepúlveda. [Estudio
preliminar de Manuel Jiménez Fernández] Caracas,
Academia Nacional de la Historia, 1962.
lxxviii, 260 p.   23 cm.   (Biblioteca de la
Academia Nacional de la Historia, 56)

19895 Casas Grieve, Luis Felipe de las.
Plan y gobierno; fundamentos para la formulación
del plan de gobierno aprista. Lima, Partido Aprista
Peruano, Secretaría Nacional de Plan de Gobierno,
1961.
190 p.   illus.   19 cm.
Includes bibliography.

19896 Casas y González, Juan Bautista.
Estudios acerca del régimen y administración de
España en Ultramar, seguidos de una disertación sobre
los carácteres de la civilización hispanoamericana.
La guerra separatista de Cuba; sus causas, medios
de terminarla y de evitar otras, por el doctor D.
Juan Bautista Casas... Madrid, Est. tipog. de San
Francisco de Sales, 1896.
xviii, 490, [1] p.   23 cm.
Half-title: La guerra separatista de Cuba.

19897 Casanta, Tereza.
Criança e literatura. Belo Horizonte, Centro
Regional de Pesquisas Educacionais João Pinheiro
[1968]
64 p.   illus.   24 cm.   (Caderno de educação, 3)

19898 Casasús de Sierra, Margarita.
Las llaves perdidas; análisis. Introducción:
Manuel J. Sierra. Ilustraciones: Elvira Gascón.
[1. ed.] México, Universidad Nacional Autónoma de
México, 1961.
280 p.   illus.   24 cm.

19899 Cascia, Adolfo.
       La apicultura en su aspecto económico (mercado de
       la miel) Pergamino, Estación Experimental Regional
       Agropecuaria Pergamino, 1973.
       30 p.   tables.   27½ cm.   (Informe técnico,
       no. 122)
       Summary in English.

19900 Cascudo, Luis da Camara, 1899-
       Dante Alighiere e a tradição popular no Brasil:
       La divina commedia, La vita nuova, Il convivio.
       Pôrto Alegre, Pontificia Universidade Católica do
       R. G. S., 1963.
       326 p.   24 cm.

19901 Case, Alden Buell, 1851-1932.
       Thirty years with the Mexicans; in peace and
       revolution, by Alden Buell Case... New York, Chicago
       [etc.] Fleming H. Revell company [c1917]
       3 p.l., 5-285 p.   front., plates.   21 cm.

19902 Casey, Alfredo.
       Adán ciego; drama en tres actos. [La Plata]
       Municipalidad de La Plata [1962]
       111 p.   18 cm.

19903 Casimir Liautaud, Jean.
       La República de Haiti; ensayo de interpretación
       sociológica. México, 1962.
       ii, 93 l.   tables.   28 cm.
       Tesis (licenciatura en ciencias sociales) -
       Universidad Nacional Autónoma de México.
       Bibliography: leaves [90]-93.

19904 Cassani, Jorge Luis.
       Metodología de la investigación histórica;
       la heurística y la clasificación de las fuentes,
       por Jorge Luis Cassani y A. J. Pérez Amuchástegui.
       Santa Fé, 1961.
       59 p.   23 cm.   (Universidad Nacional del
       Litoral. Departamento de Pedagogía Universitaria.
       Serie Extensión cultura, 2)
       Bibliographical footnotes.

19905 Cassani, Joseph, 1673-1750.
       Historia de la Provincia de la Compañía de
       Jesús del Nuevo Granada en la América. Estudio
       preliminar y anotaciones al texto por José del Rey.
       Caracas, Academia Nacional de la Historia, 1967.

xcix, 451 p.   23 cm.   (Biblioteca de la Academia
Nacional de la Historia, 85)

19906   Castagnino, Raúl H
        El teatro de Roberto Arlt [por] Raúl H. Castagnino.
        La Plata, Universidad Nacional de La Plata, Facultad
        de Humanidades y Ciencias de la Educación [1964]
        96 p.   23 cm.   (Departamento de Letras.
        Monografías y tesis, 6)

19907   Castagnino, Raúl H
        El teatro romántico de Martín Coronado. [Buenos
        Aires] Ediciones Culturales Argentinas, Ministerio
        de Educación y Justicia, Dirección General de Cultura.
        [1962]
        208 p.   illus.   25 cm.   (Biblioteca del
        sesquicentenario. Serie Cuadernos culturales)

19908   Castañé Recoud, Carlos.
        Tres acciones tácticas de la Guerra del Chaco.
        Asunción del Paraguay, Editorial El Gráfico, 1962.
        83 p.   illus.   20 cm.

19909   Castañeda, Francisco.
        El General Menéndez y sus victimarios; páginas
        de la historia contemporánea de la República de
        El Salvador. San Salvador, Dirección General de
        Publicaciones, Ministerio de Educación, 1966.
        193 p.   port.   25½ cm.   (Colección Historia,
        13)

19910   Castañeda, Gabriel Angel.
        Ismael Cerna; boreto para su estatua literaria
        previa a su fundición en bronce. 1856, centenario,
        1956. Guatemala [Tipografía Nacional] 1962.
        207 p.   illus., ports.   20 cm.   (Colección
        los de ayer, v. 3)
        "Apéndice lírico": p. 101-127.
        "La penitenciaria de Guatemala; drama histórico
        nacional en tres actos y en verso, por Ismael Cerna"
        (p. [131]-201) has special t.p. Includes bibliography.

19911   Castañeda Alarcón, José A
        Apuntes sobre derecho del trabajo; contrato de
        trabajo [por] José A. Alarcón Castañeda. Bogotá,
        1962.
        93 p.   25 cm.
        Tesis - Pontificia Universidad Javeriana, Bogotá.
        Bibliography: p. 93.

19912 Castaño, Luis.
       Temas de sociología política mexicana. México,
       Instituto de Investigaciones Sociales, Universidad
       Nacional Autónoma de México, 1961.
       165 p.   18 cm.   (Cuadernos de sociología;
       biblioteca de ensayos sociológicos)

19913 Castañón Rodríguez, Jesús.
       Los primeros 25 [i.e. veinticinco] años de indus-
       trialización en Puebla [por] Jesús Castañón R.
       México, Boletín Bibliográfico de la Secretaría de
       Hacienda y Crédito Público, 1960.
       21 p.   facsim., port.   23 cm.

19914 Casteel, J   Doyle.
       Five micro-simulations illustrating cross-cultural
       conflict in a Latin American setting [by] J. Doyle
       Casteel, Terry L. McCoy, Felicity M. Trueblood.
       [Gainesville] University of Florida, Center for
       Latin American Studies, 1978.
       25 p.   28 cm.   (Curriculum report, no. 5)

19915 Castellano, Enrique.
       La generación del 18 en la poética venezolana.
       [Caracas, Comisión Nacional del Cuatricentenario de
       la Fundación de Caracas, Comité de Obras Culturales,
       1966]
       147 p.   24 cm.   (Ediciones del cuatricentenario
       de Caracas)

19916 Castellanos, Alfredo.
       Historia hidrogeológica del río Corriente.
       Rosario, Argentina, 1959.
       30 p.   maps.   25 cm.
       At head of title: Universidad Nacional del
       Litoral, Facultad de Filosofía y Letras.
       English summary.

19917 Castellanos, Alfredo.
       Nuevos restos del género "Stromaphoropsis" Kragl.
       del Uruguay, por Alfredo Castellanos. Rosario,
       Universidad Nacional del Litoral, Instituto de
       Fisiografía y Geología, 1949.
       48 p., 22 p. of plates.   illus., tables.   26 cm.
       (Publicaciones, XXXVII)

19918 Castellanos, Alfredo.
       Restos de "Boreostracon corondanus" n. sp. descu-
       biertos en la provincia de Santa Fé (Argentina)

Tucumán, 1958.
135-189 p.   illus., tables.   23½ cm.
"Edición del autor; de Acta geológica Lilloana,
tomo II, páginas 135-189."
Abstract in English.
Appended to this is Castellanos' Anotaciones
fundamentales para el trazado geomorfológico de la
provincia de Corrientes, in Boletín de la Filial
Rosario de la Sociedad Argentina de Estudios Geográficos, no. 6, 1 April 1972.

19919   Castellanos, Alfredo.
Sedimentos neógenos del S. W. del Uruguay (nota
preliminar) Rosario [Argentina] 1948.
35 p.   illus.   28 cm.   (Universidad Nacional
del Litoral. Facultad de Ciencias Matemáticas,
Físico-Químicas y Naturales Aplicadas a la Industria.
[Publicaciones] Serie técnico-científica, publicación
no. 34)

19920   Castellanos, Diego Luis.
Manual para estudios de mercados, guía metodológica.
[Caracas, Taller Gráfico de Mersifrica, 1960]
126 p.   23 cm.

19921   Castellanos, Juan de, 1522-1607.
Elegías de varones ilustres de Indias. Introducción
y notas de Isaac J. Pardo. Caracas, Academia Nacional
de la Historia, 1962.
xcvii, 284 p.   23 cm.   (Biblioteca de la
Academia Nacional de la Historia, 57)
An abridged edition containing pt. 1, elegías 9 to 14
and pt. 2, elegías 1 to 3.

19922   Castellanos, Luis.
El alzamiento, novela. Bogotá, Ediciones Edicrón,
1962.
211 p.   20 cm.

19923   Castellanos, Zulma J   A   de.
Contribución al conocimiento biológico del
calamar argentino, Illex illecebrosus argentinus,
por Zulma J. A. de Castellanos. Mar del Plata,
1964.
35 p.   illus., map.   25 cm.   (Boletín del
Instituto de Biología Marina, no. 8)
Summary in English.
Bibliography: p. [33]-34.

19924 Castellanos, Zulma J   A   de.
       Contribución al estudio biológico de Loligo
       brasiliensis Bl. Mar del Plata, Instituto de
       Biología Marina, Universidades Nacionales de Buenos
       Aires, 1967.
       33 p.   25 cm.   (Boletín, 14)

19925 Castelli, Eugenio.
       Estructura mítica e interioridad en "Don Segundo
       Sombra" [por] Eugenio Castelli [y] Rogelio Barufaldi.
       Santa Fé, Argentina, Librería y Editorial Colmegna
       [1968]
       51 p.   18 cm.   (Colección Hispanoamérica [4])
       "Publicación del Instituto Argentino de Cultura
       Hispánica de Rosario."
       Contents. - Estructura mítica de "Don Segundo
       Sombra," por E. Castelli. - Interioridad del contorno
       regional en "Don Segundo Sombra," por R. Barufaldi. -
       Bibliografía sobre Güiraldes (p. 47-51)

19926 Castello, Jose Aderaldo.
       O movimento academicista no Brasil; 1641-1820/22.
       São Paulo, Conselho Estadual de Cultura, 1969.
             v.   (Conselho Estadual de Cultura. Coleção
       textos e documentos)
             Library has v. I, t. 3 (no. 15), v. I, t. 4 (no. 18),
       v. I, t. 5 (no. 20)

19927 Castello, Lucia.
       La edad incierta, y Confidencias de dos inmigrantes;
       [relatos] Montevideo, 1964.
       79 p.   20 cm.

19928 Castello Branco, José Moreira Brandão.
       Descobrimento das terras da região acreana.
       Rio de Janeiro, Departamento de Imprensa Nacional,
       1960.
       101 p.   illus.   23 cm.

19929 Castello Branco, Manoel Thomaz.
       O Brasil na II Grande Guerra. [Rio de Janeiro]
       Biblioteca do Exército, 1960.
       630 p.   illus., ports., maps (part fold.)
       plans, tables.   23 cm.   (Brazil. Ministerio
       da Guerra. Biblioteca do Exército, 268-269)
       Bibliography: p. [611]-614.
       Errata slip inserted.

295

19930 Castelo, José Aderaldo.
Método e interpretação. São Paulo, Conselho
Estadual de Cultura, Comissão de Literatura [1965]
147 p. 22 cm. (Coleção Ensaio, 39)

19931 Castelo, José Aderaldo, ed.
Textos que interessam à histórica do romanticismo.
São Paulo, Conselho Estadual de Cultura, Comissão
de Literatura [1961-
v. 24 cm. (Coleção Textos e documentos, 4)

19932 Castilla Rosa Pérez, Elias.
Tutoría en educación. Arequipa, Cuzzi, Impresores,
1960.
vii, 196 p. 24 cm.
Bibliography: p. [195]-196.

19933 Castillero Pimentel, Ernesto, 1918-
Panamá y los Estados Unidos. [1. ed.] Panamá
[1964]
336, cxli p. illus., facsims., maps, ports.
20 cm.
Bibliography: p. cxv-cxxv.

19934 Castillero Pimentel, Ernesto, 1918-
Política exterior de Panamá; los objectivos de
nuestra política exterior, los instrumentos o medios
para lograrlos y las bases generales del nuevo
tratado que debe la República de Panamá negociar
con los Estados Unidos de América. Panamá [Impresora
Panamá] 1961.
84 p. illus. 21 cm.
Includes bibliography.

19935 Castillero Reyes, Ernesto de Jesús, 1889-
La isla que se transformó en ciudad; historia de
un siglo de la ciudad de Colón. Panamá, 1962.
270 p. illus., ports. 22 cm.
Bibliography: p. 255-259.

19936 Castillo, Carlos José del.
Aplicación práctica de la proyección mercator
transversal universal (U. T. M.) Caracas, 1961
[i.e. 1962]
72, [93] p. illus. 23 cm.
At head of title: República de Venezuela. Ministerio de Obras Públicas. Dirección de Cartografía
Nacional.
"Proyección U.T.M. Tablas": p. [1]-[93](2nd group)

296

19937 Castillo, Domingo B
Memorias de Mano Lobo. La cuestión monetaria en
Venezuela. Caracas Presidencia de la República
1962.
423 p. port., facsims. 24 cm. (Colección
"Venezuela peregrina," 1)

19938 Castillo, Eduardo, 1889-
Obra poética. Bogotá, Edición del Ministerio de
Educación, 1965.
288 p. 24 cm.

19939 Castillo F   , Víctor M
Nezahualcóyotl, crónica y pinturas de su tiempo.
Texcoco, Gobierno del Estado de México, 1972.
197 p. illus. 24 cm.

19940 Castillo Ruiz, Rafael del.
El petróleo y el desarrollo económico de México;
análisis jurídico económico de la industria.
[México] 1963.
149, iii p. 23 cm.
Tesis (licenciatura en derecho) - Universidad
Nacional Autónoma de México.
Bibliography: p. 147-149.

19941 Castillo y Guevara, Francisca Josefa de.
Obras completas de la Madre Francisca Josefa de
la Concepción de Castillo; según fiel transcripción
de los manuscritos originales que se conservan en la
Biblioteca Luis-Angel Arango. Introducción, notas
e índices por Dario Achury Valenzuela. Bogotá,
Talleres Gráficos del Banco de la República, 1968.
2 v. illus., facsims. 28 cm.

19942 Castiñeira de Dios, José María.
El leño verde; [poemas por] J. M. Castiñeira de
Dios. Buenos Aires, Edición "4 Rumbos," 1960.
[54] p. 21 cm.

19943 Castiñeiras, Pedro F
Los precios del acero, por Pedro F. Castiñeiras.
[Buenos Aires?] Siderurgia Argentina [1967]
[22] p. illus. 22 cm.
Cover title.
"Publicado por el diario 'Clarín' de Buenos Aires
el día 25 de junio de 1967."

19944   Castonnet des Fosses, Henri Louis, 1846-1898.
        Cuba & Puerto-Rico; conférence faite à Roubaix
        le 15 février 1889, par m. H. Castonnet des Fosses...
        Lille, Imprimerie L. Danel, 1889.
        24 p.   23 cm.
        At head of cover-title: Société de géographie de
        Lille.

19945   Castorena, José de Jesús.
        Manual de derecho obrero [por] J. Jesús Castorena.
        4. ed. [aumentada y corregida] México, 1964.
        327 p.   23 cm.

19946   Castrillón Muñoz, Aurelio.
        Historial de las banderas y escudos nacionales.
        [Bogotá? Impr. de las Fuerzas Militares, 1962?]
        114 p.   illus.   22 x 29 cm.
        "Suplemento de la Revista de las Fuerzas Armadas."

19947   Castro, Américo, 1885-
        ... Conferencias dadas en el salón de honor de la
        Universidad [de Chile] en 1923 por el profesor de
        filología de la Universidad Central de Madrid, don
        Américo Castro. Santiago de Chile, Sociedad Imprenta
        y Litografía Universo, 1924.
        173 p.   25½ cm.
        Contents. - Épocas principales de la historia de
        la lengua española. - Influencia del renacimiento en
        la evolución de la lengua española. - "La Celestina"
        de Fernando Rojas, como representación del concepto
        renacentista de la vida. - Lope de Vega, sus obras. -
        Cervantes, su filosofía de la naturaleza i su técnica
        literaria. - Metodología de la enseñanza de la lengua
        y literatura españolas.

19948   Castro, Carlo Antonio.
        Intima fauna. Xalapa, México, Universidad Vera-
        cruzana, 1962.
        101 p.   20 cm.   (Universidad Veracruzana.
        Ficción 49)
        Poems.

19949   Castro, Cláudio de.
        Contribuição ao estudo das rochas granulíticas
        de Salvador-Bahía [por] Cláudio de Castro [e] Alcides
        Nobrega Sial. Recife, Universidade Federal de
        Pernambuco, Instituto de Geociências, 1971.
        18 p.   illus.   23 cm.   (Universidade Federal

de Pernambuco. Instituto de Geociências. Série B:
Estudos e pesquisas, v. 1, no. 2)

19950 Castro, Cláudio de.
Descoberta de resinas fósseis na Chapada do Araripe,
município de Porteira, Ceará [por] Cláudio de Castro,
Eldemar de A. Menor [e] Vilma Alves Campanha. Recife,
Universidade Federal de Pernambuco, Instituto de
Geociências, 1970.
11 p.   illus., tables.   23 cm.   (Série C,
Notas prévias, v. I, no. 1)
English abstract: p. 10.
"Referências bibliográficas": p. 11.

19951 Castro, Dolores.
La ciudad y el viento; novela. Xalapa, México,
Universidad Veracruzana, 1962.
111 p.   20 cm.   (Universidad Veracruzana.
Ficción, 43)

19952 Castro, José Antonio.
La bárbara memoria. Maracaibo, Facultad de
Humanidades, Universidad del Zulia [1973]
[48] p.   illus.   32 cm.
"Portada, maqueta y dibujos: José Francisco
Bellorín."
Poems.

19953 Castro, José Antonio.
Narrativa modernista y concepción del mundo.
[Maracaibo] Universidad del Zulia, Centro de Estudios
Literarios [1973]
186 p.   20 cm.

19954 Castro, José Antonio.
El proceso creador [por] José Antonio Castro.
Maracaibo, Universidad del Zulia, Facultad de Humanidades y Educación, Centro de Estudios Literarios,
1975.
148 p.   22 cm.

19955 Castro, José Félix.
Estructura de la radiodifusión. Bogotá [Editorial
Cultura] 1962.
324 p.   illus.   23 cm.   (Publicación del
Colegio Superior de Publicidad, Periodismo y Radio-
difusión)

19956   Castro, M   Vianna de.
        A aristocracia rural fluminense. Rio de Janeiro,
        Gráfica Laemmert, 1961.
        27 p.   illus., ports.   24 cm.
        Includes bibliography.

19957   Castro, Manuel de, 1896-
        Metafísica del vino, y otras poemas.   [Montevideo,
        Taller Gráfica Gaceta Comercial] 1963.
        49 p.   illus.   17 cm.

19958   Castro, Mauro Cunha Campos de Moraes e.
        O funcionário e o mandato eletivo gratuito.   [Rio de
        Janeiro] D. A. S. P., Serviço de Documentação, 1961.
        93 p.   24 cm.

19959   Castro Aguirre, Constancio de.
        Teoria psicométrica de la confiabilidad; su alcance
        en la construcción de una ciencia psicológica.   Caracas,
        Ediciones de la Biblioteca, Universidad Central de
        Venezuela, 1968.
        63 p.   16½ cm.   (Colección las ciencias)

19960   Castro Alves, Antônio de, 1847-1871.
        Castro Alves; antologia poética, com um retrato
        e uma vinheta por Adolfo Pastor.   Montevidéu,
        Instituto de Cultura Uruguaio-Brasileiro, 1968.
        65 p.   front.   20 cm.   (Coleção "Textos
        brasileiros," 2)
        Introductory material in Spanish; text in Portuguese.

19961   Castro Alves, Antônio de, 1847-1871.
        Gonzaga ou a revolução de Minas, drama em 4 atos.
        Rio de Janeiro, Serviço Nacional de Teatro, 1972.
        vi, 178 p.   21 cm.

19962   Castro Alves, Antônio, 1847-1871.
        Obra completa. Organização, estudo crítico,
        fixação de texto, cronologia e notas preliminares
        por Eugênio Gomes... Rio de Janeiro, José Aguilar
        [1966]
        794 p.   illus.   17 cm.
        "Segunda edição."

19963   Castro Bastos, Leonidas.
        Bibliografía geológica del Perú. Lima, 1960.
        317 p.   23 cm.

                            300

19964 Castro Bastos, Leonidas.
       Geohistoria del Perú; ensayo económico, político,
       social. Lima, 1962.
       324 p.   22 cm.
       Includes bibliography.

19965 Castro Bastos, Leonidas.
       Golpismo; [ensayo socio-político. Lima, D. Miranda,
       1964]
       200 p.   18 cm.

19966 Castro Contreras, Jaime.
       Política y huelga bancaria [por] Jaime Castro
       Contreras [y] Jesús Higinio Calonge. Lima, Peru,
       Universidad Nacional Federico Villarreal, 1973.
       119 p.   22 cm.

19967 Castro Leal, Antonio, ed.
       La novela de la revolución mexicana. Selección,
       introducción general, cronología, historia, prólogos,
       censo de personajes, índice de lugares, vocabulario
       y bibliografía. México, Aguilar, 1960.
       2 v.   fronts.   19 cm.
       Contents: v. 1. Mariano Azuela. Los de abajo.
       Los caciques. Las moscas. - Martín Luis Guzmán.
       El aguila y la serpiente. La sombra del caudillo. -
       José Vasconcelos. Ulises criollo. - Agustín Vera.
       La revancha. - Nellie Campobello. Cartucho. Las
       manos de mamá. - v. 2. José Rubén Romero. Apuntes
       de un lugareño. Desbandada. - Gregorio López y
       Fuentes. Campamento. Tierra. ¡Mi general! -
       Francisco L. Urquizo. Tropa vieja. - José Mancisidor.
       Frontera junto al mar. En la rosa de los vientos. -
       Rafael F. Muñoz. ¡Vámonos con Pancho Villa! Se
       llevaron el cañón para Bachimba. - Mauricio Magdaleno.
       El resplandor. - Miguel N. Lira. La escondida.

19968 Castro Leal, Antonio, ed.
       La novela del México colonial. Estudio preliminar,
       selección, biografías, bibliografía general y lista
       de los principales acontecimientos de la Nueva
       España de 1517 a 1821... Madrid, México, Buenos
       Aires, Aguilar, 1964.
       2 v.   illus.   19 cm.
       Contents: v. 1. Carlos de Sigüenza y Góngora.
       Los infortunios de Alonso Ramírez. - Anónimo.
       Xicoténcatl. - José Tomás de Cuéllar. El pecado del
       siglo. - Eligio Ancona. Los mártires del Anáhuac.
       El filibustero. Memorias de un alférez. - Heriberto

Frías. Leyendas históricas nacionales. - v. 2.
Justo Sierra O'Reilly. La hija del judío. - Vicente
Riva Palacio. Monja y casada, virgen y mártir.
Martín Garatuza. - José Pascual Almazán. Un hereje
y un musulmán. - Luis González Obregón. Leyendas de
las calles de México.

19969 Castro Nájera, Miguel Antonio.
El consentimiento del interesado. México, Univer-
sidad Nacional Autónoma de México, Facultad de
Derecho, 1962.
106 p.   23 cm.
Bibliography: p. 105-106.

19970 Castro Pineda, Lucio.
Morfología castellana. Lima [196-?]
376 p.   23 cm.
Stamped on t. p.: Librería J. Mejía Baca, Lima.

19971 Castro Romero, Jorge.
Panorama agro-pecuario y socio-económico de Boyacá.
[1. ed. Tunja] Contraloría General de Boyacá, Fondo
Rotatorio de Publicaciones, 1967.
76, [3] p.   maps.   24 cm.   (Colección Socio-
logía y economía)
Publicaciones de la Contraloría General de Boyacá,
Fondo Rotatorio de Publicaciones, v. 5.
Bibliography: p. [77]

19972 Castro Saavedra, Carlos.
Breve antología; poesías. Medellín, Universidad
Pontificia Bolivariana, 1969.
63 p.   16 cm.   (Colección Rojo y negro, 65)

19973 Castro Saavedra, Carlos.
Obra selecta. Manizales, Colombia, A. Nariño,
1962.
550 p.   19 cm.

19974 Castro Viana, Djalma, 1900-
Colcha de retalhos. Teatro-poesía. Rio de Janeiro,
Serviço Nacional de Teatro, 1972.
134 p.   21 cm.

19975 Castro y Bachiller, Raymundo de.
Centenario del nacimiento del Dr. Jorge Le-Roy y
Cassá. La Habana, Consejo Científico, Ministerio de
Salud Pública, 1968.
166 p.   front., illus.   23 cm.   (Cuadernos de

historia de la salud pública, 37)
Bibliography: p. 151-160.

19976 Casudo, Luis de Câmara.
Folclore do Brasil; pesquisas e notas. Rio de
Janeiro, Editôra Fundo de Cultura, 1967.
252 p.   illus.   20 cm.   (Biblioteca Fundo
Universal de Cultura. Estante de sociologia)

19977 Catá, Alvaro, d. 1908.
... De guerra á guerra. La Habana, La Razón [1906]
6 p.l., [15]-240 p.   18 cm.

19978 Catalán, Hilda.
Servicio social; conceptos fundamentales. Santiago,
Chile, Editorial Universitaria, 1971.
135 p.   19½ cm.   (Colección manuales y mono-
grafías, 10)
Bibliography: p. 134-135.

19979 Catalani, Wally R
Localización del Centro Universitario de Mendoza
y las redes hidrográficas del área. Rosario,
Argentina, Instituto de Fisiografía y Geología,
Facultad de Ciencias, Ingeniería y Arquitectura,
Universidad Nacional de Rosario, 1972.
16 p.   illus., maps, diagrs.   27½ cm.
(Serie A, no. 6)

19980 Catalano, Edmundo Fernando.
Productividad, por Edmundo F. Catalano y Horacio
Pousa. Buenos Aires, Banco Industrial de la República
Argentina, Dirección General de Desarrollo Industrial,
Departamento de Estudios Técnicos, 1961.
72 p.   30 cm.

19981 Catalano, Luciano R
Energía hidroeléctrica argentina, valle Calchaquí,
Provincia de Salta; estudios y anteproyectos de
construcción de varias usinas hidroeléctricas en los
Rios Chuscha y Mischi, por Luciano R. Catalano.
Buenos Aires, 1965.
86 p.   illus., fold. maps.   20 cm.   (Subse-
cretaría de Minería. Serie argentina, no. 7)

19982 Cataldi D   , Alberto.
La situación demográfica del Uruguay en 1957 y
proyecciones a 1982. Santiago, Chile, 1964.

120 p.   tables.   28 cm.   (Chile. Universidad,
Santiago. Centro Latino-americano de Demografía.
Serie C, 15)

19983   Catalogação simplificada usada na Biblioteca Pública
        do Estado, por Ida Maria Groen Caiado de Castro,
        Elisabete Maisonnave Heidrich, Frida Enk, Sara
        Roitman Jakobson. Pôrto Alegre, Departamento de
        Educação e Cultura, 1968.
        18 ℓ.   33 cm.
        At head of title: Universidade Federal do Rio Grand(
        do Sul. Departamento de Educação e Cultura & Associaçã
        Riograndense de Bibliotecários.
        "I Jornada Sul Riograndense de Biblioteconomia e
        Documentação... Tema 2: Processos técnicos."
        Bibliography: leaf [12]

19984   Catholic Church. Archdiocese of Belo Horizonte.
        Igreja para servir; guia informativo dos serviços
        da Igreja no Brasil de modo especial na Arquidiocese
        de Belo Horizonte. Uma elaboração para o Dep. de
        Informações da Arquidiocese - DIA. Belo Horizonte,
        Imp. Oficial, 1967.
        155 p.   23 cm.

19985   Catholic Church. Conferencia Episcopal de Colombia.
        La Iglesia ante el cambio; [conclusiones y
        orientaciones de la XXV Asamblea Plenaria del Episco-
        pado Colombiano, Bogotá, 1-9 de julio de 1969] Bogotá,
        Secretariado Permanente del Episcopado Colombiano
        [1969]
        160 p.   21 cm.
        "Tercera edición."

19986   Catholic Church. Society of Jesus. Institutum Histo-
        ricum Societatis Iesus, Rome.
        Bibliografía de Serafim Leite S. I. Apresentação
        de Miguel Batlori. Roma, 1962.
        105 p.   20 cm.   (Subsidia ad historiam S. I.
        Series minor, 5)

19987   Catholic Church in Chile. Comité Permanente de los
        Obispos de Chile.
        Chile, voluntad de ser. [Santiago de Chile,
        Ediciones Paulinas, Alameda Bernardo O'Higgins,
        1626, 1968]
        [25] unnumb. ℓ.   15 x 19 cm.

19988 Catholic Church in Chile. Secretariado General del
       Episcopado de Chile.
       La Iglesia y el problema del campesinado chileno;
       pastoral colectiva del episcopado de Chile. Santiago
       de Chile, Secretariado General del Episcopado de
       Chile, 1962.
       36 p.   19 cm.

19989 Catholic Church in Chile. Secretariado General del
       Episcopado de Chile.
       Los obispos de Chile hablan. El cristiano en el
       mundo actual y los medios de difusión. Santiago de
       Chile, Publicación del Secretariado General del
       Episcopado de Chile, 1962.
       [111] p.   19 cm.

19990 Cattaneo di Tirano, Pino.
       Un ciego de barro, y otros cuentos. [La Plata]
       Municipalidad de La Plata [1962]
       117 p.   18 cm.

19991 Caturelli, Alberto.
       En el corazón de Pascal. Córdoba, Facultad de
       Filosofía y Humanidades, Universidad Nacional de
       Córdoba [1970]
       53 p.   20½ cm.

19992 Caturelli, Alberto.
       La filosofía en Argentina actual. [Córdoba]
       Dirección General de Publicidad, Universidad Nacional
       de Córdoba [1963, c1962]
       113 p.   21 cm.   (Colección de ensayos y
       estudios)
       Bibliographical footnotes.

19993 Caturelli, Alberto.
       ... La filosofía en la Argentina actual...
       Buenos Aires, Editorial Sudamericana [1971]
       373 p.   21 cm.

19994 Caturelli, Alberto.
       Presente y futuro de la filosofía en la Argentina.
       Córdoba, Facultad de Filosofía y Humanidades,
       Universidad Nacional de Córdoba, 1972.
       83 p.   19½ cm.   (Colección de ensayos)

19995 Cauduro, Milia.
       Alem do silencio. Pôrto Alegre, Edición Globo, 1968.
       96 p.   21 cm.

19996 Caulin, Antonio, b. 1719.
Historia de la Nueva Andalucia. Estudio preliminar
y edición crítica de Pablo Ojer. Caracas, Academia
Nacional de la Historia, 1966.
2 v.   illus., facsims., maps (part fold.)   23 cm.
(Biblioteca de la Academia Nacional de la Historia, 81-82)
First published in 1779 under title: Historia coro-
gráphica natural y evangélica de la Nueva Andalucía.
Bibliography: v. 1, p. [xii]-xxx.

19997 Cavalcante, José Candido Marques.
Diccionário inglês-português para economistas;
elaborado para o Escritório Técnico de Estudos
Econômicos do Banco do Nordeste do Brasil S.A.
Rio de Janeiro, Livraria Freitas Bastos, 1960.
458 p.   23 cm.

19998 Cavalcante, Paulo B
A farmacopéia Tiriyó. Estudo étno-botánico [por]
Pablo B. Cavalcante [e] Protasio Frikel. Belém,
Museu Paraense Emílio Goeldi, 1973.
156 p.   table.   28 cm.   (Publicações avulsas
do Museu Goeldi, no. 24)
Summary in English, p. 144.

19999 Cavalcante, Paulo B
Frutas comestiveis da Amazônia. Vol. 1. Belém,
Brasil, Museu Paraense Emílio Goeldi, 1972)
84 p.   illus.   27 cm.   (Publicações avulsas, 1

20000 Cavalcanti, Clóvis de Vasconcelos.
... Vale de Moxotó. Análise sócio-econômica de
uma bacia de acude público. Recife, Instituto
Joaquim Nabuco de Pesquisas Sociais, Departamento
Nacional de Obras Contra as Sêcas, 1970.
273 p.   tables, graphs, maps (part fold.)   24 cm.
At head of title: Clóvis de Vasconcelos Cavalcanti;
Dirceu Murilo Pessoa.

20001 Cavalcanti, Cordélia Robalinho.
Novos métodos de pesquisa legislativa. Nuevos
enfoques en la investigación legal. New approaches
to legal research. Brasília, Biblioteca da Câmara
dos Deputados, 1970.
87 p.   22 cm.
In Portuguese, Spanish, and English.

20002 Cavalcanti, Emiliano di, 1897-
Reminiscências líricas de um perfeito carioca [por]
E. di Cavalcanti, com ilustraçoẽs do autor. Rio de
Janeiro, Editôra Civilização Brasileira [1964]

97 p.   col. illus.   21 cm.   (Coleção Rio-
quatrocentros)
Contents: Reminiscências líricas de um perfeito
carioca. - Retrato de um primo. - Poemas in espere-
damente cariocas. - Agenda de certas ruas cariocas.

20003 Cavalcanti, Péricles de Souza.
Lições de português. Rio de Janeiro, Bôlsa de
valores de Rio de Janeiro (Estado de Guanabara), 1968.
255 p.   29 cm.

20004 Cavarozzi, Marcelo.
El rol de los partidos gobernantes y organizaciones
públicas en la generación de políticas de industriali-
zación [por] Marcelo Cavarozzi. Austin, Institute
of Latin American Studies, University of Texas at
Austin, 1976.
40 p.   28 cm.   (Tecnical papers series, 2)

20005 Cavazos Garza, Israel.
Catálogo y síntesis de los protócolos del Archivo
municipal de Monterrey 1599-1700... Monterrey, 1966.
351 p.   23 cm.   (Publicaciones del Instituto
Tecnológico de Estudios Superiores de Monterrey.
Serie: Historia, 4. Índices de los archivos del
Noreste de México, II)

20006 Cavo, Andrés, 1739-1803.
Historia de México, paleografiada del texto original
y anotada por Ernesto J. Burrus, con un prólogo del
P. Mariano Cuevas. México, Editorial Patria, 1949.
491 p.   24 cm.
Bibliography: p. 21-28.

20007 Cavo, Andrés, 1739-1803.
Los tres siglos de Mejico durante el gobierno
español hasta la entrada del ejército trigarante,
obra escrita en Roma por el padre D. Andrés Cavo...
Publicada con notas y suplemento en 1836, por el
licenciado D. Carlos María de Bustamante. Jalapa,
Tip. Veracruzana de A. Ruiz, 1870.
2 p.l., iv, [9]-1115 p.   26½ cm.   (Half-title:
Biblioteca histórica mejicana)
Errors in pagination.

20008 Cazalis, Oche.
No eran los últimos. Cuento. [Maracaibo] Universidad
del Zulia, Facultad de Humanidades y Educación [1973?]
16 p.   21 cm.   (Arte y letras, LIII)

20009 Cea, José Roberto, 1939-
Codice liberado (selecciones del libro Todo el
codice) San Salvador, El Salvador, Ministerio de
Educación, Dirección General de Cultura 1968
83 p. 22½ cm. (Colección poesía, 24)

20010 Cea, José Roberto, 1939-
Naufrago genuino. San Salvador, El Salvador,
Ministerio de Educación, Dirección General de Cultura
[1968]
99 p. 22 cm. (Colección poesía, v. 26)

20011 Cea, José Roberto, 1939-
El solitario de la habitación 5 Guión 3. San
Salvador, El Salvador, Ministerio de Educación,
Dirección General de Cultura, 1970.
33 p. 21 cm. (Colección Caballito de mar, 30)

20012 Ceará, Brazil (State) Superintendência do Desenvolvi-
mento Econômico e Cultural.
Considerações preliminares das condições agrícolas
e do uso atual dos solos da zona fisiográfica de
Baturité. Fortaleza, 1967.
40 p. fold. map. 23 cm.
"Separata do v. I do Diagnóstico socio-econômico da
zona fisiográfica de Baturité."
"Trabalho apresentado no XI Congresso de Ciência do
Solo, realizado em Brasília em julho de 1967."
Bibliography: p. 36.

20013 Ceará, Brazil (State) Superintendência do Desenvolvimento Econômico e Social.
Plano trienal de investimentos, município de
Cascavel, 1968-70. Fortaleza, 1968.
35 l. tables. 28 cm.
"Elaborado pela Divisão de Cooperação Técnica
da SUDEC, através da seguinte equipe: Antonio Camilo
da Silva, Emanuel Silva Magalhães."

20014 Ceará, Brazil (State) Superintendência do Desenvolvi-
mentc Econômico e Cultural.
Tendência da urbanização e deficit habitacional na
cidade de Quixadá. Fortaleza, 1968.
59 p. fold. maps, tables (part fold.) 23 cm.

20015 Ceará, Brazil (State) Universidade Federal. Departamento de Educação e Cultura.
O reitor Antônio Martins Filho e a Universidade do
Ceará. Fortaleza [1968]
49 p. illus., plates. 23 cm.

20016　Cedeño Cenci, Diógenes F
El idioma nacional y las causas de su degeneración
en la Provincia de Bocas del Toro. Panamá, 1960.
40 p.　22 cm.

20017　Cedeño Cenci, Diógenes F
Vida y obra de don Abel Bravo (en el centenario de
su nacimiento) Panamá [Ediciones del Ministerio de
Educación, Departamento de Bellas Artes y Publica-
ciones] 1960.
248 p.　illus.　22 cm.
"Discursos y escritos del doctor Abel Bravo":
p. [153]-248.

20018　Cedulario de las provincias de Santa Marta y Cartagena
de Indias, siglo XVI. Madrid, Librería general de
V. Suárez, 1913-
v.　21 cm.　(Colección de libros y documentos
referentes a la historia de América, t. XIV)
Library has vol. 1, 1529-1535.

20019　Celli, Blas Bruni.
... Discurso de incorporación del doctor Blas Bruni
como individuo de número de la Academia Nacional de
Medicina. Discurso de contestación por el individuo
de número doctor Oscar Beaujon. Caracas, Academia
Nacional de Medicina, 1965.
35 p.　23 cm.

20020　Centellas, Isabel.
El titán de bronce; novela peruana nacionalista.
[1. ed.] Lima, 1964.
174 p.　21 cm.

20021　Centrais Elétricas de Minas Gerais, S.A. Centro de
Documentação.
A classificação de documentos na CEMIG; trabalho
apresentado no Seminário sôbre Classificação Decimal
Universal realizado em Brasília. Belo Horizonte,
1968.
1 v. (various pagings)　29 cm.

20022　Central American Bank for Economic Integration.
Central American transportation study, 1964-1965.
Report prepared for Central American Bank for
Economic Integration. T.S.C. Consortium: Trans-
portation Consultants, Inc., Washington, D.C.
Wilbur Smith and Associates, New Haven, Connecticut.
Consultecnica, Ltda., San José, Costa Rica.

309

[n.p., 1965?]
2 v.   illus., maps (part fold.), tables.   29 cm.

20023 Centro Brasileiro de Pesquisas Físicas.
       Accumulated index of publications (Notas de
       física, monografías, ciência e sociedade, teses)
       Rio de Janeiro, 1975.
       82 p.   28 cm.

20024 Centro Brasileiro de Pesquisas Físicas.
       Chacaltaya emulsion chamber experiment, by Japanese
       and Brazilian Emulsion Chamber Groups. Rio de
       Janeiro, Centro Brasileiro de Pesquisas Físicas,
       1971.
       186 p.   29 cm.   (Notas de física, v. 17, no. 1)

20025 Centro Brasileiro de Pesquisas Físicas.
       Characteristics of multiple production of mesons
       around 100 TEV from Chacaltaya cosmic-ray experiment,
       by Brazil-Japan Emulsion Collaboration. Rio de
       Janeiro, 1974.
       61 p.   diagrs.   28 cm.   (Notas de física,
       Suplemento ao Vol. XXIII)

20026 Centro das Indústrias das Cidades Industrais de Minas
       Gerais.
       Programa de integração social. Contagem, Minas
       Gerais [197-?]
       78 p.   22 cm.

20027 Centro de Documentación e Información Social Cristiano,
       La Habana.
       Socialismo, marxismo [y] bolchevismo. La Habana
       [Ediciones Obreras, 1960]
       61 p.   20 cm.

20028 Centro de Documentación Económico-Social, Lima.
       ¿Qué es la reforma agraria? [Lima] 1963.
       49 p.   illus.   17 cm.   (Serie Reforma
       agraria, 1)

20029 Centro de Educación Fundamental para el Desarrollo de
       la Comunidad en América Latina.
       La administración de los programas de desarrollo
       de la comunidad en América Latina. Patzcuaro,
       México, 1968.
       62, [9] p.   23 cm.   (Publicaciones de difusión,

20030　Centro de Educación Fundamental para el Desarrollo
de la Comunidad en América Latina.
Conceptos y métodos de la programación por zonas
para el desarrollo de la comunidad. Pátzcuaro,
México, 1968.
32 p.　23 cm.　(Publicaciones de difusión, 2)

20031　Centro de Estudios Monetarios Latinoamericanos.
Aspectos financieros del seguro social en América
Latina. México, 1963.
158 p.　illus.　22 cm.　(Estudios)

20032　Centro de Estudios Monetarios Latinoamericanos.
Cooperación financiera en América Latina. [Documentos
preparados para la última (VII) Reunión Operativa del
CEMLA, cuyo tema general fue "Contribución de los
sistemas financieros a la integración económica de
América Latina," y que se celebró en México del 3 al 14
de septiembre de 1962. 1. ed.] México, 1963.
293 p.　22 cm.　(Reuniones)

20033　Centro de Estudios Monetarios Latinoamericanos.
Coordinación monetaria regional. [Documentos
preparados para la última (VII) Reunión Operativa
del CEMLA celebrada en México en septiembre de 1962,
y cuyo tema general fué: "Contribución de los
sistemas financieros a la integración económica de
América Latina." 1. ed.] México, 1963.
211 p.　23 cm.　(Reuniones)
Continuation of Cooperación financiera en América
Latina.
Bibliographical footnotes.
Appéndices (p. [191]-208): A. Algunos artículos
del Tratado de Roma. - B. Estatuto del Comité Monetario del Consejo de la Comunidad Económica Europea.

20034　Centro de Fomento y Productividad Industrial, Guatemala.
Informe sobre el desarrollo industrial de Guatemala.
Guatemala, 1963.
57 ℓ.　tables.　28 cm.

20035　Centro de Historia del Estado Mérida.
Los primeros repartimientos de Mérida. [Mérida]
1968.
22 p.　22 cm.

20036　Centro Latino Americano de Pesquisas de Ciencias Sociais.
Bibliografía sobre estudios de comunidades en
América Latina. Bibliographie des études de commu-

311

nautés en Amérique Latine. Rio de Janeiro,
Servicio de Documentación del Centro, 1964.
ix, 24 l.   28 cm.
Foreword in English and Portuguese.

20037   Centro Latino Americano de Pesquisas de Ciências
Sociais.
Instituições de ensino e pesquisa. Instituciones
de enseñanza y investigación. Chile, México.
As ciências sociais na América Latina. Rio de
Janeiro, 1960.
1 v.   (various paging)   32 cm.   (Publicação
no. 14, ed. provisória)

20038   Centro Latino Americano de Pesquisas de Ciências
Sociais.
Situação social da América Latina: população,
natalidade, nupcialidade, saúde, educação, custo da
vida, salários, condições de trabalho. [Rio de
Janeiro, 1961?]
179 p.   maps, diagrs., tables.   23 cm.

20039   Centro Latino Americano de Pesquisas de Ciências
Sociais.
Situação social de América Latina. Rio de Janeiro,
1965.
467 p.   map.   22 cm.
Summary in English (29 p.) inserted.

20040   Centro para el Desarrollo Económico y Social de América
Latina.
La Alianza para el progreso y el desarrollo social
de América Latina; sinopsis del informe preliminar.
[Santiago, Chile] Desal [1963]
104 p.   illus., tables.   18 cm.

20041   Centro Regional de Alfabetización Funcional en las
Zonas Rurales de América Latina (CREFAL)
Bibliografía sobre alfabetización. Patzcuaro,
Michoacán, CREFAL, 1969.
2 v.   23 cm.   (Publicación de difusión, 8, 11)

20042   Centro Regional de la Unesco en el Hemisferio Occidental
Las corrientes educativas en 1960-1961. Estudio
comparado... La Habana, 1964.
60 p.   27 cm.
"Estracto del Anuario internacional de educación,
vol. XXIII, 1961."

312

20043   Centro Rural Universitário de Treinamento e de Ação
        Comunitária.
        Relatório das atividades de 1967. Programa da
        Universidade Federal do Rio Grande do Norte. Natal -
        Brasil. [Natal?] Imprensa Universitária, 1968.
        75 p.   fold. tables.   24 cm.

20044   Cepeda Ulloa, Fernando.
        La convención de Ginebra sobre la plataforma conti-
        nental; un análisis político. Nota preliminar de
        Alvaro Hernán Medina. Bogotá [Instituto Colombiano
        de Estudios Internacionales, Escuela Superior de
        Administración Pública] 1963.
        147 p.   24 cm.
        Errata slip inserted.
        Bibliography: p. 144-147.

20045   Cerda Catalán, Alfonso.
        Contribución a la historia de la sátira política
        en el Uruguay, 1897-1904. Advertencia de Eugenio
        Petit Muñoz. Montevideo, Universidad de la República
        Oriental de Uruguay, Facultad de Humanidades y
        Ciencias, 1965.
        78 p.   illus.   25 cm.   (Instituto de Investi-
        gaciones Históricas. Ensayos, estudios y monografías,
        no. 10)
        Bibliography: p. 69-78.

20046   Cerda G   , Hugo.
        Teatro de guiñol; historia, técnica y aplicaciones
        del teatro guiñol en la educación moderna [por] Hugo
        y Enrique Cerda G.   Caracas, Ministerio de Educación,
        Dirección Técnica, Departamento de Publicaciones
        [1965]
        338 p.   illus., ports.   20 cm.   (Colección
        Vigilia, 6)

20047   Cerda Silva, Roberto de la.
        El movimiento obrero en México. [1. ed.]   México,
        Instituto de Investigaciones Sociales, U.N.A.M.,
        1961.
        187 p.   24 cm.
        Includes bibliography.

20048   Cereceda, Raúl.
        Las instituciones políticas en América Latina.
        Bogotá, Oficina Internacional de Investigaciones
        Sociales de FERES, 1961.
        256 p.   22 cm.   (Documentos latino-americanos, 1)

313

20049   Cerqueira Filho, Gisálio.
        A influência das ideas socialistas no pensamento
        político brasileiro - 1890/1922. Tese de mestrado
        [Instituto Universitário de Pesquisas do Rio de
        Janeiro] [Rio de Janeiro, 1975]
        5 p.l., 108 p.   28 cm.

20050   Cerruti Aicardi, Héctor J
        La seguridad social del trabajador rural en el
        Uruguay. Montevideo, Banco de Seguros del Estado,
        1962.
        15 p.   20 cm.

20051   Cervantes de Salazar, Francisco, ca. 1514-1575.
        Crónica de la Nueva España que escribió el Dr. D.
        Francisco Cervantes de Salazar, cronista de la imperia
        ciudad de México. Madrid, The Hispanic Society of
        America, 1914.
        843 p.   26½ cm.
        Edited by M. Magallón.

20052   Cervantes Saavedra, Miguel de, 1547-1916.
        Discursos de don Quijote. [San Salvador, Departa-
        mento Editorial del Ministerio de Educación, 1961]
        28 p.   20 cm.   (Colección Azor, 5)

20053   Cervantes Tapia, Onésimo.
        La accesión en el derecho agrario. México, 1963.
        88 p.   23 cm.
        Tesis (licenciatura en derecho) - Universidad
        Nacional Autónoma de México.
        Bibliography: p. 83-84.

20054   Cervantes Villarreal, José Rafael, 1946-
        Tiempo de escalpelo. Monterrey, México, Ediciones
        Sierra Madre, 1968.
        24 p.   22 cm.   (Poesía en el mundo, 62)

20055   César, Guilhermino.
        O embuçado do Erval (mito e poesia de Pedro Canga).
        Pôrto Alegre, Faculdade de Filosofia, Universidade
        Federal do Rio Grande do Sul, 1968.
        117 p.   20 cm.

20056   César, Guilhermino.
        Historia da literatura do Rio Grande do Sul (1737-
        1902) 2.ª edição. 1.ª impressão. Pôrto Alegre,
        Editôra Globo [1971]
        414 p.   facsim.   22½ cm.

314

20057 César, Guilhermino.
Historia do Rio Grande do Sul. Período colonial.
Pôrto Alegre, Editôra Globo [1970]
327 p.   23 cm.

20058 César, Guilhermino, ed.
Primeiros cronistas do Rio Grande do Sul; estudo
de fontes primárias da historia rio-grandense accom-
panhado de varios textos. Pôrto Alegre, Brazil,
Edições da Faculdade de Filosofia, Universidade
Federal do Rio Grande do Sul, 1969.
231 p.   19 cm.

20059 Céspedes, Augusto.
Sangre de mestizos; relatos de la Guerra del Chaco.
La Paz, Bolivia [Ministerio de Educación y Bellas
Artes, Oficialía Mayor de Cultura, 1962]
239 p.   22 cm.   (Biblioteca boliviana de
autores contemporáneos, 2)
Contents. - Terciana muda. - El pozo. - La Coronela. -
Seis muertos en campaña. - El milagro. - Humo de
petróleo. - Las ratas. - La paraguaya. - Opiniones
de dos descabezados.

20060 Céspedes, Carlos Manuel de, 1871-1939.
Cartas de Carlos M. de Céspedes a su esposa Ana de
Quesada. La Habana, Instituto de Historia, Comisión
Nacional de la Academia de Ciencias de la República
de Cuba, 1964.
267 p.   22½ cm.

20061 Céspedes Ponce, Gicela, 1927-
Fermentación y refermentación del cacao cubano.
La Habana, ICIT, 1960.
45 p.   illus.   24 cm.   (Instituto Cubano
de Investigaciones Tecnológicas. Serie de estudios
sobre trabajos de investigación, no. 12)
Includes bibliography.

20062 Céspedes y Quesada, Carlos Manuel de, 1871-1939.
Carlos Manuel de Céspedes, por Carlos Manuel de
Céspedes y Quesada. Paris, Tip. de P. Dupont, 1895.
3 p.l., 346 p.   port.   21½ cm.

20063 Cevallos, Miguel Angel, 1887-
Escuela preparatoria modelo; proyecto para su
fundación [1. ed.] México, Universidad Nacional
Autónoma de México, Dirección General de Publicaciones,

315

1961.
75 p.   23 cm.

20064   Cevallos Arízaga, Benjamín.
Historia del derecho civil ecuatoriano.   Quito,
Talleres Gráficos Nacionales, 1963-64.
2 v.   23 cm.
Includes legislation.

20065   Cevallos Garcia, Gabriel.
América: teoría de su descubrimiento.   Cuenca
[Núcleo del Azuay de la Casa de Cultura Ecuatoriana]
1975.
229 p.   21 cm.

20066   Chacel, Rosa, 1898-
Ofrenda a una virgen loca; [cuentos y relatos.
1. ed. en español]   Xalapa, Universidad Veracruzana,
1961.
136 p.   20 cm.   (Universidad Veracruzana.
Ficción, 32)
Contents. - Lazo indisoluble. - Transfiguración. -
Secreto manifiesto. - Ofrenda a una virgen loca. -
Balaam.

20067   Chaclán Toc, Patrocinio Francisco.
El procedimiento penal guatemalteco; sus factores
e innovaciones.   Guatemala,   Centro Editorial "José
de Pineda Ibarra," Ministerio de Educación Pública,
1964.
218 p.   illus.   23 cm.
Tesis (licenciatura en ciencias jurídicas y
sociales) - Universidad de San Carlos de Guatemala.
Bibliography: p. 217-218.

20068   Chacon, Dulce.
Receitas mágicas.   Recife, 1973.
355 p.   24 cm.
Bibliography: p. 355.

20069   Chacón y Rumbea, Luis Roberto.
Luis Roberto Chacón y Rumbea.   Selección y nota
de Rigoberto Cordero y León.   Cuenca, Ecuador, 1965.
57-128 p.   21 cm.   (Presencia de la poesía
cuencana, 42)
"Anales de la Universidad de Cuenca."
At head of title: Universidad de Cuenca.
Cover title.

316

20070 Chagas, José.
Os telhados (poesia) [n.p.] SIOGE, 1972.
46 p. 20 cm.

20071 Chagas, Paulo Pinheiro.
Democracia & parlamento. Rio de Janeiro,
Libraria São José, 1956.
211 p. 24 cm.

20072 Chagas, Paulo Pinheiro.
Do alto desta tribuna. Capa de Santa Rosa. Rio
de Janeiro, Libraria São José, 1956.
210 p. 24 cm.

20073 Chagas, Paulo Pinheiro.
Teófilo Ottoni, ministro do povo. Prêmio "Joaquim
Nabuco" da Academia Brasileira de Letras. Ilustrações
de Percy Lau e capa de Enrico Bianco. 2.ª edição,
revista e aumentada pelo autor. Rio de Janeiro,
Libraria São José, 1956.
667 p. illus., facsims. 24½ cm.

20074 Chagas, Wilson.
Mundo e contramundo. Pôrto Alegre, Editôra da
Universidade Federal do Rio Grande do Sul, 1972.
116 p. 19½ cm.
Errata sheet before half-title.
Contents. - Solidão e comunicação na obra de Carlos
Drummond de Andrade. - Quando os deuses morrem. -
Albert Camus e a lógica do absurdo. - Amar-amaro. -
Perspectiva do nova romance: La jalousie, de Robbe-
Grillet.

20075 Chalbaud Zerpa, Reinaldo.
Instituciones sociales. Temas de sociología para
alumnos de derecho. Volumen I. Mérida, Venezuela,
Universidad de Los Andes, Facultad de Derecho [1967]
318 p. 23 cm.

20076 Chambers, D   L
Situación actual de la mosca de la fruta del
Caribe, Anastrepha suspensa Loew [by] D. L. Chambers.
México, Sociedad Entomológica Mexicana, 1976.
25-35 p. 23 cm.
Reprinted from Folia entomológica mexicana, no. 34,
1976.
Abstract in Spanish.

317

20077   Chamie, Mario.
        Palavra-levantamento na poesia de Cassiano Ricardo.
        [Rio de Janeiro] Livraria São José, 1963.
        141 p.   19 cm.
        Bibliographical references included in "Notas"
        (p. 132)

20078   Chamorro Rodríguez, Luis Emilio.
        Influencia de los estados emotivos y pasionales
        en la responsabilidad criminal. Santiago, Editorial
        Universitaria, 1957.
        79 p.   22 cm.
        Memoria de prueba (licenciatura en ciencias jurídicas
        y sociales) - Universidad de Chile, Santiago.
        Bibliography: p. 73-75.

20079   Chaney, Elsa.
        Agrarian reform and politics. [Madison, Land
        Tenure Center, University of Wisconsin] 1970.
        21 l.   28 cm.   (Land Tenure Center, University
        of Wisconsin. LTC no. 74)
        Includes bibliographical references.

20080   Chapman, Anne MacKaye, 1922-
        Los nicarao y los chorotega según las fuentes
        históricas. San José [1960]
        115 p.   fold. map.   21 cm.   (Publicaciones
        de la Universidad de Costa Rica. Serie histórica
        y geografía, no. 4)
        Part of the author's unpublished work: Studies in
        culture history of Central America.
        Bibliography: p. 111-115.

20081   Chapman, Samuel, 1859-1943.
        The postage stamps of Mexico, from the commencement
        in 1856, to the end of the provisional period in
        1868, by S. Chapman, F.R.P.S.L. With details of
        the numbers of the stamps of each issue printed
        and distributed amongst the various district post
        offices in the republic, compiled from official
        records. Published under the auspices of The
        Collectors' Club, New York City, as Handbook number
        four. Sevenoaks, England, Printed (for circulation
        amongst subscribers only) by the Caxton and Holmes-
        dale press, 1926.
        xxxi, 307 p.   23 cm.

20082   Chappert, Jacques.
        Réévaluation de la calibration du déplacement

isomérique de 57Fe, par M.M. Jacques Chappert,
Jean-René Regnard et Jacques Danon. Rio de Janeiro,
Centro Brasileiro de Pesquisas Físicas, 1971.
311-316 p.   29 cm.   (Notas de física, v. 16,
no. 21)

20083   Chardon, Roland Emanuel Paul.
        Geographic aspects of plantation agriculture in
        Yucatan. Washington, National Academy of Sciences-
        National Research Council, 1961.
        xi, 200 p.   illus., diagrs., maps.   28 cm.
        (Foreign field research program, report no. 11)
        National Research Council. Publicacion 876.
        Bibliography: p. 194-200.

20084   Charlevoix, Pierre François Xavier de, 1682-1761.
        Historia del Paraguay, escrita en francés por el
        P. Pedro Francisco Javier de Charlevoix... con las
        anotaciones y correcciones latinas del P. Muriel;
        tr. al castellano por el P. Pablo Hernández...
        Madrid, V. Suárez, 1910-16.
        6 v.   fold. map.   20 cm.   (Half-title:
        Colección de libros y documentos referentes a la
        historia de América. t. XI-XIII, XV-XVI, XVIII)
        Vol. 2 has half-title, and v. 3-6 added t.-p.:
        Los jesuitas en el Rio de la Plata, 1586-1830.
        First edition of the work published Paris, 1756.
        Forms the first part of a projected work entitled
        "Los jesuitas en el Río de la Plata", to include as
        second and third parts, respectively, a translation
        of Domingo Muriel's continuation of Charlevoix, and
        El extrañamiento de los jesuitas del Río de la Plata...
        by P. Hernández.

20085   Charria Angulo, Pedro Manuel.
        El abuso del derecho como limitación al ejercicio
        de los derechos subjetivos. Bogotá, 1964.
        122, [11] p.   24 cm.
        Tesis - Pontificia Universidad Javeriana, Bogotá.
        Bibliography: p. [125]-[129]

20086   Charry Lara, Fernando.
        Los adioses [poesía. 1. ed.] Bogotá, Ediciones
        del Ministerio de Educación, Imprenta Nacional, 1963.
        75 p.   24 cm.

20087   Chateaubriand, François René, vicomte de, 1768-1848.
        Prefacio de "Atala" y "René" - 1805... traducción
        y notas: Ma. J. Pérez Winter de Tamburini. Cuadernos

para el estudio de la estética y literatura,
dirección: Hilda Torres-Varela. Resistencia,
Chaco, Sección Literaturas Modernas, Instituto de
Letras, Facultad de Humanidades, Universidad Nacional
del Nordeste [n.d.]
14 p.   29 cm.   (Cuadernos para el estudio de
la estética y la literatura, 2)

20088 Chavarría Flores, Manuel.
       Política educacional de Guatemala. Guatemala
       [Impr. Universitaria] 1951.
       220 p.   port.   20 cm.
       Bibliography: p. 213-218.

20089 Chavarría Olivares, Daniel.
       Divisiones políticas de México, de la Colonia a la
       Constitución de 1917. México, 1963.
       170 p.   23 cm.
       Tesis (licenciatura en derecho) - Universidad
       Nacional Autónoma de México.
       Bibliography: p. 167.

20090 Chaverri Rodríguez, Gil.
       Química general... por Gil Chaverri Rodríguez y
       Guillermo Chaverri Benavides... San José, Costa
       Rica, 1966.
       3 v.   tables.   27½ cm.

20091 Chaves, Flavio Loureiro.
       Aspectos do modernismo brasileiro. [Por] Flávio
       Loureiro Chaves, Donaldo Schüler, Bruno Kiefer,
       Leonor Scliar Cabral, Tânia Franco Carvalhal, José
       Hildebrando Dacanal. Pôrto Alegre, Brasil, Comissão
       Central de Publicações, Universidade Federal do Rio
       Grande do Sul, 1970.
       217 p.   19 cm.
       Contents. - Contribuições de Oswald e Mario de
       Andrade ao romance brasileiro, by Flávio Loureiro
       Chaves. As raízes da poesia moderna, by Donaldo
       Schüler. Mario de Andrade e o modernismo na música
       brasileira, by Bruno Kiefer. As ideias lingüísticas
       de Mario de Andrade, by Leonor Scliar Cabral.
       Presença da literatura francesa no modermisno brasi-
       leiro, by Tânia Franco Carvalhal. O romance europeu
       e o romance brasileiro do modernismo, by José
       Hildebrando Dacanal.

20092 Chaves, João Gabriel.
       Didática da matemática. [Rio de Janeiro] Ministerio

320

da Educação e Cultura [1960]
105 p.   illus.   16 cm.
Includes bibliography.

20093   Chaves, Luis Fernando.
Geografía agraria de Venezuela.   Caracas, Universidad Central de Venezuela, Ediciones de la
Biblioteca, 1963.
257 p.   illus.   23 cm.   (Ediciones de la
Biblioteca, 12)
Colección Ciencias sociales, 6.
Includes bibliography.

20094   Chaves, Mário M
Sáude e sistemas.   Rio de Janeiro, Serviço de
Publicações, Instituto de Documentação, Fundação
Getúlio Vargas, 1972.
212 p.   illus.   22 cm.

20095   Chaves, Nelson.
Sexo, nutrição e vida.   Prefacio de I. de L. Neves-
Manta.   Recife, Universidade Federal de Pernambuco,
1968.
305 p.   illus.   22 cm.
Includes bibliographies.

20096   Chaves, Nelson.
Trópico e nutrição.   Recife, Universidade Federal
de Pernambuco, 1969.
70 p.   22 cm.
Summary in English.
Bibliography: p. 67-70.

20097   Chaves, Ronald.
Efectos del terremoto de Managua (23 diciembre de
1972) por Ronald Chaves y Rodrigo Saenz.   San José,
Costa Rica, Instituto Geográfico Nacional [1973?]
45-67 p.   illus.   25 cm.
Reprinted from Informe semestral, enero a junio,
1973.

20098   Chaves, Sylla M
Aspectos de relações públicas [por] Sylla M.
Chaves.   [Rio de Janeiro] D.A.S.P., Serviço de
Documentação, Seção de Publicações, 1966.
76 p.   26 cm.
Includes bibliographies.

321

20099   Chavez Hayhoe, Arturo.
        Guadalajara de antaño. Guadalajara, Ediciones del
        Banco Industrial de Jalisco [1960]
        173 p.   23 cm.
        Bibliography at end of each chapter.

20100   Chavez Suarez, Sócrates.
        Guapore, hombre y río. La Paz, Ministerio de Educaci
        y Bellas Artes, 1960.
        326 p.   19 cm.   ([Biblioteca de autores boliviano
        contemporaneos] 2)

20101   Chen, Ari.
        O sétimo dia. (Um exorcismo em dois atos e um
        epílogo) Menção Honrosa, Prêmio Servico Nacional de
        Teatro - 1966. Rio de Janeiro, Serviço Nacional de
        Teatro, 1968.
        99 p.   21 cm.

20102   Chen, Chi-Yi.
        Aspectos administrativos de la planificación;
        el sistema venezolano [por] Chi-Yi Chen [y] Ramón
        Martín Mateo. Caracas, Instituto de Investigaciones
        Económicas y Sociales, Universidad Católica Andrés
        Bello, 1973.
        203 p.   24½ cm.

20103   Chenery, Hollis B
        Development alternatives for Latin America, by
        Hollis B. Chenery and Peter Eckstein. Cambridge,
        Mass., Center for International Affairs, Harvard
        University, 1967.
        61 ℓ.   28 cm.   (Project for Quantitative Research
        in Economic Development. Memorandum 29, revised)

20104   Chertudi, Susan, ed.
        Cuentos folklóricos de la Argentina. Buenos Aires,
        Ministerio de Educación y Justicia de la Nación
        Argentina, Instituto Nacional de Filología y Folklore,
        1960-
        v.   21 cm.

20105   Chiapas en 1824. [México, 1874]
        8-10 p.   illus., map.   32 cm.
        Reprinted from Boletín bibliográfico de la Secretaría
        de Hacienda y Crédito Público, Año XX, Tercera época,
        no. 501, Septiembre de 1974.

20106   Chickering, Arthur Merton.
        Panamanian spiders of the genus Tmartus (Araneae,
        thomisidae)   Cambridge, Mass., Printed for the
        Museum, 1965.
        340-368 p.   20 cm.   (Bulletin of the Museum
        of Comparative Zoology, Harvard University. v. 133,
        no. 7)

20107   Chico, Irmão.
        Disciplina Cristã. Mensagems. Psicografia de
        Irene Guedes Trinidade. 1.ª edição. Niterói, Centro
        Espírita Casa de Lício, 1970.
        175 p.   19 cm.

20108   Chile.
        ... Informe del ajente de Chile ante el Tribunal
        arbitral anglo-chileno, creado a virtud de la Convención
        de 26 de septiembre de 1893. Santiago de Chile,
        Imprenta i librería Ercilla, 1896.
        470 p.   28 cm.
        On verso of front cover: Edición oficial.
        The claims dealt with in this report are those
        arising out of the Balmaceda revolution of 1891.

20109   Chile. Comisión de Estudios de la Seguridad Social.
        Informe sobre la reforma de la seguridad social
        chilena. Santiago, Editorial Jurídica de Chile, 1964.
        2 v. (1554 p.)   27 cm.

20110   Chile. Comisión de Planeamiento Integral de la
        Educación.
        Algunos antecedentes para el planeamiento integral
        de la educación chilena. Santiago, Ministerio de
        Educación Pública, 1964.
        327 p.   illus. (part. fold.)   25 cm.   (Publi-
        cación no. 1)

20111   Chile. Congreso. Biblioteca.
        Integración económica en América Latina. (Mercado
        Común) [por la Sección Catalogación y Referencias
        Bibliográficas] Santiago de Chile, 1961.
        11 l.   34 cm.   (Serie Bibliografías, no. 12)
        At head of title: Biblioteca del Congreso Nacional.
        Caption title.
        "Bibliografía... preparada con el objeto de faci-
        litar la consulta del material que conserva la
        Biblioteca, para la 2ª Conferencia Interparlamentaria
        Americana, Santiago, 22-29 de octubre de 1961."

20112   Chile. Congreso. Biblioteca.
        Reforma agraria; [bibliografía preparada por la
        Sección Catalogación y Referencias Bibliográficas]
        Santiago, 1961-62.
        2 pts.   33 cm.   (Serie Bibliografías, no. 11,
        supl. 1)
        Caption title.
        Part 2 is a supplementary list of publications
        received for the period April, 1967-March, 1962.

20113   Chile. Congreso. Cámara de Diputados.
        Reglamento de la Cámara de Diputados y Constitución
        Política de la República de Chile. [Santiago] 1957.
        158 p.   24 cm.

20114   Chile. Congreso. Cámara de Diputados.
        Reglamento de la Cámara de Diputados y constitución
        política de la República de Chile. [Santiago?] 1969.
        243 p.   18½ cm.

20115   Chile. Consejeria Nacional de Promoción Popular.
        División de Estudios.
        Cooperativos de producción. Realidad y perspectivas.
        Santiago, 1968.
        110 p.   19½ cm.

20116   Chile. Corporación de la Reforma Agraria.
        Cuatro años de reforma agraria. Santiago, 1968
        (i.e. 1969)
        79 p.   illus., graphs, maps (all part col.)
        30 cm.

20117   Chile. Departamento de Economía Agraria.
        La agricultura chilena en el quinquenio 1956-1960.
        Santiago, Ministerio de Agricultura, Dirección de
        Agricultura y Pesca, 1963.
        279 p.   illus., diagrs., tables (part fold.)
        27 cm.

20118   Chile. Departamento de Economía Agraria.
        Aspectos económicos y sociales del inquilinaje en
        San Vicente de Tagua. [Santiago] Departamento de
        Economía Agraria, Sección Uso y Tenencia de la Tierra,
        1960.
        75 p.   tables.   26 cm.
        At head of title: República de Chile, Ministerio de
        Agricultura, Dirección de Agricultura y Pesca.

20119 Chile. Departamento de Estudios Financieros.
Cuentas fiscales de Chile, 1925-1957. Santiago,
Talleres Gráficos "La Nación," 1959.
133 p.   tables (part fold.)   25 cm.

20120 Chile. Departamento de Navegación e Hidrografía.
... Catálogo, cartas náuticas y publicaciones
[Valparaiso] Instituto Hidrográfico de la Armada,
1969.
88 p.   maps.   29 cm.
At head of title: I.H.A. Pub. 3000.

20121 Chile. Departamento de Navegación e Hidrografía.
Derrotero de la costa de Chile. Valparaiso,
Instituto Hidrográfico de la Armada, 1956-
v.   28 cm.
At head of title: Instituto Hidrográfico de la
Armada.
Contents: v. 1. Desde Arica hasta el Canal Chacao.
Publ. 3001. 5.ª ed., 1967. - v. 2. Desde Canal Chacao
hasta Golfo de Penas. Publ. 3002. 4.ª ed., 1968. -
v. 4. Estrecho de Magallanes y aguas adyacentes desde
el Cabo Victoria al Cabo Vírgenes. Publ. 3004. 4.ª
ed., 1956. - v. 5. Tierra del Fuego y canales e islas
adyacentes. Publ. 3005. 5.ª ed., Publ. 3006. 1.ª
ed., 1962.

20122 Chile. Dirección de Abastecimiento de Petroleo.
Memoria final presentada por el Servicio y corres-
pondiente a los años 1943-1944 y 1945. Santiago,
1946.
69 p.   illus., forms, tables.   27 cm.

20123 Chile. Dirección de Bibliotecas, Archivos y Museos.
Bibliografía de las memorias de grado sobre
literatura chilena (1918-1967). Santiago, Ediciones
de la Biblioteca Nacional,1969.
39 p.   26 cm.

20124 Chile. Dirección de Bibliotecas, Archivos y Museos.
Chile: su futura alimentación; ciclo de conferencias
organizado por la Dirección de Bibliotecas, Archivos
y Museos. [Santiago] Ediciones de la Biblioteca
Nacional [1963]
233 p.   19 cm.
At head of title: Extensión cultural de la Biblioteca
Nacional.
Bibliography at end of most of the lectures.

20125   Chile. Dirección de Contabilidad.
        Cuenta jeneral de las entradas i gastos fiscales
        de la República de Chile... 1854-1925. Santiago,
        Imprenta Nacional [etc.] 1855-1927.
        41 v. in 40.   fold. tables.   27-38 cm.
        No volumes for 1856, 1859-62, 1865, 1868-70, 1872,
        1880-81, 1883, 1886-87, 1892, 1903, 1906-08, 1910-14,
        1916-24.
        Total LC holdings filmed with holding and collation
        statement.

20126   Chile. Dirección de Estadística y Censos.
            Boletín. año 1-   enero 1928-   [Santiago?]
                v. in   diagrs.   27-31 cm.   monthly
        (irregular)
        Library has v. 14-19, 1941-1946.
        Title varies: 1928-Jan./Feb. 1961, Estadística
        chilena.
        Vols. for 1928-52 issued by the Dirección General de
        Estadística; 1953-July Aug. 1959 by the Servicio
        Nacional de Estadística y Censos (1953-Sept./Oct.
        1954 under an earlier name: Servicio Nacional de
        Estadística.

20127   Chile. Inspección Jeneral de Tierras i Colonización.
            Memoria de la Inspección Jeneral de Tierras i
        Colonización... Santiago de Chile, Impr. Cervantes
        [etc.] 19-
                v.   tables (partly fold.)   25-27 cm.
        Reports on colonization are found also in the reports
        of the Minister of Foreign Relations, 1873-19-

20128   Chile. Instituto Geográfico Militar.
            Láminas de signos convencionales. [Santiago] 1950.
            41 pl.   15 x 21 cm.

20129   Chile. Instituto Hidrográfico de la Armada de Chile.
            Bahía Tongoy. Valparaiso, 1898-1904.
            map.   47 x 55 cm.
            Scale: 1:32,000.

20130   Chile. Instituto Hidrográfico de la Armada de Chile.
            Canal Concepción y Canal Oeste... Con correcciones
        hasta junio de 1969. Valparaiso, 1969.
            map.   80 x 58 cm.
            Scale: 1:200,000.

20131   Chile. Instituto Hidrográfico de la Armada de Chile.
            Canal Murray. Valparaiso, 1947-1959.

```
         map.    73 x 29 cm.
         Scale:  1:30,000.
```

20132 Chile. Instituto Hidrográfico de la Armada de Chile.
       ... Catálogo. Cartas náuticas y publicaciones.
       1969. Santiago, Instituto Hidrográfico de la
       Armada [1969?]
          88 p.   maps.   27½ cm.

20133 Chile. Instituto Hidrográfico de la Armada.
       ... Glosario de mareas y corrientes. [Valparaiso]
       Instituto Hidrográfico de la Armada, 1969.
          [39] p.   29 cm.

20134 Chile. Instituto Hidrográfico de la Armada de Chile.
       Puerto Montt. Zona portuaria. Valparaiso, 1969.
          map.   54 x 52 cm.
          Scale: 1:5,000.

20135 Chile. Instituto Hidrográfico de la Armada de Chile.
       Puertos en el territorio antárctico de Chile.
       Valparaiso, 1947-1955.
          map.   67 x 88 cm.
          Scale: 1:15,000, 1:20,000, 1:30,000.

20136 Chile. Instituto Hidrográfico de la Armada de Chile.
       Puertos en la costa de Arauco. Valparaiso,
       1910-1943.
          map.   43 x 58 cm.
          Scale: 1:15,000.

20137 Chile. Laws, statutes, etc.
       Código civil. Edición oficial al 31 de marzo de
       1970, aprobada por decreto no. 883, de 3 de junio de
       1970, del Ministerio de Justicia. [Santiago]
       Editorial Jurídica de Chile, 1970.
          802 p.   19 cm.

20138 Chile. Laws, statutes, etc.
       Código de aguas. Edición oficial, al 31 de marzo
       de 1970, aprobada por decreto no. 1897, de 10 de
       octubre de 1969 del Ministerio de Justicia. [Santiago]
       Editorial Jurídica de Chile, 1970.
          137 p.   20 cm.

20139 Chile. Laws, statutes, etc.
       Código de derecho internacional privado. Edición
       oficial al 31 de octubre de 1969, aprobada por
       decreto no. 1898 de 10 de octubre de 1969 del Minis-

terio de justicia. [Santiago] Editorial Jurídica de
Chile, 1969.
84 p. 19½ cm.

20140 Chile. Laws, statutes, etc.
Código penal (concordado, con jurisprudencia y
doctrina)... Santiago, Ediciones Encina [1968-1970]
6 v. 22 cm.
Edited by Mario Verdugo Marinkovic.
V. vi has title, Delitos contemplados en leyes
especiales.

20141 Chile. Laws, statutes, etc.
Código de procedimiento civil. Edición oficial al
31 de mayo de 1966, aprobada por Decreto no. 2078
de 21 de noviembre de 1967 del Ministerio de Justicia.
[Santiago] Editorial Jurídica de Chile, 1966.
277 p. 19 cm.
"Apéndice" (p. 197-277) contains related legislation.

20142 Chile. Laws, statutes, etc.
Código de procedimiento penal. Edición oficial
al 31 de marzo de 1970, aprobada por decreto no. 1194,
de 24 de julio de 1970 del Ministerio de Justicia.
[Santiago] Editorial Jurídica de Chile, 1970.
215 p. 20 cm.

20143 Chile. Laws, statutes, etc.
Código del trabajo. Edición oficial al 31 de mayo
de 1966, aprobada por decreto no. 1066 de 21 de junio
de 1967 del Ministerio de Justicia. [Santiago]
Editorial Jurídica de Chile, 1966.
494 p. 18 cm.

20144 Chile. Laws, statutes, etc.
D. F. L. 190, de 1960; código tributario. Nueva
organización de los servicios de impuestos internos,
creación de las direcciones regionales, giros, pagos
e intereses, medios especiales de fiscalización, de
los apremios, de las infracciones y sanciones, del
procedimiento general de las reclamaciones, del procedimiento para la aplicación de sanciones, del cobro
ejecutivo de las obligaciones tributarias, de la
prescripción, índice alfabético de materias. Edición
actualizada para 1963. [Santiago] Ediciones Gutenberg,
1963.
72 p. 25 cm. (Ediciones Gutenberg, no. 125)

20145 Chile. Laws, statutes, etc.
Recopilación de leyes y reglamentos sobre Caja de
Previsión de la Marina Mercante Nacional y Sección
Tripulantes y Obreros Marítimos. Para uso de oficiales,
empleados navieros, agentes de aduana y cabotaje,
tripulantes de naves y obreros marítimos. [1. ed.]
Valparaiso, Escuela Tip. Salesiana [1963?]
159 p.   19 cm.

20146 Chile. Laws, statutes, etc.
Recopilación y análisis de las modificaciones a la
legislación tributaria, segundo semestre, año 1967
[por] Sergio Carvallo Hederra. [Santiago] Editorial
Jurídica de Chile, 1968.
161 p.   23 cm.
On spine: Modificaciones a la legislación tributaria.

20147 Chile. Laws, statutes, etc.
La reforma tributaria; [nueva Ley de la renta.
Comentarios de] Eduardo Bell Escalona. [Valparaiso,
1964]
159 p.   20 cm.

20148 Chile. Ministerio de Educación.
Cuadernos de la superintendencia. Síntesis de la
labor desarrollada por la Superintendencia de
Educación 1964-1969. Principales normas legales y
reglamentarias relacionadas con educación 1965-1970.
[Santiago, 1970]
69 p.   34 cm.   (no. 16)

20149 Chile. Ministerio de Educación.
Programa de desarrollo de la enseñanza normal
(segunda versión)   Santiago, 1967.
108 p.   tables, graphs.   32 cm.

20150 Chile. Ministerio de Hacienda.
Cuentas fiscales de Chile (1925-1957)   Santiago,
Talleres Gráficos "La Nación", 1959.
141 p.   tables (part fold.)   27 cm.

20151 Chile. Ministerio de Hacienda.
Manual de la administración pública de Chile.
Santiago, 1959.
2 v.   tables (1 fold.)   26 cm.

20152 Chile. Ministerio de Hacienda.
Manual de la organización del gobierno de Chile.

329

Santiago, 1959.
318 p.   charts (1 fold.)   26 cm.

20153 Chile. Ministerio de Hacienda.
Memoria del ministro de hacienda presentada al
Congreso Nacional... 1835-[1931] Santiago [etc.]
1836-1931.
82 v. in 69.   fold. plans, fold. tables, fold.
diagrs.   23½-29 cm.
Title varies slightly.
Library has volumes covering years: 1835, 1839-40,
1841-46, 1848, 1850, 1852-59, 1861-85, 1887-1917,
1919-21, 1927-29, 1931.
Library lacks volumes covering years: 1836-38,
1847, 1849, 1851, 1860, 1886, 1918, 1922-26, 1930.

20154 Chile. Ministerio de Instrucción Pública.
Bases generales para el planeamiento de la educación
chilena. Santiago, 1961.
149 p.   graphs (part fold.)   27 cm.

20155 Chile. Ministerio de Marina.
Derrotero del estrecho del Magallanes, Tierra del
Fuego i canales de la Patagonia. Desde el canal de
Chacao hasta el cabo de Hornos. Redactado conforme
a los documentos mas modernos, por Ramón Serrano M.,
capitán de fragata. Santiago de Chile, Imprenta
Nacional, 1891.
xviii, 596 p.   plates (part fold.)   26 cm.
Extra numbered leaves inserted.

20156 Chile. Ministerio de Relaciones Exteriores.
La cuestión del Rio Lauca [libro blanco] Santiago,
1963.
327 p.   illus., 2 fold. col. maps.   26 cm.

20157 Chile. Oficina Central de Estadística.
Censo jeneral de la república de Chile levantado
en abril de 1854. Santiago, Imprenta del ferro-
carril, 1858.
1 p.l., 9 p.   43 tables (part fold.)   43½ x 53½ c

20158 Chile. Oficina Central de Estadística.
... Nota preliminar del censo jeneral de la
República de Chile levantado el 28 de noviembre de
1895. Santiago, Imprenta i encuadernación Barcelona,
1896.
1 p.l., xi, 254, [1] p.   fold. tables.   25½ cm.

330

Binder's title: Chile. Censo. 1895.
Preface signed: Vicente Grez.

20159   Chile. Oficina Central Estadística.
        Sesto censo jeneral de la población de Chile
        levantado el 26 de noviembre de 1885 y compilado por
        la Oficina Central de Estadística en Santiago...
        Valparaiso, Imprenta de "La Patria", 1899-90.
        2 v.   tables.   33½ cm.

20160   Chile. Oficina Central de Estadística.
        ... Statistical abstract of the Republic of Chile...
        Santiago de Chile, Sociedad Imprenta y Litografía
        Universo, 1918.
        ix, 146 p. incl. tables.   26 cm.
        At head of title: Central Statistics Bureau.
        Map on t.-p.

20161   Chile. Oficina de Estudios Tributarios.
        El sistema tributario chileno; análisis, evaluación,
        alternativas de reforma. [2. ed. Santiago, 1960]
        2 v.   graphs, tables.   27 cm.   (Informe)

20162   Chile. Oficina de Planificación Nacional.
        Balances económicos de Chile, 1960-1970. Santiago,
        Editorial Universitaria, 1973.
        258 p.   27 cm.   (ODEPLAN, ser. 4, no. 2.
        Balances económicos)

20163   Chile. Oficina de Planificación Nacional.
        Diagnóstico y estrategía para el desarrollo de la
        región del Maule; provincias de Curico, Talca,
        Linares, Maule. Santiago, 1968.
        251 p.   maps, tables.   27½ cm.

20164   Chile. Oficina de Planificación Nacional.
        Plan de reconstrucción 1971-1973, de las provincias
        de Coquimbo, Aconagua, Santiago, Valparaiso y
        O'Higgins, afectadas por el sismo del 8 de julio de
        1971. Santiago, 1971.
        256 p.   illus., maps, tables.   24 cm.   (Serie
        5, vol. 3)

20165   Chile. Oficina de Planificación Nacional.
        Política de desarrollo nacional; directivas
        nacionales y regionales. Santiago, 1968.
        149 p.   maps (part fold.)   27 cm.

20166   Chile (Colony)   Real Audiencia.   Archivo.
        ... Catálogo del Archivo de la Real Audiencia de
        Santiago... Santiago, Imprenta, litografía y encuader-
        nación Barcelona [etc.] 1898-1942.
        4 v.   24-26½ cm.
        At head of title, v. 1-3:   Biblioteca Nacional;
        v. 4:   Archivo Nacional.
        Imprint varies: v. 3, Imprenta Cervantes; v. 4,
        Dirección de talleres fiscales de prisiones.

20167   Chile.   Servicio de Seguro Social.
        Manual de consultas del SSS; ley 10.383 del 8 de
        agosto de 1952.   [San Miguel, Unidad] 1963.
        24 p.   illus.   25 cm.

20168   Chile.   Servicio Nacional de Estadística.
        Algunos resultados provinciales del XIII censo de
        población obtenidos por muestro; XIII censo de poblacié
        y II de vivienda levantados el 29 de noviembre de 1960.
        [Santiago] 1963.
        284 p.   27 cm.

20169   Chile.   Servicio Nacional de Estadística.
        Población total por provincias, Chile; 1885-1960.
        Santiago, 1964.
        11 p.   tables.   25 cm.

20170   Chile.   Servicio Nacional de Estadística.
        III [i.e. Tercero] censo nacional de manufacturas;
        datos referidos al año 1957.   [Santiago, 1960]
        132 p.   illus., map.   28 cm.
        Issued by the agency under a variant name:
        Dirección de Estadística y Censos.

20171   Chile.   Servicio Nacional de Salud.
        Enfermedades infecciosas de declaración obligatoria.
        Síntesis estadística 1952-1960.   [Santiago? 1961]
        115 p.   tables.   25 cm.

20172   Chile.   Servicio Nacional de Salud.
        Información técnica sobre higiene mental y alcoholism
        [Santiago] 1959.
        31 p.   26 cm.

20173   Chile.   Superintendencia de Bancos.
        Memoria de la Superintendencia de bancos corres-
        pondiente a los años 1940 y 1941.   Santiago, 1942.
        130 p.   21 cm.

20174 Chile. Superintendencia de Educación.
Matrícula por cursos, niveles y ramas de la
educación. 1955-1967. [Santiago] 1968.
28 p. 22 x 32½ cm.

20175 Chile. Superintendencia de Educación.
... Seminario de recursos humanos (29 de mayo al
7 de junio) Santiago, 1967.
76 p. 28 cm.

20176 Chile. Superintendencia de Educación.
La Superintendencia de Educación y la reforma
educacional chilena. [Santiago, 1969]
211 p. fold. table. 27½ cm.

20177 Chile. Superintendencia de Educación. Dirección de
Educación Secundaria.
Proposal for five experimental integral secondary
schools. Santiago, 1968.
25, 16 p. 32½ x 22 cm.

20178 Chile. Superintendencia de Educación. Oficina de
Planeamiento.
Oferta y demanda de profesores de educación básica.
Santiago, 1968.
28 p. 22 x 32 cm.

20179 Chile. Superintendencia de Educación. Oficina de
Planeamiento.
Proyecciones del gasto en educación 1967-1975.
[Santiago] 1968.
[17] p. 22 x 32½ cm.

20180 Chile. Superintendencia de Seguridad Social.
Bibliografía de la seguridad social chilena.
Santiago, 1967.
226 p. 27 cm.

20181 Chile al día. Valparaiso, J. M. Duque [192-]
unpaged. illus. 25 x 34 cm.

20182 Chinchilla V , Eduardo.
Sistema básico para la automazación de los datos
en el catastro, por Eduardo Chincilla V. y Rodrigo
Pratt G. San José, Costa Rica, Instituto Geográfico
Nacional [1973?]
23-43 p. illus., tables. 25 cm.
Reprinted from Informe semestral, enero a junio,
1973.

20183   Chirino, Otón.
        Vísperas de la luz. [Caracas, 1975]
        63 p.   24 cm.
        Inscribed by author.
        Poetry.

20184   Chirinos, Victor Manuel.
        Introducción a la teoría de la documentación.
        Maracaibo, Centro de Documentación e Información,
        Universidad del Zulia, 1968.
        101 p.   24 cm.

20185   Chubut, Argentine Republic. Dirección General de
        Estadística y Censos.
        Estadística trienal. [Rawson?]
        v.   33 cm.
        Library has 1962-1963-1964.

20186   Chumacero, Alí.
        Páramo de sueños, seguido de Imágenes desterradas.
        México [Universidad Nacional Autónoma de México]
        1960.
        107 p.   24 cm.

20187   Churcher, C   S   1928-
        Smilodon neogaeus en las barrancas costeras de Mar
        del Plata, provincia de Buenos Aires, por C. S.
        Churcher. Mar del Plata, Comisión Municipal de
        Cultura, 1967.
        245-261 p.   illus.   23 cm.   (Publicaciones
        del Museo Municipal de Ciencias Naturales de Mar del
        Plata, v. 1, no. 8)
        Summary in English.
        Bibliography: p. 257.

20188   Cicero, Marcus Tullius.
        Sobre el destino. Introducción, traducción y notas
        de Angel J. Cappelletti. Rosario [Instituto de
        Filosofía, Universidad Nacional del Litoral, Facultad
        de Filosofía y Letras] 1964.
        111 p.   23 cm.
        Translation of De fato.
        Latin and Spanish on opposite pages.
        Errata slip inserted.

20189   El Cid Campeador.
        Poema de mio Cid. Edición facsimil del Códice
        de Per Abat, conservado en la Biblioteca Nacional.

Madrid, 1961.
[5] p. facsim.: 1 v. (unpaged)   23 cm.

20190 Ciechomski, Juana D   de
Carácter del desove y fecundidad de la merluza
argentina, Merluccius merluccius hubbsi, del sector
bonaerense. Mar del Plata, Universidades nacionales
de Buenos Aires, La Plata y del Sur, P. E. de la
Provincia de Buenos Aires, Instituto de Biología
Marina, 1967.
30 p.   illus.   25 cm.   (Boletín, no. 13)

20191 Ciechomski, Juana D   de.
Huevos y larvas de tres especies de peces marinos,
Anchoa marinii, Brevoortia aurea, y Prionotus nudigula
de la zona de Mar del Plata, por Juana D. de Ciechomski.
Mar del Plata, 1968.
28 p.   illus.   26 cm.   (Boletín del Instituto
de Biología Marina, no. 17)
At head of title: Universidades Nacionales de Buenos
Aires, La Plata, y del Sur. P. E. de la Provincia
de Buenos Aires. Instituto de Biología Marina.
Summaries in Spanish and English.
Bibliography: p. 28.

20192 Ciechomski, Juana D   de.
Observaciones sobre la reproducción, desarrollo
embrionario y larval de la anchoíta argentina
(Engraulis anchoita) por Juana D. de Ciechomski.
Mar del Plata, 1965.
29 p.   illus.   26 cm.   (Boletín del Instituto
de Biología Marina, no. 9)
Summary in Spanish and English.
Bibliography: p. 21-22.

20193 Cieza de León, Pedro, 1518?-1560.
La crónica del Perú. Prólogo por Sergio Elias Ortiz.
[Bogotá] Ediciones de la Revista Ximénez de Quesada
[1971]
419 p.   24 cm.

20194 Cieza de León, Pedro, 1518?-1560.
El Señorio de los Incas; 2ª. parte de la Crónica
del Perú. Introducción de Carlos Aranibar. [1. ed.]
Lima, Instituto de Estudios Peruanos, 1967.
xcvi, 271 p.   18 cm.   (Colección de fuentes e
investigaciones para la historia del Perú. Serie:
Textos básicos, no. 1)
Bibliography: p. [lxxxv]-xcvi.

335

20195   Cincinnati. Public Library. Rare Book Department.
        A checklist of books relating to the discovery,
        exploration and description of America, from Columbus
        to Mackenzie, 1492-1801. Compiled by Yeatman
        Anderson, III, curator. [Cincinnati] Public Library
        of Cincinnati and Hamilton County, 1961.
        1 v. (unpaged)   22 cm.
        Includes bibliography.

20196   Cinta Guzmán, Alberto.
        Evolución legislativa y doctrinaria de la reforma
        agraria. México [1963?]
        116 p.   23 cm.
        Tesis (licenciatura en derecho) - Universidad Naciona
        Autónoma de México.
        Bibliography: p. 115-116.

20197   Cintra, Alarico.
        Bimbalhada e sarabandas... [crônicas]   Rio de
        Janeiro [Gráfica Tupy] 1963.
        192 p.   18 cm.

20198   Cintra de Camargo, Maria Lourdes Sampaio.
        Tratamento de publicações periódicas numa biblioteca
        São Paulo, Universidade de São Paulo, Biblioteca
        Central, 1966.
        19 p.   31 cm.

20199   Ciocchini, Héctor E
        Góngora y la tradición de los emblemas. Bahía
        Blanca [Instituto de Humanidades, Universidad Nacional
        del Sur] 1960.
        70 p.   20 cm.   (Cuadernos del Sur)
        Bibliography: p. 69-70.

20200   Ciocchini, Héctor E
        El sendero y los días [por] Héctor Ciocchini. [Bahía
        Blanca, República Argentina] Instituto de Humanidades,
        Universidad Nacional de Sur [1973]
        191 p.   22 cm.   (Cuadernos del Sur)
        Essays.
        Includes bibliographical references.

20201   Ciocchini, Héctor E
        Los trabajos de Anfión. Bahía Blanca, Instituto
        de Humanidades, Universidad Nacional del Sur [1969?]
        120 p.   24 cm.

20202 Cirigliano, Gustavo F   J
       Análisis fenomenológico de la educación [por]
       Gustavo F. J. Cirigliano. Paraná, Argentina,
       Facultad de Ciencias de la Educación, Universidad
       Nacional del Litoral, 1962 [i.e. 1963]
         191 p.   illus.   24 cm.
       Bibliography: p. [185]-188.

20203 Cirigliano, Gustavo F   J
       Universidad y pueblo. Planteos y textos. Prólogo
       de Juan Emilio Cassani. Buenos Aires, Librería del
       Colegio [1973]
         150 p.   20 cm.   (Biblioteca nueva pedagogía)

20204 Cisneros, Francisco Javier, 1836-1898.
       Relación documentada de cinco espediciones, por
       Francisco Javier Cisneros. Nueva York, Impr. de
       Hallet y Breen, 1870.
         120 p.   23 cm.
       Cover-title: Cinco espediciones á Cuba.

20205 Civeira Taboada, Miguel.
       Fray Alonso Ponce, cronista de la Nueva España.
       [México, 1974]
         broadside.   illus.   32 cm.
       Reprinted from Boletín bibliográfico de la Secretaría
       de Hacienda y Crédito Público, Año XX, Tercera época,
       no. 501, Septiembre de 1974, p. 13.

20206 Clarice [pseud.]
       Semi Rosa. [Apresentação de Paulo Bonfim et José
       Mautner. São Paulo] Martins [1963]
         109 p.   22 cm.

20207 Clark, James Hyde.
       Cuba and the fight for freedom; a powerful and
       thrilling history of the "Queen of the Antilles," the
       oppression of the Spanish government, the insurrection
       of 1868 and the compromise of 1878, and a full and
       vivid account of the present struggle of the people
       for liberty and independence... Written and edited
       by James Hyde Clark... assisted by one of the Cuban
       patriots of the "Ten years' war." Philadelphia,
       Globe Bible publishing co. [1896]
         512 p. incl. front., plates, ports., fold. map.
       20 cm.

20208 Clark, Lawrence.
       Popoluca-castellano, castellano-popoluca; dialecto

337

de Sayula, Veracruz, compilado por Lorenzo Clark y
Nancy Davis de Clark. [1. ed.] México, Instituto
Lingüístico de Verano, en cooperación con la Dirección
General de Asuntos Indígenas de la Secretaría de
Educación Pública, 1960.
165 p.   illus.   21 cm.   (Serie de vocabularios
indígenas Mariano Silva y Aceves, no. 4)
Cover title: Vocabulario populuca de Sayula.

20209 Clark, Ronald James.
Problemas y conflictos sobre propiedad de tierras
en Bolivia. Madison, Land Tenure Center, University
of Wisconsin, 1969.
17 p.   28 cm.   (LTC reprint no. 54-S)
Reprinted from Inter-American economic affairs,
vol. 22, no. 4, Spring 1969.

20210 Clark, Ronald James.
Reforma agraria e integración campesina en la
economía boliviana. Madison, Land Tenure Center,
University of Wisconsin, 1973.
5-22 p.   24 cm.   (LTC reprint no. 107)
Reprinted from Estudios Andinos, año 1, vol. I, no. 3 (197

20211 Clark, Ronald James.
Reforma agraria y participación de los campesinos
en el mercado del altiplano de Bolivia. Madison,
Land Tenure Center, University of Wisconsin, 1968.
32 p.   28 cm.   (LTC reprint no. 42-S)
Reprinted from Land economics, vol. XLIV, May 1968.

20212 Clark, Wayne E
Taxonomy and biology of spittlebugs of the genera
Aenolamia Fennah and Prosapia Fennah (Cercopidae)
in northeastern Mexico [by] Wayne E. Clark, Gregorio
E. Ibarra-Díaz, and Horace W. Van Cleave. México,
Sociedad Mexicana de Entomología, 1976.
13-24 p.   illus., map.   23 cm.
Reprinted from Folia entomológica mexicana, no. 34, 1976
Abstracts in English and Spanish.

20213 Clarke, Arthur Charles, 1917.
O vento solar; historias de era espacial; tradução
de Leonel Vallandre. Pôrto Alegre, Editôra Globo, 1973.
188 p.   23 cm.

20214 Clarke, M
The yield of sugar cane in Barbados in 1968, by
M. Clarke, C. D. Gilkes, E. L. Jones, and A. StE
Clarke... [Bridgetown?] 1968.
26 p.   33 cm.   (Barbados. Ministry of labour,
agriculture and national insurance, Bulletin, no. 46)

20215 Clarke, Robin, 1937-
       La gran experiencia; la ciencia y la tecnología
       en el segundo decenio para el desarrollo. Preparado
       para el Centro de Información Económica y Social de
       las Naciones Unidas. New York, Naciones Unidas, 1971.
       78 p.   22½ cm.   (Documento informativo para
       ejecutivos)

20216 Claro, María Elena.
       Algo sobre Virginia Woolf. [Santiago de Chile,
       Editorial Universitaria, c1967]
       98, [5] p.   port.   19 cm.   (El Espejo de papel)
       Bibliography: p. 97-[99]

20217 Claro, Samuel.
       La música virreinal en el nuevo mundo. Santiago de
       Chile, Instituto de Investigaciones Musicales,
       Facultad de Ciencias y Artes Musicales, Universidad
       de Chile, 1970.
       31 p.   illus., music.   26 cm.   (Colección de
       ensayos, 18)

20218 Claudel, Paul, 1868-1955.
       Le chemin de la croix. Monterrey, México, Ediciones
       Sierra Madre, 1969.
       28 p.   22 cm.   (Poesía en el mundo, 66)
       Parallel French and Spanish text.
       Translation by Arturo Salinas Martínez.

20219 Claudel, Paul, 1868-1955.
       Magnificat. Monterrey, México, Ediciones Sierra
       Madre, 1969.
       40 p.   22 cm.   (Poesía en el mundo, 65)
       Parallel French and Spanish text.
       Translation by Alfonso Rubio.

20220 Cleaves, Peter S
       Implementation of the agrarian and educational
       reforms in Peru [by] Peter S. Cleaves. Austin,
       Institute of Latin American Studies, University of
       Texas at Austin, 1977.
       39 p.   28 cm.   (Technical papers series, 8)

20221 Clemente, José Edmundo, ed.
       El ensayo. [Buenos Aires] Ediciones Culturales
       Argentinas, Ministerio de Educación y Justicia,
       Dirección General de Cultura [1961]
       146 p.   21 cm.   (Biblioteca des sesquicentenario.
       Colección Antologías)

20222　Cleymans, Jean.
　　　On the quark-parton fragmentation functions, by
　　　Jean Cleymans and Rudolf Rodenberg. Rio de Janeiro,
　　　Centro Brasileiro de Pesquisas Físicas, 1973.
　　　213-217 p.　　22 cm.　　(Notas de física, v. 20,
　　　no. 11)

20223　Cloud, William F
　　　Church and state, or Mexican politics from Cortez
　　　to Diaz. Under X rays. By W. F. Cloud... Kansas
　　　City, Mo., Peck & Clark, printers, 1896.
　　　274, 58 p.　　illus., pl., 4 port. (incl. front.)
　　　19½ cm.
　　　Contents. - book I. Church and state. - book II.
　　　History of Texas and of the Mexican war.

20224　Cobo, Mario.
　　　Estudio estadístico de la pesca del camarón en el
　　　Ecuador y de algunas características biológicas de
　　　las especies explotadas, por Mario Cobo y Harold Loesc
　　　... Guayaquil, 1966.
　　　25 p.　　tables, diagrs., fold. map.　　25 cm.
　　　(Ecuador. Instituto Nacional de Pesca del Ecuador.
　　　Boletín científico y técnico, vol. I, no. 6)
　　　Summaries in Spanish, French, and English)

20225　Cobo, Mario.
　　　Lista de los peces marinos del Ecuador, por Mario
　　　Cobo y Sheyla Massay. Guayaquil, 1969.
　　　26 p.　　illus.　　25 cm.　　(Ecuador. Instituto
　　　Nacional de Pesca del Ecuador. Boletín científico
　　　y técnico, vol. 2, no. 1)

20226　Cochabamba, Bolivia (Dept.) Corte Superior.
　　　Discurso informe; apertura del año judicial [por]
　　　Victor Nery Q. [1. ed.] Cochabamba [Editorial
　　　Universitaria] 1968.
　　　44 p.　　18 cm.

20227　Cock Mincapié, Olga.
　　　El seseo en el Nuevo Reino de Granada, 1550-1650.
　　　Prólogo de Guillermo L. Guitarte. Bogotá, 1969.
　　　170 p.　　24 cm.　　(Publicaciones del Instituto
　　　Caro y Cuervo, 26)
　　　Bibliography: p. [144]-151.

20228　Codazzi Aguirre, Juan Andrés.
　　　Escudo para las Islas Malvinas y adyacencias.
　　　[Rosario, Argentina, Escuela de Artes Gráficas del

Colegio Salesiano San José, 1969
77 p.   illus., coats of arms (part col.)   19 cm.
Cover title.

20229   Codex Cortesianus.
Los mayas según el Códice Trocortesiano. [l. ed.]
Mexico, 1965.
163 p.   illus.   17 cm.
Edited and translated by Felipe Fernández Encarnación.
"Principió la traducción del Códice por la página 112
que se ha mirado como la última... y así la página 1,
mirada como la primera, viene a ser la última del
Códice."

20230   Códice de Calkiní. Campeche, Gobierno del estado, 1957.
147 p.   illus., facsims.   17 cm.   (Biblioteca
Campechana, 4)

20231   Codman, John, 1814-1900.
Ten months in Brazil: with incidents of voyages
and travels, descriptions of scenery and character,
notices of commerce and productions, etc., by John
Codman. Boston, Lee and Shepard, 1867.
208 p.   front., plates.   19½ cm.

20232   Codovilla, Victorio.
Por la acción de masas hacia la conquista del poder;
informe rendido en nombre del Comité Central ante
el 12. Congreso del Partido Comunista que sesionó
desde el 22 de febrero hasta el 3 de marzo de 1963.
[Buenos Aires, Editorial Anteo, 1963]
45 p.   29 cm.

20233   Coelho, Nelly Novaes.
Tres momentos poéticos; Bocage, Vicente de Carvalho,
Mário de Andrade. São Paulo, Comissão de Literatura,
Conselho Estadual de Cultura, 1970.
165 p.   22 cm.   (Coleção ensaio, 74)

20234   Coelho, Paulo Japyassú.
Dez dias em contacto com as selvas brasileiras.
Uma excursão ao Rio Doce agosto de 1939. Juiz de
Fora, Juljo de 1940.
44 p.   illus.   24 cm.

20235   Coelho, Paulo Japyassú.
Versóides: acrósticos, trovas y coisas diversas.
2. ed. Juiz de Fora [Gráf. Comércio e Indústrial]

341

1967.
112 p.   23 cm.

20236   Coelho Netto, Henrique Maximiniano, 1864-1934.
O patinho torto ou os mistérios do sexo. Comédia em
3 atos. Rio de Janeiro, Serviço Nacional de Teatro,
1973.
viii, 52 p.   21 cm.

20237   Coelho Netto, Zita.
Coelho Netto, meu pai e grande amigo! Rio [de
Janeiro] Organização Simoes, 1964.
61 p.   16 cm.

20238   Coerr, Wymberley DeR
Forces of change in Latin America. [Washington]
Department of State [1961]
12 p.   22 x 10 cm.   ([U.S.] Department of State.
Publication 7157. Inter-American series, 64)
"Address made before the League of Women Voters of
Massachusetts."
"Reprinted from the Department of State Bulletin
of February 20, 1961.

20239   Coimbra Filho, Adelmar Faria.
Bibliografia florestal brasileira, 1. Contribuição
[por] Adelmar Faria Coimbra Filho [e] Alceo Magnanini.
[Manaus] Conselho Nacional de Pesquisas, Instituto
Nacional de Pesquisas da Amazônia, 1964.
93 p.   23 cm.   (Instituto Nacional de Pesquisas
de Amazônia. Botânica. Publicação, no. 20)

20240   Colegio de Economistas de Venezuela.
Diagnóstico de la economía venezolana. Colegio de
Economistas de Venezuela; [primera convención nacional,
Caracas, mayo de 1963. Edición al cuidado de José
Moreno Colmenares. Caracas] Universidad Central de
Venezuela [1964]
176 p.   22 cm.   (Colección Temas)

20241   Colegio de Escribanos de la Provincia de Buenos Aires.
Biblioteca Notarial.
Transferencias de fondos de comercio; homenaje al
Código de comercio en su centenario. La Plata, 1963.
496 p.   21 cm.   (Colegio de Escribanos de la
Provincia de Buenos Aires. [Publicaciones] 6)
"Apéndice: Material publicado en el suplemento
del Diario de sesiones de la Cámara de Senadores de la
Nación el 24 de setiembre de 1959": p. [277]-496.

20242   Colegio Máximo de las Academias de Colombia.
        Presencia de Francia en la cultura colombiana.
        Bogotá, 1965.
        66 p.   17 cm.   (Publicaciones, 2)

20243   Coleridge, Samuel Taylor, 1772-1834.
        Biographia literaria, capítulos XIV y XVIII...
        Traducción: Cristina Iglesia y María Elisa Latorre.
        Revisión y notas: Matilde Vucko de Goy, Enriqueta
        Varela, y Sandra Penchansky de Zapata. Cuadernos
        para el estudio de la estética y literatura, dirección:
        Hilda Torres-Varela. Resistencia, Chaco, Sección
        Literaturas Modernas, Instituto de Letras, Facultad
        de Humanidades, Universidad Nacional del Nordeste
        [n.d.]
        33 p.   29 cm.   (Cuadernos para el estudio de
        la estética y la literatura, 1)

20244   Colette, Sidonie Gabrielle, 1873-1954.
        De la poesía moderna francesa. Monterrey, México,
        Ediciones Sierra Madre, 1962.
        23 p.   25¼ cm.   (Poesía en el mundo, 36)
        Parallel French and Spanish texts.
        Translation by Jaime A. Villareal and Gerardo Rubén
        Martínez.

20245   Colimodio, José María.
        La sociedad anónima; actos constitutivos y funcionales.
        Buenos Aires, Información S.R.L. [1960]
        342 p.   23 cm.
        "Modelos de documentación": p. 225-247.
        "Legislación": p. 249-329.

20246   Colin, Mario.
        Antecedentes agrarios del municipio de Atlacomulco;
        estado de México: documentos. [1. ed.] México,
        Edición del Departamento de Asuntos Agrarios y
        Colonización, 1963.
        279 p.   illus.   24 cm.   (Testimonios de
        Atlacomulco, no. 18)

20247   Colin, Mario.
        Bibliografía general del Estado de México. Mexico
        [Editorial Jus] 1963-
        v.   facsims.   24 cm.   (Biblioteca enci-
        clopédica del Estado de México, 1)
        Contents. - t. 1. Impresos de Estado.

20248   Colina, José de la.
        La lucha con la pantera [cuentos. 1. ed.] Xalapa,
        Universidad Veracruzana, 1962.
        109 p.   20 cm.   (Ficción, 47)

20249   Coll, Pedro Emilio.
        Estudio preliminar de Rafael Angel Insausti.
        Caracas, 1966.
        xli, 413 p.   port.   18 cm.   (Colección Clásicos
        venezolanos de la Academia Venezolana de la Lengua, 14)
        Bibliography: p. xxxix-xli.

20250   Coll Cuchi, Cayetano.
        ... La ley Foraker. Estudio histórico-político
        comparado por el doctor Cay. Coll Cuchi... San Juan,
        Puerto Rico, Tip. del Boletín mercantil, 1904.
        1 p.l., ix, 206 p.   18½ cm.
        Contents. - 1. pte. Breve historia política del
        pueblo de Puerto Rico. - 2. pte. La ley Foraker.
        Comentarios. Su interpretación y aplicación. -
        3. pte. Examen de varias cartas coloniales y de la
        carta autonómica de Puerto Rico comparadas con la
        ley Foraker.

20251   Coll y Prat, Narciso, abp., 1754-1822.
        Memoriales sobre la independencia de Venezuela.
        Estudio preliminar por Manuel Pérez Vila. Caracas,
        Academia Nacional de la Historia, 1960.
        403 p.   23 cm.   (Biblioteca de la Academia
        Nacional de la Historia, 23)

20252   Collado de la Garza, Gloria, 1940-
        Juego de dos. Monterrey, México, Ediciones Sierra
        Madre, 1971.
        28 p.   illus.   22 cm.   (Poesía en el mundo, 89)

20253   Collazo, Enrique, 1848-1921.
        ... Los americanos en Cuba, por Enrique Collazo.
        La Habana, Imp. C. Martínez y comp., 1905.
        2 v.   18½ cm.
        Cover of pt. 2 dated 1906.

20254   Collell Núñez, José.
        La escuela angloamericana del derecho internacional
        privado. Santiago, Editorial Universitaria, 1962.
        90 p.   22 cm.
        Tesis (licenciatura en ciencias jurídicas y
        sociales - Universidad de Chile.
        Bibliography: p. 89.

20255   Colmerares, Germán, comp.
Fuentes coloniales para la historia del trabajo en
Colombia. Transcripciones del Archivo Histórico
Nacional de Bogotá: G. Colmenares, M. de Melo [y]
D. Fajardo. Bogotá, Ediciones de la Universidad de
Los Andes, 1968.
525 p.   25 cm.
At head of title: Universidad de Los Andes. Facultad
de Artes y Ciencias. Departamento de Historia.

20256   Coloane, Francisco A   1910-
El témpano de Kanasaka, y otros cuentos [por]
Francisco Coloane. [Santiago, Chile] Editorial
Universitaria [1968]
xii, 133 p.   19 cm.   (Colección Letras de
América, 10)
Cormorán.
Contents. - Cabo de Hornos. - El témpano de Kanasaka. -
El australiano. - El último contrabando. - Cururo. -
Perros, caballos, hombres. - La venganza del mar. -
La gallina de los huevos de luz. - Golfo de Penas. -
En el caballo de la aurora. - De como murió el chilote
Otey. - La botella de caña.

20257   Colombia. Caja de Crédito Agrario, Industrial y Minero.
Caja de Crédito Agrario, Industrial y Minero. Su
órigen, organización, obra. Tercera edición. Bogotá,
1970.
169 p.   tables.   25 cm.

20258   Colombia. Cámara de Cuentas.
Informe que la honorable Cámara de Cuentas presenta
al Congreso Nacional sobre las cuentas generales del
distrito de Santo Domingo. Ciudad Trujillo, Distrito
de Santo Domingo, Imprenta Listín Diario, 1942.
24 p.   12 fold. tables.   23 cm.

20259   Colombia. Comisión de Estudios del Plan Decenal para
el Fomento del Departamento del Chocó.
Plan de fomento regional para el Chocó, 1959-1968.
[Bogotá? 1959?]
xxxii, 705 p.   diagrs., tables, maps.
At head of title: Consejo Nacional de Política
Económica y Planeación. Departamento Administrativo
de Planeación y Servicios Técnicos.

20260   Colombia. Comité Nacional de Planeación.
Statistical survey of the economy of Colombia, 1959.

Bogotá, Imprenta de la República, 1960.
77 p. (chiefly diagrs., tables)   28 cm.

20261   Colombia. Consejo Nacional de Política Económica y
Planeación.
Colombia: plan cuatrienal de inversiones públicas
nacionales, 1961-1964 (diciembre de 1960) [Bogotá,
Imprenta Nacional, 1961]
278 p.   diagrs., tables.   30 cm.   (Documentos
del desarrollo)
At head of title: Consejo Nacional de Política
Económica y Planeación [y] Departamento Administrativo
de Planeación y Servicios Técnicos.

20262   Colombia. Consejo Nacional de Política Económica y
Planeación.
Colombia: plan general de desarrollo económico y
social. [Bogotá] 1962-
v.   diagrs., tables.   28 cm.   (Documentos
del desarrollo)
At head of title: Consejo Nacional de Política
Económica y Planeación [y] Departamento Administrativo
de Planeación y Servicios Técnicos.
Contents. - 1. pt. El programa general.

20263   Colombia. Constitution.
Constitución política de Colombia, acordada con la
reforma plebiscitaria y con los actos legislativos
1, 2, 3 y 4 de 1959. Bogotá, Imprenta Nacional, 1960.
164 p.   17 cm.
At head of title: Ministerio de Gobierno.

20264   Colombia. Constitution.
Constitución política de la República de Colombia.
10. ed. Bogotá, Editorial Voluntad [1961]
169 p.   14 cm.   (Colección "Codex brevis")

20265   Colombia. Constitution.
Constitución política de la República de Colombia.
Decimaoctava edición. [Bogotá] Voluntad [1970]
177 p.   15½ cm.

20266   Colombia. Departamento Administrativo de Planeación
y Servicios Técnicos.
Statistical survey of the economy of Colombia,
1959. Bogotá, Imprenta Banco de la República, 1960.
77 p. (p. 11-77 diagrs., tables)   map.   27 cm.

20267   Colombia. Departamento Administrativo Nacional de
        Estadística.
        La biblioteca en Colombia, 1964. 5. ed. Bogotá,
        1966.
        xiv, 110 ℓ., 111-113 p.   map, form.   27 cm.
        (Boletín no. 9)

20268   Colombia. Departamento Administrativo Nacional de
        Estadística.
        La cinematográfica en Colombia, 1965. Segunda
        edición. Bogotá, 1967.
        94 p.   tables.   28 cm.

20269   Colombia. Departamento Administrativo Nacional de
        Estadística.
        Colombia: debate agrario; documentos. Bogotá,
        1971.
        xvi, 227 p.   illus., tables, diagrs.   28 cm.

20270   Colombia. Departamento Administrativo Nacional de
        Estadística. Punto Central de Información.
        Directorio de bibliotecas y editoriales en Colombia.
        [2. ed. Bogotá, 1960]
        xv, 53 p.   tables.   25 cm.   (Boletín no. 4)

20271   Colombia. Departamento Administrativo Nacional de
        Estadística.
        Directorio nacional de explotaciones agropecuarias;
        censo agropecuario, 1960. Resumen nacional. Bogotá,
        1962.
        91 p.   33 cm.

20272   Colombia. Departamento Administrativo Nacional de
        Estadística.
        División político-administrativa de Colombia.
        [4. ed.] Bogotá, Multilith Estadual, 1960.
        213 p. of maps, tables.   23 cm.
        First edition issued in 1953 by Dirección Nacional
        de Estadística.

20273   Colombia. Departamento Administrativo Nacional de
        Estadística.
        La educación en Colombia, 1963-1964. Bogotá, 1966.
        v, 46 p.   27 cm.

20274   Colombia. Departamento Administrativo Nacional de
        Estadística.
        Estimaciones y pronósticos agrícolas: 1960-1970.

[Bogotá, 1970]
26 ℓ.   graphs.   28 cm.

20275   Colombia. Departamento Administrativo Nacional de
Estadística.
Guía industrial de Colombia, 1969. Catálogo
general de productos. Medellín, 1969.
xxiv, 455 p.   illus.   29 cm.
Published jointly with Asociación Nacional de Industriales.

20276   Colombia. Departamento Administrativo Nacional de
Estadística.
Publicaciones periódicas en Colombia, 1965.
Publicación preparada por la División de Información
y Publicaciones a cargo de Armando Moreno Mattos.
Bogotá, 1967.
62 p.   27 cm.

20277   Colombia. Departamento de Prisiones.
Realizaciones y proyectos para la reforma carcelaria
y penitenciaria, 1938-1939. Exposición del director
general de prisiones al Ministro de Gobierno. Bogotá,
Imprenta Nacional, 1939.
120 p.   20 cm.
Issued also as the department's annual report in the
Memoria of the Ministerio de Gobierno.

20278   Colombia. Dirección del Presupuesto.
Manual de preparación del presupuesto. Bogotá,
1963.
528 p.   illus.   28 cm.
Includes legislation.

20279   Colombia. División de Atención Médica.
Análisis de la información básica sobre la utilización y disponibilidad de los recursos para la
atención médica en Colombia. Bogotá, 1967.
15 ℓ., 29 tables.   29 cm.

20280   Colombia. Fondo Nacional de Ahorro para el Desarrollo
Económico y Social.
Texto del proyecto de ley como fué aprobado por
la comisión tercera del H. Senado de la República.
Bogotá, 1968.
viii, 27 p.   35 cm.

20281   Colombia. Instituto Colombiano Agropecuario.
Algunos aspectos del análisis de suelos. Segunda

edición. Bogotá, Imprenta Nacional, 1968.
55 p. illus., diagrs. 24 cm.

20282 Colombia. Instituto Colombiano Agropecuario.
Plegable de divulgación. Bogotá, no. 1-
196-
folders in 6 p. 22 cm.
Library has no. 10-23.

20283 Colombia. Instituto Colombiano de Comercio Exterior.
Decreto 617 de 1972 (18 de abril) por el cual se
reducen los gravámenes arancelarios a las importa-
ciones de algunos productos originarios y provenientes
de los paises miembros del Acuerdo de Cartagena.
Bogotá, Imprenta Nacional, 1972.
228 p. 25½ cm.

20284 Colombia. Instituto Colombiano de Energía Eléctrica.
La electrificación en Colombia. Informe del
Instituto Colombiano de Energía Eléctrica, 1966-1970.
Bogotá, 1970.
164 p. illus., tables (part fold.), graphs,
maps. 29½ cm.

20285 Colombia. Instituto Colombiano de Especialización
Técnica en el Exterior (ICETEX)
Recursos y requerimientos de personal de alto nivel,
Colombia 1964-1975; implicaciones en la política
educativa y económica. Bogotá [n.d.]
xxviii, 246 p. 22 cm.

20286 Colombia. Instituto Colombiano de la Reforma Agraria.
Búfalos de agua; su introducción a Colombia por
el INCORA. [Bogotá, INCORA, 1967]
18 p. 22 cm. (Publicación del INCORA. Serie
didáctica no. 10)

20287 Colombia. Instituto Colombiano de la Reforma Agraria.
5 [i.e. Cinco] años de reforma social agraria;
informe de actividades en 1966. [Bogotá, 1967]
39 p. illus., group ports. 28 cm. (Publicación del INCORA. Serie informes, no. 8)

20288 Colombia. Instituto Colombiano de la Reforma Agraria.
Comité de Estudios Técnicos.
Recomendaciones sobre política agraria para
Colombia; informe del Primer Comité de Estudios
Técnicos, organismo asesor del Instituto Colombiano
de la Reforma Agraria, diciembre 1961-diciembre 1962.

349

Bogotá [1963]
96 p.   24 cm.   (Publicaciones. Serie Informes,
no. 3)

20289   Colombia. Instituto Colombiano de la Reforma Agraria.
Sección de Cooperativas y Mercadeo.
Cuatro años de cooperativismo agropecuario.
[Bogotá, 1967]
40 p.   illus., map.   28 cm.   (Publicación del
Incora. Serie informes, no. 13)

20290   Colombia. Instituto Colombiano de Pedagogía.
... Informe del II. curso de capacitación para
concentraciones de desarrollo rural. Documento
elaborado por: Rebeca Bernal Zapata [y] Ernesto López
Montaña. Secretaría: Mimi León de Navas. Bogotá,
1974.
2 p.l., 313 p. and various pagination at end for
Anexos.   tables, diagrs.   32 cm.

20291   Colombia. Instituto Colombiano de Pedagogía.
Plan de emergencia para la capacitación del personal
requerido para las concentraciones de la Victoria
-Valle-, Bolívar -Cauca-, La Unión y Consaca -Nariño-.
Documento preliminar de trabajo. Bogotá, 1973.
[12], 71 p., 19 anexos.   map, fold. tables.
28 cm.
Bibliografía: p. 68-70.

20292   Colombia. Instituto Colombiano para el Fomento de la
Educación Superior.
Directorio de publicaciones periódicas colombianas.
Bogotá, 1975.
3 p.l., 199 numb. ℓ.   33½ cm.

20293   Colombia. Instituto Colombiano para el Fomento de la
Educación Superior.
La educación superior en Colombia. Documentos básico
para su planeamiento. Volumen II (versión en español)
Informes de la comisión asesora de la Universidad de
California. Bogotá, 1970.
331 p.   24½ cm.

20294   Colombia. Instituto Colombiano para el Fomento de la
Educación Superior.
La educación superior en Colombia; documentos básicos
para su planeamiento. Bogotá [1970]
2 v.   24 cm.
Earlier edition of v. 1, with title Plan básico de

la educación superior en Colombia, issued in 1968
by the División of Planeación of the Fondo Universi-
tario Nacional, earlier name of the Institute.
Volume 2, "Informes de la Comisión Asesora de la
Universidad de California," issued also in English.
Includes bibliographies.

20295   Colombia. Instituto Colombiano para el Fomento de la
        Educación Superior. Grupo de Documentación.
        Directorio de universidades colombianas. Bogotá,
        1969.
        84, 7 p.   28 cm.

20296   Colombia. Instituto Colombiano para el Fomento de la
        Educación Superior.
        Estadísticas universitarias. Estudiantes, profe-
        sores, personal administrativo. Bogotá, 1972.
        unpaged.   tables (part fold.), graphs.   32 cm.

20297   Colombia. Instituto Colombiano para el Fomento de la
        Educación Superior. Grupo do Documentación.
        Directorio de universidades colombianas. Bogotá,
        1969.
        81, 7 p.   28 cm.

20298   Colombia. Instituto Colombiano para el Fomento de la
        Educación Superior. Programa Servicio Nacional de
        Pruebas.
        Algunos aspectos del bachiller colombiano. Estudio
        preliminar basado en encuesta hecha a los bachilleres
        y en sus resultados de las pruebas nacionales de
        aptitud y conocimientos, 1968. [Bogotá? 1970]
        168 p.   tables, graphs.   24 cm.

20299   Colombia. Instituto de Investigaciones Tecnológicas,
        Bogotá.
        La industria panelera en Colombia; estudio sobre
        su mejoramiento. Bogotá, 1964.
        72 p.

20300   Colombia. Instituto de Investigaciones Tecnológicas,
        Bogotá.
        Realizaciones y programas. [Bogotá, 1963?]
        40 p.

20301   Colombia. Instituto Geográfico Agustín Codazzi.
        Departamento Agrológico.
        Estudio general de suelos del Municipio de Merca-
        deres, para fines agrícolas (Departamento del Cauca)

por James Varela [et al.] Bogotá, 1968.
v, 106, [1] p.   fold. col. map (in pocket)
28 cm.   ([Boletín] v. 4, no. 11)
Bibliography: p. [107]

20302 Colombia. Instituto Geográfico Agustín Codazzi.
Departamento Agrológico.
Estudio general de suelos y forestal de las hoyas
hidrográficas de los Rios Mulatos y San Juan. Bogotá,
Instituto Geográfico Agustín Codazzi, Departamento
Agrológico, 1963.
38 ℓ.   fold. tables, fold. map.   28 cm.
(Publicación EE-6)

20303 Colombia. Instituto Geográfico Agustín Codazzi.
Departamento Agrológico.
Formaciones vegetales de Colombia; memoria explicativa sobre el mapa ecológico. Bogotá, Instituto
Geográfico Agustín Codazzi, Departamento Agrológico,
1963.
201 p.   illus., fold. maps at end.   25½ cm.

20304 Colombia. Instituto Geográfico Agustín Codazzi.
Monografía del Departamento del Magdalena. [Bogotá,
1973]
162 p.   illus.   32 cm.
Includes bibliographies.

20305 Colombia. Instituto Geográfico Agustín Códazzi.
Plan piloto de desarrollo urbano de Girardot.
Bogotá, 1972.
ix, 114 ℓ.   illus.   22 x 28 cm.
Cover title: Plan piloto de desarrollo urbano:
Girardot.

20306 Colombia. Instituto Geográfico Agustín Codazzi.
Problemas de la colonización en el Putumayo.
[Bogotá, 1973?]
1 v. (various pagings)   illus.   28 cm.
Includes bibliography.

20307 Colombia. Instituto Geográfico Agustín Codazzi.
Santa Marta: plano aerofotogramétrico. 1 ed.
sujeta a correcciones. [Bogotá] 1963.
col. map 76 x 98 cm.
Scale 1:5,000.
Relief shown by contours at 2 and 5 meter intervals.
"Fotografías aéreas tomadas en febrero de 1962."
Inset: Santa Marta y sus alrededores. 1:25,000.

At head of title: República de Colombia, Departamento del Magdalena.

20308 Colombia. Instituto Nacional de Abastecimientos.
Informe presentado al Sr. Presidente de la República,
Doctor Alberto Lleras y a los miembros de la Junta
Directiva [Bogotá] 1961.
1 v. (various pagings)   22 cm.

20309 Colombia. Instituto Nacional de Fomento Municipal.
Plan cuatrienal de acueductos y alcantarillados
urbanos, 1962-1965. [Bogotá, 196-]
235 ℓ.   illus.   28 cm.

20310 Colombia. Instituto Nacional de Fomento Tabacalero.
Departamento Técnico.
Plagas del tabaco en Colombia y métodos para comba-
tirlas. Bogotá, Imprenta Nacional, 1959.
35 p.

20311 Colombia. Instituto Nacional de Nutrición (Colombia)
Encuesta nutricional de El Trébol, municipio de
Chinchiná, Caldas, agosto 1963. Bogotá [1966?]
v, 38 ℓ.   28 cm.   (EPI-66-03. T.R.I. 16)
Bibliography: leaf 37.

20312 Colombia. Instituto Nacional de Nutrición de Colombia.
Plan nacional del PINA Colombia. Para extender
progresivamente a todo el país el programa integrado
de nutrición aplicada. [Bogotá, n.d.]
iii, 26 p.   map, diagrs.   29½ cm.   (DIR-65-10
[4]; R.R.P. 11)

20313 Colombia. Instituto Nacional de Nutrición de Colombia.
Plan of operations for the programme of protection
of pre-school children (P.P.P.) which will be carried
out by the Ministry of Public Health and the National
Institute of Nutrition with financial cooperation
from the United Kingdom committee of the freedom
from hunger campaign. [Bogotá, n.d.]
various pagination.   29 cm.   (DIR-65-34;
T.R.P. 54)

20314 Colombia. Instituto Nacional de Nutrición de Colombia.
Sección de Epidemiología.
Encuesta alimentaria de la vereda de San Bernardo,
municipio de Dagua, Valle, 1965. Bogotá [1966?]
i, 30 ℓ.   28 cm.   (EPI-66-07. T.R.I.17)
Bibliography: leaf 30.

20315   Colombia. Instituto Nacional de Nutrición de Colombia.
Sección de Epidemiología.
Encuesta nutricional de San Jacinto, Bolívar, 1967.
[Bogotá, 1968]
42, [2] p.   illus.   28 cm.
Bibliography: p. [43]-[44]

20316   Colombia. Laws, statutes, etc.
Código de procedimiento civil, compilado por Jorge
Ortega Torres. Bogotá, Editorial Temis, 1963.
422 p.   16 cm.   (Códigos de bolsillo Temis)

20317   Colombia. Laws, statutes, etc.
Código de sociedades [por] José Ignacio Narváez.
[Codificación de todas las disposiciones vigentes,
desde las constitucionales hasta las simplemente
reglamentarias. Con citas de tratadistas, extractos
de jurisprudencia, concordancias y comentarios del
autor al pie de cada artículo. Bogotá] Legislación
Económica [1960]
444 p.   25 cm.

20318   Colombia. Laws, statutes, etc.
Código de sociedades; legislación, doctrinas,
modelos de minutas. 3. ed. Bogotá, 1961.
xxii, 797 p.   25 cm.

20319   Colombia. Laws, statutes, etc.
Código penal y código de procedimiento penal,
con notas, concordancias, jurisprudencia de la Corte
Suprema y del Tribunal de Bogotá y normas legales
complementarias por Jorge Ortega Torres. 10. ed.,
actualizada. Bogotá, Temis, 1961.
5 p.l., 13-960, [2] p.   21 cm.

20320   Colombia. Laws, statutes, etc.
Código sustantivo del trabajo y Código procesal
del trabajo. 13. ed. Bogotá, Editorial Voluntad
[1964]
843 p.   14 cm.   (Colección "Codex brevis")

20321   Colombia. Laws, statutes, etc.
Código sustantivo del trabajo y Código procesal
del trabajo, compilados por Jorge Ortega Torres.
Bogotá, Editorial Temis, 1964.
548 p.   16 cm.   (Códigos de bolsillo Temis)

20322 Colombia. Laws, statutes, etc.
Decretos 182, 703, 719 y 2602 de 1968; 461, 810
y 2117 de 1969; y acuerdo no. 10 de 1968. Uso de
aguas y distritos de riego; arrendatarios y aparceros;
adquisición de tierras; incremento de producción
agropecuaria; cooperativas de la reforma agrícola;
adjudicación de baldíos; reguardos indígenas; reglamento sobre valorización. [Bogotá] INCORA [1970]
unpaged. 24 cm. (Publicación del INCORA,
Asesora jurídica, Serie jurídica no. 19)

20323 Colombia. Laws, statutes, etc.
Decretos reglamentarios de la Ley 135 de 1961, sobre
reforma social agraria. Bogotá, Ministerio de
Agricultura, 1962.
1 v. (various pagings) 32 cm.

20324 Colombia. Laws, statutes, etc.
Derecho colombiano de familia; compilación legis-
lativa. Elaborada por Fernando Hinestrosa. Bogotá,
Imprenta Nacional, 1969.
286 p. 24 cm.
At head of title: Ministerio de Justicia.

20325 Colombia. Laws, statutes, etc.
Legislación sobre medicina del trabajo y seguridad
industrial [por] la División de Medicina del Trabajo
y Seguridad Industrial. [Bogotá] Ministerio del
Trabajo, Sección de Divulgación [1963]
163 p. 24 cm.
Cover title.

20326 Colombia. Laws, statutes, etc.
Legislación tributaria; compilación legal. [La
compilación, las notas marginales y la dirección
estuvieron a cargo del Dr. Jaime Jiménez Ramírez,
jefe del Departamento de Asuntos Jurídicos de la
ANDI] Medellín, Biblioteca ANDI, 1962.
319 p. 22 cm.
At head of title: Asociación Nacional de Industriales.

20327 Colombia. Laws, statutes, etc.
La nueva legislación agraria. Bogotá, Imprenta
Nacional, 1962.
339 p.

355

20328　Colombia. Laws, statutes, etc.
Reforma del Código del trabajo. Bogotá, Imprenta
Nacional, 1960.
454 p.　25 cm.　(Biblioteca del Ministerio
del Trabajo)
Initiated by the Minister of Labor, Otto Morales
Benítez.

20329　Colombia. Laws, statutes, etc.
La reforma judicial. Bogotá, 1964.
327 p.　24 cm.
Name of editor, Luis F. Serrano A., at head of title.
Consists of Law 27 of 1963 and 18 decrees relating
to judicial reform.

20330　Colombia. Laws, statutes, etc.
La reforma social agraria; la Ley 135 de 1961 y
los otros estatutos legales que la complementan y
desarrollan. Bogotá, 1962.
x, 392 p.　25 cm.
Name of editor, Luis F. Serrano A., at head of title.
"Apartes de la ponencia para segundo debate del
Proyecto de Ley sobre reforma social agraria, presentad
al Senado por el senador doctor Carlos Lleras Restrepo"
p. [1]-54.

20331　Colombia. Laws, statutes, etc.
Reforma social agraria; leyes 135 de 1961 y 1ª
de 1968. [Bogota] INCORA [1968]
79 p.　22 cm.　(Publicación del INCORA, Asesoría
Jurídica. Serie jurídica, no. 11)
"Se han intercalado en los artículos pertinentes
de la Ley 135 de 1961 las modificaciones y adiciones
de que trata la Ley 1ª de 1968."

20332　Colombia. Laws, statutes, etc.
... La reforma tributaria: ley 81 de 1960, decreto
437 de 1961... Bogotá, Editorial Voluntad [1961]
403, [1] p.　14 cm.　(Colección "Codex brevis")

20333　Colombia. Laws, statutes, etc.
Regimen de propiedad intelectual y de prensa;
leyes, decretos y resoluciones vigentes sobre la
materia. Compilación, concordancias y notas de
Eduardo Santa. Bogotá, Imprenta Nacional, 1962.
283 p.　21 cm.

At head of title: República de Colombia. Ministerio
de Gobierno.

20334 Colombia. Laws, statutes, etc.
El servicio civil y la carrera administrativa en
Colombia; compilación de las disposiciones constitucionales y legales sobre la materia, precedida de
una información explicativa y seguida de los índices
correspondientes, hecha por la Oficina de Divulgación
e Información del Servicio Civil. Bogotá, Imprenta
Nacional, 1961.
   xxiv, 195 p.   illus.   25 cm.
   At head of title: República de Colombia. Departamento Administrativo del Servicio Civil.

20335 Colombia. Ministerio de Agricultura.
Plan cuatrienal para la exportaciones de algodón,
azúcar, banano, y tabaco, 1968-1971. Preparado por:
Alvaro Ramírez S., sub-jefe Oficina de Planeamiento,
Coordinación, y Evaluación [y] Guillermo A. Guerra E.,
asesor económico del Ministro. Con la asesoría de
Alberto Franco. En colaboración con: Oficina de
Planeamiento, Coordinación, y Evaluación del Ministerio,
Departamento Administrativo de Planeación, F.A.O.,
y grupos de trabajo de los sectores público y privado.
Bogotá, 1968.
   iii, 3, 81 p.   28 cm.   (Serie de planeamiento,
no. 12)
   Bibliographical footnotes.

20336 Colombia. Ministerio de Agricultura. Oficina de Planeamiento, Coordinación y Evaluación.
Programas para el desarrollo agropecuario en el
Departamento del César, 1968-1971. Preparado por:
Alberto García M. [et al.] de la Oficina de Planeamiento, Coordinación, y Evaluación. Con la asesoría
de Alberto Franco [y] Guillermo A. Guerra. Bogotá,
1968.
   72, 24 p.   2 fold. maps.   28 cm.   (Ministerio
de Agricultura. Serie: Estudios regionales, no. 3)

20337 Colombia. Ministerio de Agricultura. Servicio
Técnico Agrícola Colombiano Americano.
Compendio de legislación agropecuaria y organismos
agrícolas de Colombia. Bogotá, 1962.
   v, 157 p.   25 cm.

20338   Colombia. Ministerio de Educación Nacional. Oficina
        de Planeamiento, Coordinación y Evaluación.
        Directorio de establecimientos de educación
        oficiales y privados, educación media y superior.
        Bogotá, 1960.
        88 ℓ.   22 cm.
        Cover title.
        At head of title: Ministerio de Educación Nacional.
        Oficina de Planeamiento Educativo. Sección de Esta-
        dística.

20339   Colombia. Ministerio de Educación Nacional. Oficina
        de Planeamiento, Coordinación y Evaluación.
        Informe del proyecto para el I. Plan quinquenal.
        Bogotá, 1957-58.
        4 v. in 5.   maps, forms, tables.   28 cm.
        (Centro de Documentación e Información. Documento
        no. 0.10 (0.55))
        Cover title.
        Issued by the office under its earlier name:
        Oficina de Planeación.
        "Agenda del seminario: Proyecto del Plan quinquenal"
        3 leaves inserted in v. 1.
        "Over-all planning for education, VI Inter-American
        Seminar on Education, June, 1958": 12 p. inserted in
        v. 1.
        Includes legislation.

20340   Colombia. Ministerio de Educación Nacional. Sección de
        Orientación Pedagógica.
        Manual de orientación y consejería escolar. Bogotá,
        1972 (1972 on half-title)
        3 ℓ., 92, 2 numb. ℓ.   28 cm.

20341   Colombia. Ministerio de Educación Nacional. Sección de
        Orientación Psicopedagógica.
        El departamento de bienestar y orientación en la
        educación media. Bogotá, 1973.
        67 ℓ.   fold. diagr.   28 cm.

20342   Colombia. Ministerio de Minas y Petróleos.
        Proyecto de ley sobre petróleos y código de minas.
        Bogotá, Imprenta nacional, 1943.
        86 p.   24 cm.

20343   Colombia. Ministerio de Minas y Petróleos. Empresa
        Colombiana de Minas.
        Ley 20 de 1969 "Por la cual se dictan algunas dis-
        posiciones sobre minas e hidrocárburos". Bogotá,

1970.
46 p.   24 cm.

20344 Colombia. Ministerio de Obras Públicas.
Programa de construcción y reconstrucción de
carreteras nacionales de la República de Colombia,
1951-1954. [Bogotá, Imprenta Departamental, 1951]
49 p.   maps (part col.)   diagrs.   35 cm.

20345 Colombia. Ministerio de Salud Pública.
Investigación nacional de morbilidad: Accidentes.
Bogotá, 1968.
76 p.   illus., maps.   26 cm.   (Estudio de
recursos humanos para la salud y educación médica en
Colombia)
At head of title: Ministerio de Salud Pública.
Asociación de Facultades de Medicina.
Bibliography: p. 37.

20346 Colombia. Ministerio de Salud Pública.
Investigación nacional de morbilidad: Atención
médica. Bogotá, 1968.
118 p.   illus., maps.   26 cm.   (Estudio de
recursos humanos para la salud y educación médica en
Colombia)
At head of title: Ministerio de Salud Pública.
Asociación de Facultades de Medicina.
Bibliography: p. 42.

20347 Colombia. Ministerio de Salud Pública.
Investigación nacional de morbilidad: Evidencia
clínica. Bogotá, 1969.
110 p.   illus.   26 cm.   (Estudio de recursos
humanos para la salud y educación médica en Colombia)
At head of title: Ministerio de Salud Pública.
Asociación de Facultades de Medicina.
Includes bibliographies.

20348 Colombia. Ministerio de Salud Pública.
Investigación nacional de morbilidad: morbilidad
oral. Bogotá, 1971.
83 p.   illus.   26 cm.   (Estudio de recursos
humanos para la salud y educación médica en Colombia)
At head of title: Ministerio de Salud Pública.
Asociación de Facultades de Medicina.
Includes bibliographies.

20349 Colombia. Ministerio del Trabajo.
Problemas campesinos. Bogotá, División Técnica

de la Seguridad Social Campesina, 1960.
64 p.   27 cm.   (Biblioteca del Ministerio del
Trabajo)

20350   Colombia. Registraduría Nacional del Estado Civil.
Organización y estadísticas electorales, marzo 15 de
1964. [Bogotá, Reginal Publicaciones, 1965]
148 p.   23 cm.
Cover title.

20351   Colombia. Servicio Nacional de Aprendizaje.
Estudio socio-económico: área de Boyacá. Elaborado
por Pedro Nel Barrera M. [Bogotá, Servicio Nacional
de Aprendizaje] Dirección Nacional, 1963.
76 ℓ.   illus., map.   29 cm.   (Publicaciones
"SENA")
At head of title: Sección de Investigaciones.

20352   Colombia. Servicio Nacional de Aprendizaje.
Estudio socio-económico: área del Quindío. Informe
preparado por Pedro Nel Barrera. [Bogotá, 1961]
21 ℓ.   illus.   30 cm.
At head of title: Servicio Nacional de Aprendizaje
"SENA." Dirección Nacional.

20353   Colombia-U.S. Workshop on Science and Technology,
Fusagasugá, 1968.
Seminario sobre Ciencia y Tecnología para el
Desarrollo; informe final en español y en inglés.
[Bogotá, 1968]
2 v.   28 cm.
At head of title: Ministerio de Educación Nacional.
Added t.p. in English.
Includes bibliographies.
Contents. - v. 1. Informe final. - v. 2. Trabajos
presentados.
Library has v. 2 only.

20354   Colombo, Haydée.
Volver de si misma; novela. [Buenos Aires] Institut
Amigos del Libro Argentino [1964]
100 p.   20 cm.

20355   Colomina de Rivera, Marta.
El huésped alienante; un estudio sobre audiencia
y efectos de las radio-telenovelas en Venezuela.
[Maracaibo, Editorial Universitaria, 1968]
150 p.   tables, graphs.   23 cm.   ([Maracaibo.
Universidad del Zulia. Facultad de Humanidades y

Educación. Escuela del Periodismo] Centro Audio-
visual. Colección ensayos no. 1)

20356 Colón, Fernando, 1488-1539.
... Historia del almirante don Cristobal Colón,
por su hijo don Hernando; traducida nuevamente del
italiano... Madrid, V. Suárez, 1932.
2 v. pl. 18 cm. (Colección de libros raros
o curiosos que tratan de América. 1. ser. t. V-VI)
This work written in Spanish was first published
in the Italian translation by Alfonso Ulloa, a copy
of which with imprint "In Venetia, Per il Prodocimo,
1569" is found in the library of Princeton university.
The original Spanish manuscript was never printed.
"Proemio; vida y escritos de don Hernando Colón
[por Manuel Serrano y Sanz]": v. 1, p. [v]-clxi.
"Relación de fray Ramón acerca de las antigüedades
de los indios, las cuales, con diligencia, como hombre
que sabe el idiomas de éstos, recogió por mandato del
almirante": v. 2, p. [35]-90.

20357 Coloratlas Kapelusz. Orbe físico-político-económico-
estadístico. Buenos Aires, Editorial Kapelusz
[1969]
56 p. maps. 32½ cm.

20358 Coltrinari, Lylian.
Contribuição a geomorfologia da região de Guara-
tingueta-Aparecida. São Paulo, Instituto de Geografia,
Universidade de São Paulo, 1975.
156 p. illus., maps (part fold.), tables (part
fold.) diagrs. (part fold.) 26 cm. (Série teses
e monografias, no. 17)
"Bibliografia": p. 133-144.

20359 Comadrán Ruiz, Jorge.
Bibliotecas cuyanas del siglo xviii. Mendoza,
Argentina, 1961.
143 p. 24 cm.

20360 Comadrán Ruiz, Jorge.
Evolución demográfica argentina durante el período
hispano, 1535-1810. Buenos Aires Editorial
Universitaria de Buenos Aires [1969]
xi, 120 p. 23 cm. (Temas de EUDEBA)
Bibliographical footnotes.

20361 Comas, Juan, 1900-
La antropología física en México, 1943-1959;

inventario y programa de investigaciones, por Juan
Comas y Santiago Genovés T. [1. ed.] México,
Universidad Nacional Autónoma de México, 1960.
66 p.   24 cm.   (Cuadernos del Instituto de
Historia. Serie antropológica, no. 10)
Universidad Nacional Autónoma de México. Publica-
ciones del Instituto de Historia, 1. ser., no. 59.
Summary in English.
Full name: Juan Comas Camps.

20362 Comas, Juan, 1900-
Características físicas de la familia lingüística
maya. Apéndice de Ilse Schwidetzky. [1. ed.] México,
Universidad Nacional Autónoma de México, 1966.
95 p.   illus., maps, ports.   23 cm.   (Universid
Nacional Autónoma de México. Instituto de Investiga-
ciones Históricas. Cuadernos. Serie antropológica,
no. 20)
Bibliography: p. 36-45.
Full name: Juan Comas Camps.

20363 Comas, Juan, 1900-
Una década de Congreso Internacionales de America-
nistas, 1952-1962. [1. ed.] México, Universidad
Nacional Autónoma de México, 1964.
128 p.   ports.   24 cm.   (Universidad Nacional
Autónoma de México. Instituto de Investigaciones
Históricas. 1. ser.: Publicación no. 93. Cuadernos
del Instituto de Investigaciones Históricas. Serie
antropológica, no. 18)
"Contribución de la Universidad Nacional Autónoma
de México al XXXVI Congreso Internacional de
Americanistas, España, 1964."
Continuation of Los Congresos Internacionales de
Americanistas; síntesis histórica e índice biblio-
gráfico general, 1875-1952.
Full name: Juan Comas Camps.

20364 Comas, Juan, 1900-
Dos microcéfalos "aztecas"; leyenda, historia y
antropología. México, Instituto de Investigaciones
Históricas, Universidad Nacional Autónoma de México,
1968.
134 p.   plates (out of text)   23 cm. (Serie
antropológica, 22)
Full name: Juan Comas Camps.

20365 Comas, Juan, 1900-
Manual de antropología física. [2. ed. renovada,

en español] México, Universidad Nacional Autónoma de
México, Instituto de Investigaciones Históricas,
Sección de Antropología, 1966.
    710 p.   illus., facsims., maps.   23 cm.
(Universidad Nacional Autónoma de México. Sección de
Antropología. Serie antropológica, 10)
    Bibliography: p. 653-671.
    Full name: Juan Comas Camps.

20366 Comas, Juan, 1900-
        El origen del hombre americano y la antropología
    física. [1. ed.] México, Universidad Nacional
    Autónoma de México, 1961.
        53 p.   24 cm.   (Universidad Nacional Autónoma
    de México. Publicaciones del Instituto de Historia.
    1. serie, no. 67. Cuadernos: Serie Antropológica
    no. 13)
        "Redactado como base de discusión de uno de los
    puntos del Temario para los II Encontros Intelectuals
    celebrados en São Paulo, Brasil, del 21 al 26 de
    agosto de 1961."
        Includes bibliography.
        Full name: Juan Comas Camps.

20367 Comas, Juan, 1900-
        Las primeras instrucciones para la investigación
    antropológica en México: 1862. [1. ed.] México,
    Universidad Nacional Autónoma de México, 1962.
        43 p.   24 cm.   (Universidad Nacional Autónoma
    de México. Publicaciones del Instituto de Historia.
    Publicaciones, 1. ser., no. 77. Cuadernos del
    Instituto de Historia. Serie antropológica, no. 16)
        Bibliography: p. 41.
        Full name: Juan Comas Camps.

20368 Comas, Juan, 1900-
        Somatometría de los indios triques de Oaxaca,
    México [por] Juan Comas y Johanna Faulhaber. Con
    44 cuadros numéricos, 65 gráficas y 40 fotografías.
    [1. ed.] México, Universidad Nacional Autónoma de
    México, Instituto de Investigaciones Históricas,
    Sección de Antropología, 1965.
        191 p.   illus., map.   24 cm.   (Universidad
    Nacional Autónoma de México. Sección de Antropología.
    Serie antropológica, no. 9)
        Summary in French, English, and German.
        Bibliography: p. [93]-96.
        Full name: Juan Comas Camps.

20369 Comisión de Integración Eléctrica Regional. Subcomité
de Operación de Sistemas Eléctricos.
Operación de sistemas eléctricos en los países
miembros de la CIER; informe del coordinador técnico
del Subcomité de Operación de Sistemas Eléctricos de
la CIER, Leo Sudak. Buenos Aires, 1968.
4 v.   illus., maps.   28 cm.
Spanish or Portuguese.
Library has v. 4 only.

20370 Comisión de Integración Eléctrica Regional.. Subcomité
de Recursos Energéticos, Montevideo.
Informe del coordinador técnico Américo Hartmann.
Montevideo, 1969.
3 v.   28 cm.
Contents. - v. 1: Recursos energéticos no renovables
de Argentina, Bolivia, Brasil, Colombia, Chile,
Ecuador, Paraguay, Perú, Uruguay y Venezuela. -
Vol. 2: Recursos energéticos renovables de Argentina,
Bolivia, Brasil, Colombia, Chile, Ecuador, Paraguay,
Perú, Uruguay y Venezuela. - Vol. 3: Recursos ener-
géticos de los países de la CIER; panorama y conclu-
siones generales.

20371 Comitas, Lambros.
Caribbeana 1900-1965. A topical bibliography.
Published for Research Institute for the study of
man. Seattle and London, University of Washington
Press [1968]
1, 909 p.   25 cm.
Opposite title page: Editorial research assistant:
Carol Feist Dickert. Consultant on Netherlands
Caribbean: Annemarie de Waal Malefijt.
Map on lining papers.

20372 Comité Nacional de Guatemala para el Año Geofísico
Internacional.
Proyecto de programa del Comité Nacional de
Guatemala para el Año Geofísico Internacional, 1957-
1958. Guatemala, 1957.
54 p.   28 cm.
Spanish and English.

20373 Committee for Economic Development.
Economic development of Central America; a statement
on national policy by the Research and Policy Committee
of the Committee for Economic Development. [New York]
1964.

123 p.   28 cm.
English and Spanish.

20374   Compaña Barrera, Aníbal.
Breve manual de consulta del afiliado al Seguro
Social ecuatoriano; preguntas y respuestas.   Quito,
Imprenta Caja del Seguro, 1962.
55 p.   20 cm.

20375   Companhia de Desenvolvimento do Estado de Goiás.
A economia goiana no PRODOESTE.   Goiânia, 1972.
253 p.   maps. (part fold.), tables.   22 cm.

20376   Companhia de Desenvolvimento do Estado de Goiás.
A economia goiana no PROTERRA.   Goiânia, 1972.
176 p.   maps (part fold.), tables, diagrs.   22 cm.

20377   Companhia de Industrialização do Estado da Paraíba.
Distritos industriais da Paraíba, normas.
João Pessoa, 1968.
32 p.   23 cm.

20378   Companhia de Industrialização do Estado da Paraíba.
Legislação - estatutos - regulamentos.   FUNDESP
CINEP.   [n.p.] 1968.
25 p.   23½ cm.

20379   Companhia do Desenvolvimento do Planalto Central.
Estudos setoriais.   Aspectos urbanísticos, saneamento,
communicações, comercio (produtos não alimentícios),
turismo, instituições financeiras, serviços diversos.
[Brasília, 1972]
283 p.   tables, graphs,   21 cm.

20380   Companhia do Desenvolvimento do Planalto Central.
Estudos setoriais - 1972 - Educação.   Volume I.
[Brasília, 1972]
138 p.   tables, graphs.   21 cm.

20381   Companhia do Desenvolvimento do Planalto Central.
Estudos setoriais - 1972 - Habitação.   Volume II.
[Brasília, 1972]
132 p.   tables, graphs.   21 cm.

20382   Companhia do Desenvolvimento do Planalto Central.
Estudos setoriais - 1972 - Saúde e saneamento.
Volume IV.   [Brasília, 1972]
286 p.   tables, graphs.   21 cm.

20383   Companhia do Desenvolvimento do Planalto Central.
        Estudos setoriais 1972. Transporte, energia
        elétrica, comunicações, turismo, instituições
        financeiras. Volume III. [Brasília, 1972]
        112 p.   tables, graphs.   21 cm.

20384   Compañía Colombiana de Seguros.
        El estado y la empresa privada.   [Bogotá, 1963]
        78 p.   24 cm.

20385   Compañía de Acero del Pacífico.   Santiago, Chile.
        Léxico siderúrgico; español-inglés, inglés-español.
        Preparado por la Comisión de Terminología Siderúrgica.
        Santiago, Chile, 1965.
        144 p.

20386   Compañía de Seguros El Comercio de Córdoba.
        Memoria y balance general.   Córdoba.
        v.   27 cm.   annual.
        Report year ends June 30.

20387   Compayré, Gabriel, i.e. Jules Gabriel, 1843-1913.
        ... Herbart y la educación por la instrucción de
        la serie "Los grandes educadores," por Gabriel
        Compayré... Buenos Aires, Tip. el comercio, 1906.
        134 p.   18 cm.   (Libros para el maestro,
        edición hecha por el Monitor de la educación común, V)
        Translated from French.
        "Bibliografía": p. [127]-129.

20388   El Comunismo en la América Hispana [por] J. F. C.
        [Madrid, Instituto de Estudios Políticos, 1961]
        169 p.   22 cm.   (Empresas políticas, 2)

20389   Concepción, Chile. Universidad.
        Cien años de la novela chilena.   Concepción,
        Ediciones Revista Atenea, 1961.
        259 p.   21 cm.

20390   Concepción, Chile. Universidad.
        Homenaje de la Universidad de Concepción al ex
        rector Edgardo Enríquez y al ex vice-rector Galo
        Gómez, forjadores de la reforma universitaria.
        [Concepción] 1972.
        47 p.   illus.   23½ cm.   (Cuadernos de difusión.
        Serie documentos universitarios, no. 6)

20391   Condillac, Étienne Bonnot de, 1715-1780.
        La lógica, e Los primeros elementos del arte de

366

pensar. Estudio preliminar por Guillermo Morón.
Caracas, Academia Nacional de la Historia, 1959.
194 p.   23 cm.   (Biblioteca de la Academia
Nacional de la Historia, 18)
"Este libro fue traducido por Don Bernardo María de
la Calzada... impreso en Caracas, en nueva edición,
en 1812, en la imprenta de Juan de Baillío."

20392   Conejo Guevara, Adina, 1930-
Henri Pittier presentado por Adina Conejo Guevara.
San José, Costa Rica, Ministerio de Cultura, Juventud
y Deportes, Departamento de Publicaciones, 1975.
162 p.   illus.   19½ cm.   (Serie ¿Quién fué
y qué hizo? no. 20)

20393   Confederação Brasileira de Basketball.
... Régras de basketball. [n.p., n.d.]
70 p.   17 cm.
At head of cover-title: Divisão de educação
fisica - M.E.C. Confederação Brasileira de Basketball.

20394   Confederação Brasileira de Basketball.
Regras oficiais de basquetbol. [Brasília?]
Ministério da Educação e Cultura [1973?]
72 p.   illus.   19 cm.

20395   Confederação Brasileira de Desportes.
Regras oficiais de atletismo. [Brasília?]
Ministerio da Educação e Cultura, 1973.
120 p.   illus.   19 cm.

20396   Confederación General Económica de la República Argentina.
Informe económico. Buenos Aires, 1955.
192 p.   illus.   24 cm.

20397   Confederación General Económica de la República Argentina.
Transferencia de bancos y empresas industriales
nacionales a similares extranjeros. [Buenos Aires,
1967]
8 p.   22 cm.

20398   Conference on the Role of Books in Human Development,
Airlie House, 1964.
Books in human development; the final report.
Edited by Ray Eldon Hiebert. Washington [Produced by
Dept. of Journalism, American University, 1965]
131 p.   23 cm.
"Sponsored by the American University and the Agency
for International Development."

Bibliography: p. 129-131.
-- Supplement to the report; recommendations for
action. [Washington? 1965?]
11 p.   23 cm.

20399 Conferencia de Facultades (Escuelas) de Derecho
(Ciencias Jurídicas, Políticas y Sociales) Latino-
americanas, 3d, Santiago de Chile and Valparaiso,
1963.
Tercera Conferencia de Facultades (Escuelas) de
Derecho (Ciencias Jurídicas, Políticas y Sociales)
Latinoamericanas (Chile: Santiago-Valparaiso,
abril de 1963); [memoria. Santiago] Facultad de
Ciencias Jurídicas y Sociales, Universidad de Chile.
[1964?]
928 p.   illus.   27 cm.
Cover title: Tercera Conferencia de Facultades de
Derecho Latinoamericanas.
Includes bibliographical footnotes.

20400 Conferencia Interamericana de Seguridad Social.
Secretaría General.
Bibliografía de seguridad social. México, 1966.
133 p.   23 cm.

20401 Conferencia Latinoamericana de Ciencias Políticas y
Sociales, 2d, Santiago de Chile, 1966.
Segunda Conferencia Latinoamericana de Ciencias
Políticas y Sociales. [Santiago de Chile] Editorial
Jurídica de Chile, 1967.
762 p.   26 cm.
At head of title: Universidad de Chile. Facultad
de Ciencias Jurídicas y Sociales.
"Celebrada en octubre de 1966 en Santiago de Chile,
en cumplimiento de un acuerdo del Instituto Latino-
americano de Ciencias Políticas y Sociales, y con el
patrocinio del Banco Interamericano de Desarrollo y
el Ministerio de Relaciones Exteriores de Chile."
Includes bibliographical references.

20402 Conferência Nacional dos Bispos do Brasil. Secretariado
Regional Leste 1.
Cultos afro-brasileiros; candomblé, umbanda,
observações pastoris. [Rio de Janeiro] 1972.
66, [3] p.   23 cm.
Cover title: Macumba: cultos afro-brasileiros.
Bibliography: p. [67]

20403 Conferencia sobre los Problemas de la Urbanización en
Guatemala. 1st, Guatemala, 1965.
Problemas de la urbanización en Guatemala.
Guatemala, Departamento Editorial "José de Pineda
Ibarra," Ministerio de Educación, 1965.
290 p.   20 cm.   (Seminario de Integración
Social Guatemalteca. Publicación no. 16)
Includes bibliographies.

20404 Congreso Continental Anticomunista. 4th, Antigua,
Guatemala, 1958.
IV [Cuarto] Congreso Continental Anticomunista:
actas de las sesiones, version taquigráfica, resoluciones; 12 a 16 de octubre de 1958, Antigua, Guatemala.
Guatemala, 1961.
418 p.   illus., ports.   26 cm.

20405 Congreso de Academias de la Lengua Española, 3d,
Bogotá, 1960.
Actas y labores.   Bogotá, Academia Colombiana de
la Lengua, 1960.
688 p.   24 cm.

20406 Congreso de Indios de Venezuela, 2d, 14-17 April 1972.
Memoria.   Caracas, Imprenta del Congreso de la
República, 1972.
95 p.   illus.   21½ cm.

20407 Congreso de Instituciones Hispánicas. 1st, Madrid, 1963.
Presente y futuro de la lengua española; actas de
la asamblea de filología del I Congreso de Instituciones Hispánicas.   Madrid, Ediciones Cultura Hispánica,
1964.
2 v.   maps (part col.)   26 cm.   (Publicación
de la Oficina Internacional de Información y Observa-
ción del Español)
Includes bibliographies.

20408 Congreso Hispanoamericano de Historia, 3d, Cartagena,
1961.
Tercer Congreso Hispanoamericano de Historia,
Segundo de Cartagena de Indias.   [Cartagena, Talleres
Gráficos Mogollón] 1962.
421 p.   illus.   25 cm.

20409 Congreso Internacional de Literatura Iberoamericana,
13th, Los Angeles and Caracas, 1967-1968.
Homenaje a Rubén Darío (1867-1967); memoria del
XIII Congreso Internacional de Literatura Ibero-

americana (Primera Reunión) Universidad de California, Los Angeles, California (18-21 de enero, 1967) Edición al cuidado de Aníbal Sánchez-Reulet. Los Angeles, Centro Latinoamericano, Universidad de California, 1970.
298 p.   23 cm.   (Latin American studies, v. 16)
At head of title: Instituto Internacional de Literatura Iberoamericana.

20410   Congreso Jurídico Guatemalteco. 1st. Guatemala, 1960.
Primer Congreso Jurídico Guatemalteco; [resoluciones, declaraciones y recomendaciones] Guatemala, Colegio de Abogados de Guatemala, 1960.
86 p.   23 cm.

20411   Congreso Nacional de Ediles, 5th, Paysandú, Uruguay, 1970.
V [i.e. Quinto] Congreso Nacional de Ediles, realizado el 8 y 9 de agosto de 1970 en la ciudad de Paysandú. [Montevideo] Junta Departamental de Montevideo [1970 or 71]
205 p.   22 cm.

20412   Congreso Nacional de Exportadores, 2d, Bogotá, 1968.
Discursos, documentos, ponencias, informes, bibliografía. [Bogotá] Cámara de Comercio de Bogotá y Fondo de Promoción de Exportaciones [1968]
659 p.   24 cm.

20413   Congreso Nacional de Filosofía, Córdoba, Argentina, 1971.
Actas. Tomo I. Sesiones plenarias. Buenos Aires, Editorial Sudamericana [1973]
710 p.   23 cm.

20414   Congreso Nacional de Filosofía, Córdoba, Argentina, 1971.
Temas de filosofía contemporánea. Buenos Aires, Editorial Sudamericana [1971]
279 p.   21 cm.

20415   Congreso Notarial Argentino, 1st, Buenos Aires, 1917.
Actas y antecedentes. La Plata, 1967.
432 p.   21 cm.
At head of title: Colegio de Escribanos de la Provincia de Buenos Aires.

20416   Congreso Panamericano de Ferrocarriles.
Estatutos de la Asociación del Congreso Panamericano

de Ferrocarriles. Aprobados en la 1.ª sesión plenaria del XI Congreso celebrado en México, 18 al 31 de octubre de 1963. Buenos Aires, Asociación del Congreso Panamericano de Ferrocarriles, 1963.
11 p.   24 cm.

20417   Congreso Sindical. 1st, Madrid, 1961.
El 1er Congreso Sindical. [Madrid, 1961]
172 p.   27 cm.

20418   Congreso Venezolano de Petroleo. 1st, Caracas, 1962.
Aspectos de la industria petrolera en Venezuela. Caracas, Sociedad Venezolana de Ingenieros de Petroleo, 1963.
xxiii, 850 p.   illus., maps (part fold.) profiles.   24 cm.
Organized by the Sociedad Venezolana de Ingenieros de Petroleo.
Includes bibliographies.

20419   Congreso Venezolano de Salud Pública. Caracas, 1961.
Discursos en las sesiones inaugural y de clausura, los días 25 de febrero y 3 de marzo de 1961, respectivamente. Caracas, Imprenta Nacional, 1960 [i.e. 1961]
87 p.   illus., ports.   23 cm.   (Publicaciones de la Secretaría General de la Presidencia de la República)

20420   Congresso Brasileiro do Cacua, I, Itabuna, 28-30 July 1967.
... Anais. Bahía [1967]
407 p.   24 cm.
At head of title: Confederação Nacional da Agricultura [e] Federação da Agricultura do Estado da Bahía.

20421   Congresso Brasileiro de Crítica y História Literaria, 1.º, Recife - 7 a 14 de agôsto de 1960.
[Exposição realizada em Recife de 7 a 14 de agôsto de 1960] [Rio de Janeiro?] Biblioteca Nacional [1960?]
53 p.   illus.   24 cm.

20422   Congresso Eucarístico Nacional, 8th, Brasília, 1970.
Revista. Ed. única. Editor: Carlos Rodrigues. Brasília, 1970.
[48] p.   illus., facsims., ports. (part col.) 30 cm.

20423 Congresso Nacional de Botânica, 25th, Mossoró, 1974.
Anais da Sociedade Botânica do Brasil. Escola
Superior de Agricultura de Mossoró, Mossoró, RN,
20 a 26 de janeiro de 1974. Recife, Editôra Universitária da Universidade Federal de Pernambuco, 1976.
394 p.   illus.   27½ cm.
Summaries in English.

20424 Congresso Nacional de Polícia, 2d, Rio de Janeiro, 1967.
Sumário. Belo Horizonte, Secretaria de Estado da
Segurança Pública, 1967.
43 ℓ.   mimeo.   32 cm.
"Trabalhos apresentados pelo corregedor geral de
polícia, Zaluar de Campos Henriques."

20425 Congresso Nacional do Café, 3°, 8 a 11 de abril de 1970,
Moços de Caladas, M.G.
Ánais. [n.p., n.d.]
662 p.   illus., diagrs., maps.   33 cm.

20426 Congresso Nacional dos Instituto de Previdência Estaduais
2d, Recife, 1968.
Anais e documentos básicos. Recife, IPSEP, 1968.
2 v. (unpaged)   tables.   27 cm.
Cover title.

20427 Conrado, Aldomar.
0 apocalípse ou 0 capeta de caruaru. Mençao Honrosa,
1967. Rio de Janeiro, Serviço Nacional de Teatro, 1968
74 p.   21 cm.

20428 Consalvi, Simón Alberto.
Gonzalo Picón Febres; los delitos de la imaginación.
Caracas, Instituto Nacional de Cultura y Bellas Artes,
1969.
31 p.   21½ cm.   (Colección homenajes, 5)

20429 Consejo de Bienestar Rural, Caracas.
Estado actual y posibilidades del desarrollo agrícola
en Venezuela. Caracas, 1967.
xiii, x, 266 p.   illus., maps.   28 cm.

20430 Consejo Episcopal Latinoamericano.
Iglesia y universidad en América Latina. Bogotá,
Secretariado General del CELAM [1976]
143 p.   21 cm.   (Documento CELAM, no. 22)

20431 Consejo Nacional de la Universidad Peruana.
Memoria, 1973. [Lima, 1973?]
286 p.   diagrs., tables (1 fold.)   22 cm.

20432 Consejo Superior de las Cámaras Oficiales de Comercio, Industria y Navegación de España. Problemas y perspectivas del desarrollo económico de la República de Bolivia. Madrid, 1963. 83 p. 22 cm.

20433 Consejo Superior Universitario Centroamericano. Actas de la Segunda Reunión Extraordinaria, celebrada en San José, Costa Rica, del 22 al 23 de junio de 1961. San Salvador, Editorial Universitaria [1962] 135 p. 18 cm.

20434 Consejo Superior Universitario Centroamericano. Memoria de las actividades desarrolladas por la Secretaría Permanente, 1964. Ciudad Universitaria Rodrigo Facio, Costa Rica, 1965. 190 p. 27 cm. annual.

20435 Consejo Superior Universitario Centroamericano. El sistema educativo en El Salvador; situación actual y perspectivas. San José, Costa Rica, 1965. xviii, 140 p. graphs, tables. 28 cm. (Estudio de recursos humanos en Centroamérica, 5)

20436 Consejo Superior Universitario Centroamericano. El sistema educativo en Guatemala; situación actual y perspectivas. [Ciudad Universitaria, Costa Rica, 1964] xxii, 283 p. 27 cm. (Estudio de recursos humanos en Centroamérica, no. 2)

20437 Consejo Superior Universitario Centroamericano. El sistema educativo en Honduras; situación actual y perspectivas. [San José? Departamento de Publicaciones, Universidad de Costa Rica] 1965. xxiii, 119 p. illus. 27 cm. (Estudio de recursos humanos en Centroamérica, no. 3)

20438 Consejo Superior Universitario Centroamericano. El sistema educativo en Nicaragua; situación actual y perspectivas. [Ciudad Universitaria, Costa Rica] 1965. xxiv, 115 p. illus. 28 cm. (Estudio de recursos humanos en Centroamérica, no. 4)

20439 Consejo Superior Universitario Centroamericano. Comisión Centroamericana en pro de los Estudios Generales. Los estudios generales en Centroamérica. [Actas,

trabajos y recomendaciones de sus tres primeras
sesiones. Ciudad Universitaria "Rodrigo Facio",
Costa Rica, 1963.
402 p.   24 cm.   (Publicaciones de la Secretaria
Permanente del Consejo Superior Universitario Centroamericano)
On cover: 1964.

20440   Consejo Superior Universitario Centroamericano. Proyecto
de Recursos Humanos en C. A.
El sistema educativo en Costa Rica, situación actual
y perspectivas. [Ciudad Universitaria "Rodrigo Facio"]
1964.
x, 242 p.   illus.   27 cm.   (Consejo Superior
Universitario Centroamericano. Estudio de recursos
humanos en Centroamérica, no. 1)
"Anexo de cuadros":   p. [101]-242.

20441   Consiglio, Dulce Damasceno de Brito.
Hollywood, nua e crua. Rio de Janeiro, Editôra O.
Cruzeiro, 1968.
183 p.   21 cm.

20442   Consortium of Universities of the Metropolitan Washington
Area.
A union list of serials in the libraries of the
Consortium of Universities of the Metropolitan
Washington Area. Washington, D. C., The Catholic
University of America press, 1967.
370 p.   31 cm.

20443   Consuegra, José.
Doctrina de la planeación colombiana, el ciclo
económico y la planeación. Bogotá, Fundación Universidad de América, Facultad de Arquitectura, 1960.
150 p.   24 cm.
Includes bibliography.

20444   Conti, Haroldo, 1925-
Alrededor de la jaula, novela. Xalapa, Universidad
Veracruzana, 1966.
135 p.   20 cm.   (Universidad Veracruzana.
Ficción, 72)

20445   Conti, José Bueno.
Circulação secundária e efeito orografico na génese
das chuvas na região les nordeste paulista. São Paulo,
Instituto de Geografia, Universidade de São Paulo,
1975.

374

85 p. fold. maps, fold. diagrs. 26 cm.
(Série teses e monografias, no. 18)
"Referencias bibliográficas": p. 79-82.

20446 Continentino, M A
One-electron propagators for actinide metals:
strong correlation limit, by M. A. Continentino and
A. A. Gomes. Rio de Janeiro, Centro Brasileiro de
Pesquisas Físicas, 1973.
87-107 p. 29 cm. (Notas de física, v. 20, no. 6)

20447 Continentino, M A
Remarks on the conditions for magnetic instabilities
in actinides; Hartree-Feck approach, by M. A. Continentino and A. A. Gomes. Rio de Janeiro, Centro
Brasileiro de Pesquisas Físicas, 1973.
63-84 p. 29 cm. (Notas de física, v. 20, no. 4)

20448 Continentino, M A
Remarks on the conditions for magnetic instabilities
in actinides; strong correlations, by M. A. Continentino
and A. A. Gomes. Rio de Janeiro, Centro Brasileiro de
Pesquisas Físicas, 1973.
163-197 p. 29 cm. (Notas de física, v. 20, no. 9)

20449 Continentino, M A
Remarks on the electronic structure and electron
correlations in actinides, by M. A. Continentino,
L. C. Lopes and A. A. Gomes. Rio de Janeiro, Centro
Brasileiro de Pesquisas Físicas, 1972.
106-140 p. 29 cm. (Notas de física, v. 19, no. 4)

20450 Contino, Francisco.
Elementos sobre algunos rapaces del Noroeste argentino.
Salta, Argentina, Instituto de Investigación de los
Recursos Naturales Renovables, 1972.
57 p. xxii plates. 22 cm. and 47 cm. (Serie
fauna, 1)

20451 Contos Maranhenses. [Maranhão, n.d.]
141 p. 23 cm.

20452 Contreras R , J Daniel.
Breve historia de Guatemala. Con ilustraciones y
un mapa de lugares arqueológicos. 2. ed. Guatemala,
Centro Editorial del Ministerio de Educación Pública
"José de Pineda Ibarra," 1961.
143 p. illus. 21 cm. (Colección Libro escolar,
35)

20453 Contreras, Raúl.
Presencia de humo. Prólogo de Juan Guzmán Cruchaga.
[1. ed.] San Salvador, Ministerio de Cultura,
Departamento Editorial [1959]
114 p. 22 cm. (Colección Poesía, v. 10)

20454 Contreras Cervantes, Rubén.
Los subsidios federales en México. México, 1962.
109 p. tables. 23 cm.
Tesis (licenciatura en economía) - Universidad
Nacional Autónoma de México.
Bibliography: p. 107-109.

20455 Contreras Nino, Victor.
Financiación pública del transporte; carreteras
nacionales en Colombia. [Bogotá] 1962.
124 ℓ. illus. 29 cm. (Universidad de los
Andes. Centro de Estudios sobre Desarrollo Económico.
Monografía, 12)
Tesis de grado - Universidad de Bogotá "Jorge Tadeo
Lozano."
Includes bibliography.

20456 Cony, Carlos Heitor.
Da arte de falar mal; crónicas. [Rio de Janeiro]
Editôra Civilização Brasileira [1963]
152 p. 21 cm.
"Publicadas no Correio da Manhã, no periodo de 1961,
1963."

20457 Cooper, Blair.
Estudo ecônomico da cultura do Maracujá no Estado do
Pará. [Por] Blair Cooper [e] Richard Brostowicz.
Belém, Divisão de Documentação, Assessoria de Programação e Coordenação, Superintendência do Desenvolviment
da Amazônia, 1971.
119 p. 27½ cm.

20458 Cooper, H   H   A
Comentarios sobre la nueva legislación penitenciaria
en el Perú. Lima, Dirección Universitaria de Bibliotec
y Publicaciones, Universidad Nacional Mayor de San
Marcos, 1972.
114 p. 25 cm.

20459 Coral Miranda, Reynoldo.
El aluvión de Huaraz; relatorio de una tragedia.
1. ed. Lima, 1962-

v.   illus., map.   16 cm.
Library has v. 1, 1962.

20460   Corcuera, Arturo.
Primavera triunfante; [poemas] Lima [Ediciones de
La Rama Florida] 1963.
[19] p.   22 cm.

20461   Cordeiro, Copernico de Arruda, 1914-
Estudio sobre nivel y standard de vida de algunas
familias de agricultores en seis comunidades rurales
de Costa Rica. Turrialba, Costa Rica, Instituto
Interamericano de Ciencias Agrícolas de la O.E.A.,
Centro Tropical de Investigación y Enseñanza para
Graduados, 1961.
vii, 77 (i.e. 111) ℓ.   maps.   28 cm.
Summary in Spanish, English and Portuguese.
Tesis (M.A.) - Inter-American Institute of Agricul-
tural Sciences, Turrialba, Costa Rica.
Bibliography: ℓ. 72-73.

20462   Cordeiro Álvarez, Ernesto.
Tratado de los privilegios. 2.ª edición ampliada
y actualizada. Prólogo del Dr. Ivan M. Díaz Molina...
Buenos Aires, Ediciones Depalma, 1969.
681 p.   24 cm.

20463   Cordero, Héctor Adolfo.
La educación en San Fernando; reseña histórica sobre
el origen de las primeras escuelas.   Buenos Aires,
Ediciones Delta [1963]
148 p.   21½ cm.

20464   Cordero Dávila, Gonzalo.
Gonzalo Cordero Dávila. Selección y nota de
Rigoberto Cordero y León. Cuenca, 1960.
378 p.   21 cm.   (Presencia de la poesía cuencana,
24)
"Anales de la Universidad de Cuenca."

20465   Cordero y León, Ramona María.
El Condor del Aconcagua. Escrito por Mary Corylé
[pseud.] Cuenca de los Andes, Ecuador [1964]
74 p.   port.   23 cm.

20466   Cordero y León, Ramona María.
Mundo pequeño. Cuenca [Núcleo del Azuay de la Casa
de la Cultura Ecuatoriana] 1978.
153 p.   22 cm.

"Mary Corylé llega al cielo" [por] Rigoberto Cordero
y León: p. 9-12.
Short stories.

20467   Cordero y León, Ramona María.
Romancero de Bolívar. Scripto por Mary Corylé [pseud
Cuenca [Núcleo del Azuay de la Casa de Cultura Ecuatoriana, 1961]
63 p.   illus.   21 cm.

20468   Cordero y León, Rigoberto.
Meditaciones sobre Beethoven. Cuenca, Ecuador,
1962.
31 p.   23 cm.   (Publicaciones de la Universidad
de Cuenca)

20469   Cordoba Pineda, Carlos.
La United Fruit Company en Honduras y su influencia
económica y política. México, 1962.
142 ℓ.   21 cm.
Tesis (licenciatura en ciencias politicas) -
Universidad Nacional Autónoma de México.
Bibliography: leaves 141-142.

20470   Córdoba, Argentine Republic. Academia Nacional de Cienci
Academia Nacional de Ciencias, Córdoba. Centenario
de su fundación, 1869 - 11 de septiembre - 1969.
Córdoba, 1969.
78 p.   illus.   24 cm.

20471   Córdoba, Argentine Republic. Cabildo.
Actas capitulares; libros cuadragesimo quinto y
cuadragesimo sexto. Córdoba, 1960.
xviii, 630 p.   24 cm.
At head of title: Archivo Municipal de Córdoba.

20472   Córdoba, Argentine Republic (Province) Dirección General
de Estadística, Censos e Investigaciones.
Resultados provisionales para la Provincia de
Córdoba del censo minero, industrial y comercial.
[Córdoba, 1955?]
87 p.   diagrs., tables.   27 cm.
Cover title: Cifras provisorias para la Provincia
del censo minero, industrial y comercial, 1954.

20473   Córdoba, Argentine Republic. Universidad Nacional.
Dirección General de Publicidad.
La educación y las ciencias en la sociedad de masas
[por Juan Carlos Agulla et al.] Córdoba [1961]

144 p.   illus.   24 cm.   (Grandes problemas
contemporáneos)
Includes bibliographies.
Contents. - La educación en la sociedad de masas,
por J. C. Agulla. - La política en la sociedad de
masas, por J. Medina Echavaria. - La técnica en la
sociedad de masas, por A. Poviña. - Medicina y sociedad
de masas, por J. Orgaz. - La filosofía en la sociedad
de masas, por A. Raggio.

20474 Córdoba, Argentine Republic. Universidad Nacional.
Facultad de Arquitectura y Urbanismo.
Planeamiento: cinco enfoques; [conferencias]
Córdoba, 1963.
150 p.   15 cm.

20475 Córdoba, Argentine Republic. Universidad Nacional.
Instituto de Matemática, Astronomía y Física.
Informe sobre el seminario para profesores de física
realizado en IMAF - Córdoba - del 29 de abril at 7 de
junio de 1968. Producido por: Ing. Rafael E. Ferreyra.
[Córdoba? 1968?]
various pagination.   tables (part fold.), graphs.
36 cm.

20476 Córdova, Carlos J
El canto cuencano; reseña comparativa del habla de
Cuenca del Ecuador. Cuenca [Casa de la Cultura Ecuatoriana, Núcleo del Azuay] 1975.
39 p.   2 fold. maps.   21 cm.

20477 Córdova-Bello, Eleazar.
Aspectos históricos de la ganadería en el oriente
venezolano y Guayana. Caracas, 1962.
54 p.   22 cm.
"Este trabajo, resumen de una extensa obra, inédita,
sobre la ganadería en Venezuela, del profesor Eleazar
Córdova-Bello."

20478 Cordua, Carla.
Mundo, hombre, historia; de la filosofía moderna
a la contemporánea. Santiago de Chile, Ediciones de
la Universidad de Chile, 1969 [i.e. 1968]
223 p.   19 cm.
Includes bibliographical references.

20479 Cormier, Gerald H
Labor in Brazil [by Gerald H. Cormier and Louise E.
Butt] Washington, U.S. Department of Labor, Bureau

of Labor Statistics, 1962.
iv, 35 p.   tables.   27 cm.   (BLS report, no. 19
Cover title: "Revises and brings up to date an earli
report, Summary of the labor situation in Brazil,
published in 1955, [by the Bureau of Labor Statistics]"

20480   Cornejo Acosta, María.
Bibliografía de la educación en Chile. Santiago,
Centro de documentación pedagógica, Superintendencia de
educación pública, 1967.
65 p.   32 cm.

20481   Cornejo Franco, José.
La calle de San Francisco. [Guadalajara, Ediciones
del Banco Industrial de Jalisco] 1945.
218 p.   50 pl., [4] ℓ.   23½ cm.

20482   Cornoa Núñez, J
Arqueología; occidente de México. Guadalajara,
Planeación y Promoción, 1960.
71 p.   22 cm.   (Jalisco en el arte)

20483   Corona Morfín, Enrique.
Al servicio de la escuela popular [por] Enrique
Corona M. [2. ed. México, Instituto Federal de
Capacitación del Magisterio] 1963.
181 p.   21 cm.   (Biblioteca Pedagógica de Per-
feccionamiento del Magisterio, 14)

20484   Coronado Aguilar, Manuel.
Influencia de España en Centro América, ensayo
histórico jurídico por Manuel Coronado Aguilar...
[Guatemala, Tipografía Sánchez & de Guise, 1943]
cover-title, 3 p.l., 5-113 p.   22 cm.

20485   Coronado Padilla, Ricardo.
La Sociedad Mexicana de Entomología a través de sus
veinticinco años de vida [por] Ricardo Coronado Padilla
[México, 1977]
5-18 p.   23 cm.
Reprinted from Folia entomológica mexicana, no. 37,
1977.

20486   Coronel Urtecho, José.
Reflexiones sobre la historia de Nicaragua; de
Gaínza a Somoza. [León, Nicaragua, Tall. Tip. de la
"Editorial Hospicio"] 1962-
v.   21 cm.   (Publicaciones del Instituto
Histórico Centro-americano)

Contents. - 1. Alrededor de la independencia. -
2. La guerra civil de 1824.

20487 Corporación Autónoma Regional de la Sábana de Bogotá y
de los Valles de Ubate y Chiquinquira.
Autopista Bogotá-Medellín y sistema vial afluente.
Evaluación preliminar. Octubre 1961. Bogotá, SAMEL,
A.D. Salgado, Meléndez & cia. ltda., ingenieros, 1961.
various pagination.   maps (part fold.), tables
(part fold.)   29 cm.

20488 Corporación Autónoma Regional de los Valles del Magdalena
y del Sinú.
C.V.M. Departamento de Ingeniería, División Información
Básica. [Bogotá, 1962?]
1 v. (chiefly tables)   (Boletín informativo, no. 1)

20489 Corporación Autónoma Regional de los Valles del Magdalena
y del Sinú.
Informe al gobierno nacional y a las asambleas de los
departamentos de Antioquia, Atlántico, Bolívar, Córdoba,
Magdalena y Santander. Rodrigo Botero M., director
ejecutivo. Mayo 1961-mayo 1962. [Bogotá, 1962?]
159 p.   illus., maps.   24 cm.

20490 Corporación Autónoma Regional de los Valles del Magdalena
y del Sinú.
Justificación, desarrollo y proyecciones; informe
general de labores. Bogotá.
v.   28 cm.
Library has 1964-1965.

20491 Corporación Autónoma Regional del Cauca.
Análisis económico de 109 fincas en el área del
proyecto Roldanillo-La Union-Toro: 1961-1962.
[Cali, 1962]
iv, 128 ℓ.   28 cm.
Bibliographical footnotes.

20492 Corporación Autónoma Regional del Cauca. Departamento
de Aguas.
Boletín hidrológico, Valle del Cauca, 1956-1970.
247 p.   fold. map, tables.   29 cm.   (Informe
CVC 71-10)

20493 Corporación Autónoma Regional del Cauca. Departamento
de Aguas.
Precipitación diaria en milimetros, 1956-1969.
Cali, 1970.

235 p.   fold. map, tables.   29 cm.   (Informe
CVC 70-14)

20494 Corporación Autónoma Regional del Cauca. Departamento
de Aguas.
Precipitación diaria en milimetros, 1970-1971.
Cali, 1972.
178 p.   fold. map, tables.   29 cm.   (Informe
CVC 72-9)

20495 Corporación Autónoma Regional del Cauca. División de
Planeación Regional.
La industria del papel en Colombia; un resumen de
informaciones sobre la situación. Cali, 1965.
25 l.   28 cm.
Introduction signed Juan Manuel Ruiz de Torres.
Bibliography: leaf 3.

20496 Corporación de Fomento de la Producción.
Chile; sus recursos naturales, producción y comercio.
Santiago, Chile, 1967.
140 p.   illus. (part col.), col. graphs, tables.
17 cm.

20497 Corporación Financiera Colombiana.
La Corporación Financiera Colombiana en el país;
cinco años de labores. Bogotá, 1966.
180 p.   illus.   29 cm.
Cover title.

20498 Corporación Financiera Colombiana de Desarrollo Industria
Cofinanciera, Bogotá. [Colombian Finance Corporation
for Industrial Development, Bogotá, Colombia. Bogotá,
Editorial Balzac, 1962]
93 p.   23 cm.
Cover title.

20499 Corporación Venezolana de Fomento.
Cuadernos de la CVF. [Caracas, 1967]
v.   maps.   23 cm.
Library has: Nos. 8, 9, 10, 11, and "número especial"
of December 1967.

20500 Corporación Venezolana de Fomento.
Mani. Base del desarrollo agro-industrial de la
mesa de Guanipa. [Caracas, n.d.]
18 l.   illus., graphs, maps.   21 x 22 cm.

20501   Corporación Venezolana de Fomento.
         Program for the acceleration of industrial deve-
         lopment. [Caracas, n.d.]
         [12] p.   illus.   20 cm.

20502   Corporación Venezolana de Fomento. Departamento de
         Estudios y Planificación.
         El consumo y abastecimiento de energía en Venezuela,
         1945-57; 1958. Caracas, Ediciones C.V.F., 1959.
         148 p.   diagrs., forms, tables.   23 cm.
         At head of title: Electrificación del Caroni.
         Bibliographical footnotes.

20503   Corporación Venezolana de Fomento. Departamento de
         Relaciones Públicas.
         Industrial promotion. [Caracas, 1964]
         [22] p.   fols. chart with map (part col.)   22 cm.

20504   Corporación Venezolana de Fomento. División de Estudios
         Generales.
         Industria de bebidas gaseosas. Este trabajo ha
         sido realizado por la economista Antonieta Monasterio
         Camacho; personal de encuesta: Anador Rojas Cardozo
         [et al.] bajo la supervisión del Dr. Francisco J.
         Rincón, jefe de la División. Caracas, 1964.
         117 p.   illus., maps, graphs, tables.   30 cm.

20505   Corporación Venezolana de Fomentos. Sub-gerencia de
         Servicios Técnicos. División de Estudios Generales.
         Estudio económico sobre turismo en Venezuela.
         Caracas [n.d.]
              v.   maps, illus., tables.   23 cm.
         Contents. - Zona occidental. Zona central.
         Zona sub-oriental. Compendio.

20506   Corradi, Hugo.
         ... Guía antigua del oeste porteño. Buenos Aires,
         Municipalidad de la Ciudad de Buenos Aires, 1969.
         118 p.   24 cm.   (Cuadernos de Buenos Aires, XXX)

20507   Corradine Angulo, Alberto.
         Algunas consideraciones sobre la arquitectura
         Zipaquirá. Bogotá, Facultad de Artes, Universidad
         Nacional de Colombia, 1969.
         39 p.   illus.   25½ cm.

20508   Corradine Angulo, Alberto.
         Santa Cruz de Mompox. Estudio histórico y crítico
         sobre su arquitectura colonial presentado por la

Universidad Nacional de Colombia y el profesor
Alberto Corradine Angulo a través de la Sección de
Historia de la Facultad de Artes a Corporación
Nacional de Turismo. Bogotá, Sección de Historia,
Departamento do Arquitectura, Facultad de Artes,
Universidad Nacional de Colombia, 1969.
52 p.   illus., diagrs., maps.   24 x 26 cm.

20509   Corrêa, Conceição Gentil.
Estatuetas de cerâmica na cultura Santarém,
classificação e catálogo das coleções do Museu Goeldi.
Belém, Pará, Brazil, 1965.
88 p.   10 pl., fold. table.   22 cm.   (Museu
Paraense Emílio Goeldi, Publicações avulsas, no. 4)

20510   Corrêa, Lia.
Paisagem do longe.   Poemas.   [Pôrto Alegre?] 1975.
126 p.   23½ cm.
Portrait of author on back cover.
Letter from author tipped in.

20511   Corrêa, Lia.
Prece ao vento; poesias.   Pôrto Alegre, Imprensa
Oficial do Estado, 1964.
135 p.   20 cm.

20512   Corrêa, Lia.
Uma rosa no tempo; poemas.   Pôrto Alegre, Brasil,
Departamento de Imprensa Oficial do Estado, 1972.
123 p.   23 cm.
Inscribed by author.

20513   Correa, Luis, 1884-1940.
Terra patrum; páginas de historia y crítica literari
[Prólogo y nota de Domingo Miliani.   3. ed., ampliada]
Caracas, Ediciones del Ministerio de Educación,
Dirección de Cultura y Bellas Artes, Departamento de
Publicaciones, 1961.
431 p.   19 cm.   (Biblioteca popular venezolano,
79)
Includes bibliography.

20514   Corrêa, Nereu.
O canto do cisne negro, e outros estudos.   Florianópolis, Departamento de Cultura, Secretaría de Educaçã
e Cultura de Santa Catarina, 1964.
162 p.   20 cm.

20515 Corrêa, Nereu.
Cassiano Ricardo; o prosador e o poeta. São Paulo,
Comissão de Literatura, Conselho Estadual de Cultura,
1970.
90 p. 22 cm. (Coleção ensaio, 71)

20516 Corrêa, Nereu.
Discursos na Academia Catarinense de Letras [por]
Nereu Corrêa y Luiz Gallotti. Florianópolis, 1971.
67 p. 24 cm.

20517 Correa, Pancho.
El libro de un chacerero (hijo de la soledad);
poesía y prosa. [Montevideo] 1964.
267 p. 20 cm.
At head of title: Libertad, tierra y amor.
Cover title.
Errata slip inserted.

20518 Correa Reyes, Sergio.
Acción del estado en la agricultura nacional hasta
el año 1959. Santiago, Editorial Universitaria, 1962.
152 p. 22 cm.
Tesis (licenciatura en ciencias jurídicas y sociales) -
Universidad de Chile.
Bibliography: p. 148-150.

20519 Correas, Edmundo, 1901-
Prólogo y epílogo de la batalla de Maipú. Mendoza,
1968.
32 p. 27 cm.
At head of title: Junta de Estudios Históricos de
Mendoza.
Bibliographical footnotes.

20520 Corredor, Berta.
Transformación en el mundo rural latino-americano;
consecuencias económicas y sociales de las estructuras
agrarias [por] Berta Corredor y Sergio Torres.
Bogotá, Oficina Internacional de Investigaciones
Sociales de FERES, 1961.
143 p. illus. 22 cm. (Documentos latino-
americanos, 2. Centro de Investigaciones Sociales.
Serie socio-económica, 2)

20521 Corredor, R   C
... Los microelementos como fertilizantes y la
traslocación del fosfato marcado (P^{32}) en injertos
de frutales. Bogotá, Instituto de Asuntos Nucleares,

Sección de Aplicación de Radioisótopos a la agricultura
1970.
27 p.   illus., tables.   28 cm.
At head of title: IAN-A-9.

20522 Correo de Arauco. Registro oficial de la Suprema Junta
Interior Gubernativa. 1824-1825. Santiago, Chile,
Biblioteca Nacional, 1965.
442 p.   28 cm.   (Colección de antiguos periódicos
chilenos)
A reissue of two periodicals published in Santiago.
The first, El Correo de Arauco, was published irregu-
larly in 50 no. plus special and supplementary issues
over the period Jan. 30, 1824 - June 24, 1825. The
second, Registro oficial de la Suprema Junta Interior
Gubernativa, was issued in 6 no. during 1825.

20523 Correo del Orinoco.
La prensa heroica: selección del Correo del Orinoco
en homenaje al sesquicentenario del periódico de
Angostura, 1818-1822. [Caracas, 1968]
342 p.   facsim.   24½ cm.

20524 Corrientes, Argentine Republic. Universidad Nacional
del Nordeste. Escuela de Derecho.
"Casos prácticos" de derecho penal; curso de seminar:
año lectivo de 1958. Corrientes, 1959.
156 p.   (Trabajos docentes, 1)

20525 Corro, Guillermo del.
Breve historia de la geología argentina. Buenos
Aires, Museo Argentino de Ciencias Naturales "Bernardi
Rivadavia" e Instituto Nacional de Investigación de
las Ciencias Naturales, 1972.
23 p.   25½ cm.   (Publicaciones de extensión
cultural y didáctica, 18)

20526 Corro, Guillermo del.
Un nuevo microbioterio (marsupalia) del eoceno de
Patagonia, por Guillermo del Corro. Buenos Aires,
1977.
31-33 p.   illus.   28 cm.
Reprinted from Revista del Museo Argentino de Cienci
Naturales "Bernardino Rivadavia" e Instituto Nacional
de Investigación de las Ciencias Naturales, Paleonto-
logía, t. II, no. 2.
Summary in English.

20527　Corro, Guillermo del.
　　　　Parásitos, marsupiales y deriva continental, por
　　　Guillermo de Corro.　Buenos Aires, 1977.
　　　　35-68 p.　　27 cm.
　　　　Reprinted from Revista del Museo Argentino de Ciencias
　　　Naturales "Bernardino Rivadavia" e Instituto Nacional de
　　　Investigación de la Ciencias Naturales, Paleontología,
　　　tomo II, no. 3.

20528　Cortada de Kohan, Nuria.
　　　　Estadística aplicada [por] Nuria Cortada de Kohan [y]
　　　José Manuel Carro.　[Buenos Aires] Editorial Universi-
　　　taria de Buenos Aires [1968]
　　　　368 p.　　illus.　　23 cm.　　(Ediciones previas.
　　　Psicología)
　　　　Includes bibliographies.

20529　Cortázar, Julio.
　　　　Cuentos.　Selección y prólogo [por] Antón Arrufat.
　　　[La Habana] Casa de las Américas [1964]
　　　　xvi, 323 p.　　19 cm.　　(Colección Literatura
　　　latinoamericana, 13)
　　　　Contents. - Bestiario. - Final de juego. - Las
　　　armas secretas. - Historias de cronopios y de fauna.

20530　Cortázar, Julio.
　　　　Libro de Manuel.　Buenos Aires, Editorial Sudamericana,
　　　1973.
　　　　386 p.　　21 cm.

20531　Cortés, Carlos E
　　　　Bibliografía da historia do Rio Grande do Sul;
　　　periodo republicano, por Carlos E. Cortes e Richard
　　　Kornweibel.　Pôrto Alegre, Faculdade de Filosofia,
　　　Universidade Federal do Rio Grande do Sul, 1967.
　　　　58 p.　　23 cm.　　(Publicações da Cadeira de
　　　História do Brasil)

20532　Cortés, Hernando, 1485-1547.
　　　　Cartas de relación de la conquista de Méjico...
　　　Madrid, Espasa Calpe, 1942.
　　　　2 v. in 1.　　illus., 2 maps.　　19 cm.　　(On cover:
　　　Viajes clásicos)

20533　Cortés, Jesús M
　　　　Indice alfabético general de los Sueños de Luciano
　　　Pulgar, por Jesús M. Cortés.　[Bogotá] Imprenta del
　　　Banco de la República, 1956.
　　　　ix, 343 p.　　25 cm.

"El presente trabajo está ceñido exactamente a los índices parciales de las ediciones de los Sueños lanzadas por la Librería Voluntad."
The editions of the volumes indexed are: v. 1-2, 3. ed., 1941; v. 3-6, 2. ed., 1941; v. 7, 2. ed., 1942; v. 8, 2. ed., 1943; v. 9, 2. ed., 1945; v. 10-12, 1. ed. 1940.

20534 Cortés Lee, Carlos, 1859-1928.
Sermones inéditos (escritos religiosos, morales y literarios) Bogotá [Ministerio de Educación Nacional] Ediciones de la Revista Bolívar, 1954-
v.   20 cm.   (Biblioteca de Cultura Colombiana, v. 2)
Library has v. 1-4.

20535 Cortés López, Idulio.
La desocupación en el campo y la reforma agraria. México, 1963.
86 p.   23 cm.
Tesis (licenciatura en derecho) - Universidad Nacional Autónoma de México.

20536 Cortés Pinto, Raúl.
Bibliografía anotada de educación superior. Valparaiso, Chile, Universidad Técnica "Federico Santa María," 1967.
31 p.   20 cm.

20537 Cortés Santos, Rodulfo.
... J. F. Reyes Baena... Caracas, Escuela de biblioteconomía y archivos, Facultad de humanidades y educación, Universidad Central de Venezuela, 1969.
103 p.   front. (port.)   17½ cm.
At head of title: Serie bibliográfica, 9)

20538 Cortez, Irlemar Chiampi.
Narração e metalinguagem em Grande Sertão: Veredas. [Sao Paulo, 1973]
63-91 p.   24½ cm.
Reprinted from Língua e literatura, revista dos departamentos de letras de Faculdade de Filosofia, Letras e Ciências Humanas da Universidade de São Paulo, ano II, no. 2, 1973.

20539 Cortez, Nati, 1914-
Teatro espacial. O natal no espaço sideral, comédia. A guerra dos planetas, drama sideral em 3 atos. Rio de Janeiro, Serviço Nacional de Teatro, 1972.

vi, 68 p.   21 cm.
Full name: Maria Natividade Cortez Gomes.

20540 Cortez, Roberto.
Diálogo ceremonial e diálogo mitológico entre os
Tiriyó [por] Roberto Cortez. Belém, Museu Paraense
Emilio Goeldi, 1975.
25 p.   23 cm.   (Antropologia. Boletim, 61.)

20541 Cortez, Roberto.
O índio na consciência urbana [por] Roberto Cortez.
Belém, Museu Paraense Emílio Goeldi, 1975.
18 p.   23 cm.   (Antropologia. Boletim, 59)

20542 Corvalán, Juan M   M
Programación de obras y proyectos por el método
P.E.R.T. ("critical path method")   La Plata, Biblioteca
y Publicaciones, 1964.
20 p.   diagrs., tables.   27 cm.   (Provincia
de Buenos Aires. Ministerio de Obras Públicas.
Dirección de Vialidad. Publicación, no. 40)

20543 Coscarón, Sixto.
Notas sobre tabanidos argentinos, xl. Sobre los
géneros "Leucotabanus" Lutz, "Pseudacanthocera" Lutz,
"Bolbodimyia" Bigot y "Pachyschelomyia" Barretto
(diptera, insecta) por Sixto Coscarón. Buenos Aires,
Imprenta Coni, 1976.
89-103 p.   illus.   27 cm.
Reprinted from Revista del Museo Argentino de
Ciencias Naturales "Bernardino Rivadavia", Entomología,
T. V, no. 5.
Abstract in English.

20544 Coscia, Adolfo A
Comercialización y demanda del maíz del area Caseros-
Constitución. Pergamino, 1974.
39 p.   tables, diagrs.   26 cm.   (Estación
Experimental Regional Agropecuaria Pergamino,
Informe técnico, no. 123)
Summary in English.

20545 Coscia, Adolfo A
El lino en su aspecto económico [por] Adolfo A.
Coscia. Pergamino, 1975.
40 p.   tables, diagrs.   26 cm.   (Estación
Experimental Regional Agropecuaria Pergamino. Informe
técnico, no. 130)
Summary in English.

20546 Coscia, Adolfo A
El maní en su aspecto económico [por] Adolfo Coscia.
Pergamino, 1974.
35 p.   tables, diagrs.   26 cm.   (Estación
Experimental Regional Agropecuaria Pergamino, Informe
técnico, no. 129)
Summary in English.

20547 Coscia, Adolfo A
La productividad de la mano de obra en el trigo
[por] Adolfo A. Coscia [y] Miguel A. Cacciamani.
Pergamino, 1978.
15 p.   tables, diagrs.   26 cm.   (Estación
Regional Agropecuaria Pergamino. Informe técnico,
no. 141)
Summary in English.

20548 Cossio Esturo, Adolfino.
El alzamiento del 9 de octubre en Macaca...
Santiago de Cuba, Universidad de Oriente, 1968.
43 p.   23 cm.

20549 Costa, Aída.
0 De republica e o "Princeps" ciceroniana (notas de
leitura) [São Paulo, 1973]
133-144 p.   24½ cm.
Reprinted from Língua e literatura, revista dos
Departamentos de Letras da Faculdade de Filosofia,
Letras e Ciências Humanas da Universidade de São
Paulo, ano II, no. 2, 1973.

20550 Costa, Cassio.
Gávea. [Rio de Janeiro] Estado de Guanabara,
Departamento de História e Documentação [1963?]
76 p.   12 cm.   (His Historia dos subúrbios)
Bibliography: p. [75]-76.

20551 Costa, Dias da, ed.
0 bumba-meuboi (registros) compilação de Dios da
Costa. Rio de Janeiro, Campanha de Defesa do
Folclore Brasileiro, Departamento de Assuntos
Culturais, Ministério da Educação e Cultura, 1973.
7 p.   24 cm.   (Cadernos de Folclore, 16)

20552 Costa, Didio Iratym Affonso da, 1881-
Riachuelo, 11 de junho de 1865 [por] Didio Costa.
[9. ed. Rio de Janeiro, Serviço de Documentaçao-Geral
da Marinha, 1967]
48 p.   illus.   23 cm.

20553 Costa, Dídio Iratym Affonso da, 1881-
... Tamandaré, almirante Joaquim Marques Lisboa.
Rio de Janeiro, Imprensa Naval, 1953.
84 p.   illus., pl.   18½ cm.

20554 Costa, José Marcelino Monteiro da.
Acre e Rondônia, diagnóstico econômico, por José
Marcelino Monteiro da Costa e José das Neves Capela.
Belém, Superintendência do Desenvolvimento da
Amazônia, 1968.
27 ℓ.   tables.   27 cm.   (Doc. GASPLAM 68/09)
Bibliographical references included in "Notas"
(leaves 24-27)

20555 Costa, Manoel Fernandes da.
Perspectivas para o aproveitamento integral da
palmeira acaí [por] Manoel Fernandes da Costa, Maria
Regina Couto Loureiro, Carlos Roberto Abreu de
Albuquerque, Zebino Pacheco do Amaral Filho. Belém,
Instituto do Desenvolvimento Econômico-Social do
Pará, 1974.
84 p.   diagrs. (part fold.)   21 cm.   (Série
Monografías, 14)
Errata sheet at end.

20556 Costa, Miguel.
O cana-de-açúcar em Minas Gerais. Rio de Janeiro,
Instituto do Açúcar e do Alcool, 1963.
415 p.   illus., group port., maps, facsim.   24 cm.
Bibliography: p. 397-415.

20557 Costa, Newton C   A   da.
... On the theory of inconsistent formal systems.
Recife, Universidade Federal de Pernambuco, Instituto
de Matemática, 1972.
27 p.   28 cm.   (Notas e comunicações de matemática, no. 41)

20558 Costa, Rubens Vaz da.
Avaliação financeira do sistema de incentivos
fiscais no Nordeste. Fortaleza, Banco do Nordeste do
Brasil, 1968.
18 p.   21 cm.

20559 Costa, Rubens Vaz da.
O BNB e o desenvolvimento do Nordeste. Fortaleza,
Banco do Nordeste do Brasil, 1968.
36 p.   21 cm.

"Exposição... perante a Comissão de Economia da Câmara dos Deputados, no dia 28.05.68, Brasília."

20560 Costa, Rubens Vaz da.
Demographic explosion in the world and in Brazil.
Rio de Janeiro, Secretaria de Divulgação, Banco
Nacional de Habitação, 1973.
49 p.   tables, diagrs.   21 cm.

20561 Costa, Rubens Vaz da.
Demographic growth and environmental pollution.
Rio de Janeiro, Secretaria de Divulgação, Banco
Nacional de Habitação, 1973.
59 p.   tables, diagrs.   21 cm.

20562 Costa, Rubens Vaz da.
O economia do Nordeste e o desenvolvimento nacional.
Fortaleza, Banco do Nordeste do Brasil, 1968.
28 p.   tables.   21 cm.

20563 Costa, Rubens Vaz da.
Economic development and urban growth in Brazil.
Rio de Janeiro, 1972.
66 p.   tables.   23 cm.

20564 Costa, Rubens Vaz da.
O que o Nordeste espera de São Paulo.   2. impr.
Fortaleza, Banco de Nordeste do Brasil, 1968.
22 p.   tables.   21 cm.

20565 Costa, Zeferino da.
Amor real. Rio de Janeiro, 1964.
97 p.   19 cm.
Errata slip inserted.

20566 Costa e Silva, Arthur, 1902-
Mensagem ao Ceará [por] Arthur da Costa e Silva.
Fortaleza, Imp. Universitária do Ceará, 1966.
13 p.   23 cm.
"Discurso pronunciado... a 23 de julho de 1966, no
Náutico Atlético Cearense."

20567 Costa Pôrto, José da, 1909-
Os tempos de Rosa e Silva.   Recife, Universidade
Federal de Pernambuco, 1970.
219 p.   23 cm.

20568 Costa Rica. Constitution.
Constitución política de la República de Costa Rica,

392

7 de noviembre de 1949. [San José] Imprenta Nacional, 1959.
>76 p.   19 cm.
>At head of title: Ministerio de Gobernación.

20569 Costa Rica. Constitution.
>Constitution of the Republic of Costa Rica, 1949 (as amended) Washington, Pan American Union, 1961.
>36 p.   23 cm.

20570 Costa Rica. Dirección General de Estadística y Censos.
>Anuario estadístico de Costa Rica. San José.
>v.   26 cm.   annual.
>Library has 1968, 1975 and 1976.

20571 Costa Rica. Dirección General de Estadística y Censos.
>Cantón 3º, Santo Domingo [Provincia de Heredia] Revisión: Enero de 1962. [San José, C. R., 1962]
>map on sheet 75 x 108 cm.
>Scale ca. 1:12,500.
>Reproduced photographically.

20572 Costa Rica. Dirección General de Estadística y Censos.
>Cantón 9º, San Pablo [Provincia de Heredia] Dibujo: G. Ulate M., Nov. 25, 1960. [San José, C. R., 1960]
>map.   89 x 82 cm.
>Scale ca. 1:6,000.
>Reproduced photographically.

20573 Costa Rica. Dirección General de Estadística y Censos.
>Censo de población 1864. [San José] 1964.
>xl, 103, 71 p.   facsims., port.   27 cm.
>Cover title.
>Facsim. reproduction.
>Original t. p. reads: Censo general de la República de Costa Rica, 27 de noviembre de 1864. San José de Costa Rica, 1868.

20574 Costa Rica. Dirección General de Estadística y Censos.
>Censo de población 1973. Tomo I. San José, 1974.
>500 p.   27 cm.

20575 Costa Rica. Dirección General de Estadística y Censos.
>Censo de vivienda, 1963. San José, Sección de Publicaciones, Dirección General de Estadística y Censos, 1966.
>458 p.   27 cm.

20576   Costa Rica. Dirección General de Estadística y Censos.
         Censo de vivienda 1973. San José, 1974.
         447 p.   tables, diagrs., forms.   28½ cm.

20577   Costa Rica. Dirección General de Estadística y Censos.
         Comercio exterior de Costa Rica.   San José.
         v.   28 cm.
         Library has 1968, 1969, 1970 and 1977.

20578   Costa Rica. Dirección General de Estadística y Censos.
         IV Censo de manufactura 1975. Tomo 1. Resultados
         por división territorial administrativa. San José,
         1977.
         62 p.   tables.   27 cm.

20579   Costa Rica. Dirección General de Estadística y Censos.
         Ingresos y gastos de las familias del Area Metropo-
         litana de San José, según encuesta preliminar de
         1958. San José, Costa Rica, Impreso en la Sección
         de Publicaciones, 1960.
         57 p.   graphs, maps.   21 cm.

20580   Costa Rica. Dirección General de Estadística y Censos.
         Población de la república de Costa Rica por provincias
         cantones y distritos. Estimación al: 1 de enero de
         1974. [San José, 1975]
         28 p.   27 cm.

20581   Costa Rica. Dirección General de Estadística y Censos.
         Población total de la república de Costa Rica por
         provincias, cantones y distritos. Cálculo al 1° de
         octubre de 1968. Cálculo al 1° de enero de 1969.
         San José, 1970.
         19, 18 p.   22 x 29 cm.   (Costa Rica. Ministerio
         de industria y comercio. Dirección general de esta-
         dística y censos. Nos. 14-15)

20582   Costa Rica. Dirección General de Estadística y Censos.
         II [i.e., Segundo] censo de comercio de Costa Rica,
         1958. San José, 1961.
         xxxiv, 106 p.   diagrs., tables.

20583   Costa Rica. Dirección General de Estadística y Censos.
         II [i.e. Segundo] censo de industria en Costa Rica,
         1958. Boletín informático [San José, Sección de
         Publicaciones, 1961]
         25 p.   27 cm.

394

20584 Costa Rica. Dirección General de Estadística y Censos.
II censo de industrias en Costa Rica, 1958. San
José, 1962.
xxxv, 322 p.   tables.   27 cm.

20585 Costa Rica. Instituto de Educación Política.
Instituto de Educación Política: Qué es? Qué busca?
Qué ha realizado? Información general. San José,
Costa Rica [Imprenta Tormo Limitada] 1961.
31 p.   19 cm.

20586 Costa Rica. Instituto Geográfico Nacional.
Informe semestral. San José, 1970-
v.   26 cm.
Library has July-December 1969, January-June 1970.

20587 Costa Rica. Instituto Geográfico Nacional.
El Instituto Geográfico de Costa Rica; un organismo
público al servicio de la comunidad y la ciencia
geográfica. [San José] 1961.
21 p.   illus., maps.   25 cm.

20588 Costa Rica. Instituto Geográfico Nacional.
Publicaciones del Instituto Geográfico Nacional
(1954-1972) Índice bibliográfico. San José, 1973.
24 p.   25 cm.
Mounted at end is "Índice de mapas topográficos"
and price list.

20589 Costa Rica. Instituto Nacional de Aprendizaje.
Diagnóstico sobre la utilización de los recursos
humanos en Costa Rica y su relación con las necesidades
educativas. San José, 1972.
54 p.   tables (1 fold.)   28½ cm.

20590 Costa Rica. Laws, statutes, etc.
Código de trabajo. Edición revisada por Atilio
Vincenzi. San José, Imprenta Trejos, 1966.
314 p.   25 cm.

20591 Costa Rica. Laws, statutes, etc.
Ley orgánica del Registro Civil y Código electoral.
Promulgadas en el año 1952. San José, Imprenta
Nacional, 1961.
95, xviii p.   25 cm.
At head of title: Tribunal Supremo de Elecciones.
República de Costa Rica.

20592 Costa Rica. Laws, statutes, etc.
Leyes bancarias y otras de orden económico y
financiero. Publicación ordenada por el sistema
bancario nacional. [San José, Imprenta Trejos] 1960.
266 p.   26 cm.

20593 Costa Rica. Ministerio de Educación Pública.
Algunas estadísticas educativas. San José, 1973.
[1] p.   23 tables.   29 cm.

20594 Costa Rica. Ministerio de Educación Pública.
Artes industriales. III ciclo. San José, 1972.
31 p.   23 cm.   (Plan nacional de desarrollo
educativo)

20595 Costa Rica. Ministerio de Educación Pública.
Artes plásticas. I ciclo [v. 2:   II ciclo]
San José, 1974.
2 v.   23 cm.   (Plan nacional de desarrollo
educativo)

20596 Costa Rica. Ministerio de Educación Pública.
Ciencias. I ciclo [v. 2:   II ciclo] San José, 1974.
2 v.   23 cm.   (Plan nacional de desarrollo
educativo)

20597 Costa Rica. Ministerio de Educación Pública.
Educación física. I y II ciclos. San José, 1974.
58 p.   23 cm.   (Plan nacional de desarrollo
educativo)

20598 Costa Rica. Ministerio de Educación Pública.
Educación musical. I y II ciclos. San José, 1974.
47 p.   music.   23 x 29 cm.

20599 Costa Rica. Ministerio de Educación Pública.
Educación musical. III ciclo. San José, 1972.
31 p.   23 cm.   (Plan nacional de desarrollo
educativo.

20600 Costa Rica. Ministerio de Educación Pública.
Español. I. ciclo [v. 2: II ciclo. v. 3: III
ciclo] San José, 1974.
3 v.   23 cm.   (Plan nacional de desarrollo
educativo)

20601 Costa Rica. Ministerio de Educación Pública.
Estudios sociales. III ciclo. San José, 1974.
48 p.   23 cm.   (Plan nacional de desarrollo
educativo)

20602　Costa Rica. Ministerio de Educación Pública.
　　　　Francés. San José, 1972.
　　　　36 p.　23 cm.　(Plan nacional de desarrollo
　　　　educativo.

20603　Costa Rica. Ministerio de Educación Pública.
　　　　Inglés. San José, 1974.
　　　　43 p.　23 cm.　(Plan nacional de desarrollo
　　　　educativo)

20604　Costa Rica. Ministerio de Educación Pública.
　　　　Matemática. I ciclo. [v. 2: II ciclo] San José,
　　　　1972.
　　　　2 v.　23 cm.　(Plan nacional de desarrollo
　　　　educativo.

20605　Costa Rica. Ministerio de Educación Pública.
　　　　Plan nacional de desarrollo educativo. Decreto
　　　　No. 3333-E. [San José, 197]
　　　　91 p.　22 cm.
　　　　Cover title.

20606　Costa Rica. Ministerio de Educación Pública.
　　　　Planeamiento del desarrollo educativo. Diagnóstico.
　　　　San José, 1971.
　　　　249 p.　map, tables, diagrs.　25½ cm.

20607　Costa Rica. Ministerio de Educación Pública.
　　　　Planeamiento del desarrollo educativo. Programación.
　　　　San José, 1971.
　　　　196 p.　tables (1 fold.), diagrs.　25½ cm.

20608　Costa Rica. Ministerio de Educación Pública. Dirección
　　　　General de Desarrollo Educativo.
　　　　Estadísticas del sistema educativo costarricense
　　　　1969-1972. San José, 1973.
　　　　136 p.　tables, diagrs.　28 cm.

20609　Costa Rica. Ministerio de Educación Pública. Dirección
　　　　General de Planeamiento Educativo.
　　　　Centros educativos de Costa Rica. 1973. San José
　　　　[1973?]
　　　　201 p.　tables.　22½ x 35 cm.

20610　Costa Rica. Ministerio de Hacienda.
　　　　Memoria anual. Ministerio de Hacienda, 1969.
　　　　San José, 1970.
　　　　205 p.　tables.　28½ cm.　annual.

20611　Costa Rica. Ministerio de Obras Públicas.
Estudios sobre la primera etapa del Plan Vial.
[San José] 1961.
156 p.　maps (part fold.)　diagrs., tables.
26 cm.

20612　Costa Rica. Ministerio de Trabajo y Bienestar Social.
Memoria. 1968. San José, Imprenta Nacional [1969]
83 p.　25 cm.

20613　Costa Rica. Ministerio de Trabajo y Bienestar Social.
Seminario - mesa redonda. La armonía obrero-patronal
como factor de desarollo... 3-6 diciembre de 1968.
San José, Imprenta Nacional, 1969.
64 p.　24½ cm.

20614　Costa Rica. Oficina Nacional del Censo.
Censo de población de Costa Rica, 11 de mayo de 1927.
San José, 1960.
115 p.　diagrs., tables.　28 cm.

20615　Costa Rica. Oficina de Planificación. Departamento
de Planes a Largo y Mediano Plazo.
La economía de Costa Rica en 1966. San José, 1967.
iii, 52 p.　tables (part fold.)　23 cm.

20616　Costa Rica. Superintendencia de Bancos.
Informe anual 1941. San José, Imprenta Nacional,
1942.
52 p., 20 tables.　21 cm.

20617　Costa Rica. Universidad. Escuela de Ciencias Económicas.
Estudio integral de las necesidades de la Universidad
de Costa Rica para un período de diez años. Ciudad
Universitaria, 1962.
98 p.　20 cm.　(Publicaciones de la Universidad
de Costa Rica. Serie miscelánea, 75)

20618　Costales Samaniego, Alfredo.
Diccionario de modismos y regionalismos centro-
ame⁚icanos (Costa Rica, Nicaragua, Honduras, El
Salvador y Guatemala) Ciudad Universitaria "Rodrigo
Facio," Costa Rica [1962?]
83 p.　27 cm.
At head of title: Instituto Universitario Centro-
americano de Investigaciones Sociales y Económicas
(Organismo regional del Consejo Superior Universitario
Centroamericano)

20619 Costanzo, G   A
Programas de estabilización en América Latina.
México, Centro de Estudios Monetarios Latinoamericanos,
1961.
143 p.   22 cm.

20620 Cotelo, Julio César.
Influencia del pensamiento de Artigas en el Congreso
de abril de 1813. Montevideo, Biblioteca, Junta
Departamental de Montevideo, 1968 [i.e. 1969]
109 p.   20½ cm.

20621 Cotlar, Mischa.
Introducción a la teoría de la representación grupos.
[Buenos Aires] 1963.
xv, 288 p.   28 cm.   (Universidad de Buenos Aires.
Departamento de Matemática. Cursos y seminarios de
matemática, fasc. 11)
Cover title.
Bibliography: p. xv.

20622 Cotmier, Gerald H
Labor in Brazil. Washington, Bureau of Labor
Statistics, U. S. Department of Labor, 1962.
35 p.   22 cm.   (BLS report, 191)

20623 Cotrim Garaude, Lupe.
Poemas ao outro. Prefácio de André Carneiro.
São Paulo, Conselho Estadual de Cultura, Comissão de
Literatura [1970]
79 p.   19 cm.   (Coleção Poesia, 8)

20624 Cotta de Varela, Laura B
La grafología en la escuela primaria [por] Laura B.
Cotta de Varela. La Plata, Ministerio de Educación
de la Provincia de Buenos Aires, 1957.
119, [8] p.   illus.   24 cm.   (Suplemento de
la Revista de educación, no. 6)
Bibliography: p. [121]-[123]

20625 Couffon, Claude.
Orihuela y Miguel Hernández. Traducción de Alfredo
Varela. Buenos Aires, Editorial Losada [1967]
186 p.   illus., ports.   18 cm.   (Biblioteca
clásica y contemporánea, 334)
Includes poems and letters of Miguel Hernández.

20626 Cousseau, María Berta.
Contribución al conocimiento de la biología del surel
(Trachurus picturatus australis) del área de Mar del

399

Plata (pisces, fam. carangidae) Mar del Plata, Universidades nacionales de Buenos Aires, La Plata y del Sur, P. E. de la Provincia de Buenos Aires, Instituto de Biología Marina, 1967.
38 p. illus., graphs. 25 cm. (Boletín, no. 15)

20627 Coutin Correa, Donis Pablo.
Características de la zeolitización en rocas sedimentarias de origen volcánico en Cuba oriental, por Donis Pablo Coutin Correa [y] Amelia Brito Rojas. La Habana, Academia de Ciencias de Cuba, Instituto de Geología y Paleontología, 1975.
26 p. map, tables, diagrs. 27 cm. (Serie geológica, no. 20)
Abstract in English.

20628 Coutin Correa, Donis Pablo.
Tres nuevos tipos de materias primas no metálicas en la provincia de Oriente, por Donis Coutin, Elemer Nagy y Guillermo Pantaleón. La Habana, Academia de Ciencias de Cuba, Instituto de Geología y Paleontología, 1976.
19 p. illus., diagrs. 27 cm. (Serie geológica, no. 25)

20629 Coutinho, Afrânio.
Introdução à literatura no Brasil. 4. ed. Rio de Janeiro, Liv. São José, 1968.
392 p. 22 cm.
Bibliography: p. [311]-359.
"Compõem êste livro as seis introduções escritas pelo seu autor para a Literatura no Brasil."

20630 Coutinho, Afrânio.
Recepção de Afrânio Coutinho na Academia Brasileira de Letras. Rio de Janeiro [Soc. Gráf. Vida Domestica] 1962.
68 p. 23 cm.
"Discurso do Sr. Afrânio Coutinho. Discurso do Sr. Levi Carneiro."

20631 Coutinho, Aluizio Bezerra.
Genética e evolução. [Por] Aluizio Bezerra Coutinho [e] André Freire Furtado. Vol. I. (Genética) 2ª edição. Recife, Universidade Federal de Pernambuco, 1972.
173 p. illus. 24 cm.

20632 Coutinho, Evaldo.
O espaço da arquitetura. Recife, Universidade
Federal de Pernambuco, 1970.
253 p. 23½ cm.

20633 Coutinho, Evaldo.
A imagem autônoma; ensaio de teoria do cinema.
Recife, Brasil, Universidade Federal de Pernambuco,
1972.
299 p. 24 cm.

20634 Couto, Gabriel P   Bueno.
O homen ea sua realização; o roteiro da felicidade
[por] Gabriel P. Bueno Couto. São Paulo, Ed. Paulinas,
1968.
99 p. 18 cm. (Coleção Caminho, verdade e vida, 6)
Bibliographical footnotes.

20635 Couture, Eduardo J   , 1906-1956.
Tres conferencias [que el decano de la Facultad de
Derecho de la Universidad de Montevideo dicto en
nuestra Universidad durante la Escuela de Temporada
de 1955. Panamá, Ediciones del Ministerio de Educación,
Departamento de Bellas Artes y Publicaciones] 1956
71 p. 22 cm. (Universidad de Panamá. Escuela
de Temporada. [Publicaciones])

20636 Couture, Eduardo J   1906-1956.
Vocabulario jurídico, con especial referencia al
derecho procesal positivo vigente uruguayo. Edición
a cargo de Jorge Peirano Facio y José Sánchez Fontana.
Montevideo, 1960.
606 p. 25 cm. (Biblioteca de publicaciones
oficiales de la Facultad de Derecho y Ciencias
Sociales de la Universidad de la República. Sección
3, 113)

20637 Cova-García, Pablo.
La legislación antimalárica venezolana y proyecto
de reglamentación. Caracas, Ministerio de Sanidad y
Asistencia Social, 1940.
34 p. 26 cm. (Publicaciones de la División de
Malariología, no. 6)
Tesis - Universidad Central de Venezuela.
Bibliography: p. [27]-34.

20638 Covarrubias, Miguel, 1902-1957.
El poeta. Monterrey, México, Ediciones Sierra Madre,

1969.
24 p.   22 cm.   (Poesía en el mundo, 69)

20639 Cox, Paul.
Venezuela's agrarian reform at mid-1977, by Paul
Cox. Madison, Land Tenure Center, University of
Wisconsin, 1977.
v, 66 p.   28 cm.   (R. P. no. 71)

20640 Coyner, Mary Susan (Coiner)
Agriculture and trade of El Salvador. Washington,
1971.
vii, 27 p.   map.   27½ cm.   (U.S. Dept. of
Agriculture. Economic Research Service. ERS Foreign
323)

20641 Coyner, Mary Susan (Coiner)
Agriculture and trade of Honduras. Washington,
Regional Analysis Division, Economic Research Service,
Dept. of Agriculture, 1962.
23 p.   27½ cm.   (U.S. Dept. of Agriculture.
Economic Research Service. ERS Foreign 33)

20642 Coyner, Mary Susan (Coiner)
El Salvador: its agriculture and trade. Washington,
U.S. Dept. of Agriculture, Economic Research Service,
Regional Analysis Division, 1963.
iv, 30 p.   illus., map.   26 cm.   (ERS Foreign,
49)

20643 Crabbé, Pierre, 1928-
Ciencia y sociedad. Monterrey, México, 1973.
20 p.   22 cm.   (Nuevo León. Departamento de
Relaciones Culturales. Cuadernos de asuntos culturales.
Série ciencias. 2)

20644 Craveiro, Paulo Fernando.
A fábula da guerra; crônicas. Recife, Universidade
Federal de Pernambuco, 1970.
257 p.   23 cm.

20645 Craviotto, José A
Quilmes a través de los años. Quilmes, Argentina,
Secretaría de Gobierno y Cultura, Municipalidad de
Quilmes, 1966.
340 p.   18½ cm.

20646 Crazut, Rafael J
El Banco Central de Venezuela; notas sobre la historia

y evolución del Instituto: 1940-1970. Caracas,
Banco Central de Venezuela, 1970.
316 p.   24 cm.

20647   Creelman, James, 1859-1915.
Entrevista Díaz-Creelman. Prólogo por José María
Juján. Traducción de Mario Julio de Campo. [1. ed.]
México, Universidad Nacional Autónoma de México, 1963.
5 p., facsim. (231-277 p. illus., ports.), 9-50 p.
24 cm.   (Publicaciones del Instituto de Historia,
Universidad Autónoma de México. 1. ser., no. 81.
Cuadernos: Serie documental, no. 2)
Original caption title reads: President Díaz,
hero of the Americas.
"En forma facsimilar el original publicado por el
Pearson's magazine y a continuación la traducción."

20648   Creimer, Diana.
El truque, y otros cuentos. [La Plata] Municipalidad
de La Plata [1962]
118 p.   18 cm.
Contents. - El truque. - Vacaciones. - La gota. -
Tia Gemma. - Un baño en el arroyo. - Descubrimiento. -
El piropo.

20649   Crespo, María R   ed.
Selección del nuevo cuento cuencano (prólogo de María
R. Crespo) Cuenca [Núcleo del Azuay de la Casa de la
Cultura Ecuatoriana] 1979.
186 p.   19½ cm.
Includes short stories by Eliecer Cardenas Espinoza,
Jorge Dávila Vázquez, Osvaldo Encalada Vázquez,
Nelly Peña de Venegas, Ivan Petroff Rojas, David
Ramírez Olarte, Juan Valdano Morejón.

20650   Crespo, Osvaldo Víctor.
Aproximaciones para una sociogeografía de las tierras
áridas de América Latina. [Santiago de Chile, 1971]
113-124 p.   24½ cm.
Reprinted from Revista chilena de historia y
geografía, no. 139, 1971.

20651   Crêspo, Rodrigues.
Banco das cismas.   Belo Horizonte, Editôra Gênesis
[1955?]
216 p.   20 cm.

20652   Crespo Ordóñez, Roberto.
El descubrimiento del Amazonas y los derechos terri-

toriales del Ecuador; conferencia sustentada en el
Núcleo del Azuay de la Casa de la Cultura Ecuatoriana.
Cuenca, Núcleo del Azuay de la Casa de Cultura
Ecuatoriana, 1961.
55 p.   22 cm.

20653   Crespo Ordóñez, Roberto.
Discursos históricos y literarios. 2. ed. Cuenca
[Casa de la Cultura Ecuatoriana, Núcleo del Azuay]
1961.
339 p.   illus.   23 cm.
First published in 1944 under title: Discursos
literarios.

20654   Crespo Paniagua, Renato.
La universidad y las necesidades actuales de la
enseñanza superior; [discurso pronunciado en oportunidad
de la inauguración del año académico en fecha 30 de
abril de 1964, por] Renato Crespo P. Cochabamba,
Bolivia [Universidad Mayor de San Simón] 1964.
36 p.   19 cm.

20655   Crespo Toral, Remigio, 1860-1939.
Bolívar, el héroe y el genio de América. Compilación
y prólogo de Victor Manuel Albornoz. Cuenca [1960]
183 p.   (Publicaciones del Centro de Estudios
Históricos y Geográficos de Cuenca)

20656   Crispolti, Francisco María, 1834-1887.
El mensaje de 24 de enero y el dictámen de 21 de
febrero en el Congreso de Nicaragua en 1882. Relativos
a la cuestión "jesuitas" de 1881. Exámen histórico-
jurídico con algunos documentos anotados y comentados,
por el p. F. M. Crispolti... Nueva York, 1882.
3 p.l., iv, [5]-170 p.   22½ cm.
Errata slip inserted.

20657   Croce, Benedetto, 1866-1952.
A poesia. Introdução à crítica e história da poesia
e da literatura. Tradução de Flávio Loureiro Chaves.
Supervisão e revisão de Angelo Ricci. Pôrto Alegre,
Edições da Faculdade de Filosofia da Universidade
Federal do R. G. do Sul, 1967.
226 p.   19½ cm.

20658   Cronistas de la independencia y de la República
[Selecciones] Puebla, J. M. Cajica Jr. [1960]
650 p.   22 cm.   (Biblioteca ecuatoriana mínima.
La colonia y república)

20659 Croquevielle Brand, Teodoro.
La reforma presupuestaria del DFL no. 47, de 1959.
Santiago, Editorial Universitaria, 1962.
153 p.   22 cm.
Tesis (licenciatura en ciencias jurídicas y sociales) -
Universidad de Chile.
Bibliography: p. 146-148.

20660 Crosby, Elisha Oscar, 1818-1895.
Memoirs of Elisha Oscar Crosby; reminiscences of
California and Guatemala from 1849 to 1864, edited by
Charles Albro Barker. San Marino, Calif., The
Huntington library, 1945.
xxvi, 119 p.   front. (port.) plates.   23½ cm.
(Half-title: Huntington library publications)
"Bibliographical note on the Crosby papers":
p. xxiii-xxvi.

20661 Cross, Elsa, 1946-
Peach Melba. Monterrey, México, Ediciones Sierra
Madre, 1970.
24 p.   illus.   22 cm.   (Poesía en el mundo, 82)

20662 Cruchaga Gandarillas, Vicente.
La igualdad jurídica de los estados. [Santiago de
Chile] Editorial Jurídica de Chile, 1968.
113 p.   23 cm.   (Universidad Católica de Chile.
Facultad de Ciencias Jurídicas, Políticas y Sociales.
Memoria, no. 31)
Bibliography: p. 109-110.

20663 Cruchaga Santa María, Angel, 1893-
Noche de las noches; [poema en prosa. Santiago de
Chile, 1963]
47 p.   15 cm.   (Colección El Viento en la llama, 6)

20664 Cruz, Arlete Nogueira da.
As cartas. Rio de Janeiro, Liv. São José, 1969.
58 p.   18 cm.

20665 Cruz, Ernesto Horácio da, 1898-
Historia de Belém. Belém, Universidade Federal do
Pará, 1973.
2 v.   24 cm.   (Coleção amazônica. Série José
Veríssimo)

20666 Cruz, Ernesto Horácio da, 1898-
Historia do Pará [por] Ernesto Cruz. [Belém]
Universidade do Pará [1963-

405

v. 23 cm. (Coleção amazônica. Série José Veríssimo)
Bibliographical references included in "Notas".

20667 Cruz, Jorge de la.
Dos nuevas especies de acaros (Acarina: Chriodiscidae, Labidocarpinae) parásitos de murciélagos de Cuba.
La Habana, Instituto de Zoología, Academia de Ciencias de Cuba, 1974.
8 p. illus. 24½ cm. (Poeyana, no. 127)
Abstract in English.

20668 Cruz, Jorge de la.
Dos nuevos especies de peces dulceacuícolas del género Rivulus Poey (Cyprinodontidae) de Cuba e Isla de Pinos [por] Jorge de la Cruz y A. M. Dubitsky.
La Habana, Instituto de Zoología, Academia de Ciencias de Cuba, 1976.
6 p. 23 cm. (Poeyana, no. 155)
Abstract in English.

20669 Cruz, Jorge de la.
Notas adicionales a la fauna de garrapatas (Ixodoidea) de Cuba. I. Argasidae de las aves. La Habana, Instituto de Zoología, Academia de Ciencias de Cuba, 1974.
3 p. 24½ cm. (Poeyana, no. 129)
Abstract in English.

20670 Cruz, Jorge de la.
Notas adicionales a la fauna de garrapatas (Ixodoidea) de Cuba. II. Nuevo status para Parantricola Cerny, 1966. La Habana, Instituto de Zoología, Academia de Ciencias de Cuba, 1974.
4 p. 24½ cm. (Poeyana, no. 130)
Abstract in English.

20671 Cruz, Jorge de la.
Notas adicionales a la fauna de garrapatas (Ixodoidea) de Cuba. V. Una nueva especie del género Antricola Cooley y Kohls. 1942 (Argasidae) La Habana, Instituto de Zoología, Academia de Ciencias de Cuba, 1976.
8 p. illus. 23 cm. (Poeyana, 151)
Abstract in English.

20672 Cruz, Jorge de la.
Nueva especie de acaro (Acarina: Listrophoridae)

Parásito de murciélagos cubanos. La Habana, Instituto de Biología, 1969.
8 p.   illus.   23½ cm.

20673   Cruz, Jorge de la.
Nueva especie de acaro del género Geckobia Megnin, 1878 (Acarina: Pterygosomidae) parásito de la Tarentola americana (Gray) de Cuba. La Habana, Instituto de Zoología, Academia de Ciencias de Cuba, 1973.
6 p.   illus.   24½ cm.   (Poeyana, no. 102, 27 April 1973)
Abstract in English.

20674   Cruz, Jorge de la.
Una nueva especie de Olabidocarpus Lawrence, 1948 (Acarina, Chirodiscidae) parásita de murciélagos de Cuba. La Habana, Instituto de Zoología, Academia de Ciencias de Cuba, 1973.
4 p.   illus.   24½ cm.   (Poeyana, no. 122, 20 Noviembre 1973)
Abstract in English.

20675   Cruz, Jorge de la.
Nuevos géneros y especies de acaros de la superfamilia Listrophoroidea (Acarina: Chirodiscidae y Labidocarpidae) parásitos de mamíferos cubanos. La Habana, Instituto de Zoología, Academia de Ciencias de Cuba, 1973.
10 p.   illus.   24½ cm.   (Poeyana, no. 115, 23 August 1973)
Abstract in English.

20676   Cruz, Jorge de la.
Los tábanos (Diptera: Tabanidae) de Cuba, por Jorge de la Cruz e Israel García Ávila. La Habana, Instituto de Zoología, Academia de Ciencias de Cuba, 1974.
91 p.   illus.   24½ cm.   (Poeyana, no. 125)
Abstract in English, p. 1.

20677   Cruz, Olga.
A serra do mar e o litoral na área de Caraguatatuba-SP. Contribuição à geomorfologia litorânea tropical. São Paulo, Instituto de Geografia, Universidade de São Paulo, 1974.
181 p.   illus., maps (part fold.), tables, diagrs. (part fold.)   26 cm.   (Série teses y monografias, no. 11)
"Bibliografia": p. 169-177.

20678 Cruz, Raul de la.
       Ritos y costumbres de nuestros pueblos primitivos.
       Prólogo: Héctor Cardenas Rodríguez. Ilus.: Román
       Domíguez [!] Rivero. [1. ed.] México, 1964.
       143 p.   illus.   24 cm.
       Bibliography: p. 143.
       "Apéndice: Proceso y actualidad indigenista. Fiestas
       populares de México": p. 129-141.

20679 Cruz Coronado, Guillermo de la, 1921-
       Pórtico al Quijote; estudio estructural del primer
       capítulo. Curitiba, Conselho de Pesquisas da Univer-
       sidade Federal do Paraná, 1968.
       111 p.   24 cm.
       Bibliographical footnotes.

20680 Cruz Costa, João.
       Panorama da história da filosofia no Brasil. São
       Paulo, Editôra Cultrix [1960]
       132 p.   22 cm.   (Coleção Letras brasileiras)

20681 Cruz Larena, Jorge.
       Fundación de Antofagasta y su primera década.
       Antofagasta, Municipalidad de Antofagasta, 1966.
       133 p.   20 cm.

20682 Cruz Reyna, Gonzalo de la.
       Trascendencia del pensamiento de don Andrés Molina
       Enríquez en el proceso histórico del derecho agrario.
       México, 1963.
       101 p.   28 cm.
       Tesis (licenciatura en derecho) - Universidad
       Nacional Autónoma de México.
       Bibliography: p. 101.

20683 Cuadra, Pablo Antonio, 1912-
       Cantos de Cifar. Avila, España, Institución Gran
       Duque de Alba, 1971.
       133 p.   illus.   16 x 17 cm.   (Colección El toro
       de granito, 18)

20684 Cuadra, Pablo Antonio, 1912-
       Doña Andreita y otros retratos. Caracas, Ediciones
       Poesía de Venezuela, 1971.
       20 p.   19 cm.   (Poesía de Venezuela, 32)

20685 Cuatrecasas, José.
       Cunoniáceas, por José Cuatrecasas, Lyman B. Smith
       e Roberto M. Klein. Florianópolis, Universidade

Federal de Santa Cararina, Divisão de Botânica, 1976.
21 p.   illus.   23 cm.   (Flórula da Ilha de
Santa Catarina, planejada e coordenada por Ranulpho
José de Souza Sobrinho e Antônio Bresolin)

20686   Cuba.   Administración General de Café y Cacao.
El cultivo del cacao; recopilación de trabajos sobre
el cacao.   La Habana, Imprenta Nacional, 1961.
223 p.   illus.   24 cm.

20687   Cuba.   Comisión Nacional de la UNESCO.
Historia de una ciénaga.   [La Habana, 1961]
unpaged.   illus.   15 x 23 cm.

20688   Cuba.   Comisión Nacional de la UNESCO.
Methods and means utilized in Cuba to eliminate
illiteracy.   [La Habana, 196-]
79 p.   fold. diagr.   29 cm.

20689   Cuba.   Convención Constituyente, 1900-1901.
Diario de sesiones de la Convención constituyente
de la isla de Cuba.   No. 1-52, 6 de noviembre de
1900-10 de septiembre de 1901.   La Habana, 1900-01.
651 p.   32 cm.
"Proyectos de bases para la constitución de la
República de Cuba, apéndice especial al número 15"
inserted between p. 158 and 159.

20690   Cuba.   Departamento de Asuntos Económicos Internacionales.
La posición del azúcar cubano en los Estados Unidos
de América.   La Habana, 1960.
32 p.   illus.   24 cm.

20691   Cuba.   Dirección Nacional de Bibliotecas.
Guía de bibliotecas de la República de Cuba.   2. ed.,
aumentada y corregida.   La Habana, Departamento
Metódico, Biblioteca Nacional José Martí, 1966.
107 p.   21 cm.

20692   Cuba.   Intendencia de Ejército y Hacienda.
Estados relativos a la producción azucarera de
la isla de Cuba, formados competemente y con autori-
zación de la Intendencia de Ejército y Hacienda, por
Carlos Rebello.   La Habana, 1860.
1 p.l., 106 p., 2 ℓ.   30 x 24½ cm.

20693   Cuba.   Laws, statutes, etc.
Ley de 7 de septiembre de 1938, sobre jubilaciones
y pensiones de empleados de bancos de la república

de Cuba... La Habana, Imprenta Compañía editora de
libros y folletos, 1938.
23 p.   22 cm.
"Publicada en la Gaceta oficial de 12 de septiembre
de 1938."

20694   Cuba. Laws, statutes, etc.
Proclamas y leyes del gobierno provisional de la
revolución, 1º a 31 de enero de 1959. 4. ed. La Habana,
Editorial Lex, 1959.
111 p.   16 cm.   (Folletos de divulgación legislativa, 1)

20695   Cuba. Ministerio de Agricultura.
Precio promedio definitivo 1959; antecedentes relacionados con la formación de los precios promedios
oficiales de la zafra de 1959. [La Habana, 1960?]
8, [63] ℓ. (chiefly tables)   36 cm.

20696   Cuba. Ministerio de Educación.
Cursos de superación para maestros. La Habana,
Editora del Ministerio de Educación, 1963-1964.
8 v.   illus., maps, tables, diagrs., facsims.
20 cm.

20697   Cuba. Ministerio de Salubridad y Asistencia Social.
Asistencial social en Cuba. [La Habana, 1960]
38 p.   illus.   20 cm.

20698   Cuba. Ministerio del Trabajo.
La Revolución en el campo laboral. 5 leyes básicas
en materia de trabajo, dictadas por el Gobierno Revolucionario de Cuba. [La Habana, 1960]
245 p.   22 cm.

20699   Cuba. Provisional Governor, 1906-1909 (Charles E. Magoon)
Annual report of Charles E. Magoon, provisional
governor of Cuba, to the secretary of war   [Dec. 1]
1907. Washington, Government printing office, 1908.
94 p.   23 cm.
Included is a letter of submittal by the secretary
of war, William H. Taft, addressed to the President
[Theodore Roosevelt] dated January 10, 1908.
--- --- Washington, Government printing office, 1908.
96 p.   23 cm.   ([U.S.] 60th Cong., 1st sess.
Senate. Doc. 155)
The "Letter of submittal" is dated Jan. 13, 1908.
The President's reply of the same date is included,
also his message transmitting the report to Congress,

January 14, 1908.
--- --- ... Report of the provisional governor of
Cuba from December 1, 1907, to December 1, 1908...
Washington, Government printing office, 1909.
    viii, 121 p. incl. tables.   23 cm.   ([U.S.] 60th
Cong., 2d sess. House. Doc. 1457)
    Luke E. Wright, secretary of war.

20700 Cuba, territorio libre de América. [Fotos, cortesía de:
revista Bohemia, Norbert Frýd, José Collado. Textos:
Pavel Stránsky y José Forné Farreres] Praga
[Publicado por] Artia [para la Imprenta Nacional de
Cuba, c1961]
    [4] p., 24 photos.   23 x 33 cm.

20701 Cuba en su puesto, discursos pronunciados por el sr.
presidente de la república, y los jefes de la
"Coalición socialista democrática," en la reunión
celebrada el día 10 de octubre de 1941, en el Palacio
presidencial Coronel F. Batista, dr. Gustavo Cuervo
Rubio, dr. Eduardo Suárez Rivas [y otros]... La
Habana, Cuba, Comité ejecutivo nacional de Partido
"Unión revolucionaria comunista" [1941]
    23 p.   20 cm.

20702 Cuba Socialista. La Habana.
    nos.   35 cm.
    Library has nos. 1, 3-4, 6-17, 19-23, Sept. 1961-
July 1963.

20703 The Cuban question in its true light; a dispassionate
and truthful review of the situation in the island
of Cuba, and the position of the United States
toward the insurrection, by an American. New York,
1895.
    48 p.   23½ cm.

20704 Cubas Alvariño, Ana M
    Reforma agraria: bibliografía. Catálogo colectivo
1962-1972 [por] Ana M. Cubas Alvariño. La Molina,
Perú, Universidad Nacional Agraria, Taller de
Estudios Andinos [1976]
    6 p.l., 89 p.   30 cm.

20705 Cué Sarquís, Irma.
    Estudio de algunos aspectos del juicio de amparo.
México [196-?]
    93 p.   23 cm.

Tesis - Universidad Nacional Autónoma de México.
Bibliography: p. 92-93.

20706 Cuenca, Humberto.
Derecho procesal civil. Caracas, Universidad Central
de Venezuela, Ediciones de la Biblioteca, 1965-
v. 23 cm. (Ediciones de la Biblioteca, 18.
Colección ciencias jurídicas, 1)
Contents. - t. 1. Parte general.

20707 Cuenca, Humberto.
La revolución cubana. Caracas, Editorial Cultura
Contemporánea [1962]
108 p. 17 cm.

20708 Cuenca, Humberto.
La universidad colonial. Prólogo: Luis Villalba-
Villalba. [Caracas] Universidad Central de Venezuela
[1967]
140 p. 16 cm. (Colección Avance, 16)
Ediciones de la Biblioteca.

20709 Cuentistas jovenes de Centro América y Panamá. [San
Salvador] Esso Standard Oil [1967]
85 p. 20 cm.

20710 Cuervo, Angel, 1838-1896.
La dulzada. Edición dirigida por Mario Germán
Romero. Introducción por Eduardo Guzmán Esponda.
Glosario por Ricardo Pardo. Bogotá, Instituto Caro
y Cuervo, 1973.
xciv, 217 p. front. (port.), facsim. 22½ cm.
(Biblioteca colombiana, VI)

20711 Cuervo, Angel, 1838-1896.
Epistolario de Angel y Rufino José Cuervo con
Rafael Pombo. Edición, introducción y notas de
Mario Germán Romero. Bogotá, Instituto Caro y Cuervo,
1974.
cxxiv, 407 p. ports., facsims. 24 cm.
(Archivo espistolar colombiano, VII)

20712 Cuervo, Rufino José, 1844-1911.
Epistolario de Rufino José Cuervo y Emilio Teza.
Edición, introducción y notas de Ana Hauser y Jorge
Páramo Pomareda. Bogotá, 1965.
lix, [1], 454 p. illus., facsims., ports. 24 cm.
(Publicaciones del Instituto Caro y Cuervo. Archivo
epistolar colombiano, 1)

Spanish and Italian.
Bibliography: p. [lx]

20713 Cuervo, Rufino José, 1844-1911.
Epistolario de Rufino José Cuervo y Hugo Schuchardt.
Edición, introducción y notas de Dieter Bross.
Bogotá, Instituto Caro y Cuervo, 1968.
294 p.   illus., facsims.   24 cm.   (Publicaciones
del Instituto Caro y Cuervo. Archivo epistolar
colombiano, II)

20714 Cuervo, Rufino José, 1844-1911.
Epistolario de Rufino José Cuervo con Luis María
Lleras y otros amigos y familiares. Edición, intro-
ducción, y notas de Guillermo Hernández de Alba.
Bogotá, 1969.
398 p.   ports.   24 cm.   (Publicaciones del
Instituto Caro y Cuervo. Archivo epistolar colombiano,
3)
Bibliography: p. 20.

20715 Cuervo, Rufino José, 1844-1911.
Epistolario de Rufino José Cuervo y Miguel Antonio
Caro con Antonio Gómez Restrepo. Edición, introducción
y notas de Mario Germán Romero. Bogotá, Instituto
Caro y Cuervo, 1973.
ix, 297 p.   illus., facsim.   24½ cm.   (Publica-
ciones del Instituto Caro y Cuervo. Archivo Epistolar
Colombiano. VI)

20716 Cuervo, Rufino José, 1844-1911.
Epistolario de Rufino José Cuervo con filólogos de
Alemania, Austria y Suiza, y noticias de las demás
relaciones de Cuervo con estos países y sus represen-
tantes, por Günther Schütz. Bogotá, Instituto Caro
y Cuervo, 1976.
2 v.   illus., ports., facsims.   23 cm.
(Archivo epistolar colombiano, IX)

20717 Cuervo, Rufino José, 1844-1911.
Epistolario de Rufino José Cuervo y Miguel Antonio
Caro con Belisario Peña. Compilación, introducción
y notas de Vicente Pérez Silva. Bogotá, Instituto
Caro y Cuervo, 1977.
xx p., 1ℓ., 271 p.   ports., facsims.   23½ cm.
(Publicaciones del Instituto Caro y Cuervo. Archivo
epistolar colombiano, IV)

20718   Cuervo, Rufino José, 1844-1911.
        Epistolario de Rufino José Cuervo con Miguel Antonio
        Caro. Edición, introducción y notas de Mario Germán
        Romero. Bogotá, Instituto Caro y Cuervo, 1978.
        lii, 315 p.   illus., ports., facsims.   24½ cm.
        (Publicaciones del Instituto Caro y Cuervo. Archivo
        epistolar colombiano, XIII)

21719   Cuesta y Cuesta, Alfonso
        Homenaje al decano de la Facultad de Humanidades y
        Educación de la Universidad de los Andes. Doctor Carlo
        César Rodríguez. Mérida, Venezuela, Marzo 19, 1968.
        28 p.   illus.   20 cm.

21720   Cueva Tamariz, Agustín.
        Abismos humanos. Cuenca [Casa de la Cultura
        Ecuatoriana, Núcleo del Azuay] 1976.
        219 p.   19½ cm.
        Contents. - Semblanza biotipológica de Alfonso
        Moreno Mora. - Ensayo de interpretación de Medardo
        Angel Silva. - Las ideas biológicas del P. Solano. -
        El sentido psicológico de Werther de Goethe. - La
        psicología de Nietzsche. - Psicología de Oscar Wilde.

21721   Cueva Tamariz, Agustín.
        Evolución de la psiquiatría en el Ecuador. Cuenca
        [Núcleo del Azuay, Casa de la Cultura Ecuatoriana]
        1966.
        173 p.   illus.   23 cm.
        Bibliography: p. 157-173.

21722   Cueva Tamariz, Agustín.
        Genio y figura de Remigio Romero y Cordero. Cuenca,
        Casa de la Cultura Ecuatoriana, Núcleo del Azuay,
        1968.
        37 p.   front. (port.)   23 cm.

21723   Cueva Silva, Jaime.
        Comercialización del banano ecuatoriano. Quito
        [AECA] 1964.
        234 p.   22 cm.
        Bibliography: p. 233-234.

21724   Cuevas, Mariano, 1879-1949.
        Historia de la Nación Mexicana. 3. ed. México,
        Editorial Porrúa, 1967.
        xxix, 1090 p.   24 cm.
        "Bio-bibliografía del P. Mariano Cuevas, S. J.":
        p. xiii-xiv.

21725   Cuevas Herrera, Luis.
        Estatuto jurídico del comercio farmacéutico.
        Santiago, Editorial Universitaria, 1958.
        151 p.   22 cm.
        Memoria de prueba (licenciatura en ciencias jurídicas
        y sociales) - Universidad de Chile, Santiago.
        Bibliography: p. 147.

21726   Cuevas Paralizábal, Carlos.
        El cocinero presidencial; [relatos políticos]
        Ilus.: Antonio Cardoso. [1. ed.] México, 1963.
        166 p.   illus.   18 cm.

21727   Culleré, Jaime.
        Las tres vertientes de la historia de la cultura.
        [Córdoba, Argentina] Dirección General de Publicidad,
        Universidad Nacional de Córdoba [c1961]
        101 p.   21 cm.   (Colección de ensayos y estudios)
        Contents. - Las tres vertientes de la historia de
        la cultura. - La sociología de la cultura de Alfred
        Weber. - Historia de la cultura y culturología. -
        La idea del tiempo-eje en Karl Jaspers.

21728   Cultura venezolana; revista mensual. año 1-47; junio
        1918-sept./oct. 1934. Caracas, Venezuela, 1918-34.
        47 v.   illus., plates, ports.   22½ cm.
        Editor: June 1918-   J. A. Tagliaferro.
        Lacks no. 118, v. 47.
        Suspended April 1932-May 1934.

21729   Cumaná, Venezuela. Universidad de Oriente.
        Universidad de Oriente: bases, organización,
        proyectos. Provisional. Cumaná [Editorial Arte] 1961.
        46 p.   map.   21 cm.

21730   Cummings, Edward Estlin, 1894-
        10 [Dez] poemas. [Rio de Janeiro, 1960]
        37 p.   20 cm.

21731   Cundinamarca, Colombia (Dept.)
        Plan de rectificación y pavimentación de carreteras
        departamentales. Bogotá [Imprenta Departamental]
        1950.
        45 p.   illus., part. col. map., diagrs.   32 cm.

21732   Cunha, Alarico José da.
        Barra do Corda, uma experência de colonização [por]
        Alarico da Cunha, Jr., Eudes Alves Simões [e] Levon
        Debelian. Rio de Janeiro, Instituto Nacional de
        Imigração e Colonização [1959]

124 p. illus. 22 cm. (INIC. Departamento de Estudos e Planejamento. Série "Colonização, 2/1959)

21733 Cunha, Celso Ferreira da.
Lingua e verso; ensaios. [Por] Celso Cunha. 2. ed. rev. e aumentada. Rio de Janeiro, Livraria São José, 1968.
142 p. 22 cm.
Bibliographical footnotes.

21734 Cunha, Fernando Whitaker Tavares de.
A seara de bronze; estudos e ensaios. Préfacio de Carlos Burlamaqui Kopke. São Paulo, Editôra Cupolo, 1960.
201 p. 21 cm.
Contents. - A vida trágica de Lacenaire (O romantismo de assassinato) - Influências indus em Cruz e Souza. - O drama da redenção em Rimbaud. - Processualistica e deontología em Franz Kafka. - Desequilíbrio e arte.

21735 Cunha, Lygia da Fonseca Fernandes da.
... A coleção de estampas Le grand théâtre de l'univers. Rio de Janeiro, Divisão de Publicações e Divulgação, Biblioteca Nacional, 1970.
188 p. illus. 22 cm.
At head of title: Biblioteca Nacional, Coleção Rodolfo Garcia.

21736 Cunha, Odaléa de Queiroz, 1907-
O amante de minha mulher. Peça em três atos e três quadros. Rio de Janeiro, Serviço Nacional de Teatro, 1974.
viii, 68 p. 21 cm.

21737 Cunha, Osvaldo Rodriguez da.
... Ofidios da Amazônia. I -- A ocorrencia de Bothrops bilineatus (Wied) nas matas dos arredores de Belém, Pará (ophidia, crotalidae) Belém, Museu Paraense Emilio Goeldi, 1967.
12 p. 23 cm. (Museu Paraense Emilio Goeldi, Boletim, nova série, Zoologia, no. 66)

21738 Cunha, Persivo.
Criminalística médico-legal. Recife, Universidade Federal de Pernambuco, 1970.
v. illus. (Biblioteca universitaria pernambucano. Coleção jurídica, 2)
Contents. - v. 1. Asfixiología forense.

21739 Cunha, Rui Vieira da, 1926-
... Figuras e fatos da nobreza brasileira. Rio de
Janeiro, Arquivo Nacional, 1975.
220 p. 23 cm. (Publicações históricas, 1.ª
serie, 80)

21740 Cunha, S F da.
Diffusion and solubility of Zn in GaSb, by S. F.
da Cunha and J. Bougnot. Rio de Janeiro, Centro
Brasileiro de Pesquisas Físicas, 1973.
185-196 p. diagrs. 29 cm. (Notas de
física, v. 21, no. 10)

21741 Cunha, S F da.
Transport properties of LI-compensated gallium
antimonide, by S. F. da Cunha and S. Almairac. Rio
de Janeiro, Centro Brasileiro de Pesquisas Físicas,
1973.
167-181 p. diagrs. 29 cm. (Notas de
física, v. 21, no. 9)

21742 Curitiba. Universidade Federal do Paraná. Departamento
de História.
Arquivos Paranaenses Boletim no. 9. Contribuição
do Núcleo Regional do Paraná da APUH ao V Simpósio
Nacional dos professôres universitarios de história.
Curitiba, 1969.
428 p. 24 cm.

21743 Currie, Lauchlin Bernard.
El algodón en Colombia; problemas y oportunidades.
Bogotá, Federación Nacional de Algodoneros, 1963.
165 leaves. 28 cm.

21744 Curso Nacional sobre Juventudes Rurales en Costa Rica.
1st, Turrialba, Costa Rica, 1962.
Fundamentos del trabajo con juventudes rurales;
materiales del Primer Curso Nacional sobre Juventudes
Rurales para Costa Rica, Turrialba, Costa Rica, feb.
12 a marzo 3, 1962. Editado por Earl Jones [et al.]
Turrialba, Costa Rica, Departamento de Economía y
Extensión, Centro Tropical de Investigación y Enseñanza
para Graduados, Instituto Interamericano de Ciencias
Agrícolas de la OEA, 1962.
275 p. 27 cm.
"Organizado por el Servicio de Extensión Agrícola
del Ministerio de Agricultura y Ganadería de Costa
Rica en colaboración con el Centro Tropical de Inves-
tigación y Enseñanza para Graduados... y el Programa

417

Interamericano para la Juventud Rural."
Includes bibliographies.

21745   Curtis, Thomas D   1935-
        Land reform, democracy, and economic interest in
        Puerto Rico, by Thomas D. Curtis. Tucson, Division of
        Economic and Business Research, College of Business
        and Public Administration, University of Arizona,
        1966.
        viii, 64 p.   23 cm.
        Bibliography: p. 62-64.

21746   Curutchet, Marta I   K
        Eficiencia funcional de los centros urbanos, por
        Marta I. K. Curutchet. Buenos Aires, Imprenta de la
        Facultad de Filosofía y Letras, 1976.
        35 p.   maps, diagrs.   22 cm.   (Buenos Aires.
        Universidad. Facultad de Filosofía y Letras. Instituto
        de Geografía "R. Adissone". Serie cuadernos de geo-
        grafía, no. 1)

21747   Cuyo; anuario de historia del pensamiento argentino.
        Mendoza, Argentina, Instituto de Filosofía, Universidad
        Nacional de Cuyo.
        v.   20-23 cm.
        Library has v. 10-11 (1974-78) and v. 12 (1979)

21748   Cuza Malé, Belkis.
        El viento en la pared; poemas. [Santiago de Cuba]
        Universidad de Oriente [1962]
        55 p.   22 cm.   (Colección Poesía)

21749   Cuzán, Alfred G
        A tale of two sites: political structure and policy
        performance in Costa Rica and El Salvador [by] Alfred
        G. Cuzán. Austin, Office of Public Sector Studies,
        Institute of Latin American Studies, University of
        Texas at Austin, 1977.
        2 p.l., 12 p.   28 cm.   (ILAS Tecnical papers
        series, no. 12)

21750   Cvitanovic, Dinko, ed.
        La idea del cuerpo en las letras españolas (siglos
        XIII a XVII) Bahía Blanca, Instituto de Humanidades,
        Universidad Nacional del Sur, 1973.
        211 p.   23 cm.

21751   Cvitanovic, Dinko, ed.
        El sueño y su representación en el barroco español.

Estudios reunidos y presentados por Dinko Cvitanovic.
Bahía Blanca, Instituto de Humanidades, Universidad
Nacional del Sur [1969]
    188 p.   22 cm.

21752 Cysneiros, Lúcia Maria Rosa.
       Bigodes. Recife, Museu do Açúcar, 1967 ¡
       [15] p.   ports.   23 cm.
       Cover title.
       Bibliography: p. [15]

19664 Camargo, Cándido Procopio de.
       Aspectos sociológicos del espiritismo en São Paulo.
    Con una introducción histórica del Dr. Fray Buena-
    ventura Kloppenburg y una introducción sociológica
    de Jean Labbens. Friburgo, Suiza, Oficina Inter-
    nacional de Investigaciones Sociales de FERES, 1961.
       125 p.   illus.   22 cm.   (Estudios sociológicos
    latino-americanos, 17)